BY ROGER CROWLEY

Conquerors: How Portugal Forged the First Global Empire

City of Fortune: How Venice Ruled the Seas

Empires of the Sea: The Siege of Malta, the Battle of Lepanto, and the Contest for the Center of the World

1453: The Holy War for Constantinople and the Clash of Islam and the West

Conquerors

Conquerors

HOW PORTUGAL FORGED THE FIRST
GLOBAL EMPIRE

Roger Crowley

RANDOM HOUSE

NEW YORK

Published in the United States by Random House, an imprint
and division of Penguin Random House LLC, New York.

RANDOM HOUSE and the HOUSE colophon are registered
trademarks of Penguin Random House LLC.

LIBRARY OF CONGRESS CATALOGING-IN-PUBLICATION DATA
Crowley, Roger, author.
Conquerors : how Portugal forged the first global empire / Roger Crowley.
pages cm
Includes bibliographical references and index.
ISBN 978-0-8129-9400-1 — ISBN 978-0-8129-9401-8 (ebook)
1. Portugal—Colonies—History—16th century.
2. Imperialism—History. I. Title.
JV4214.C76 2015
909'.0971246905—dc23
2015008152

Printed in the United States of America on acid-free paper

randomhousebooks.com

2 4 6 8 9 7 5 3 1

First Edition

Book design by Caroline Cunningham

To Pascal,
who inspired and encouraged the voyage,
with many thanks

The sea with limits may be Greek or Roman;

The sea without end is Portuguese.

—FERNANDO PESSOA

CONTENTS

CONTENTS

PART III

Conquest

THE LION OF THE SEA

CONTENTS

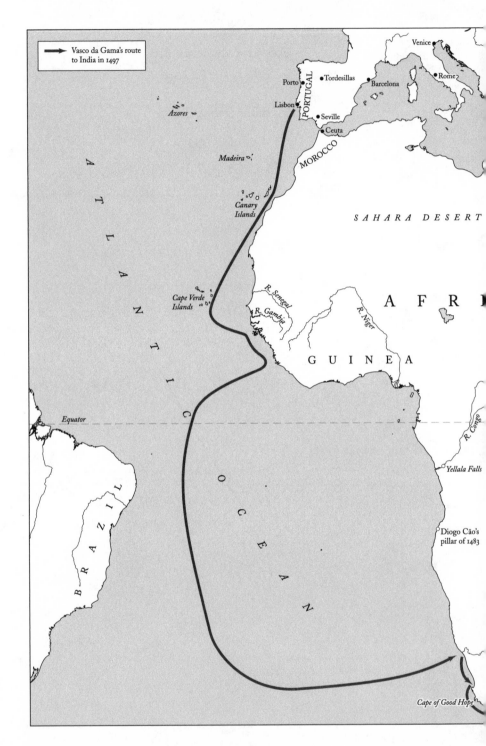

From Portugal to India c. 1500

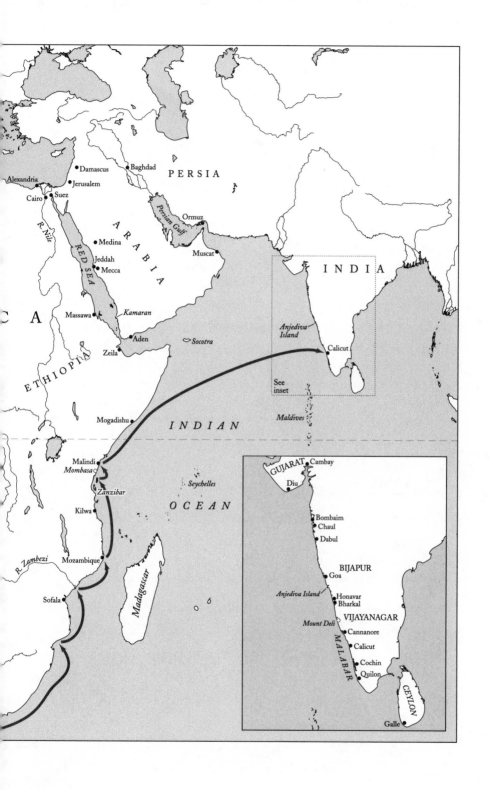

Damascus
Baghdad
PERSIA
Alexandria
Jerusalem
Cairo
Suez
Ormuz
Persian Gulf
A R A B I A
Medina
Muscat
INDIA
Jeddah
Mecca
RED SEA
Anjediva
Island
Calicut
Massawa
Kamaran
A
Socotra
Aden
See
inset
Zeila
ETHIOPIA
Mogadishu
INDIAN
Maldives
Malindi
GUJARAT
Cambay
Mombasa
Seychelles
Diu
Zanzibar
OCEAN
Kilwa
Bombaim
Chaul
R. Zambezi
Dabul
Mozambique
BIJAPUR
Goa
Madagascar
Anjediva Island
Honavar
Sofala
Bharkal
VIJAYANAGAR
Mount Deli
Cannanore
MALABAR
Calicut
Cochin
Quilon
CEYLON
Galle

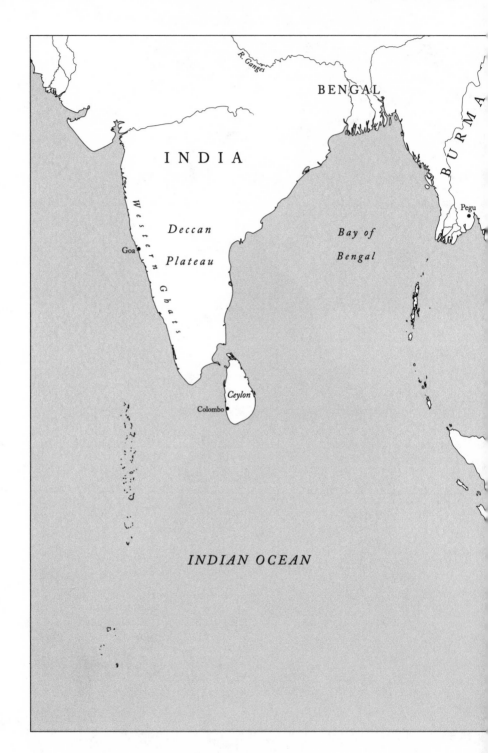

From India to China c. 1500

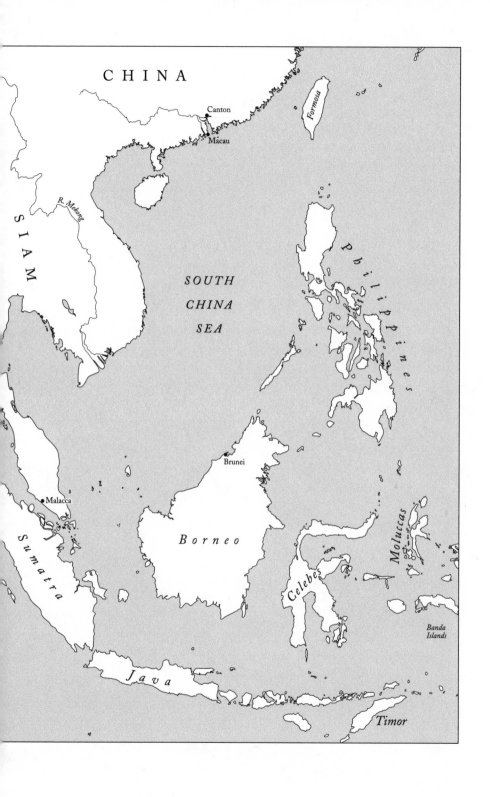

CHINA

Canton

Macau

Formosa

SIAM

R. Mekong

SOUTH
CHINA
SEA

Philippines

Malacca

Brunei

S u m a t r a

B o r n e o

Celebes

Moluccas

Banda
Islands

J a v a

Timor

PROLOGUE

The Prow of Europe

ON SEPTEMBER 20, 1414, the first giraffe ever seen in China was approaching the imperial palace in Beijing. A crowd of eager spectators craned their heads to catch a glimpse of this curiosity "with the body of a deer and the tail of an ox, and a fleshy boneless horn, with luminous spots like a red cloud or a purple mist," according to the enraptured court calligrapher and poet Shen Du. The animal was apparently harmless: "its hoofs do not tread on living creatures . . . its eyes rove incessantly. All are delighted with it." The giraffe was being led on a halter by its keeper, a Bengali; it was a present from the far-away sultan of Malindi, on the coast of East Africa.

The dainty animal, captured in a contemporary painting, was the exotic trophy of one of the strangest and most spectacular expeditions in maritime history. For thirty years at the start of the fifteenth century, the emperor of the recently established Ming dynasty, Yongle, dispatched a series of armadas across the western seas as a demonstration of Chinese power.

The fleets were vast. The first, in 1405, consisted of some 250 ships carrying twenty-eight thousand men. At its center were the treasure ships: multi-decked, nine-masted junks 440 feet long with innovative watertight buoyancy compartments and immense rudders 450 feet square. They were accompanied by a retinue of support vessels—horse

transports, supply ships, troop carriers, warships, and water tankers—
with which they communicated by a system of flags, lanterns, and
drums. As well as navigators, sailors, soldiers, and ancillary workers,
they took with them translators, to communicate with the barbarian
peoples of the West, and chroniclers, to record the voyages. The fleets
carried sufficient food for a year—the Chinese did not wish to be
beholden to anyone—and navigated straight across the heart of the
Indian Ocean from Malaysia to Sri Lanka, with compasses and cali-
brated astronomical plates carved in ebony. The treasure ships were
known as star rafts, powerful enough to voyage even to the Milky Way.
"Our sails," it was recorded, "loftily unfurled like clouds, day and night
continued their course, rapid like that of a star, traversing the savage
waves." Their admiral was a Muslim named Zheng He, whose grand-
father had made the pilgrimage to Mecca, and who gloried in the title
of the Three-Jewel Eunuch.

These expeditions—six during the life of Yongle, and a seventh in
1431–33—were epics of navigation. Each lasted between two and
three years, and they ranged far and wide across the Indian Ocean
from Borneo to Zanzibar. Although they had ample capacity to quell
pirates and depose monarchs and also carried goods to trade, they were
primarily neither military nor economic ventures but carefully choreographed displays of soft power. The voyages of the star rafts were
nonviolent techniques for projecting the magnificence of China to the
coastal states of India and East Africa. There was no attempt at military
occupation, nor any hindrance to the area's free-trade system. By a
kind of reverse logic, they had come to demonstrate that China wanted
nothing, by giving rather than taking: "to go to the [barbarians'] countries," in the words of a contemporary inscription, "and confer presents
on them so as to transform them by displaying our power." Overawed
ambassadors from the peripheral peoples of the Indian Ocean returned
with the fleet to pay tribute to Yongle—to acknowledge and admire
China as the center of the world. The jewels, pearls, gold, ivory, and
exotic animals they laid before the emperor were little more than a
symbolic recognition of Chinese superiority. "The countries beyond
the horizon and at the end of the earth have all become subjects," it
was recorded. The Chinese were referring to the world of the Indian

Ocean, though they had a good idea what lay farther off. While Europe was pondering horizons beyond the Mediterranean, how the oceans were connected, and the possible shape of Africa, the Chinese seemed to know already. In the fourteenth century they had created a map showing the African continent as a sharp triangle, with a great lake at its heart and rivers flowing north.

The year after the giraffe arrived in Beijing and twenty-one thousand sea miles away, a different form of power was being projected onto the shores of Africa. In August 1415, a Portuguese fleet sailed across the Strait of Gibraltar and stormed the Muslim port of Ceuta, in Morocco, one of the most heavily fortified and strategic strongholds in the whole Mediterranean. Its capture astonished Europe. At the start of the fifteenth century, Portugal's population numbered no more than a million. Its kings were too poor to mint their own gold coins. Fishing and subsistence farming were staples of the economy, but the nation's poverty was matched only by aspiration. King João I, "John the Bastard," founder of the ruling house of Aviz, had snatched the country's crown in 1385 and asserted the country's independence from neighboring Castile. The assault on Ceuta was designed to soak up the restless energies of the noble class in a campaign that combined the spirit of medieval chivalry with the passions of crusade. The Portuguese had come to wash their hands in infidel blood. They fulfilled their contract to the letter. Three days of pillage and massacre had ransacked a place once described as "the flower of all other cities in Africa . . . [its] gateway and key." This stunning coup served notice to European rivals that the small kingdom was self-confident, energetic—and on the move.

Three of João's sons, Duarte, Pedro, and Henrique, had earned their spurs at Ceuta during a day of fierce fighting. On August 24, in the city's mosque, which had been ritually cleansed with salt and renamed Our Lady of Africa, they were knighted by their father. For the young princes, it was a moment of destiny. In Ceuta, the Portuguese had been afforded a first glimpse of the wealth of Africa and the Orient. The city was the roadhead for the caravans trafficking gold across the Sahara from the Senegal River, as well as the most westerly entrepôt of the

Islamic spice trade with the Indies. Here, wrote a Portuguese chronicler, came all the merchants of the world, from "Ethiopia, Alexandria, Syria, Barbary, Assyria . . . as well as those from the Orient who lived on the other side of the Euphrates River, and from the Indies . . . and from many other lands that are beyond the axis and that lie beyond our eyes." The Christian conquerors had seen for themselves the stores of pepper, cloves, and cinnamon, then wantonly destroyed them in a search for buried treasure. They had looted the booths of an apocryphal twenty-four thousand traders and smashed their way into ornately carpeted dwellings of rich merchants and beautifully vaulted and tiled underground cisterns. "Our poor houses looked like pigsties compared to those of Ceuta," wrote an eyewitness. It was here that Henrique, particularly, first perceived the wealth that might be reached "beyond the axis" if the Islamic barrier could be outflanked down the coast of Africa. Ceuta marked the beginning of Portuguese expansion, the threshold of a new world.

It was Portugal's fate and fortune to be locked out of the busy Mediterranean arena of trade and ideas. On the outer edge of Europe, peripheral to the Renaissance, the Portuguese could only look enviously at the wealth of cities such as Venice and Genoa, which had cornered the market in the luxury goods of the Orient—spices, silks, and pearls—traded through the Islamic cities of Alexandria and Damascus and sold on at monopoly prices. Instead they faced the ocean.

Twenty miles west of the seaport of Lagos, the coast of Portugal ends in a rocky headland looking out over the Atlantic, Cape St. Vincent. This is the prow of Europe, the continent's southwesternmost point. In the Middle Ages, certainty about the world ended here. From the cliffs the eye takes in a vast sweep of water and feels the buffet of the wind. The horizon curves west to a vanishing point where the sun sinks into an unknown night. For thousands of years, the inhabitants of the edge of the Iberian Peninsula had looked out from this coastline into nothingness. In dirty weather the rollers pound the cliffs with a terrifying ferocity, and the tops of the waves rear and dip with the long-range rhythm of a vast sea.

The Arabs, whose extensive knowledge of the world stopped a little beyond the Strait of Gibraltar, called this the Green Sea of Darkness:

mysterious, terrifying, and potentially infinite. Since ancient times it had been the source of endless speculation. The Romans knew of the Canary Islands, a smattering of rocks off the coast of Morocco, which they called the Fortunate Islands and from which they measured longitude—all points to the east. To the south, Africa faded into legend, its bulk and point of termination unknown. In ancient and medieval maps painted on strips of papyrus or vellum, the world is usually a circular dish, surrounded by ocean; America is uninvented, the extremities of the earth separated by an unsurmountable barrier of dark water. The classical geographer Ptolemy, whose influence in the Middle Ages was profound, believed that the Indian Ocean was enclosed, unreachable by ship. Yet for the Portuguese, the prospect from Cape St. Vincent was their opportunity. It was along this coast, over a lengthy apprenticeship in fishing and voyaging, that they learned the arts of open-sea navigation and the secrets of the Atlantic winds that were to give them unequaled mastery. In the wake of Ceuta, they started to use this knowledge to make voyages down the African coast that would eventually crystallize in the attempt to reach the Indies by sea.

The crusading enterprises against Muslims in North Africa would be deeply intertwined with the Portuguese maritime adventure. In a symmetrical arc, the royal house of Aviz started its ascent at Ceuta in 1415 and was destroyed nearby 163 years later. In between, the Portuguese pushed faster and farther across the world than any people in history. From a standing start they worked their way down the west coast of Africa, rounded the Cape, and reached India in 1498; they touched Brazil in 1500, China in 1514, and Japan in 1543. It was a Portuguese navigator, Fernão de Magalhães (Magellan), who enabled the Spanish to circumnavigate the earth in the years after 1518. The Ceuta campaign was the starting point for these projects; it was conceived in secret as an outlet for religious, commercial, and nationalistic passions, fueled by a background hatred of the Islamic world. In the crusades to North Africa, several generations of Portuguese conquistadors were first blooded. Here they learned the martial appetite and reflex violence that would overawe the peoples of the Indian Ocean and allow small numbers of invaders enormous leverage. In the fifteenth century, Portugal's whole population was hardly more than that of the one Chinese city of Nanjing, yet its ships exercised a more frightening power than the armadas of Zheng He.

The astonishing tribute fleets of the Ming were comparatively as advanced and as expensive as moon shots—each one cost half the country's annual tax revenue—and they left as little behind as footprints in the lunar dust. In 1433, during the seventh expedition, Zheng He died, possibly at Calicut, on the Indian coast. He was most likely buried at sea. After him, the star rafts never sailed again. The political current in China had changed: the emperors strengthened the Great Wall and shut themselves in. Oceangoing voyages were banned, all the records destroyed. In 1500 it became a capital offense to build a ship with more than two masts; fifty years later, it was a crime even to put to sea in one. The technology of the star rafts vanished with Zheng He's body into the waters of the Indian Ocean; they left behind a power vacuum waiting to be filled. When Vasco da Gama reached the coast of India, in 1498, the local people were able to give only garbled accounts of mysterious visitors with strange beards and incredible ships who had once come to their shores. Zheng He left just one significant monument to his voyages: a commemorative tablet written in Chinese, Tamil, and Arabic, offering thanks and praises to Buddha, Shiva, and Allah respectively: "Of late we have dispatched missions to announce our mandates to foreign nations, and during their journey over the ocean they have been favored with the blessing of your beneficent protection. They escaped disaster or misfortune, and journeyed in safety to and fro." It was an open-palmed gesture of religious tolerance, set up at Galle, near the southwestern tip of Ceylon (now Sri Lanka), where the fleets made their turn up the west coast of India into the Arabian Sea.

   The Portuguese came with no such blessings or magnificence. All of Gama's tiny ships, with some 150 men, could have fitted inside one of Zheng He's junks. The gifts they offered to a Hindu king were so pitiful that he refused to inspect them, but they announced their intentions with red crosses painted on their sails and bronze cannons. Unlike the Chinese, they shot first and never went away; conquest was a rolling national project, year after year deepening their position until they became impossible to dislodge.

The Galle monument still exists. It is crested by two Chinese dragons contesting the world, but it was Portuguese seamen from primitive Europe who first linked the oceans together and laid the foundations for a world economy. Their achievement has largely been overlooked. It is a long-range epic of navigation, trade, and technology, money and crusade, political diplomacy and espionage, sea battles and shipwrecks, endurance, reckless courage, and extreme violence. At its heart was an astonishing burst of some thirty years that forms the subject of this book, when these few Portuguese, led by a handful of extraordinary empire builders, attempted to destroy Islam and control the whole of the Indian Ocean and the world's trade. In the process, they launched a maritime empire with planatary reach and the great age of European discoveries. The Vasco da Gama era of history set in motion five hundred years of Western expansion and the forces of globalization that now shape the world.

PART I

Reconnaissance

THE ROUTE TO THE INDIES

1483–1499

1

The India Plan

1483–1486

13°25'7" S, 12°32'0" E

I n August 1483, a group of weather-beaten sailors was hauling a stone pillar into an upright position on a headland on the coast of what is now Angola. It was five and a half feet tall and surmounted by an iron cross, fixed into a socket with molten lead. Its cylindrical shaft was fashioned at the top into a cube, whose facets were carved with a coat of arms and an inscription in Portuguese:

> In the era of 6681 years from the creation of the world, 1482 years since the birth of Our Lord Jesus, the most High and Excellent and Mighty Prince, King D. João II of Portugal, sent Diogo Cão squire of his House to discover this land and plant these pillars.

This monument, a minute pinprick on the enormous bulk of Africa, marked the most southern point of European exploration beyond the shores of the Mediterranean. It was both an immodest act of possession and a baton being carried south, headland by headland, down the west coast of Africa, in search of a seaway to India. It proclaimed its own mythologies about time, identity, and religious mission. Cão planted a succession of these stone memorials as he sailed south at his king's command. Carved probably a year earlier—hence the mismatch with the dates—in the green hills of Sintra, near Lisbon, and carried four thousand sea miles in a pitching caravel, they represented acts of profound intention, like an American flag packed in a spacecraft in anticipation of a lunar landing. As Cão looked south from this pillar, the coast appeared to curve away east. He seems to have thought he was close to the end of Africa. The way to India was in sight.

This pillar marked the terminal point of Diogo Cão's voyages down the coast of West Africa. It was erected at Cape Cross in Namibia in January 1486 and subsequently removed to Berlin in 1893.

Like an *Apollo* space mission, this moment represented decades of effort. In the aftermath of Ceuta, Prince Henrique, who has passed into the bloodstream of history as Henry the Navigator, began to sponsor expeditions down the coast of Africa in search of slaves, gold, and spices. Year by year, headland by headland, Portuguese ships worked their way down the southwestward-sloping bulge of West Africa, cautiously sounding with plumb lines as they went, forever wary of shoals and reefs, over which the sea broke in pounding surf. In the process they began to delineate the shape of a continent: the desert coasts of Mauretania, the lush tropical shores of the region they called Guinea, the "Land of the Blacks," and the great rivers of equatorial Africa: the Senegal and the Gambia. Under Henrique's direction, exploration, raiding, and trading went hand in hand with ethnographical curiosity and mapping. Each successive cape and bay was pinned to a chart with the name of a Christian saint or a visible feature or an event.

These expeditions were modest affairs: two or three vessels, under the direction of a squire of Henrique's household, though the navigation and ship management were the responsibility of an experienced and, usually, anonymous pilot. Each carried a few soldiers, crossbows at the ready as they approached an unknown shore. The ships themselves, caravels, were a Portuguese development possibly of Arab origin. Their triangular lateen sails allowed them to sail close to the wind, invaluable for battling back from the Guinea coast, and their shallow draft made them ideal for nosing up estuaries. They were well suited for exploration, even if their small size—hardly eighty feet long, twenty wide—limited their space for supplies and rendered long sea voyages a trial.

Henrique's motivations were mixed. Portugal was small and impoverished, marginal to European affairs, and hemmed in by its powerful neighbor Castile. At Ceuta the Portuguese had glimpsed another world. Henrique and his successors hoped to access the sources of African gold, to snatch slaves and spices. He was influenced by medieval maps produced in Majorca by Jewish cartographers that showed glittering rivers leading to the kingdom of the legendary Mansa Musa, "king of kings" who had ruled the kingdom of Mali early in the fourteenth century and controlled the fabled gold mines of the Senegal River. The maps suggested that some rivers crossed the whole continent and linked into the Nile. They nourished the hope that Africa might be traversed via internal waterways.

The royal household projected these voyages to the pope as

crusades—continuations of the war with Islam. The Portuguese had
expelled the Arabs from their territory far earlier than their neighbors
in Castile and established a precocious sense of national identity, but
the appetite for holy war remained undimmed. As Catholic monarchs,
those in the royal house of Aviz sought legitimacy and parity on the
European stage as warriors for Christ. In a Europe that felt itself increasingly threatened by militant Islam, particularly after the fall of
Constantinople in 1453, they obtained from the papacy spiritual and
financial concessions and territorial rights over explored lands in the
name of Christ. The crusading remit from Rome was "to invade, search
out, capture, vanquish and subdue all Saracens and pagans whatsoever,
and other enemies of Christ . . . and to reduce their persons to perpetual slavery."

They were impelled, too, by a desire to do great deeds. Henrique
and his brothers were half English—their mother was Philippa of Lan-
caster, granddaughter of Edward III; their cousin was Henry V, the
victor at Agincourt. An atmosphere of knightly chivalry, fueled by
their Anglo-Norman ancestry and medieval romances, hung heavily
around the royal court and infused its restless nobility with a high-
octane mixture of prickly pride, reckless courage, and a desire for glory,
linked to crusading fever. This noble group, in Portuguese the *fidalgos,*
literally "the sons of someone," lived, fought, and died by an honor
code that would accompany the Portuguese across the world.

Behind the Africa initiative lay a very old dream of militant Christendom: that of outflanking Islam, which blocked the way to Jerusalem and the wealth of the East. Some of the maps portrayed a regal
figure dressed in a red robe with a bishop's miter on his head, his
throne glowing with burnished gold. This was the legendary Christian
king Prester John—John the Priest. The myth of Prester John reached
far back into the Middle Ages. It constituted a belief in the existence
of a mighty Christian monarch who resided somewhere beyond the
barrier of the Islamic world, and with whom Western Christendom
might link up to destroy the infidel. It had been conjured out of travelers' tales, literary forgery—in the shape of a famous letter purporting
to come from the great king himself in the twelfth century—and a
blurred knowledge that there were actual Christian communities be-

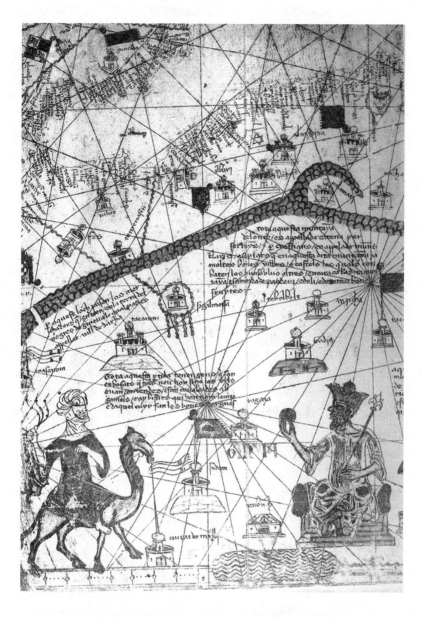

Detail from the Catalan Atlas of 1375, produced in Majorca, showing
Mansa Musa holding up a gold nugget. To the north, the mythical
River of Gold, the coast of North Africa, and southern Spain.

yond Europe: Nestorians in Central Asia, followers of St. Thomas in the Indies, and an ancient Christian kingdom in the highlands of Ethiopia. Prester was held to command vast armies, and he was immensely wealthy, "more powerful than any other man in the world and richer than any in gold, and in silver and in precious stones," according to a fourteenth-century account. The roofs and interiors of the houses in his country were said to be tiled with gold, and the weapons of his army were forged in it. By the fifteenth century the Prester figure had been superimposed onto the actual Christian kings of Ethiopia, and the maps suggested that his kingdom could be reached by river through the heart of Africa. For more than a century, this dazzling mirage would maintain a powerful hold over the imagination and strategies of the Portuguese.

The maps, the travelers' tales, confused images of great rivers that could penetrate to the heart of Africa, fabulous rumors of gold, word of mighty Christian rulers with whom an alliance might be forged against the Islamic world—this swirl of half-truths, wishful thinking, and mistaken geography leached into the worldview of the Portuguese. It was what lured them ever farther south down the African coast, hunting for the River of Gold or the river that would take them to Prester John. Each gulf, each river mouth seemed promising to their inquisitive ships, but the push down the coast was hard-won. The pounding surf made landings treacherous; the reception from the local people was always edgy. The sailors encountered vast lagoons and tortuous mangrove swamps at the mouths of the rivers, dense fogs and calms and violent equatorial rainstorms. The fever zone struck the sailors heavily. Within the Gulf of Guinea, the contradictory local winds and a strong current from east to west hampered forward progress, but they were for a long time spurred on by the eastward trend of the coast. Slowly they evolved a belief that they were inching toward the southern tip of Africa and that the riches of India might be reached by sea rather than by river, but the shape and sheer size of the continent, fifty times as big as the Iberian Peninsula, would baffle and confound their preconceptions for almost eighty years.

The idea of outflanking Islam's grip on Europe was both economic and ideological. To trade directly with the peoples of sub-Saharan Af-

rica, to source gold and possibly spices—spurred on by the image of
the gold nugget in the hand of the Malian king—was an enormously
powerful attraction; to link up with Prester John and his mythical army
and attack Islam from the rear was equally persuasive. When Henrique
died, the initiative faltered for a while, until pushed forward again in
the 1470s by his grandnephew Prince João. It was when João became
king, in 1481, that the Africa project received a whole new impetus.

Black-bearded and long-faced, well-built, and somewhat melan-
choly in expression, with "an air of such gravity and authority that
everyone recognized him as king," João was "a man who commanded
others and who was commanded by no one." He was perhaps the most
remarkable European monarch of the early modern age. To the Portuguese people he would pass into history as the Perfect Prince. His rival
Isabella, queen of Castile and then the unified kingdom of Spain, gave
him the ultimate accolade. She simply referred to him as "the Man."
João was preoccupied with "the deep desire to do great things," and
the first of the great things to which he stretched out his hand was the
exploration of Africa. On his accession he embarked on an intense
five-year period of state-funded exploration in which he hoped to
fulfill two objectives: find a route to the Indies and reach the fabled
kingdom of Prester John. It was Diogo Cão, erecting pillars along the
west coast of Africa, to whom he had entrusted this task.

João II: "The Perfect Prince"

However, by the 1480s other theories about a possible route to the Indies were circulating along the Lisbon waterfront. The city was the frontier of exploration, a laboratory for testing ideas about the world. Across Europe, astronomers, scientists, mapmakers, and merchants looked to Portugal for the latest information about the shape of Africa. Jewish mathematicians, Genoese merchants, and German cartographers were being attracted to the hubbub of its streets, its vistas of boundless ocean beyond the mouth of the River Tejo (or Tagus), from where Portuguese caravels returned with black slaves, brilliantly colored parrots, pepper, and handmade maps. João's interest in navigation led to the formation of a scientific committee drawing on these intellectual resources. This included José Vizinho, a pupil of the great Jewish astronomer and mathematician of the age, Abraham Zacuto, and the German Martin Behaim, later the creator of a prototype terrestrial globe. In the interests of scientific inquiry, both men made voyages on Portuguese ships to undertake solar observations.

While Cão was inching down the coast in the summer of 1483, the Genoese adventurer Cristoforo Colombo—known to the Spanish as Cristóbal Colón and in English as Christopher Columbus—was at the royal court in Lisbon proposing a counterstrategy for reaching the Indies. It was one that João already knew. A decade earlier, he had prompted a letter and a map on the subject from the famed Florentine mathematician and cosmographer Paolo Toscanelli. Toscanelli had proposed "a sea route from here to India, the land of spices; a route which is shorter than that via Guinea." His reasoning was that because the world was spherical, it was possible to reach the Indies by sailing in either direction, and that it was a shorter voyage to sail west. Apart from the as yet invisible barrier of the Americas, Toscanelli had made a fundamental error: he had undercalculated the circumference of the earth. But the letter and the map were destined to become a potent ingredient in the accelerating race for the world that gripped the Iberian Peninsula in the final decades of the century. Columbus knew, or had a copy of, Toscanelli's letter, and he now boldly approached João for the resources to make the attempt. The king was prepared to keep an open mind. He turned the formidably self-confident Columbus's proposition over to his committee of savants and mathematicians for consideration, and waited for Cão's return.

Cão was back in Lisbon by early April the following year, 1484, with his reports of the eastward-inclining coast. João closely questioned his explorer and was sufficiently pleased with the results to award him a large annual pension and elevation to the nobility, with his own coat of arms. Cão chose the emblem of two pillars crested by crosses for his device. For João, the Indies were just around the corner. It seemed that one more expedition must decide it.

Cão's report was the immediate end of Columbus's hopes. Both the manner and the mathematics of the Genoese were considered faulty. João's committee judged that Columbus had compounded Toscanelli's error about the size of the world: he had shrunk the globe by 25 percent in his estimation of the distance to the Indies, and his certainty was found insufferable—as, probably, were his demands for recompense. "The king, because he saw this Cristóvão Colombo to be boastful and pushy in talking up his abilities, and deluded and fanciful about the [position of] the island of Japan, gave him little credence," recorded the Portuguese historian João de Barros, "and with this disappointment he left the king and took himself off to Spain, where he also went hawking his petition." Columbus set to work there lobbying Isabella and Ferdinand, taking advantage of the rivalry between the two kingdoms to leverage his project.

Meanwhile João was confident of success. In May or June 1485, Cão, accompanied by Martin Behaim, was sent out again with more pillars to plant on the extremity of Africa. A few months later, the Portuguese king was trumpeting to the world that his seamen were close to the final breakthrough. In November, his orator, Vasco Fernandes de Lucena, was making the king's submission to the new pope, Innocent VIII, in a ringing statement of nationalist PR and holy crusade. He spoke of Prester John and

the well-founded hope of exploring the Arabian Sea where the kingdoms and nations of those who inhabit Asia, only obscurely known to us, practice with great devotion the holy faith of the savior, in relation to whom, if it's true what the most learned geographers propound, Portuguese navigation is within a few days' reach. In fact, having explored the greater part of the African coast, our

men came close to the Prassus Promontory [the end of Africa] only
last year, where the Arabian sea begins; having explored all the rivers,
coasts and ports for a distance of more than 4,500 miles from Lisbon, from the most rigorous observation of the sea, the land and the
stars. Once this region is explored, we will see an enormous accu-
mulation of wealth and honor for all the Christian people and especially you, most Holy Father.

Lucena went on to quote Psalm 72:"He shall have dominion also from
sea to sea, and from the river unto the ends of the earth." The river was
the Jordan; it might just as well have stood for the Tejo in João's increasingly global vision.

However, even as Lucena was speaking, the king's hopes were again
being baffled. Thousands of miles away, Cão discovered that the eastward trend of the land was illusory, just a large bay that quickly turned
south yet again in an apparently unending coastline. That autumn he
placed a farther pillar, on a headland 160 miles south; the coast gradually shifted from equatorial forest to low-lying barren sand hills, sparse
vegetation, and semidesert. Cão reached the farthest limit of endurance in January 1486 at a place he called Cape Cross, in modern Namibia, where he planted his last pillar, among a colony of seals basking
on the black rocks. It seemed that Africa would continue forever, and
Cão himself slips through the cracks of history at this point and van-
ishes. Either he died on the return journey or he made it back to
Lisbon and João, furious and embarrassed by the failure of this publicly
touted mission, condemned him to disgrace and obscurity.

Whatever his fate, Cão had added another 1,450 miles of coast to the
mapmakers' lexicon. The Portuguese seemed indefatigable in their endurance and their willingness to push themselves over the edge of the
known world, riding the rough seas in their agile caravels or probing
the enormous rivers of West Africa in pursuit of the elusive kingdom of
Prester John and an inland route to the Nile. Many perished in the attempt. They died in foundering ships, of malaria and poisoned arrows
and isolation, leaving their small markers as talismans against oblivion.

No more poignant memorial to Cão's attempts exists than that at

The main inscription carved on the rocks at the Yellala Falls

the Yellala Falls, up the Congo River. Whoever came here sailed or rowed a hundred miles upstream from the sea, past mangrove swamps and densely forested riverbanks. As they progressed, the current increased in ferocity until they reached a rocky gorge and thunderous waterfalls, a colossal torrent of water pouring out of the heart of Africa. When they could sail no farther, they abandoned their ships and scrambled ten miles over the rocks in the hope of finding navigable water upstream, but the succession of rapids defeated them. On the face of an overhanging cliff high above the crashing torrent, they left a carving, a monument of a different sort. The coat of arms of King João, a cross, and some words: "Here arrived the ships of the illustrious monarch Dom João the Second of Portugal, Diogo Cão, Pedro Anes, Pedro da Costa, Álvaro Pyris, Pêro Escolar A . . ." To the lower right and carved by a different hand, other names: "João de Samtyago, Diogo Pinheiro, Gonçalo Alvares, of sickness João Alvares . . ."; elsewhere, just a Christian name: "Antam" (Anthony).

All these inscriptions are broken off, their circumstances as ambiguous as a last entry in the diary of a polar explorer. They give us the names of the men who captained the ships—Diogo Cão and the others carved by the cross—but the commanders were probably not present. It is likely that Cão ordered a side trip to probe the navigability of the Congo; it is these men who form the second group of names. Both sets of inscriptions are incomplete, as if interrupted at the same moment. Evidently, men were ill or dead—probably of malaria. Were they too weak to continue? Were they surprised or attacked as they scratched away at the rock? Unusually, there is no date; nor is there any contemporary record of this exploit, which was unknown until European explorers stumbled on the inscription in 1911.

The Portuguese notion of a river or land route across Africa, fueled by the suppositions of ancient geographers and the enticing gold-leaved pages of medieval cartographers, died hard. The belief that the great rivers of West Africa linked to the Nile, that the kingdom of Prester John was just out of reach across a continent whose width they had miscalculated, doomed the Portuguese to decades of enduring, baffled effort. João dispatched multiple overland missions for information, gold, and prestige. The probe up the Congo was mirrored repeatedly. Caravels sailed five hundred miles up the Senegal River but were halted by the Felu rapids; when a similar expedition was thwarted at the Barrakunda Falls, on the Gambia, João sent engineers to break up the rocks on the riverbed, but the scale of the task defeated them. At the same time, servants and squires of the royal household set off into the interior on foot. Small teams of men crossed the Mauretanian desert to Wadan and to Timbuktu; to the realms of Jolof and Tokolor; to the Mandinka king they knew as Mandi Mansa, on the upper Niger. Some returned with reports of kingdoms and trade routes; others vanished.

But João was undeterred, daunted by neither the obdurate rapids of the Gambia and the Congo nor the ever receding coastline of Africa nor the uncertain location of a semimythical Christian king. The scope, coherence, and persistence of his India project were astonishing. In 1486, with his committee of geographers in Lisbon poring ever more intently over misshapen maps of the world and Columbus now lobbying the monarchs of Spain for his western route, the king simply intensified his efforts. The same year the noun *descobrimento,* "discovery," is recorded in written Portuguese for the first time.

2

The Race

1486–1495

THE CASTLE OF ST. George in Lisbon, situated on a rocky promontory with far-reaching views over the Tejo River, contained among its treasures a sumptuous world map. It had been commissioned thirty years earlier by King João's father, Afonso, from a cartographer monk in Venice with the brief to summarize the best geographical knowledge of the day.

Fra Mauro produced an extraordinary work of art, microscopically detailed and brilliant with gold leaf, wavy seas of vivid blue, and the images of castellated cities. Like an enormous circular shield, ten feet across and oriented to the south, in the Arab tradition, it showed something that no European map had before: it portrayed Africa as a freestanding continent with a southern cape, which he called Cape Diab. Although Africa is seriously distorted and many details had already been outdated by Portuguese discoveries in João's time, Fra Mauro had attempted to apply an evidence-based approach. Venice, with its deep trading contacts with the Orient, was the clearinghouse for information and travelers' tales about the world beyond Europe.

The picture is peppered with hundreds of textual commentaries in red and blue ink, drawn principally from the eyewitness accounts of Marco Polo and a fifteenth-century traveler called Niccolò de' Conti, as well as "information of all new discoveries made or projected by the

Portuguese." "Many have thought, and many have written, that the sea does not encompass our habitable and temperate zone on the south," Mauro notes on his map, "but there is much evidence to support a contrary opinion, and particularly that of the Portuguese, whom the king of Portugal has sent on board his caravels to verify the fact by ocular inspection." Special attention is drawn to the spice islands and ports of the Indian Ocean—of particular interest to the Portuguese— and he tackles head-on a key assertion of Ptolemaic geography: that the Indian Ocean was a closed sea. The particular evidence he produces for an all-water route to the Indies includes the ancient geographer Strabo's account of such a voyage, as well as a tale, probably from Conti, of the journey of a Chinese junk that was said to have sailed round Africa.

Fra Mauro's map crystallized, in visual form, the Portuguese ambition to find a sea route to the Indies. It also highlighted how little Europeans knew. Never had the world been more divided. The Europeans of the Middle Ages had less contact with the Orient than had the Roman Empire. Marco Polo had walked and ridden there down silk roads controlled by the Mongols and returned across the Indian Ocean in a Chinese junk. His account remained hugely influential, because by the fifteenth century almost all direct links with the East had been severed. The Mongol Empire had collapsed, destroying the long-range land routes; in China, its successor, the Ming dynasty, after the spectacular voyages of the star rafts, had been seized by xenophobia and closed its frontiers. With the exception of Conti's reports, almost all European knowledge was nearly two hundred years old. Islam hemmed Christian Europe in. The Ottomans had crossed into Europe and barricaded the land routes. The Mamluk dynasty, in Cairo, controlled the desirable wealth of the East and traded it through Alexandria and Damascus at monopoly prices. Of the exact sources of the spices, silks, and pearls sold to the Venetians and Genoese, there were only muffled rumors.

Undeterred by Cão's failure to round Africa, João persisted. The scope of his inquiry became increasingly wide-ranging. Nothing was ruled out. At his command, two monks set out across the Mediterranean to seek information about Prester John in the East. About Columbus's proposed western route, João hedged his bets. He licensed a Flemish adventurer called Fernão de Ulmo with the concession to sail west for forty days with two caravels at his own expense and the right to whatever land he discovered, at a 10 percent payment of all revenues to the crown. The king effectively leased out to private enterprise a venture that he deemed speculative but could not definitively dismiss. Nothing came of these initiatives. It seems Ulmo was unable to raise the funds; the monks were turned back at Jerusalem by their inability to speak Arabic. Nothing daunted, João tried again.

The king had gathered around him a loyal generation of highly talented pilots, seamen, and adventurers, chosen for their talents rather than their social status, on whom he now called for a final push. In 1486 he energetically planned a triple-pronged approach to solving the India problem and locating Prester John. He would tackle the problem at both ends. A more focused expedition would sail on past Cão's pillars and attempt to round Africa; along the way it would drop Portuguese-speaking native Africans to seek information about the legendary Christian king in the interior of the continent; and João would rectify the failure of his overland initiative to the East by recruiting Arabic speakers who could penetrate the heartlands of the Indies to learn about spices, Christian kings, and the possibility of sailing routes to the Indian Ocean.

In October 1486, soon after Cão's return—or the return of his ships—João appointed a knight of his household, Bartolomeu Dias, to command the next expedition down the African coast. At about the same time, he chose replacements for an overland expedition to the Indian Ocean.

The man he recruited for this task was Pêro da Covilhã. Covilhã was about forty years old, a quick-witted, multitalented adventurer of lowly birth, an adept swordsman, a loyal servant of the Portuguese kings, and a spy. As well as Portuguese, he spoke Castilian fluently and, more valuably, Arabic, which he had probably learned from the Arab population of Spain. He had performed undercover operations for João there, and undertaken secret negotiations in Morocco with the king of Fez. It was Covilhã and another Arabic speaker, Afonso de Paiva, to whom the king now entrusted a daring operation.

In the spring of 1487, while Dias was preparing his ships, the two men were being briefed by the bishop of Tangiers and two Jewish mathematicians, members of the commission that had turned down Columbus. The adventurers were presented with a navigational map of the Middle East and the Indian Ocean, presumably the best guess available within Europe as to the world beyond the Mediterranean, probably drawing heavily on Fra Mauro's work. On May 7 they had a last secret audience with the king at his palace at Santarém, outside Lisbon, where they were given letters of credit to pay their way on the sea voyage to Alexandria. Among those privy to this audience was the eighteen-year-old duke of Beja, Dom Manuel, the king's cousin, for whom the memory of this expedition was to have a special importance. Over the summer they took a ship from Barcelona to the Christian island of Rhodes, where they acquired a stock of honey to enable them to pass themselves off in the Arab world as merchants. From there they caught another vessel to Alexandria, portal to the Islamic world.

Back in Lisbon, Dias was putting the finishing touches to his matching expedition down the west coast of Africa. He was given two caravels belonging to the crown and also, because of the long-range nature of the voyage and the limited hold size of the caravels, a square-rigged store ship, "to carry extra provisions, because on many occasions the [lack of them] weakened the ships that were exploring on their return journey." Following Cão's expedition, the ships also carried a number of carved stone pillars, to mark the stages of the voyage. Dias himself was a highly experienced seaman, and he took with him the best pilots of the day, among them Pêro de Alenquer, destined to play a key role in the India ventures. Alenquer was evidently highly regarded by King João, who called him "a man who by his experience and navigating skill deserved to be honored, favored and well rewarded." The supply ship's pilot was João de Santiago, recorded on the inscription at the Yellala Falls, who would be invaluable in retracing Cão's voyage back to its terminal point.

This little flotilla sailed out of the Tejo sometime in late July or early

August 1487. It was to prove one of the most significant expeditions in the history of exploration, but also one of the most mysterious. It went almost unnoticed in contemporary records, as if Portuguese chroniclers were looking the other way. There is just a scattering of marginal notes on maps and books and casual mentions in the chronicles. Otherwise its details, its scope, and its achievement would wait sixty years to be recorded, by the sixteenth-century historian João de Barros. If the exact details of Dias's sailing instructions are lost, their substance can be reconstructed: first, to push south beyond Cão's last marker in pursuit of the elusive Prassus Promontory, the definitive end of Africa. Second, to land people along the coast to seek further information about an inland or river route to the kingdom of Prester John. This, in conjunction with the journeys of Paiva and Covilhã, constituted a determined and coherent strategy for solving the mystery of Asia.

To this end, Dias carried with him six Africans, two men and four women, who had been kidnapped by Cão on one of his journeys and taught Portuguese, because, according to João de Barros, "the king ordered that they were to be dropped all the way down this coast, finely dressed and supplied with displays of silver, gold, and spices." The intention was "that going into the villages, they would be able to tell the people about the grandeur of his kingdom, and the wealth that he had there, and how his ships were sailing all along this coast, and that he sought the discovery of India, and especially of a king called Prester John." Women were particularly chosen, as they would not be killed in tribal disputes.

In Alexandria, the two spies, Covilhã and Paiva, were dying of fever.

Dias sailed down the west coast of Africa, past Cão's last pillar, naming the capes and bays after the saints' days as he went, from which the expedition's progress can be dated: successively the Gulf of St. Marta (December 8), St. Tomé (December 21), and St. Victoria (December 23); by Christmas Day they had reached a bay they called the Gulf of

St. Christopher. They had been at sea for four months, zigzagging against a southwest wind blowing along the shore, with a current setting to north. At various places along the way they must have landed their unfortunate ambassadors, though one had already died on the voyage; of the others, nothing further is recorded. It was at this point that they decided to leave their supply ship with nine men on board, to be collected on their return, on the shores of Namibia.

For several more days the two caravels plugged past a desolate coast of low hills. Then the pilots took a startling decision. At about twenty-nine degrees south, they gave up the attritional battle with the adverse winds and currents. Instead they turned their ships away from the shore, lowered their sails to half-mast, and flung themselves out into the void of the westerly ocean with the counterintuitive aim of sailing east. No one knows exactly why this happened; it may have been a maneuver worked out in advance, or it may have been a moment of genius, an intuition about the Atlantic winds based on previous experience of sailing home from the Guinea coast. This involved a tack to the west away from the African coast, taking the ships out in a wide loop into the central Atlantic, where they picked up westerly winds that carried them east back to Portugal. Maybe, they reasoned, the same rhythm applied in the southern Atlantic. Whatever the logic, this was a decisive moment in the history of the world.

The caravel: ideal for exploration but cramped for long voyages

For thirteen days, and nearly a thousand miles, the half-masted caravels plowed out into nothingness. As they entered the Antarctic latitudes, it became very cold. Men died. At about thirty-eight degrees south, the intuition paid off. The winds became more variable. They turned their ships to the east with the hope and expectation of hitting an infinitely elongated African coast they imagined to still run north–south. They sailed on for several days. No land blurred the horizon. It was decided to turn the ships north again in the hope of finding land. Sometime toward the end of January, they spied high mountains; on February 3, 1488, they came ashore at a point they christened the Bay of the Cowherds. They had been on the open sea for nearly four weeks; their great loop had carried them past both the Cape of Good Hope and Cape Agulhas—the Cape of the Needles—Africa's southernmost point, where the Atlantic and the Indian Oceans meet.

Landfall was fraught. They saw a large herd of cows guarded by people "with woolly hair, like those of Guinea." They were unable to communicate with these pastoralists. Nine years later, the pilot Pêro de Alenquer was there again and remembered what happened. When the Portuguese placed gifts on the beach, the natives just ran away. The place was evidently provided with a spring, but "when Dias was taking in water, close to the beach, they sought to prevent him, and when they pelted him with stones from a hill, he killed one of them with the arrow of a cross-bow."

After this skirmish they sailed on another two hundred miles, and the coast unmistakably turned to the northeast. It was now apparent for the first time that they must have rounded the tip of Africa; the water was getting warmer, but the battering of the seas had taken its toll. On March 12, they reached a bay, where they planted their last pillar; at this moment the exhausted crews "with one voice began to murmur, and asked that they should not proceed further, saying that the supplies were being exhausted [and] that they needed to get back to the store ship, which they left behind with provisions, which was now so distant they would all be dead by the time they got there." Dias wanted to go on but was bound by his sailing instructions to consult with the other officers on matters of importance. They agreed to con-

tinue for just three more days; when they came to a river, which they
christened the Rio Infante, they turned about. It seems clear that Dias
was disappointed, but he abided by the democratic decision. The historian João de Barros, writing sixty years later, accords Dias a backward
glance as he retraced his steps: "when [he] departed from the pillar
which he had erected there, he was overcome by great sadness and
deep emotion, as if he was saying goodbye to a son banished forever;
he remembered the great danger faced by him and all his men, how
long they had journeyed to come only to this point, then that God had
not granted him the main prize." "He saw the land of India," said another chronicler, "but could not enter it, like Moses in the Promised
Land." But these were retrospective imaginings.

Back in Lisbon, King João, while waiting for news from Dias or Covilhã, was still hedging his bets. He could not definitively rule out the
advantages of the westerly route, and he was acutely aware of the
growing rivalry with Spain. On March 20, he granted Columbus a
safe-conduct to return to Lisbon, where he was subject to a warrant
for debt. Meanwhile Covilhã and Paiva had made a miraculous recovery from the fever that had struck them down in Alexandria. They
took a boat down the Nile to Cairo, a caravan across the desert to the
Red Sea, and then sailed to Aden, at its mouth. Here the two men
parted, Paiva to make his way to Ethiopia, to what he believed to be
the kingdom of Prester John, Covilhã to voyage on to India.

Turning his ships east now to sail home, Dias caught sight of the
Cape of Good Hope for the first time. It was a historic moment: this
definitive proof of the end of Africa demolished forever a tenet of
Ptolemy's geography. According to Barros, Dias and his companions
named it the Stormy Cape, which King João changed to the Cape of
Good Hope, "because it promised the discovery of India, so long desired and sought for over so many years." Dias left the Cape with a
good stern wind.

The men on the supply ship had been marooned on the desert
shores of Namibia for nine months, waiting forlornly for a sight of the
caravels that might never return. By the time these arrived on July 24,

1488, of the nine men, only three were still alive. The others had been killed by the local people in a squabble over the trading of goods. Among the dead may well have been Bartolomeu's own brother, Pêro. For one of the survivors, Fernão Colaço, the ship's clerk, weak with illness, the sight of the caravels proved too much. He is said to have died "from the joy of seeing his companions." The supply ship was rotten with worms; after transferring its contents, they burned it on the beach and headed for home. The battered caravels reentered the Tejo in December 1488. Dias had been away sixteen months, discovered 1,260 miles of new coast, and rounded Africa for the first time.

We know of his return only because of a famous marginal note written in a book by Christopher Columbus, still in Lisbon under safe-conduct. He was evidently a witness to the complete debriefing Dias gave to the king:

> Note, that in December of this year, 1488, there landed at Lisbon Bartolomeu Didacus [Dias], the commander of three [*sic*] caravels, whom the King of Portugal had sent to Guinea to seek out the land, and who reported that he had sailed 600 leagues beyond the furthest reached hitherto, that is, 450 leagues to the south and then 150 leagues to the north, as far as a cape named by him the Cape of Good Hope, which cape we judge to be in Agisimba, its latitude, as determined by the astrolabe, being 45° S., and its distance from Lisbon 3100 leagues. This voyage he [Dias] had depicted and described from league to league upon a chart, so that he might show it to the king; at all of which I was present.

The latitudes that Columbus mentioned have been the subject of heated historical debate, but there seems no doubt that he was present as the king and his cosmographers pored over the details of the voyage, whose features would quickly seep into contemporary maps. Dias had achieved two major breakthroughs. He had shown definitively that Africa was a continent with a seaway to India, abolishing some of the precepts of Ptolemy's geography; and by his inspirational swing out to sea, he had unlocked the final part of the riddle of the winds and suggested the way to get there—not by slogging down the African coast but by arcing out into the empty Atlantic in a widening loop and trusting to the reliable westerlies to carry ships around the continent's tip. It was the culmination of sixty years of effort by Portuguese sailors, but it is not clear that the achievement was apparent to the men to whom Dias told his tale. After so many false dawns, they were perhaps more cautious. There were no meritorious honors for Dias, no public pronouncements that the promised land had been glimpsed, as if they couldn't quite believe the revealed evidence: the warmer seas, the curve of the coast. Still holding to the shreds of classical geography, the consensus seems to have been that there might still be a farther point to be passed. The following year in another speech, which was almost a repeat of the earlier one made to the pope, it was claimed that "every day we are trying to reach those headlands . . . and also the sands of the Nile, by which one reaches the Indian Ocean and from there the Barbarian gulf, source of infinite riches." It would be another nine years before the value of Dias's voyage would become manifest. As for Columbus, he sensed that João's interest had died. He returned to lobbying the Spanish court.

Far away in the Indian Ocean itself, Covilhã was still traveling. In the autumn of that year, he caught a trading dhow across the Indian Ocean to Calicut (now Kozhikode), the hub of the spice trade and the terminus for much of the long-distance commerce from farther east. By early 1488 he was probably in Goa; he then sailed north to Ormuz, at the mouth of the Persian Gulf, another hub of the Indian Ocean. Crisscrossing the ocean, collecting and secretly recording information about sailing routes, winds, currents, ports, and politics, he picked up a ship going from the east coast of Africa to Sofala, far to the south, opposite Madagascar, the farthest point of Arab navigation in the southern Indian Ocean. He was attempting to find out about the feasibility of rounding Africa by sea, and navigation along its east coast. By the time he returned to Cairo, in 1490 or early 1491, he had been traveling for almost four years; he had scouted the major trade routes of the Indian Ocean and was in a position to provide the king with a detailed account.

Back in Cairo he learned that Paiva had died, somewhere on the way to Ethiopia. Meanwhile, João had sent out two Jews, a rabbi and a shoemaker, to look for his lost spies. Mysteriously, they somehow found and recognized Covilhã in the hubbub of Cairo and brought him letters from the king. The order was to return to Lisbon, but not before "he had seen and found out about the great king Prester John." Covilhã wrote the king a long letter, sent back with the shoemaker, detailing everything he had seen and knew—about the trade and navigation of the Indian Ocean, and adding that João's "caravels that frequent Guinea, by sailing from place to place and seeking the coast of the isle of Madagascar and Sofala, could easily enter these eastern seas and reach the shore of Calicut, because there is sea all the way."

By this time Covilhã seems to have been bitten by incurable wanderlust. He decided to finish off Paiva's business but interpreted João's orders freely. Accompanying the rabbi to Aden and Ormuz, he then made his own heavily disguised tour of the holy places of Islam— Mecca and Medina—before striking out for the Ethiopian highlands. Here he became the first Portuguese to meet the man they knew as Prester John, the Christian emperor of Ethiopia. The current ruler, Eskender, received him honorably but refused to let him leave. He was discovered in the country thirty years later by a Portuguese expedition, to whom he would tell his story. He remained in Ethiopia until the day he died.

Dias and Covilhã between them had effectively joined up the dots on a possible sea route to the Indies. The India plan was complete, though it is not clear when or even if Covilhã's report reached the king, nor what the silence surrounding Dias's achievement meant in court circles. However, in the interim, by coincidence, an Ethiopian priest came to Lisbon, forwarded by the pope. João returned him with a letter addressed to Prester John, stating "the desire he had for his friendship and of how he had explored the whole coast of Africa and Ethiopia." This wording might suggest that he had received news from Covilhã. By the early 1490s, João probably had all the necessary information to make the final push to the Orient and link up the world.

Instead, nothing happened. There would be a pause of eight years before the Portuguese followed up their decades of patient investigation. In the years after Dias's return, João was beset by problems. He was involved in bitter campaigns in Morocco toward the end of the 1480s—always a religious duty for crusading Portuguese kings; he was starting to be afflicted by the kidney disease that would finally kill him; and he was hard hit by unexpected turns of fortune. In 1491 his only son and heir, Afonso, died in a riding accident. In 1492, when the Jews were expelled from Spain, they fled in large numbers to Portugal, and this influx, despite the benefit of a large number of industrious and educated people, involved careful attention.

The following year came another heavy blow: on March 3, 1493, one battered ship struggled into the harbor at Restelo, near Lisbon, the traditional anchorage for returning vessels, but it was not Portuguese. It was Columbus returning with news of a voyage to the "Indies" in the *Santa Maria*—in fact, the modern-day Bahamas, Cuba, Haiti, and the Dominican Republic—made under the patronage of rival Spain. It is unclear if Columbus, an unreliable fabulist who reinvented his own past, was blown accidentally into the Tejo by a violent storm or if this visit was intended as a calculated snub to the king who had refused him. The man waiting to interview him was Bartolomeu Dias, whose voyage had scuppered Columbus's chances of Portuguese patronage. According to Columbus, who claimed to have reached islands close to Japan, he was then royally received by the king.

The Portuguese account was more muted. Columbus was insufferably condescending. The royal court found him "puffed up in manner, and continuously exceeding the bounds of truth in his account, and making the expedition much more significant in terms of gold, silver and riches than it actually was" and upbraiding the king for lack of belief. João was shaken by the apparent proof of the native hostages he produced. In appearance they were not African; they seemed more like what he imagined the people of the Indies to be, but no one could be certain exactly what the self-promoting Genoese had found. The king's advisers had a simple solution: kill him discreetly and the Spanish discoveries would die. João ruled it out; it was both morally wrong

and bad diplomacy, at a time when relations between the two monarchies were already strained.

What he did do was send a severe and rapid letter to Ferdinand and
Isabella in Seville to the effect that Columbus had encroached on Portuguese territory. In 1479, to end an earlier war, the two monarchies
had agreed to draw a horizontal frontier through the Atlantic Ocean,
ratified by the pope, that defined areas of exclusive exploration. João
believed that Columbus had discovered land within his domain and
prepared to send his own expedition. The Spanish appealed to Alexander VI, the Spanish Borgia pope, who found in their favor, cutting
Portugal out of huge swaths of the Atlantic Ocean that they believed
they had carved out for themselves. Suddenly Portuguese Atlantic hegemony was threatened, and they were not about to have their decades
of investment snatched away. João threatened war. The two sides agreed
to face-to-face negotiations, bypassing the pope, to defuse a major
diplomatic row.

At the small and ancient town of Tordesillas, on the plains of central
Spain, a delegation from each side met to bargain for the world. Here
they simply cut the globe in two with a vertical line through the Atlantic Ocean "from the Arctic to the Antarctic pole"; to the east of this line
was to be Portuguese; to the west, Spanish. João and his team of astronomers and mathematicians, probably more experienced and skillful,
forced their opponents to have this line moved from its original position,
proposed by the pope, more than a thousand miles to the west—midway
between the Portuguese Cape Verde Islands and the Caribbean islands,
discovered by Columbus, which he believed to be part of the coast of
Asia. Conveniently, this alteration was to bring the coast of Brazil, as yet
apparently undiscovered, within the Portuguese ambit. Since there was
no way of accurately fixing the longitude of the Tordesillas meridian, the
exact position of the line continued to be fiercely disputed. It would
remain so until 1777.

Like 1492 itself, the treaty marked a decisive moment in the end of
the Middle Ages. Although what was agreed at Tordesillas was later
ratified by Pope Pius III, rights to the world had effectively been removed from the hegemony of the papacy. They had been calculated by

Dividing up the world: the fierce Portuguese-Spanish rivalry for discoveries beyond the Atlantic Ocean led to a series of running disputes. King João was correct in his belief that Columbus had encroached on Portuguese territory south of the 1479 line. The pope's solution was highly favorable to Spain. In a series of bulls in 1493 he decreed that the space was to be divided by a vertical line running from pole to pole fixed 100 leagues west of the Azores and the Cape Verde Islands. This gave the Spanish the right to all discoveries west of the line, even as far as India, and seemed to grant Portugal no matching rights to any land by sailing east. Potential exclusion from India was unacceptable to João. At Tordesillas the line was moved 170 leagues west to include the apparently as-yet-undiscovered coast of Brazil. It also gave Portugal back rights to undiscovered lands east of the line. The Tordesillas settlement led to further disputes on the far side of the world when the Spanish reached the Moluccas in 1521 by sailing west, which the Portuguese had reached by sailing east in 1512.

scientists and carved up according to secularized national interests. In effect, the two Iberian powers at the cutting edge of exploration had turned everywhere beyond Europe into a privatized political space, to the bemusement of other monarchs. "Show me the clause in Adam's will," snorted Francis I of France derisively sometime later. Yet no one else by 1500 had the Atlantic access or the experience to challenge the Iberian pioneers. And Columbus had unknowingly sailed into a cul-de-sac, barred by the Americas, in his race for the Indies. Only the Portuguese knew enough to find a sea route there and to link up the world. They had a window of opportunity denied to their Spanish competitors.

Although João had been badly shaken by Columbus's claims, he revived his India plan and prepared a new expedition. But for him it was too late. "The Man is dead," Isabella of Spain was said to have murmured when she heard the news in 1495. She had hoped to marry her daughter to João's son, Afonso, but he had already died. The throne passed to the young Dom Manuel, duke of Beja, who had witnessed the final briefing of Paiva and Covilhã. Manuel fortuitously inherited a crown, eighty years of accumulated exploration experience, and the launchpad for the final push to India. He had even been gifted the wood to build the ships. If João passed into Portuguese history as the Perfect Prince, Manuel was destined to be the Fortunate King.

3

Vasco da Gama

October 1495–March 1498

THE NEW KING HAD inherited a streak of messianic destiny that ran deep in the Portuguese royal house of Aviz. Born on the feast day of Corpus Christi and christened with the luminous name Emmanuel, "God is with us," he read mystical significance into his coronation. He was twenty-six years old, round-faced, and possessed of disproportionately long arms, which hung down to his knees, giving him an apelike appearance. It had taken extraordinary circumstances to place him on the throne: the death or exile of six people, including the mysterious riding accident that killed João's son, Afonso, and the murder of his brother Diogo at João's own hands. He saw his kingship as a sign that he had been chosen by God.

In the dying years of the century, with the nearing of the fifteen hundredth anniversary of Christ's birth, apocalyptic tendencies swept Europe, particularly the Iberian Peninsula, where the expulsion of both the Muslims and the Jews from Spain was taken as a sign. In this atmosphere Manuel believed, and was encouraged to believe, that he was predestined for extraordinary things: the extermination of Islam and the worldwide spread of Christianity under a universal monarch. "Among all the western princes of Europe," wrote the mariner Duarte Pacheco Pereira, "God only wanted to choose Your Highness." The possibility that great deeds might be accomplished by tiny Portugal could itself be justified by biblical quotation: "the first shall be last; and the last shall be first."

King Manuel I as the universal monarch with the motto "[we turn] to God in heaven but to You on earth." He is flanked by the royal coat of arms with its five escutcheons and the armillary sphere, the mystical symbol of the Portuguese exploration of the world.

The India plan, which had faltered in the later troubled years of João's reign, became the primary outlet for these dreams. Manuel believed he had inherited the mantle of his granduncle Henrique, "the Navigator." Since the fall of Constantinople, Christian Europe had felt itself increasingly hemmed in. To outflank Islam, link up with Prester John and the rumored Christian communities of India, seize control of the spice trade, and destroy the wealth that empowered the Mamluk sultans in Cairo—from the first months of his reign, a geostrategic vision of vast ambition was already in embryo; it would, in time, sweep the Portuguese around the world. If it was forged in the spirit of crusade, it also had a material dimension: not only to wrest trade from the Mamluks but also to replace the Venetians as the mart for the luxury goods of the Orient. The project was at the same time imperial, religious, and economic. It was in this spirit that Manuel started to assemble the expedition to reach the Indies, a vaguely defined space, given the lack of detailed knowledge, that in the European imagination probably encompassed the whole of the Indian Ocean and wherever spices might grow.

The idea was not wholeheartedly endorsed. When Manuel called a general council in December 1495, a few weeks after his coronation, there was fierce opposition from a noble class that had been bullied by King João and saw no glory and much risk in such a long-range venture, compared to the easy rewards from crusading in Morocco. During his reign, Manuel would prove at times to be vacillating and indecisive, but he could also be authoritarian. He claimed an inherited obligation to pursue the discoveries and drew on his sense of divine mission to overrule all objections.

> And giving as an overriding reason, to those who cited the difficulties if India were discovered, that God, in whose hands he put this matter, would provide the means for the well-being of the kingdom [of Portugal], finally the king decided to proceed with this discovery, and when he was later in Estremoz, he appointed Vasco da Gama, *fidalgo* of his household, as captain-major [the commander's title] of the ships he would send there.

It seems that Vasco da Gama was initially only the second choice for this venture. Manuel first requisitioned Gama's older brother Paulo, who pleaded ill health but agreed to come on the voyage anyway, under Vasco's command. Gama, "an unmarried man and of the age to be able to weather the trials of such a voyage," was then in his thirties. His early career and experience and the reasons for his choice remain somewhat mysterious. He appears in few records prior to 1496; his seafaring knowledge is largely unknown. He came from minor nobility in the seaport of Sines, south of Lisbon, and probably had a background in corsairing along the Moroccan coast. Whatever he was or had been subsequently became, like the life of Columbus, enshrouded in myth. He was apparently short-tempered. At the time of his appointment, he had an outstanding charge of violent affray against his name. The obdurate nature of his personality would unfold in the voyage ahead: implacably steeped in the crusading tradition of hatred of Islam, enduring before the hard life of the sea, but crucially impatient of diplomatic niceties, he came to be described as "bold in action, severe in his orders and very formidable in his anger." Gama had probably been chosen more to command men and negotiate with the unknown kings of the Orient than to sail ships.

Vasco da Gama

By the 1490s, the exploration along the African coast had transformed Lisbon into a city buzzing with activity and expectation. The unloading of exotic produce on the gently sloping banks of the Tejo—spices, slaves, parrots, sugar—conjured up the expectation of new worlds beyond the breakwater. By 1500, probably 15 percent of the population were Guinea blacks—there were more slaves in the city than anywhere else in Europe. Lisbon was exotic, dynamic, colorful, and purposeful, "bigger than Nuremberg and much more populous," said the German polymath Hieronymus Münzer, who came here in 1494. The city was the cutting edge of new ideas about cosmography and navigation, the shape of the world and how it might be imaged on maps. After their expulsion from Spain in 1492, a wave of Jewish immigrants, many of them learned or entrepreneurial, further enriched the city's dynamism. Although their welcome did not last long, it brought a remarkable fund of knowledge. The refugees included the Jewish astronomer and mathematician Abraham Zacuto, whose creation of a maritime astrolabe and a book of tables for charting the position of celestial bodies would in time revolutionize navigation at sea.

For Münzer, Lisbon was a city of marvels. Here he could see an impressive synagogue with ten great chandeliers holding fifty or sixty candles each; the body of a crocodile hanging as a trophy in the choir of a church; the beak of a pelican and the enormous serrated saw of a swordfish; mysterious outsized canes gathered on the shores of the Canary Islands (which Columbus had also inspected and taken as proof of lands in the far west). He also got to see "an enormous and extraordinarily well-made golden map, fourteen palms in diameter"—it was Fra Mauro's map of 1459, displayed in the city's castle. He could meet seamen who could tell hair-raising tales of survival and escape, and talk with a contingent of German cannon founders and artillery men, held in great esteem with the king.

The wealth of produce for sale in the port startled him: great piles of oats, walnuts, lemons, and almonds, enormous quantities of sardines and tuna for export across the Mediterranean world. He visited the offices that controlled the import of goods from this new world, where he saw the merchandise of Africa: dyed cloth from Tunis, carpets, metal basins, copper cauldrons, beads of colored glass, and, from the Guinea coast, big bunches of fiery pepper, "of which they gave us a lot," the tusks of elephants, and black slaves.

What Münzer witnessed was not just a glimpse of an exotic world beyond the earth's curve but the industrial infrastructure of shipbuilding, seafaring provision, and arsenal facilities that gave Portugal its maritime punch. He saw

> an enormous workshop with many furnaces where they make an-
> chors, colubrinas [cannons] and so on, and everything necessary for
> the sea. There were so many blackened workers around the furnaces
> that we thought ourselves to be among the Cyclops in the cave of
> Vulcan. Afterward we saw in four other buildings innumerable very
> large and superb colubrinas, and also throwing weapons, javelins,
> shields, breastplates, mortars, hand guns, bows, lances—all very well
> made and in great abundance ... and what enormous quantities of
> lead, copper, saltpetre and sulfur!

The ability to produce high-quality bronze cannons and techniques for deploying them effectively at sea had probably been developed by the energetic King João, whose inquisitive mind and wide-ranging interests included practical experiments in shipborne artillery. He had developed the use of large bombards on caravels and carried out test firings to determine their most effective use on the decks of pitching ships. The solution was to fire the guns horizontally at water level; any higher and the likelihood was that the shots would whistle overhead. In some cases, if the guns were positioned sufficiently low down in the bows, the cannonballs could be made to ricochet off the surface of the water, thus increasing their range. The Portuguese also developed *ber-ços*, lightweight breech-loaded bronze swivel guns, which could be carried by ship's boats and had the advantage over the conventional muzzle-loaders in their rate of fire—up to twenty shots an hour. The superiority of their artillery, which was augmented by recruitment of German and Flemish cannon founders and gunners, was to prove a telling advantage in the events about to unfold.

The expedition in prospect was modest in scale but carefully pre-pared. It was based on decades of incremental learning. All the skill and knowledge acquired over many years in ship design, navigation, and provision for Atlantic voyages went into building two stout ships, and Manuel drew on a talented generation of practical experience in their construction. The caravel had been the agent and instrument of

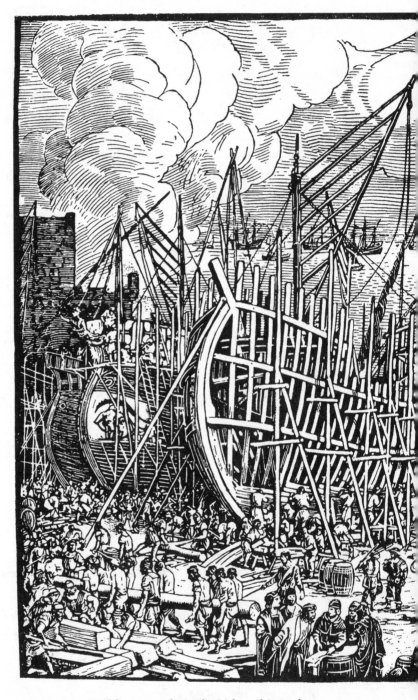

Building carracks in the Lisbon shipyard.
A caravel is beached in the center right of the picture.

all this exploration, ideal for nosing up tropical rivers and battling back up the African coast against the wind, but horribly uncomfortable on long voyages across huge seas. Dias's rounding of the Cape had exposed their operational limits: the crews would go no farther.

It was Dias who was charged with designing and overseeing the construction of two stout carracks, the sailing ships the Portuguese called *naus,* to lead the voyage. The brief was clear: they had to be durable enough to withstand the pounding seas of the southern Atlantic; roomy enough to accommodate and provision the crews better than the rolling decks of a caravel; small enough to maneuver in shallows and harbors. The ships under construction on the banks, their frameworks chocked up by wooden scaffolding, had tubby rounded hulls, high sides, a tall aftercastle, and three masts; they were nevertheless of shallow draft, and not outsized. They were about eighty feet long, and each probably weighed about 100 to 120 tons. Their square sails made them less maneuverable in a contrary wind; the compensation was their sturdiness against the unpredictable battering of unknown seas. A supply ship, intended to be broken up near the Cape, was also constructed.

It seems that no expense was spared in the construction or provisioning of these ships, or the recruitment and payment of the crews. "They were built by excellent masters and workmen, with strong nails and wood," remembered the mariner Duarte Pacheco Pereira.

Each ship had three sets of sails and anchors and three or four times as much other tackle and rigging as was usual. The cooperage of the casks, pipes and barrels for wine, water, vinegar and oil was strengthened with many hoops of iron. The provisions of bread, wine, flour, meat, vegetables, medicines, and likewise of arms and ammunition, were also in excess of what was needed for such a voyage. The best and most skillful pilots and mariners in Portugal were sent on this voyage, and they received, besides other favors, salaries higher than those of any seamen of other countries. The money spent on the few ships of this expedition was so great that I will not go into detail for fear of not being believed.

The barrels rolled up the gangplanks on the shores of the dockyard contained sufficient food for three years. Gama received two thousand gold cruzados for the venture, a huge sum; his brother Paulo, the same. The seamen's wages were raised, and some of the money paid in advance to support their families. It was perhaps a recognition that many of them would not be coming back. No detail was omitted. The ships carried the best navigational aids available: as well as sounding leads and hourglasses, astrolabes and the most up-to-date maps—and possibly copies of Abraham Zacuto's recently printed tables for determining latitudes from the height of the sun. Twenty cannons were hoisted aboard, both large bombards and the smaller breech-loaded *berços,* along with plentiful supplies of gunpowder tightly sealed against the sea air and quantities of cannonballs. The skilled craftsmen—carpenters, caulkers, forgers of iron, and barrelmakers—who would ensure the security of the ships were recruited in pairs, in case death thinned out their ranks. There were interpreters to speak Bantu and Arabic; musicians to lead sea chanteys and blow ceremonial fanfares; gunners and men-at-arms and skilled seamen, supported by an underclass of "deck fodder." These comprised African slaves, orphans, converted Jews, and convicted men, enrolled for the menial heavy work: hauling on ropes, raising anchors and sails, pumping out the bilges. The convicts were particularly expendable; they had been released from prison specifically to be put ashore to make first inquiries on uncharted and potentially hostile coasts; priests also went, to lead the prayers and consign the souls of the dead to the sea with a Christian burial.

There were four ships in all: the two carracks, christened *São Gabriel* and *São Rafael* after the archangels, according to a vow made by King João before his death; with them went a caravel, the *Bérrio,* and the two-hundred-ton supply ship. Gama called on seamen he knew and relatives he could trust, to lessen the possibility of dissent in a tightly knit expedition. These included his brother Paulo, commander of the *Rafael,* and two Gama cousins. His pilots and leading seamen were the most experienced of the age. They included Pêro de Alenquer and Nicholas Coelho, who had rounded the cape with Bartolomeu Dias, and Dias's own brother Diogo. Another pilot, Pêro Escobar, whose name was carved at the Yellala Falls, had been a navigator with Diogo Cão. Bartolomeu Dias was also scheduled to accompany the expedition on the first leg of the voyage in a ship bound for the Guinea coast.

The expense of this modest, speculative, but high-cost probe into the unknown was met with gold from the Guinea coast—and a windfall: in 1496 the reluctant expulsion of the Jews who would not convert to Christianity had been the bride price of Manuel's marriage to Princess Isabella of Spain. Their goods and property provided unexpected resources.

It was midsummer 1497 by the time the expedition was ready; the sails emblazoned with the red cross of the crusading Order of Christ, the barrels rolled aboard, the heavy cannons winched into position, the crews assembled. The small flotilla was floated out from the shipyards and anchored off the beach at Restelo, a fishing village downstream from Lisbon. In the stifling heat, Manuel had retreated to his hilltop castle at Montemor-o-Novo, some sixty miles inland, and it was here that Vasco da Gama and his captains made their way to receive their sailing instructions and a ritual blessing from the king. On bended knees, Gama was solemnly invested with the command of the expedition and a silk banner also emblazoned with the cross of the Order of Christ. He was given his instructions: to seek out Christian kings in India at a city called Calicut, to whom he was to hand a letter written in both Arabic and Portuguese, and to establish a trade in spices and "the oriental riches so celebrated by ancient writers, but which have made such great powers as Venice, Genoa and Florence." Another letter was addressed to Prester John. The mission was both sacred and secular, overtones of crusade mixed with commercial rivalry.

Restelo, on the banks of the Tejo outside the city walls, had been the traditional point of departure for Portuguese voyagers since the time of Henry the Navigator; its gently shelving beach provided a wide stage for the religious ceremonies and emotional rituals of departure: "a place of tears for those going, of joy for those who return." On the hill above, surveying the wide sweep of the Tejo that led west to the open sea, was Henrique's chapel, dedicated to Santa Maria de Belém, "Our Lady of Bethlehem," for the purpose of bestowing the sacraments on departing mariners. The whole crew, something between 148 and 166 men, spent the hot summer night before departure there in prayer and vigil.

July 8, 1497. A Saturday. The mission to rediscover India, "for so many centuries hidden." The day, consecrated to the Virgin Mary, had been chosen by court astrologers as auspicious for departure. A month earlier, the pope had granted Manuel perpetual ownership of lands conquered from the infidel on which other Christian kings did not already have claims. People came flocking out of Lisbon to send off their friends and relatives. Gama led his men in a devotional procession from the chapel down to the beach, organized by the priests and the monks of the Order of Christ. The navigators wore sleeveless tunics and carried lighted candles. The priests walked behind, chanting the litany, and the people called in response. When they reached the water's edge, silence fell on the crowd. Everyone knelt to make a general confession and to receive absolution, according to the papal bull Henrique had obtained for those who died "in this discovery and conquest." "In this ceremony everyone wept," according to João de Barros.

Then the men were ferried out to the ships in small boats. The sails were hoisted to the rhythmic clashing of cymbals, the vessels cast off, and the royal standard run up on Gama's flagship, the *Gabriel;* with the sailors raising their fists to the sky and chanting the traditional cries— "Safe voyage!"—and the blowing of whistles, the flotilla caught the wind, led by the two carracks, with the beautifully painted wooden figureheads of the archangels Gabriel and Raphael at their prows. People waded into the water to catch a last glimpse of their loved ones across the widening gap. "And with one party looking back at the land, the others to the sea, but all equally absorbed by their tears and the thought of the long voyage, they remained like this until the ships were far from port." The ships slid away down the Tejo until they passed the mouth and felt the first sting of the ocean.

And on the *Rafael* one man, whose identity has never been conclusively established, was preparing to take notes. The anonymous writer starts his terse journal, the only eyewitness account of everything that followed, with an abrupt lurch:

Artist's reconstruction of the *São Gabriel*

In the name of God. Amen!

In the year 1497, King Dom Manuel, the first of that name in Portugal, dispatched four ships to discover and go in search of spices.

We left Restelo on Saturday July 8, 1497. May God our Lord permit us to accomplish this voyage in his service. Amen!

If one goal—the search for spices—was clear, the curiously intransitive verb *descobrir*, "to discover," undefined by objective, hints at the extent to which this was a leap into the unknown.

Catching the favorable winds down the African coast, they sighted the Canary Islands within a week. Aware of likely weather conditions, Gama had given orders that if the ships became separated they should rendezvous at the Cape Verde Islands a thousand miles farther south. By the following night, the *Rafael* had become lost in fog; when it cleared next day, the others had vanished. It sailed on. By July 22, when the *Rafael* sighted the scattered outer islands of Cape Verde and the other ships came into view, it was the *Gabriel*, with their commander, that was now missing. Frustrated, they sat there becalmed for four days, on a flat sea. When the *Gabriel* was sighted, on July 26, something like relief broke out among the fleet. "And having got speech with him in the evening we gave expression to our joy by many times firing our bombards and sounding our trumpets." An edginess marks the early days of the expedition. A week was spent on the Cape Verde island of Santiago, making repairs to masts and taking on board meat, wood, and as much water as they could store in their barrels for the ocean sailing ahead.

"On Thursday 3 August we left in an easterly direction," recorded the anonymous writer in a routine voice. In fact, the expedition was about to embark on a maneuver for which there is no known precedent and only the sketchiest record. Some seven hundred miles south of the Cape Verdes, about seven degrees from the equator, instead of following the familiar contours of the African coast into the doldrums of Guinea, the *Gabriel* and its following vessels turned their rudders toward the southwest and plunged into the center of the Atlantic in a huge looping curve. The land had vanished. The ships driving briskly on into the unknown were swallowed up in the vastness of the ocean. The sails crackled in the salt wind.

Gama's course followed the counterintuitive truth established by Bartolomeu Dias nine years earlier—that to round Africa it was necessary to swing away out into the ocean to pick up westerly winds that would carry ships past the Cape—but the *Gabriel's* tack was a huge magnification of the earlier experiment. It is evident that by the end of the century, Portuguese navigators must have had a clear idea of how the winds of the southern Atlantic worked, but how they acquired this knowledge in the southwest quadrant of the sea remains unknown. The possibility of secret exploratory voyages in the interval since Dias's return remains speculative; the confidence to commit the ships to the deep ocean, relying on solar navigation to judge position, must have come from somewhere.

If it was deeply frightening, the unemotional journal contains no hint. On August 22, they saw heronlike birds flying south-southeast "as if making for the land," but by this time they were eight hundred leagues, over two thousand miles, out to sea. They clung to a sense of passing time by the calendar of saints' days; otherwise, their world was a blank of sea and sky, sun and wind. It would be another two months before the diarist saw anything else worth recording that might suggest they were not lost in an enormous void: "On Friday 27 October, the eve of St. Simon and St. Jude, we saw many whales."

Even before the pilots put their hands to the tiller to turn southwest, the ships felt the weight of the sea. Six hundred miles south of Santiago, the *Gabriel* cracked its main yardarm, "and we lay to under foresail and lower mainsail for two days and a night." The toughness of the crews must have been tested to the maximum. Each man watched four hours on, four hours off, day and night, the time being counted by the glass and called out by the ship's boys: "the watch is changed, the glass is running." The more unskilled work—pumping out the bilges, raising sails, hauling on ropes, swabbing decks—fell to the convicts and the dispossessed. The men would be fed on an unbalanced diet of biscuits, meat, oil and vinegar, beans, and salted fish—and fresh fish, when they could be caught. All foodstuffs deteriorated as the long days passed, the biscuits more wormy, the rats hungrier—though it was usual for ships to carry cats, and sometimes weasels, to control the rodent population. The one likely hot meal a day, if conditions were reasonable, would be cooked in a sandbox. It was not food that would run short but drinking water, which became increasingly foul as the voyage progressed and had to be mixed with vinegar. As the barrels emptied, they would be refilled with seawater to maintain the balance of the ship.

The aristocrats of the ships, the captains and the navigators, wearing the badges of their offices—a whistle hanging from a golden chain, capes of black velvet—ate and slept in their private cabins, the others according to their status: experienced seamen in the forecastle, men-at-arms under the bridge. If nights were fetid in cabins, they were worse for the convicts and outcasts, out on deck shivering under goat-skins or oilcloths as the ships ran south of the equator, into colder seas. Everyone slept on mattresses of straw in clothes stiff with salt, which in wet weather would never dry. Their oilcloth blankets would double as shrouds if they had to be cast to the depths. They defecated and urinated into buckets or directly overboard, as the sea dictated. No one washed. The round of the day was marked by the calling of the watch, the hours of meals, the emergencies to fix running repairs, the routine prayers morning and night. In stormy weather the sailors would be aloft, hanging from the rigging above a dipping and rearing sea, adjust-ing the sails, hauling in or resetting yards of heavy canvas, feeling the lash of rain and wind. When the ships were running well and the sea was stable, men would put themselves to their amusements. Gambling with cards, a ready source of trouble, was forbidden. The men might fish, catch up on sleep, read (if they could), sing and dance to pipe and drum, or hear the priest read the lives of the saints. Processions around the deck might be organized to mark the days of the saints, and Mass was said without consecration, for fear that the chalice might be over-turned and the contents profaned. The role of the musicians was to entertain and preserve morale.

Increasingly emaciated, thirsty, sleep-deprived, and weakened by seasickness, those unused to the shipboard life succumbed to dysentery and fever, and, almost unnoticed, despite whatever dried fruit, onions, or beans were initially included in their diet before they became ined-ible, the whole crew experienced the slow but steady advance of the sailor's disease. Without adequate vitamin C, symptoms present themselves after sixty-eight days; men start to die after eighty-four; in 111 days, scurvy wipes out a whole crew. For Gama's men, the clock was ticking.

Despite the ravages of the sea—the hot days of the equator, the increasingly cold, violent waters to the south—the ships sailed on, averaging about forty-five miles a day. At a latitude of perhaps twenty degrees south, the navigators felt the pull of variable winds, turned their prows to the southeast, and began to sweep back in the hope of rounding the Cape. On Saturday, November 4, the laconic diarist picks up his pen again with hardly a mention of the voyage behind: "we had soundings in 110 fathoms, and at nine o'clock we sighted the land. We then drew near to each other, and having put on our gala clothes, we saluted the captain-major by firing our bombards, and dressed the ships with flags and standards." The release of pent-up emotion behind the terse words was evident. They had been out of sight of land for ninety-three days, sailed some forty-five hundred miles across open sea, and endured. It was a remarkable feat of navigation. Columbus's crossing to the Bahamas took a mere thirty-seven.

They had, in fact, fallen slightly short of the Cape and landed in a broad bay 125 miles to the northwest. Landfall was the opportunity for scrupulous repairs: cleaning the ships, mending sails and yardarms, hunting for meat, and taking on water. It seems that for the first time they were able to assemble their astrolabe, unusable on the shifting deck of a ship, and take accurate readings of the latitude. There were edgy meetings with the natives, "tawny colored" men, according to the diarist, who was surprised that "their numerous dogs resemble those of Portugal, and bark like them." They captured one man, brought him to the ship, and fed him. However, the local language proved inaccessible to the interpreters: "they speak as if they have hiccups," the diary recorded. These were the Khoikhoi, pastoral people of southwest Africa, whom Europeans would later come to label Hottentots, in imitation of the sound of their words. Initially the exchanges were friendly—the diarist acquired "one of the sheaths which they wore over their penises"—but relations ended with a skirmish, in which Gama was lightly wounded by a spear. "All this happened because we looked upon these people as men of little spirit, quite incapable of violence, and had therefore landed without first arming ourselves." It was perhaps a seminal moment for the expedition. Henceforth, landfalls would be extremely cautious and heavily armed. The tendency was to shoot at the slightest provocation.

It took six days and several attempts to battle round the Cape of Good Hope in stormy weather. When they landed again, at the Bay of Cowherds—now rechristened St. Brás—where Dias had been nine years earlier, it was with shows of force: breastplates, drawn crossbows, and swivel guns loaded in the longboats to show the people who had come to see them "that we had the means of doing them an injury, although we had no desire to employ them." The mutual incomprehension of these meetings, which had marked many previous encounters down the coast of West Africa, contrasted with entrancing moments of shared humanity across the barriers of culture and language. Here the crew started to transfer goods from the supply ship, which they then burned on the beach.

On December 2, a large number of the natives, about two hundred, came down to the beach.

> They brought with them about a dozen oxen and cows and four or five sheep. As soon as we saw them we went ashore. They forthwith began to play on four or five flutes, some producing high notes and other low ones, thus making a pretty harmony for Negroes who are not expected to be musicians; and they danced in the style of Negroes. The captain-major then ordered the trumpets to be sounded, and we, in the boats, danced, and the captain-major did so likewise when he rejoined us.

The Africans and the Europeans were temporarily united by rhythm and melody, but the mutual suspicion remained. It ended days later with the Portuguese, fearful of ambush, firing their *berços* from the longboats to scatter the pastoralists. Their last sight of the bay, as they sailed away, was of the Khoikhoi demolishing the stone pillar and cross they had just erected. To relieve their feelings, the ships' crews used their cannons to blast a colony of seals and flightless penguins as they went.

The little flotilla paid a high price for not having cleanly rounded the Cape. The ships became temporarily separated by a storm; on December 15, they battled past Dias's last pillar against the prevailing current. By December 20, they had been swept back there again. It was here that Dias's men had refused to go on. Gama's ships were released from this coastal labyrinth only by an overpowering stern wind that swept them forward. "Henceforward it pleased God in His mercy to allow us to make headway!" the journal writer recorded with relief. "May it please Him that it be thus always!"

However, the contest to round Africa had frayed both men and ships. The *Rafael*'s main mast cracked near the top; then it lost an anchor. Drinking water was running low. Each man was now down to a third of a quart a day, and their thirst was not helped by having the food cooked in seawater. Scurvy was beginning to ravage the crews. The respite of a welcoming landfall was urgent.

On January 11, 1498, they reached a small river. Immediately they sensed that they had entered a different world. The clustering groups of tall people who came to meet them were quite unlike the Khoikhoi. They were unafraid and received the strange white men hospitably. These were Bantu people, with whom the interpreters were able to strike up some kind of communication. Water was taken on board, but a stay could not be prolonged, as the wind was favorable. By January 22, they had reached a low, thickly wooded coast and the delta of a much vaster river, in which crocodiles and hippopotamuses lurked. "Black and well-made" people came out in dugout boats to see them and to trade, though some of their visitors, described in the journal as "very haughty ... valued nothing which we gave them."

By this time, the ravages of scurvy were advanced and many of the crew were in a ghastly state. Their hands, feet, and legs were monstrously swollen; their bloody and putrid gums grew over their teeth, as if devouring them, so that they could not eat. The smell from their mouths became intolerable. Men started to die. Paulo da Gama went continuously to comfort and doctor the sick and the dying with his own medical supplies. What saved the whole expedition from annihi-

lation was not Paulo's ministrations nor the healthy air, as some believed, but, more accidentally, the abundance of fruits growing on the
banks of the Zambezi River.

They spent a month anchored off the immense delta, careening the
hulls of the ships, repairing the *Rafael*'s mast, refilling their water barrels, and recovering from the intense battering of the seas. Before they
left, they erected a pillar dedicated to St. Raphael and christened the
Zambezi the River of Good Omens. There was in the air, in the greater
warmth and the perceived higher level of civilization of the native
people, a sense of expectation. After seven months at sea, Gama's men
were on the threshold of the Indian Ocean.

The ships left on February 24 and were now within the Mozambique
Channel, the wide strait between the coast of East Africa and the island
of Madagascar, whose eddies and currents could pose a serious hazard
to sailing ships. The heat was mounting; the sky and sea a brilliant blue;
the view to landward a fringe of green trees, white sand, breaking surf.
Cautious of shoals, they sailed only by day. By night they anchored up.
Their progress was unhindered until they sighted a large bay, on
March 2. The light caravel, the *Bérrio,* testing the depths, mistook the
channel and became temporarily wedged on a sandbank. As Coelho,
the pilot, was extricating the ship and anchoring, they noticed a deputation of men in dugout canoes approaching from a nearby island to
the sound of brass trumpets. "They invited us to proceed further into
the bay, offering to take us into port if we desired it. Those among
them who boarded our ships ate and drank what we did, and went on
their way when they were satisfied." The port, they learned, was called
Mozambique, and the language of communication was Arabic. They
had entered the Muslim world. It was now that the complexity of their
dealings took a fresh turn.

4

"The Devil Take You!"

March–May 1498

THOUSANDS OF MILES AWAY, on the walls of the royal palace of St. George in Lisbon, the great circular map of Fra Mauro projected its own image of the world. Its Africa was grossly distorted, its India less a defined subcontinent than the torn edge of a vast and circular Asia. Many of its annotations and place-names derived from the wanderings of Niccolò de' Conti, the fifteenth-century Venetian traveler. But it clearly showed an Indian ocean to be crossed, and it marked the coastal city of Calicut, which Conti had identified as the hub of Indian commerce, with the promising legend "here pepper grows." The spy Pêro da Covilhã also claimed to have sent back details of his mission to India in a letter handed over in Cairo, before vanishing into the uplands of Ethiopia. This should have given the Portuguese much information about the world into which they had now sailed, but it remains unclear to this day whether Covilhã's letter made it back to Lisbon or was ever transmitted beyond King João, and whatever secret instructions, maps, destinations, or mental geography Gama carried with him were probably hidden from the anonymous writer on his voyage. Gama seems to have been furnished with a letter addressed only vaguely to "the Christian king of India" in Calicut; that it was written in Arabic suggests that the Portuguese were aware of a significant Muslim presence in the Indian Ocean. Beyond this, it appears from everything that ensued that their knowledge of this world—its weather systems, its ancient trading networks, the intricate cultural relations between Islam and Hinduism, its conventions for doing business and its politics—was woefully limited. Their blunders and misunderstandings would be multiple and have long-term consequences.

The Indian Ocean, thirty times the size of the Mediterranean, is shaped like an enormous M, with India as its central V. It is flanked on its western edge by the arid shores of the Arabian Peninsula and the long Swahili coast of East Africa; on its east, the barrier islands of Java and Sumatra and the blunt end of Western Australia separate it from the Pacific; to the south run the cold and violent waters of the Antarctic. The timing and trade routes of everything that moved across its surface in the age of sail were dictated by the metronomic rhythm of the monsoon winds, one of the great meteorological dramas of the planet, by whose seasonal fluctuations and reversals, like the operation of a series of intermeshing cogs, goods could be moved across great stretches of the globe. The traditional ship that plied the waters of the western Indian Ocean was the dhow—that is, any of a large family of long, thin vessels with triangular lateen sails of various sizes and regional designs, ranging from coastal craft of between five and fifteen tons up to oceangoing ships of several hundred tons that could overtop Gama's carracks. Historically, these were sewn vessels, held together by coir ropes, made from coconut fiber without the use of nails.

Unlike Columbus, the Portuguese had not burst into silent seas. For thousands of years, the Indian Ocean had been the crossroads of the world's trade, shifting goods across a vast space from Canton to Cairo, Burma to Baghdad, through a complex interlocking of trading systems, maritime styles, cultures and religions, and a series of hubs: Malacca, on the Malay Peninsula, larger than Venice, for goods from China and the farther spice islands; Calicut, on the west coast of India, for pepper; Ormuz, gateway to the Persian Gulf and Baghdad; Aden, at the entrance to the Red Sea and the routes to Cairo, the nerve center of the Islamic world. Scores of other small city-states dotted its shores. It dispatched gold, black slaves, and mangrove poles from Africa, incense and dates from Arabia, bullion from Europe, horses from Persia, opium from Egypt, porcelain from China, war elephants from Ceylon, rice

from Bengal, sulfur from Sumatra, nutmeg from the Moluccas, dia-
monds from the Deccan Plateau, cotton cloth from Gujarat. No one
had a monopoly in this terrain—it was too extensive and complex,
and the great continental powers of Asia left the sea to the merchants.
There was small-scale piracy but there were no protectionist war fleets,
and little notion of territorial waters prevailed; the star fleets of the
Ming dynasty, the one maritime superpower, had advanced and withdrawn. It constituted a vast and comparatively peaceful free-trade zone:
over half the world's wealth passed through its waters in a commercial
commonwealth that was fragmented between many players. "God," it
was said, "had given the sea in common."

This was the world of Sindbad. Its key merchant groups, distributed
thinly around its shores, from the palm-fringed beaches of East Africa
to the spice islands of the East Indies, were largely Muslims. Islam had
been spread, not at the point of a sword, but by missionaries and merchants from the deck of a dhow. This was a polyethnic world, in which
trade depended on social and cultural interaction, long-range migra-
tion, and a measure of mutual accommodation among Islam, Hinduism, and Buddhism, local Christians and Jews; it was richer, more
deeply layered and complex than the Portuguese could initially grasp.
Their mindset was defined by the assumption of monopoly trading
rights, as developed on the west coasts of Africa and by holy war in
Morocco. The existence of Hinduism appears to have been occluded,
and their default position when checked was aggression: hostage taking and the lighted taper ever ready at the touchhole of a bombard.
They broke into this sea with their fast-firing, ship-mounted cannons,
a player from outside the rules. The vessels they would encounter in
the Indian Ocean lacked any comparable defenses.

It became immediately apparent as Gama's ships approached the
town of Mozambique that this was different from the Africa of their
previous experience. The houses, thatched with straw, were well built;
they could glimpse minarets and wooden mosques. The people, evidently Muslim merchants richly dressed in caftans fringed with silk
and embroidered with gold, were urban Arabic speakers with whom
their translators could communicate. The welcome was unusually
friendly. "They came immediately on board with as much confidence

as if they were long acquainted and entered into familiar conversation." For the first time the Portuguese heard news of the world they had come to find. Through the interpreters they learned of the trade of the "white Muslims"—merchants from the Arabian Peninsula; there were four of their vessels in the harbor, bringing "gold, silver, cloves, pepper, ginger and silver rings ... pearls, jewels and rubies." "Further on, where we were going," the anonymous writer added with a justifiable note of incredulity, "they abounded, and ... precious stones, pearls and spices were so plentiful that there was no need to purchase them as they could be collected in baskets." This heady vision of wealth was encouraging enough; but they also learned of a large presence of Christians along the coast and that "Prester John resided not far from this place; that he held many cities along the coast, and that the inhabitants of those cities were great merchants and owned big ships." Whatever might have been lost in translation, "we cried with joy and prayed God to grant us health, so that we might behold what we so much desired."

Gradually it dawned on the Portuguese that they themselves were also assumed to be Muslim merchants. Initially the sultan came on board in the spirit of friendship, and despite Gama's attempts to lay on a show—probably not easy, given the battered appearance of both ships and men—he was disappointed by the quality of the presents on offer. The Portuguese, apparently ignorant of the wealth of this new world, had departed from Lisbon with trinkets to delight a West African chief: brass bells and basins, coral, hats, and modest garments. The sultan wanted scarlet cloth. With the failure of these curious and emaciated sailors to establish their credibility as traders or people of substance, questions arose about their identity and intentions. Initially the sultan took them for Turks and was keen to see their famed bows and their Korans. Gama was forced to dissimulate: they were from a country near Turkey and had not wished to entrust their sacred books to the sea; but he did lay on an impressive firing of crossbows and a display of armor, "with all of which he was much pleased, and greatly astonished."

They had already learned how treacherous the coast could be—the *Bérrio* had grounded entering the harbor—and that the way ahead was dotted with shoals. Gama asked the sultan for the loan of a pilot. He provided two, to be paid in gold; inherently suspicious of the intentions of Muslims, Gama insisted that one should always remain on board. If doubt was growing in their hosts' mind, the mood soon darkened. On Saturday, March 10, when the ships were moved from the town to an island three miles away with the aim of conducting a secret Mass there, one of the pilots absconded. Gama sent two boats to hunt for him, but they were met by six armed vessels coming from the island with an order for them to return to Mozambique town. At this point the Christians probably thought that their cover had been blown. The one pilot they had was trussed up to prevent escape, and the bombards put the Muslims to flight. It was time to move on.

However, the weather thwarted their departure. The wind turned. They were forced back to the island. The sultan tried to make peace overtures but was refused. Ten nervy days ensued. The water on the island was brackish, and the ships were running short. They were forced to return to the port of Mozambique on March 22. At midnight they attempted a secret landing to collect water, taking with them the remaining pilot. He either could not or would not locate the spring. In the lingering daylight the following evening, they tried again and found it guarded by twenty men. The bombards roared and put the men to flight. The battle for water continued. The next day they still found the source guarded, and this time the men were protected by a palisade. They bombarded the site for three hours, until the people fled. By March 25, the continuous threat of cannon fire kept all the inhabitants inside. Watering again, the Portuguese left, having snatched a few hostages from a boat, with some parting shots at the town for good measure.

A pattern of frustration and aggressive response was emerging. The captains were increasingly short-tempered and suspicious, desperate for reliable provisions and the friendly welcome of a Christian port. None was forthcoming.

Progress north was slow. They were forced back by contrary winds, sounding the channels with extreme caution for shoals and sandbanks, as they distrusted their captive pilot. They overshot the port of Kilwa, which they believed to contain many Christians, whipped the

man for deceiving them, accidentally grounded the *Rafael,* and finally reached the island port of Mombasa. It was Palm Sunday. "We
anchored here with much pleasure," recounted the diarist, "for we
confidently hoped that on the following day we might go on land
and hear mass jointly with the Christians reported to live there under
their own judge in a quarter separate from that of the Moors." The
comfortable notion of being among fellow Christians died hard.

Landfall at Mombasa followed the pattern they had begun to establish. There was an initial welcome from the sultan. Two men, probably
convicts chosen for the role, went ashore and were well received. For
the first time they met "Christians," "who showed them a paper, an
object of their adoration, on which was a sketch of the Holy Ghost."
It was to prove one of the deepest, almost comical, early misconceptions of the Portuguese that Hindus, of whom they apparently had no
knowledge, with their own images of gods, were Christians of a deviant sect. The Portuguese had come into the Indian Ocean expecting
to find estranged Christians; these men with their unfamiliar anthro-
pomorphic images neatly fitted a fixed preconception.

The sultan sent them some samples of spices as a trading gambit, but
it may well be that their reputation had preceded them. Lulled by this
welcome, the small squadron prepared to enter port under local guidance, but then the *Gabriel* started to drift and struck the next ship. In
the confusion, the pilots on board panicked. Probably fearing further
punishment, they leaped into the sea and were picked up by local
boats. The Portuguese were now jumpy. That night they tortured two
of their hostages by dropping boiling oil onto their skin to make them
"confess" that the order had been given to capture the ships as revenge
for the bombardment of Mozambique. "And when this torture was
being applied a second time, one of the Muslims, although his hands
were tied, threw himself into the sea, whilst the other did so during the
morning watch." The risk of death by drowning seemed preferable.

Toward midnight, the lookouts on the ships detected what they
took to be a rippling shoal of tuna moving through the moonlit sea.
These turned out to be men swimming silently toward the ships.
Reaching the *Bérrio,* they began to cut the cable; others managed to
climb up onto the rigging, but "seeing themselves discovered, they si-

lently slipped down and fled." On the morning of April 13, the flotilla
set sail again for Malindi, seventy miles up the coast, in pursuit of better luck and a reliable pilot. The anonymous account relates that the
sick had shown good signs of recovery, "because the climate of this
place is very good." The cause was more likely the vitamin C from a
good supply of oranges. Even so, the expedition was faltering. The
crew were so exhausted by hauling up the anchors that their strength
failed and they were compelled to cut the rope and leave one on the
seabed. As they worked their way up the coast, they came upon two
boats "and at once gave chase, with the intention of capturing them,
for we wanted to secure a pilot who would guide us where we wanted
to go." One escaped, but they ran down the other. All seventeen passengers, including a distinguished old man and his wife, preferred to
throw themselves overboard rather than be taken by pirates, but they
were scooped up out of the water, along with "gold, silver, and an
abundance of maize and other provisions" from the boat. By now hostage taking had become the default strategy in a world perceived to be
hostile.

By the evening of April 14, they had reached Malindi. With perhaps
a note of homesickness, the diarist remarked that its high whitewashed
houses with their many windows, set among fertile fields and greenery,
reminded him of a town back home on the banks of the Tejo. The following day was Easter Sunday. No one came out to inspect the strange
ship. Their reputation had preceded them. Gama landed the old man
on a sandbank in front of the town as a cautious go-between and
waited for him to be rescued. The initial response from the sultan was
similar to that of the two previous landfalls. The old man came back
with word that the sultan "would rejoice to make peace with him . . .
and willingly grant to the captain-major all his country afforded,
whether pilots or anything else." Gama moved the ships closer to the
town but remained standoffish, trying to read the signs. He refused all
invitations to step ashore, saying that "he was not permitted by his
master to go on land." Negotiations were conducted from adjacent
rowboats, but the words remained friendly. The sultan sent out sheep
and spices. He asked for the name of their king to be written down
and desired to send him an ambassador or a letter.

Weighing these words, Gama eased his position and released the boat hostages as a show of goodwill. Unwittingly, the Portuguese were learning their first lesson in the political diplomacy of the Indian Ocean. The sultan was seeking allies in a contest with Muslim trading rivals up and down the coast; the Christian incomers would in time understand how to leverage such alliances across the fault lines of religion to splinter opposition. The two parties engaged in courteous honorific ceremonies, safely separated by an expanse of water. The sultan, "much pleased, made the circuit of our ships, the bombards of which fired a salute." There was an exchange of visitors—the convicts again being sent ashore—and the sultan, seated on a bronze throne on the beach and serenaded by musicians, ordered his horsemen to stage mock fights along the sand. Gama refused repeated entreaties to come ashore and visit the sultan's old father.

Meanwhile the Portuguese were heartened to hear that four ships of Indian Christians had arrived recently in Malindi, and in due course these "Christians" came aboard. When they were shown a picture of Christ on the cross and his mother, "they prostrated themselves, and as long as we were there they came to say their prayers in front of it, bringing offerings of cloves, pepper, and other things." Their ships evidently possessed cannons and gunpowder; they lit up the night sky with a spectacular display of rockets and bombards in honor of their coreligionists; their shouts of "Christ! Christ!" split the air, and they warned Gama, via an exchange in imperfect Arabic, neither to go ashore nor to trust Muslims. They were unlike any Christians the Portuguese had ever seen. "These Indians are tawny men," he noted in his diary. "They wear but little clothing and have long beards and long hair, which they braid. They told us that they ate no beef." In the midst of this cultural confusion, it is likely that these long-hoped-for coreligionists were actually shouting, "Krishna! Krishna!"

There was something of a festive atmosphere to the Europeans' reception in Malindi. "We remained in front of this town during nine days, and all this time we had fetes, sham-fights, and musical performances." But Gama was anxious to obtain a pilot, and it took another hostage seizure to extract one. The sultan dispatched a "Christian" who was willing to steer the expedition across the ocean to their desired destination. He was more likely a Gujarati Muslim, possessed of a chart of the western Indian coast and familiar with quadrants for taking astronomical observations. Five hundred years later, Arab dhow captains would still be cursing this Muslim pilot who first let the Franks, the Europeans they called the *ferengi,* into the secrets of the ocean's navigation.

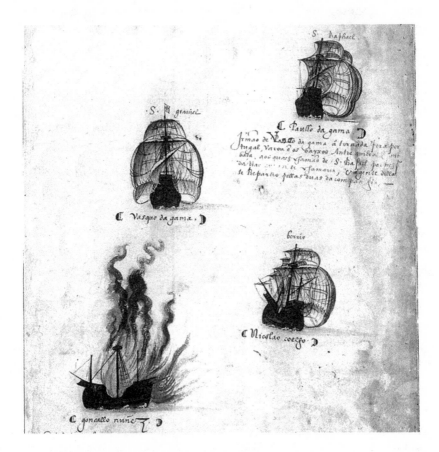

Gama's small flotilla. The supply ship was burned
after rounding the Cape.

On April 24, with the monsoon winds turning in their favor, the crews headed out to sea "for a city called Calicut." The turn of phrase suggests that the diarist at least was hearing this name for the first time—and perhaps the whole expedition, blindly breaking into the

Indian Ocean, had only the vaguest sense of their destination. With a continuous following wind, the diagonal crossing of this new sea was astonishingly quick. They were heading northeast. On April 29 they were comforted by the return of the polestar to the night sky, lost to view since the South Atlantic. On Friday, May 18, after only twenty-three days away from land and twenty-three hundred miles of open water, they spied high mountains. The following day shattering rain thundered on the decks, blotting out visibility; fierce flashes of lightning split the sky. They had hit the early prelude to the monsoon. As the storm cleared, the pilot was able to recognize the coast: "he told us that they were above Calicut, and that this was the country we desired to go to." Through the breaking rain, they surveyed India for the first time: high peaks looming through the murk. These were the Western Ghats, the long chain of mountains belting southwestern India, on the Malabar Coast; the men could see densely forested slopes, a narrow plain, surf breaking on white sand.

It must have been an emotional sight. They had watched their loved ones wading into the sea at Restelo 309 days ago. They had sailed twelve thousand miles and already lost many men. Behind lay a much longer voyage, one that reached back decades, to the first explorations of Prince Henrique, the hard slog down the African coast, the river explorations, the ships lost, the generations of men who had sailed and died. This first blurred view of India stands as a significant moment in world history. Gama had ended the isolation of Europe. The Atlantic was no longer a barrier; it had become a highway to link up the hemispheres. This was a signal moment in the long process of global convergence, yet there is no sense of any larger achievement in the resolutely factual anonymous journal, and there are only muted hints in slightly later Portuguese accounts: Vasco da Gama paid off the pilot handsomely, called the crew to prayers, and gave "thanks to God, who had safely conducted them to the long-wished-for place of his destination."

They had arrived unseasonally with the first blast of the monsoon, at a time when no ships called on this coast. From the shore there was immediate interest, sparked by both the novelty of the ships themselves, unlike anything sailing the Indian Ocean, and their unlikely timing. Four boats came out to see the strange visitors and pointed out Calicut some way off; the following day, the boats were back. Gama sent one of his convicts ashore with the visitors, a man called João Nunes, a converted Jew, destined to make the most famous landfall in Portuguese history.

The crowd on the beach took him for a Muslim and led him to two Tunisian merchants, who spoke some Castilian and Genoese. The encounter was one of mutual astonishment. Nunes found himself addressed in a language of his own continent: "The Devil take you! What brought you here?"

It was almost anticlimactic, a moment in which the world must have shrunk. The Portuguese had girdled the earth only to be spoken to almost in their own tongue. The commonwealth of Islamic trade, from the gates of Gibraltar to the China Sea, was far more extensive than the Portuguese could yet grasp.

"We came," replied Nunes, with considerable presence of mind, "in search of Christians and spices."

It was probably a fair description of Manuel's sailing instructions. The Tunisians were equally incredulous. They could not understand how the journey had been made or why by the Portuguese: "Why does not the king of Castile, the king of France, or the Signoria of Venice send men here?"

Nunes, upholding the dignity of his adopted land, replied that the king of Portugal would not permit it. The two men took him to their house and fed him delicacies—wheat bread and honey—then enthusiastically accompanied him back to the ships. "Good fortune! Good fortune!" one of them broke out as soon as he had clambered aboard. "Many rubies, many emeralds! You should give many thanks to God for having brought you to a land where there are such riches!" "We were so amazed at this that we heard him speak and we could not believe it," said the anonymous diarist, "that there could be anyone so far away from Portugal who could understand our speech."

The meeting with the friendly Muslims was probably as deeply disorienting as anything that was about to follow. It was as if the Portuguese were looking at their own world down the wrong end of a telescope. It was Europe that was ignorant and isolated, not this sea into which they had stumbled. And they were extraordinarily lucky. One of the Tunisians, a man they called Monçaide (perhaps Ibn Tayyib), would help them interpret this new world. He had a nostalgia for the Portuguese, whose ships he had seen trading on the North African coast in the reign of João II. He offered guidance to the labyrinthine manners and customs of Calicut that would prove invaluable. The city, he told them, was ruled by a king, the *samudri raja,* "the Lord of the Sea," who would "gladly receive the general as ambassador from a foreign king; more especially if the objects of his voyage were to establish a trade with Calicut, and if the general had brought with him any merchandise proper for that purpose; since the advantages which the samudri derived from the customs upon trade formed the chief source of his revenue."

Calicut, despite the lack of a good natural harbor, had established itself as the premier center for the trading of spices along the Malabar Coast because of its rulers' reputation for good governance and fair dealing with merchants. "In Calicut," one fifteenth-century visitor had noted, "no matter where a ship is from and where it is headed, if it docks there, they treat it like any other ship and subject it to no more or no less duty." It had a sizable and deeply settled Muslim trading community, whose people, known as the Mappilas, were the offspring of Muslim sailors and low-caste Hindus, as well as traveling merchants from the Arabia Peninsula, the "Mecca merchants"; all lived in harmony with their high-caste Hindu overlords to the mutual benefit of both religious groups. This reciprocal arrangement had been noted during one of the great Chinese maritime expeditions. "Formerly," wrote the chronicler Ma Huan, "there was a king who made a sworn compact with the Muslim people: You do not eat the ox; I do not eat the pig; we will reciprocally respect the taboo. [This] has been honored right down to the present day." It was this harmonious arrangement that the Portuguese were destined to disrupt.

The samudri customarily lived with other high-caste Hindus in a palace some distance from the city; he had another residence within Calicut itself, situated on a vantage point from which he could look down on the harbor and survey the comings and goings of ships—and enforce his tax dues. It was here that he was accustomed to meet foreign merchants and ambassadors. As he was out of the city, Gama sent two convict emissaries with Monçaide to press his case.

The samudri's reply was prompt and welcoming: he presented the messengers with gifts, expressed his willingness to meet the curious arrivals, and set off with his retinue to the city. He also provided a pilot to lead their ships to a better anchorage some distance away, in a secure harbor at a settlement the Portuguese would call Pandarani. Gama agreed to move his ships, but following his experiences along the African coast, he was cautious and would not proceed right into the berth that the pilot indicated. Suspicion and the tendency to misread motives would dog Portuguese actions in this new world.

On board there followed a heated debate among the captains about how to proceed. They already assumed the worst of the Islamic merchants. The majority verdict was that it was too risky for the captain-major to step ashore. Even if, as they believed, the majority of the population were Christians, the commercial and religious enmity of Muslim traders in the city would make any landfall by their leader highly dangerous. Gama, in a speech probably created for him by the chroniclers, insisted that there was now no other way. They had reached India as the king's ambassador. He must negotiate in person even at the risk of his life. He would take a few men with him and stay for only a short while: "It is not my intention to stay long on shore, so as to give opportunity to the Muslims to plot against me, as I propose only to talk with the king and to return in three days." The rest must remain at sea under his brother's command; an armed boat should be sent close to the shore each day to try to maintain communication; if any harm should befall him, they should sail away.

On the morning of Monday, May 28, a week after their arrival, Gama set out with thirteen men. The party included interpreters and the anonymous writer, well placed to provide an authentic eyewitness account. "We put on our best attire," he recorded, "placed bombards in our boats, and took with us trumpets and many flags." Splendor was to be matched by armed defense. In a scene that would be romanticized by nineteenth-century painters, the battered sailors, still rocking with the pitch of the ships, set foot on the Indian subcontinent, "so long obscured," in the best style they could muster, to the blare of trumpets.

They were greeted in contrasting style by the samudri's *bale*—his governor. To the groggy sailors, the sight of the reception committee was alarming: a large number of men, some with big beards and long hair, their ears pierced with glinting gold, many naked to the waist and holding drawn swords. These men were Nayars, members of the Hindu warrior caste, sworn from youth to protect their king until death. The Portuguese took them for Christians, and the reception seemed friendly. A palanquin, the means of transport reserved for dignitaries, shielded by an umbrella, was waiting for Gama. It was hoisted onto the shoulders of six men, organized in relays, and set off at a run. The rest of the party had to follow as best they could. Calicut was some distance off, and they attracted a growing crowd as they went. After some time they were set down at a house and fed on rice with much butter and excellent boiled fish. Gama, watchful or already impatient, declined food; the *bale* and his entourage retired for food in an adjacent house, the separation perhaps required by the dictates of the caste system.

Then the visitors were transferred to two boats lashed together and paddled down a river between palm trees, with a floating cavalcade of other craft following and people watching from the bank; they passed large ships drawn up high and dry on the banks. "They had all come to see us," observed the journal writer. "When we disembarked, the captain-major once more entered his palanquin." As they approached the city, the crowds thickened; women came out of their houses carrying children and followed them down the road. A note of claustrophobia and disorientation enters the narrative. The writer's eyes were swiveling in his head as he tried to take everything in: the unfamiliar appearance of the people, "of a tawny complexion," so unlike the Portuguese experience of Africans; the men variously shaved or heavily bearded; the women, "as a rule, short and ugly" in his estimation, but heavily festooned with gold necklaces and bracelets, and with toe rings set with precious stones that seemed to speak of the wealth of the Indies. In general he found the people "well-disposed and apparently of mild temper," but above all he was struck by their vast numbers.

Entering the city, they were guided to "a large church . . . as large as a monastery, all built of hewn stone and covered with tiles." There is nothing in this account to suggest that the Hindu temple they were led into was not a church of some deviant Christian sect. Outside there were two pillars, probably lingams of the god Shiva. Inside, they saw a sanctuary chapel in the center with a bronze door; "within this sanctuary stood a small image which they said represented Our Lady." It is impossible to know what was being lost in translation: probably from the Arabic of the Portuguese to an Arabic-speaking native, who then translated into Malayalam, the language of the Malabar Coast. Gama knelt down and prayed; the priests sprinkled holy water and "gave us some white earth, which the Christians of this country are in the habit of putting on"; Gama set his to one side. The diarist noticed, as they left, the saints on the walls, wearing crowns and "painted variously, with teeth protruding an inch from the mouth, and four or five arms."

Out on the street, the crowd continued to build until it became impossible to move for the press of people; the guests had to be sequestered in a house while a guard was called to clear a way through the throng by beating drums, blowing trumpets and bagpipes, and firing muskets. People crowded onto the roofs to see them go by. It was nearly sunset when they reached the palace. "We passed through four doors, through which we had to force our way, giving many blows to the people." Men were wounded at the entrance. At last they came into the king's audience chamber, "a great hall, surrounded with seats of timber raised in rows above one another like our theaters, the floor being covered by a carpet of green velvet, and the walls hung with silk of various colors." Before them sat a man they believed to be the Christian king they had come twelve thousand miles to find.

5

The Samudri

May 1498–August 1499

T HE FIRST SIGHT OF a Hindu monarch was, to Portuguese eyes, remarkable:

The king was of a brown complexion, large stature, and well advanced in years. On his head he had a cap or miter adorned with precious stones and pearls, and had jewels of the same kind in his ears. He wore a jacket of fine cotton cloth, having buttons of large pearls and the button-holes wrought with gold thread. About his middle he had a piece of a white calico, which came only down to his knees; and both his fingers and toes were adorned with many gold rings set with fine stones; his arms and legs were covered with many golden bracelets.

The samudri reclined in a posture of Oriental ease on a green velvet couch, chewing betel leaves, the remnants of which he spat into a large gold spittoon. "On the right side of the king stood a basin of gold, so large that a man might just encircle it with his arms; this contained the herbs. There were likewise many silver jugs. The canopy above the couch was all gilt."

Gama had evidently been coached by Monçaide as to how to return the king's greeting with the appropriate gestures: not to approach too near and to speak with his hands in front of his mouth. The guests were fed with fruits and given water. When asked to drink from the jug without touching it to their lips, "some poured the water into their throats and fell a coughing, while others poured it beside upon their faces and clothes, which much amused the king." In the crowded auditorium, it was a situation of cultural disadvantage that probably pricked Gama's sense of pride.

When he was asked to address the assembled company, Gama asserted his dignity and requested to speak in private. Withdrawing into an inner room with just their interpreters, he talked up his mission: to come to the land of India, which they had been seeking for sixty years on behalf of his king, "the possessor of great wealth of every description," to find Christian kings. He promised to bring Manuel's letters to the samudri next day. By this time Gama had evidently assumed the samudri to be a Christian.

By now a great deal of time had passed. As was the custom, the samudri asked if Gama would like to lodge with the Christians (in fact, the Hindus) or the Muslims. Gama warily asked for his men to lodge on their own. It was about ten o'clock at night. The rain was pouring down in the dark, churning up the street. He was carried on the palanquin under an umbrella; they wound through the streets followed by a large crowd so slowly that Gama lost patience and complained. They were taken out of the rain for a while, but the Oriental palaver continued. He was offered a horse to ride but without a saddle; he refused. Presumably he traveled on in the palanquin until they reached their lodgings, to which his bed had been delivered by sailors from the boat, along with the presents for the king. It was the end of a long and confusing day of overwhelming impressions: the massed crowds, the lack of breathing space, the unfamiliar rituals, the monsoon rain stirring rich smells. Probably still moving to the pitch and roll of a ghostly ship, they fell into exhausted sleep.

Whatever credibility had been gained with the samudri quickly evaporated. If the gifts with which the Portuguese had been furnished in Lisbon were snubbed in Mozambique and Malindi, here it was worse. The following morning, Gama collected the items to send to the palace: twelve pieces of striped cloth, four scarlet hoods, six hats, four strings of coral, six hand-washing basins, a case of sugar, two casks each of honey and oil. These were objects to impress an African chief, not a potentate used to the rich trading culture of the Indian Ocean. The *bale* just laughed: "the poorest merchant from Mecca, or any other part of India, gave more ... if he wanted to make a present it should be in gold." He flatly refused to forward these paltry items to the Sovereign of the Sea. Furious backpedaling was required. Gama retorted that "he was no merchant but an ambassador ... if the king of Portugal ordered him to return he would entrust him with far richer presents." Some Muslim merchants came to further disparage the wretched objects.

Gama asked to go and explain the situation in person. This could be done, he was told, but he must wait for a short time and then he would be taken to the palace. He waited impatiently. No one returned. Behind the scenes, something was going on. The Muslim merchants had sensed a threat from the Christian incomers; they may have received reports of the foreigners' aggressive tactics and bombardment of the Swahili coast. For all the credited openness of Calicut to trade, there were vested interests to protect; there is evidence that the Muslims had been instrumental in driving Chinese merchants out of the city decades earlier. They probably secured an audience with the samudri to relay the suggestion that Gama was at best a chancer, more likely a pirate. The Portuguese subsequently believed that the Muslims requested Gama's death. All day Gama waited, his temper rising. Evidently their captain's inability to relax was not shared by his companions. "As to us others," said the diarist, "we diverted ourselves, singing and dancing to the sound of trumpets, and enjoyed ourselves much."

In the morning they were taken back to the palace, where they waited four hours. To Gama, now thoroughly worked up, it was a calculated snub. Finally word came that the king would see only the captain-major and two others. The whole party thought "this separation portended no good." Gama stepped through the doorway, heavily guarded by armed men, with his secretary and interpreter.

The second interview was frosty and perplexing. The samudri wanted to know why Gama had not come the previous day. Unable to understand what motives these strangers could have if not to trade, his questions followed in quick succession to the effect that if he were from a rich country, why had he not brought gifts? And where were his letters? Gama was forced to extemporize answers about how he had brought nothing because this was a voyage of discovery. It would be followed up by others, with rich gifts. He did at least have the letters at hand. The king probed the gift mystery again: "What had he come to discover: stones or men?" he demanded ironically. "If he came to discover men, as he said, why had he brought nothing?" He had evidently been told that one of the ships contained a golden image of St. Mary. "Not golden" was the reply—the image was probably of gilded wood—to which the stoutly resistant Gama added "that even if she were he would not part with her, as she had guided him across the ocean, and would guide him back to his own country." When it came to the reading of the Arabic copy of the letter, Gama did not trust the Muslims to translate from Arabic to Malayalam; but although the "Christian" boy who was his interpreter could speak both languages, he was unable to read either. When it was finally translated, the samudri was partially appeased. Gama had at least established authentic credentials. Finally there was the issue of the merchandise: Gama might return to the ships, land, and sell it as best he could. He never saw the samudri again.

Tension, uncertainty, and mistrust increased on the lengthy journey back to the ships. Gama, perhaps conscious of status, again refused a horse and demanded a palanquin. The monsoon rain battered the streets. The anonymous writer and his companions trudged behind and got lost in the downpour. Eventually they reached the seaside port of Pandarani, exhausted, and caught up with their captain, sheltering in a guesthouse. By this time Gama was again in a foul mood. He asked for a boat to take them back to the ships. The *bale* replied, quite reasonably, that it was dark and it might be difficult to locate the ships standing some way offshore. Mutual antagonism between the two men was ratcheted up. The party was exhausted; they were given a meal, which "we ate, notwithstanding our fatigue, having been all day on our feet."

The following morning, Gama asked again for boats. The *bale* requested the ships to be brought closer inshore to make the transfer easier in the monsoon weather. The Portuguese feared a trap, orchestrated by the Muslim faction in the city; the *bale* suspected that these strange visitors might try to leave without paying their customs dues.

"The captain said that if he ordered his vessels to approach, his brother would think that he was being held a prisoner, and that he gave this order on compulsion, and would hoist the sails and return to Portugal." He demanded to return, with his complaints, to the samudri, "who was a Christian like himself." The *bale* agreed but then placed a heavily armed guard on the doors, "none of us being allowed to go outside without being accompanied by several of these guards." The *bale* requested that if the ships remained offshore, they should give up their rudders and sails so as not to make off. Gama refused. When he declared that they would die of hunger, the reply was that "if we died of hunger we must bear it." There was a tense standoff.

In the midst of this, Gama did contrive to slip a man out to meet up with a boat waiting offshore "with orders to go back to the ships and put them in a secure place." The messenger boat was pursued by local craft but managed to return to the ships. A measure of paranoia infected the hostages. Gama feared that if the ships came into port, "once inside they could easily be captured, after which they would first kill him, and then us others, as we were already in their power."

The journal recorded a day of tightening fear, offset by an ability to live in the moment.

We passed all that day most anxiously. At night more people surrounded us than ever before, and we were no longer allowed to walk in the compound, within which we were, but confined within a small tiled court, with a multitude of people around us. We quite expected that on the following day we should be separated, or that some harm would befall us, for we noticed that our jailers were much annoyed with us. This, however, did not prevent our making a good supper off the things found in the village. Throughout that night we were guarded by over a hundred men, all armed with swords, two-edged battle-axes, shields and bows and arrows. While some of these slept, others kept guard, each taking his turn of duty throughout the night.

There was an anxiety that this might be their last night on earth.

Next morning, the whole problem inexplicably vanished. Their captors came back, with "better faces," as the journal writer said. They would do as the king had requested: if the Portuguese landed their goods, they might go. They explained what the bristling Gama had failed to understand: that "it was the custom of the country that every ship on its arrival should at once land the merchandise it brought, as also the crews, and that the vendors should not return on board until the whole of it had been sold." Gama promptly sent a message to his brother to send "certain things"—not all. Some goods were landed; two men remained behind to manage and sell them, the prisoners were released back to their ships. "At this we rejoiced greatly, and rendered thanks to God for having extricated us from the hands of people who had no more sense than beasts."

The samudri probably remained uncertain how to play these strange visitors; they fitted no known category of merchant, yet they evidently came from a great king, and the commercially oriented monarch, whose wealth derived from the trading vessels that came to his open port, was reluctant to snub a potential opportunity out of hand. At his shoulder the Muslim merchants were undoubtedly hostile to the infidel intruders; whether they were plotting the murder of the Portuguese is uncertain, but their antagonism was probably as much commercial as religious. The Portuguese had come to the Indian coast with their visors lowered. Hardened by decades of holy war in North Africa, their default strategies were suspicion, aggressive hostage taking, the half-drawn sword, and a simple binary choice between Christian and Muslim, which seemed genuinely not to have factored into calculation the existence of Hinduism. These impatient simplicities were ill suited to the complexities of the Indian Ocean, where Hindus, Muslims, Jews, and even Indian Christians were integrated into a polyethnic trading zone.

Only a portion of the goods had been landed—not the complete stock, as was the custom—and displayed at a house in Pandarani. The king sent merchants to inspect the goods; they sniffed at the pathetic items on sale. "They spat on the ground, saying 'Portugal! Portugal!'" Gama complained to the king and asked if he might have his stock carried to Calicut itself. In a show of goodwill, the samudri ordered his *bale* to have the goods transferred at his own expense. "This was done," said the diarist, voicing perpetual Portuguese suspicion and the tendency to misread motives, "because it was intended to do us some ill turn, for it was reported to the king that we were thieves and went about to steal."

Nevertheless, the situation now provided the visitors with a chance to participate, in a modest way, in the commercial life of the city. The seamen had come with a small stock of goods to trade on their own behalf—"bracelets, clothes, new shirts and other articles"—and they were allowed ashore in threes by turn. They were largely disappointed with the results. Finely worked shirts fetched a tenth of their value back home, as did their other items, but they were able to buy small quantities of spices and precious stones in return. In the weeks that followed, they started to unravel the different strata of Malabar society. Along the road to Calicut they came in contact with the low-caste fisher families ("Christians"), who were far from unwelcoming. They were invited in "to eat or to sleep"—which was probably a euphemism for the easy sexual favors of Malabar women—and people came on board with their children to exchange fish for bread, so many that "sometimes it was night before we could get rid of them." These people were evidently poverty-stricken. They snatched biscuits out of the hands of sailors mending their sails "and left them nothing to eat." As a matter of policy, Gama ordered adults and children who came aboard to be fed, "to induce them to speak well of us and not evil."

The culturally curious Portuguese were starting to note the divisions in society, and they were quick learners. These weeks of informal dealing allowed them to glimpse the mechanisms and rhythms of the Indian Ocean trade and an outline of the supply networks, information they would store for future reference. Calicut itself was a major producer of ginger, pepper, and cinnamon, although better quality of the latter could be had from "an island called Ceylon, which is eight days journey to the south." Cloves came from an "island called Malacca." "The Mecca vessels" (from the Arabian Peninsula, fifty days' sailing away) would carry spices to the Red Sea, and then, via a series of transshipments, successively to Cairo and up the Nile to Alexandria, where the galleys of Venice and Genoa would load up. The Portuguese noted all the checks and barriers in this trade: the inefficient transshipments, the robbery on the road to Cairo, the exorbitant taxes paid to

the sultan there. It was this complex supply chain that they were keen
to disrupt.

July and August were dead months for trade in Calicut, too early for
the monsoon winds to carry the dhows from Arabia and the Persian
Gulf, but the visitors must have smelled the spices perfuming the
humid air and seen the stocks of merchandise ready for their arrival,
along with porcelain and lacquer from China, copper and worked
metals, sulfur and precious stones. It was hardly surprising that they
received so little trade.

They also heard tales, dating back many years, of mysterious visitors
who "wore their hair long like Germans, and had no beards except
around the mouth." Evidently these men had come with formidable
technical resources.

> They landed, wearing a cuirass, helmet, and visor, and carrying a
> certain weapon attached to a spear. Their vessels are armed with
> bombards, shorter than those in use with us. Once every two years
> they return with twenty or twenty-five vessels. They are unable to
> tell what people they are, nor what merchandise they bring to this
> city, save that it includes very fine linen cloth and brass-ware. They
> load spices. Their vessels have four masts like those of Spain.

It was a garbled account of the great Chinese star fleets of the Ming
dynasty, long withdrawn, leaving a power vacuum in the Indian Ocean
waiting to be filled—but, like all the wandering voyagers of the sea,
they had left a genetic imprint. There was a Chinese mix in the population of Calicut and along the Malabar Coast.

By the start of August, Gama was ready to leave. Whatever trade
could be effected had been accomplished, and he was probably keen
to get away before a heavy influx of Arab ships arrived and the winds
became too unfavorable for departure. The problem was that the expedition was seriously out of sync with the climatic rhythms of the
ocean.

Encouraged, at least, that some trade had gone on, Gama made an
attempt to create a small permanent commercial presence in the city.
He sent the samudri presents and informed him that he wished to

depart but to leave some men behind to carry on trade. At the same time, he requested ambassadors (or hostages) to accompany the ships back to Portugal. In return for the presents, he asked for some sacks of spices, which would be paid for "if he [the samudri] desired it."

Communications with the samudri had turned frosty again. Gama's messenger, Diogo Dias, waited four days before being admitted to his presence. The samudri did not deign to look at the presents; they should have been sent to his agent. Then he demanded a trading tax from the Portuguese, saying "that then he might go: this was the custom of the country and of those who came to it." Dias replied that he would return to Gama with this message, but he found himself detained in the house with his merchandise by armed men, and orders were given that no boats were to approach the Portuguese ships. The samudri was evidently concerned that they would sail away without paying.

Once more relations unraveled. Gama failed to understand that all merchants were obliged to pay port taxes and that the poor goods they had left onshore provided no surety. Instead, the interpretation of this behavior was that "the Christian king" had been influenced by the Muslims for commercial purposes; that they had told the samudri "that we were thieves, and that if once we navigated to his country, no more ships would come from Mecca . . . nor from any other part . . . that he would derive no profit from this [trade with the Portuguese] as we had nothing to give, and would rather take away, and that thus his country would be ruined." The basic strategic assumption would prove accurate, even if Portuguese fears that the Muslims had offered "rich bribes to the king to capture and kill us" might not. During all this period, Gama continued to receive advice and insights from the two Tunisian Muslims they had met on first landing, and who played a significant part in their understanding of this confusing world.

Meanwhile, the detainees managed to slip a message out to the ships to the effect that they were being held as hostages. Because Gama now knew this and the samudri's people were unaware that he did, he was able to develop a stealthy plan. On August 15, a boat appeared carrying some men offering to sell stones; in reality they had probably come to sense the mood on the ships. Gama gave no hint that he knew of the hostages; he wrote a letter to Diogo Dias ashore, as if nothing were amiss. Seeing no threat, more merchants came out to visit the ships: "all were made welcome by us and given to eat." On August 19, twenty-five men came out, including "six persons of quality" (high-caste Hindus). Gama saw his chance and promptly kidnapped eighteen of them and demanded his men back. On August 23, he bluffed that he was leaving for Portugal, sailed away, and waited twelve miles offshore. The next day he returned and anchored within sight of the city.

Cagey negotiations ensued. A boat called to offer to exchange Dias for the hostages. Suspicious as ever, Gama chose to believe that his man was dead and that this was just a delaying tactic "until the ships of Mecca able to capture us had arrived." He was playing tough, threatening to fire his bombards and to decapitate the hostages unless the men were returned. He bluffed a farther retreat down the coast.

In Calicut there was evidently consternation. The samudri sent for Dias and tried to untie the knot. He offered to return him for the hostages on board, and via a double interpretation process—Malayalam to Arabic, Arabic to Portuguese—he dictated a letter, addressed to King Manuel and written by Dias with an iron pen upon a palm leaf, "as is the custom of the country." The gist read: "Vasco Gama, a gentleman of your household, came to my country, whereat I was pleased. My country is rich in cinnamon, cloves, ginger, pepper and precious stones. That which I ask of you in return is gold, silver, corals and scarlet cloth." The samudri was perhaps hedging his bets against future trade. He also permitted the erection of a stone pillar—the ominous calling card of Portuguese intentions.

Offshore, the bargaining went on. Dias was brought out and the hostages were exchanged in a rowboat, as none of the accompanying people dared step aboard the *Rafael*. The stone pillar was winched into the boat, and six of the hostages were released. The other six Gama "promised to surrender if on the morrow the merchandise was restored to him." The following day he received a surprise visitor. Monçaide, the Tunisian, begged to be taken on board. His help to the unwelcome visitors had turned people against him, and he feared for his life. Later, seven boats approached with the merchandise, with many men. The bargain had been to swap the men for the goods, but

Gama broke it. He summarily decided to abandon the goods and carry the hostages off to Portugal. He left with a parting shot: "be careful, as he hoped shortly to be back in Calicut, when they would know whether we were thieves." Gama was not one to forgive or forget. "We therefore set sail and left for Portugal, greatly rejoicing at our good fortune in having made so great a discovery," the diarist reported with satisfaction.

They had already left behind them a bitter legacy. The samudri was furious at the broken bargain and sent a swarm of boats in pursuit. They caught the Portuguese, becalmed farther up the coast, on August 30. "About seventy boats approached us . . . crowded with people wearing a kind of cuirass made of red cloth." As they came within range, the Portuguese fired their bombards. A running fight ensued for an hour and a half, until "there arose a thunderstorm which carried us out to sea; and when they could no longer do us harm they turned back, while we pursued our route." It was to be the first of many naval engagements in the Indian Ocean.

It took further entanglements before the little flotilla could cut out to sea; the vessels were not in good shape, and they needed water. They worked their way slowly up the coast, hunting for water sources and receiving a friendly reception from the local fishermen, bartering for food and being able to cut cinnamon growing wild along the coast. On September 15, they erected the third of their pillars on an island. A few days later they landed on one of a cluster of small islands with plentiful water sources, the names of which they misheard from local Hindus as Anjediva.

During this time, their movements were being closely observed. On September 22, they sustained a second attack from a flotilla from Calicut, but Portuguese gunnery crippled the lead ship and the others fled. The presence of these alien vessels was causing continuous interest and suspicion, and Gama was finding the coast increasingly uncomfortable. On the following two days, deputations of boats came waving flags of friendship. Gama beat them off with warning shots. Visitors to the ships provided contradictory accounts of the comings and goings. Another friendly visitation, this one bringing gifts of sugarcane, was repulsed. There was a growing sense that curiosity was

usually a front for some evil intention. They were warned by local
fishermen that one of these attempts had been made by a noted pirate
of the region, called Timoji, a man who would figure prominently in
the subsequent doings of the Portuguese.

While they were careening the *Bérrio* on the beach, they received
yet another visitor—an extremely well-dressed man who spoke the
Venetian dialect and addressed Gama as a friend. He had a tale to tell.
He was a Christian who had been captured and converted to Islam,
"although at heart still a Christian." He was in the service of a rich
lord, from whom he sent a message—that "we might have anything in
his country which suited us, including ships and provisions, and that if
we desired to remain permanently it would give him much pleasure."
Initially his claims seemed plausible, but as time went on the Portuguese noticed that he talked "so much and about so many things, that
at times he contradicted himself."

Paulo da Gama, meanwhile, was checking the mysterious visitor's
credentials with the Hindus who had accompanied him: "they said he
was a pirate who had come to attack us." The Venetian was seized and
beaten. After he had been "questioned" three or four times, a different
story emerged. He admitted that there were a growing number of
ships gathering to attack, but he could not be broken down further.

It was evidently time to get out. The coast was becoming too hot to
handle. Soon Muslim trading ships would start to arrive from the Arabian Peninsula, and Anjediva was a frequented stopover for water. The
Portuguese ships, with the exception of the *Rafael,* had been careened;
fresh water had been loaded; boatloads of cinnamon had been collected, with the help of local fishermen. In a final act of contempt,
Gama refused a handsome offer from its captain for the return of a
vessel he had captured. He "said that it was not for sale, and as it belonged to an enemy he preferred to burn it." Such intransigence was a
foretaste of what was to come.

On October 5, the ships put out to sea, carrying away with them the
enigmatic Venetian spy; he might prove useful. They now had no pilot.
No one who had knowledge of the monsoon winds would have set

out to sail west at this time. They probably had little choice, given the circumstances, but whether Gama was aware that it would prove a terrible mistake is unknown. When six hundred miles were between them and India, the "Venetian" finally confessed, though his story would unfold in stages. He was indeed the agent of a rich lord, the sultan of Goa. He had been dispatched to assess whether the ships could be taken by the sultan, rather than by a privateer, with the aim of employing the Portuguese in his wars with neighboring kings. For Gama, this shed an interesting light on the politics of western India, which would later be put to advantage, and it flagged the importance of Goa. The Venetian's story became increasingly surprising as the voyage went on. He was a Polish Jew, a victim of the pogroms of central Europe whose wanderings had led him through successive identities. During the voyage he acquired another: by the time he reached Portugal, he had been baptized a Christian in the name of Gaspar da Gama.

The return across the Indian Ocean descended into nightmare. The details are muffled in the anonymous journal, which refers only briefly to "frequent calms and foul winds," but the reality of being imprisoned in the Indian Ocean for three months can be read between the lines: dispiriting and contrary breezes pushing them back, then the far more terrible calms, with the ships sitting unmoving for days on a sea of hot zinc; nights lit by an unpitying moon; the men bickering over whatever shade was afforded by the bulwarks or the dejected sails, tortured by thirst and hunger, calling on the saints for aid; vermin crawling from the biscuits; the water fouled. It would have been necessary to keep wetting the planks to stop the wood from splitting and rendering the ships unseaworthy.

The dread symptoms of scurvy reappeared: "all our people again suffered from their gums, which grew over their teeth, so that they could not eat. Their legs also swelled and other parts of the body, and these swellings spread until the sufferer died." The high-caste Hindu hostages would probably have been the first to go, forbidden under Brahmanic law from eating on the high seas; one by one the dead were lowered over the side, with a soft splash and the murmuring of prayers; those left alive just tottering. "Thirty of our men died in this manner—

an equal number having died previously—and those able to navigate each ship were only seven or eight." "We had come to such a pass that all bonds of discipline had gone" was the diarist's tight-lipped comment on what appears to have been a mutiny in the making. There was evidently a call to return to India, possibly even a plot to take control of the ships. The commanders agreed in principle to turn back, should a westerly wind prevail. Another fortnight, according to the anonymous writer, and they would all have been dead.

Then, as despair reached its zenith, a favorable wind picked up and carried them west for six days. On January 2, 1499, the battered ships sighted the African coast. It had taken just twenty-three days to make the voyage across; the return took ninety-three. The lessons of the seasonal monsoon were hard won.

Sailing down the African coast, they passed the Muslim port of Mogadishu; Gama, still seized with anger at the Muslims of the Malabar Coast, gratuitously bombarded the town and swept on. On January 7, the tattered ships arrived at Malindi, where again they received a warm welcome. Oranges were supplied, "much desired by our sick," but for many it was too late. Amity with the sultan of Malindi resulted in an exchange of gifts, including an elephant tusk for King Manuel; a stone pillar was erected, and a young Muslim taken on board who "desired to go with us to Portugal." They passed on, skirting inhospitable Mombasa, but by January 13 it became apparent that there were too few men to sail all three ships. The *Rafael,* which had not been careened on the Indian coast, was the most worm-eaten. They transferred all her goods and the graceful red-and-gold figurine of the archangel and burned the ship on the beach. At Zanzibar they made peaceful contact with the sultan, then stopped at the island of St. George, near Mozambique, to say Mass and erect their last pillar, but "the rain fell so heavily that we could not light a fire for melting the lead to fix the cross, and it therefore remained without one."

Picking up colder winds, they made a stop at the bay of St. Brás on March 3, rounded the Cape on March 20, though "at times nearly dead from the cold . . . [and] pursued our route with a great desire of reaching home." Here the anonymous account breaks off abruptly on April 25, in unknown circumstances, near the shoals at the mouth of

the Gambia, off the coast of West Africa. The conclusion of the voyage
was recorded in other sources. The *Bérrio* and the *Gabriel* got separated
in a storm, but by this time Gama had deeper concerns. His brother
Paulo was dying. At the island of Santiago, he relinquished the *Gabriel*
to his pilot, João de Sá, chartered a caravel, and hurried Paulo to the
island of Terceira, in the Azores. The *Bérrio* sailed into the mouth of
the Tejo and landed at Cascais, near Lisbon, on July 10, 1499, with the
news; the *Gabriel* followed soon after. Paulo, who had faithfully accompanied his brother on the epic voyage, died the day after reaching
Terceira and was buried there. The mourning Vasco did not make it
back to Lisbon until, probably, the end of August. He spent nine days
in retirement with the monks at the chapel of Santa Maria de Belém
mourning the death, before making a triumphant entry into Lisbon in
early September.

The voyage had been epic; they had been away a year, traveled twenty-
four thousand miles. It was a feat of endurance, courage, and great luck.
The toll had been heavy. Two-thirds of the crew had died. Unaware of
the rhythms of the monsoon, they had been fortunate to survive;
scurvy and adverse weather could have taken all of them in the Indian
Ocean, leaving ghost ships floating on an empty sea.

Gama was received with great acclamation; he was made grants of
land and money, elevated to the higher nobility, and given the further
honorific title of admiral of the Indies. Manuel ordered processions and
ritual Masses across the land and, with a sure instinct for public relations, set about projecting Portugal's great success to the papacy
and the royal houses of Europe. He took sly delight in informing Ferdinand and Isabella of Spain that his ships "did reach and discover
India" and had bought quantities of "cinnamon, cloves, ginger, nutmegs
and pepper . . . also many fine stones of all sorts, such as rubies and others." "We are aware," he disingenuously continued, "that Your Highness
will hear of these things with much pleasure and satisfaction"—with
certain enjoyment that the opposite would be the case. To Pope Alexander Borgia and his cardinals, he wrote trumpeting the discovery of
a Christian India: "His Holiness and Your Reverence must publicly

rejoice and give many praises to God." The fact that much of the information about this world had come via Gaspar da Gama, a converted
Jew, was taken as a sign that "God ordered and wished to constitute
Portugal as a kingdom for a great mystery of His service and for the
exaltation of the Holy Faith." Manuel saw in this the hand of destiny.

The ennobled Gama's coat of arms

The commercial implications spread quickly across Europe. Even as
the first ships docked in Lisbon, faint whispers reached Venice. On
August 8, the Venetian diarist Girolamo Priuli recorded a rumor from
Cairo that "three caravels belonging to the king of Portugal have arrived at Aden and Calicut in India and that they have been sent to find
out about the spice islands and that their captain is Columbus ... this
news affects me greatly, if it's true; however I don't give credence to it."
In Lisbon, Italian merchants were soon gathering detailed firsthand

information to confirm the expedition and its true commander from returning sailors. The prospect of the wealth of the Indies being in direct reach was immediately obvious—as were its commercial advantages and its ability to threaten vested interests in Europe. The Florentine Girolamo Sernigi pointed out that the taxes and transportation costs of the present Red Sea route raised purchase prices sixfold.

> And it all goes to pay the carriers, the ships and the dues of the sultan. So going the other way it's possible to strip out all these costs and middlemen. Which is why I hold that the sultan, these kings and the Muslims will do all they can to rebuff the Portuguese king in this business. If the king . . . continues it will be possible to sell spices at the port of Pisa many times more cheaply than at Cairo, because it's possible to get them there [via Lisbon] at a much lower cost.

The net result would be that the Venetians and Genoese would lose their spice monopoly. Sernigi added, "I don't doubt that they will do all they can to destroy this venture."

Vasco da Gama's voyage had taken everyone by surprise. It had added eighteen hundred new places to Europe's gazetteer of the world and revealed a mine of new information about the Indies. It would quickly compel all interested parties across a vast stretch of the globe—Christian, Muslim, and Hindu—to make fresh strategic calculations, and it would lead inevitably to commercial conflict and outright war. As for Manuel, it increased his confidence. To his existing titles, "King of Portugal and of the Algarves on this side and beyond the sea in Africa, and Lord of Guinea," he added "Lord of the Conquest, Navigation and Commerce of Ethiopia, Arabia, Persia and India." It was a bold claim to the monopoly of trade, and an intimation of Portuguese intentions: that the sea should be owned. Even before Gama's return, the king had been laying down keels for the next departure. By the same token, he had ordered the suppression of all the sailing charts of Gama's voyage on pain of death. Knowledge was wealth and power.

PART II

Contest

MONOPOLIES AND HOLY WAR

1500–1510

6

Cabral

March 1500–October 1501

JUST SIX MONTHS AFTER Gama's return, a vastly larger fleet was
ready to depart from the shores of Belém: thirteen ships, twelve
hundred men, and a capital investment by Florentine and Genoese
bankers, now eager to participate in the opportunities of the Indies.
Manuel could be irresolute, easily swayed, and perverse, but the year
1500 resounded with messianic portents, the eyes of Europe were
turning toward Lisbon, and this new armada, led by the *fidalgo* Pedro
Álvares Cabral as captain-major, was a swift follow-up aimed at winning material advantages and the crusading admiration of the Catholic
world.

Cabral's expedition marked the shift from reconnaissance to commerce and then conquest. In the first five years of the sixteenth century, Manuel would dispatch a volley of overlapping fleets of increasing
size, eighty-one ships in all, to ensure success in a life-and-death struggle for a permanent position in the Indian Ocean. It was a supreme
national effort that called on all the available resources of manpower,
shipbuilding, material provision, and strategic vision to exploit a window of opportunity before Spain could react. In the process, the Portuguese took both Europe and the peoples of the Indies by complete
surprise.

Cabral was able to apply all the knowledge gained from Gama's voyage. The timing of departure was no longer decided by the auspicious calculations of court astrologers but by the rhythm of the monsoon. The route was to follow the looping westward sweep undertaken by the ships in 1497, and to draw on the experience of pilots and captains such as Pêro Escobar, Nicholas Coelho, who had accompanied Gama, and Bartolomeu Dias himself. Cabral's fleet carried back Malayalam-speaking Indians who had been taught Portuguese, with the aim of cutting out the Arabic-speaking middlemen. The Jewish convert Gaspar da Gama was aboard, knowledgeable about the intricate politics of the Malabar Coast, and another converted Jew, Master John, Dom Manuel's physician, sailed as astronomer to the fleet, with the duty of studying the stars of the Southern Hemisphere for the purposes of future navigation. After the hideous embarrassment of the gifts offered at Calicut, Cabral carried choice items to entrance the samudri. It appears that the Portuguese persisted in believing that the samudri was a Christian king, albeit of an unorthodox kind, and in accord with the remit of the pope, a delegation of Franciscan friars accompanied the expedition to correct his errors, so that "the Indians ... might more completely have instruction in our faith and might be indoctrinated and taught in matters pertaining to it, as befits the service of God and the salvation of their souls."

Equally important was the commercial mission. The personnel, secretarial resources, and goods to establish a trading post in Calicut accompanied the expedition. With the cautionary example of the failures of the previous voyage, calculated attempts were made to load wares that might be attractive to the Malabar Indians. These included coral, copper, vermilion pigment, mercury, fine and coarse cloth, velvets, satins, and damasks in a whole range of colors, and gold coins. A highly experienced factor, Ayres Corrêa, who spoke Arabic, headed up this commercial initiative, supported by a team of clerks and secretaries to keep records and accounts. These literate subordinates—such as Pêro Vaz de Caminha, who wrote the first account of Brazil—provided some of the most riveting, and sometimes heartbreaking, narratives of the deeds of the Portuguese in the years ahead.

Cabral himself was no seaman, rather a diplomat with a carefully framed set of instructions, some of which had been drawn up by Gama to smooth the troubled waters in the wake of his expedition to Calicut and to establish peaceful and lucrative relations with the "Christian" samudri. Vastly better informed than his predecessor, Cabral could consult this multi-page document, which contained branching options in the case of a whole range of eventualities. It also directed him to take peremptory and high-handed action against perceived enemies that was likely to lead to trouble.

The departure from Belém, on March 9, 1500, took place with full pageantry. There was a penitential Mass and the blessing of the royal banner, emblazoned with five circles symbolic of Christ's wounds. This time Manuel was there in person to hand it to Cabral; then the procession was led by the friars, "and the king went with them to the beach, where all the people of Lisbon were gathered, each to see their husbands and sons," and they watched the longboats casting off to the carracks offshore from the Restelo beach and the unfurling of sails. Manuel accompanied the fleet by boat to the mouth of the Tejo, where the departing ships felt the hit of the sea and swung their prows to the south.

Using Gama's experience, the pilots took a more direct route. No stop was made as they passed through the Cape Verde Islands in fair weather. With sea conditions good, the sudden disappearance of one of the ships was a mystery and an omen. Their orders were to follow the previous looping course: "when they have the wind behind them make their way toward the south. And if they must vary their course let it be in the southwest direction. And as soon as they meet with a light wind they should take a circular course until they put the Cape of Good Hope directly east." They must have enlarged their loop, because on April 21 they caught sight to the west "first of a large mountain, very high and round, and of other lower lands to the south of it, and of flat land, with great groves of trees."

This landfall proved to be as peaceful as it was unexpected. The naked inhabitants were vividly different from the tribes encountered on the shores of Africa: "these people are dark, and they go nude without shame, and their hair is long, and they pluck their beards. And their eyelids and over their eyebrows are painted with figures of white and black and blue and red. They have the lip of the mouth, that is, the lower lip pierced." It was noted that "women likewise go nude without shame, and they are beautiful of body, with long hair." For the first time the Portuguese saw hammocks—"beds set up like looms." The people appeared to be docile; they danced to Portuguese bagpipe music, were willing to mimic the actions of the Mass performed on the tropic shore, and became easily frightened, "like sparrows at a feeding place." To the proselytizing, they seemed promising material for conversion.

This place, which they christened the Land of the True Cross, had plentiful fresh water and fruit, and strange animals. They ate the flesh of the manatee, "large as a barrel [with] a head like that of a pig and small eyes, and it had no teeth and had ears the length of an arm"; they saw brilliantly colored parrots, "some as large as hens; and there are other very beautiful birds." A ship was detached to sail back to Portugal with news for Manuel of this newly claimed land. It contained a letter from Master John, the astronomer, of his observations of the southern stars, and a frank account of the difficulty of taking sightings using the newfangled astronomical instruments and latitude tables: "it seems impossible to me to take the height of any star on the sea, for I labor much at it and however little the ship rolls, one errs by four or five degrees, so that it cannot be done except on land." Another letter, from the secretary Pêro Vaz de Caminha, provided Manuel with a minutely observed and brilliantly written account of all the wonders of this new world and the Tupinamba people who inhabited it. It was the start of the history of Brazil, and one of the last things Caminha could have written. On May 2, after nine days of trade and replenishment, they set sail, leaving two convicts ashore. "They began to weep and the men of the land comforted them and showed that they pitied them."

Cabral's fleet was sailing latitudes farther south than Gama's, with the estimation of cleanly rounding the Cape. On May 12, they observed a comet "with a very long tail in the direction of Arabia," visible for over a week, which they took ominously. Disaster struck twelve days later. On May 24, they entered the high-pressure zone of the South Atlantic. The wind appeared to be steadily behind them when

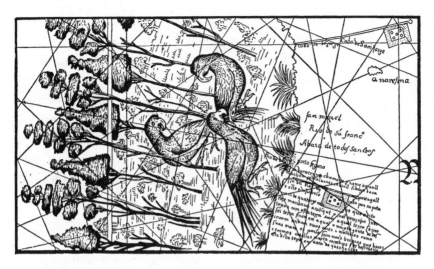

Redrawn extract from a famous Portuguese world map, the Cantino
Planisphere, smuggled out of the country around 1501. Detail shows the
coast of Brazil for the first time, and its parrots "large as hens".

they were hit head-on by a squall. The fury and direction of the blast
caught them totally unprepared: "so sudden that we knew nothing of
it until the sails were across the masts." In a flash "four ships were lost
with all on board, without our being able to give them aid in any way."
Among those swallowed up by the sea was Bartolomeu Dias, somewhere off the cape that he had been the first to round, twelve years
earlier. The remainder of the fleet was scattered into three groups and
ran before the storm for twenty days without a sail raised.

The battered remnants, seven ships, finally regathered at Mozambique on June 20; an eighth, that of Diogo Dias, Bartolomeu's brother,
sighted Madagascar for the first time but failed to find the fleet and
eventually hobbled back to Lisbon. The reception Cabral's ships received along the east coast of Africa was barely better than before. The
sultan of Mozambique, now wary of Portuguese cannons, was at least
more amenable. They were able to water and obtain pilots to steer to
Kilwa, the most important trading city on the coast, where the sultan
greeted them without enthusiasm. Like the Muslims of Calicut, he
had no need of interlopers on his commercial territory. They avoided
Mombasa altogether. It was only at Malindi that they received a wel-

come; men were again ill with "the mouth sickness," "whom the oranges made well," and a pilot was secured for the crossing to India.

It was when they reached the Anjediva islands, four hundred miles north of Calicut, that the tenor of Cabral's instructions became clear. These islands provided a frequent stopover for ships seeking supplies and water on their way to Calicut. Vasco da Gama had careened and replenished his vessels there; Cabral did likewise. It was also known that it was on the route for Arab vessels from the Red Sea—referred to by the Portuguese as the Mecca ships. Cabral was to do all he could to establish friendly relations with the samudri; but beyond his territory he was ordered to wage war against Arab shipping:

> If you encounter ships belonging to the aforesaid Muslims of Mecca at sea, you must endeavor as much as you can to take possession of them, and of their merchandise and property and also of the Muslims who are in the ships, to your profit as best you can, and to make war upon them and do them as much damage as possible as a people with whom we have so great and so ancient an enmity.

Cabral was to inform the samudri of these orders. By now the Portuguese were fully aware of the real advantage of their gunnery. They were to pummel Arab ships with their cannons rather than engage them at close quarters. Pilots and captains, valuable human resources, were to be taken alive; directions for the passengers were more vague. At the worst "you shall put them all in one of the ships, the most dismantled that there is, and shall let them go in it and you shall sink or burn all the others." These instructions, which would be freely interpreted, were effectively bipolar: to establish peaceful trade with the "Christian" samudri, giving to the Muslim traders within the harbor there a cordial welcome ("food and drink and all other good treatment"), while engaging in aggressive all-out war with his Muslim subjects once they had sailed beyond his shores. These instructions set the future pattern of Portuguese operations in the Indian Ocean and began an irreversible train of events. Cabral waited fifteen days at the Anjediva islands to ambush Arab shipping. None came. He sailed on to Calicut, presumably anchoring, according to the persnickety instructions, "with your ships close together and placed in good order, decorated with your banners and standards and as fine as you can make them."

Since Gama's visit, the old samudri had died; it was now his nephew who ruled the kingdom, but relations proved no easier. It became quickly apparent that the Malabars to whom they had taught Portuguese were useless as interpreters, since they were all of low-caste origin and forbidden to sully the king's presence. The Portuguese opened, as before, with an aggressive demand for hostage taking. Cabral was under strict orders not to disembark without this precaution. It required several days of tetchy negotiations and standoffs to arrange an exchange by which the commander could land. Cabral followed his instructions to the letter, while the samudri was upset by the prospect of high-caste Hindus being detained on the sea, where, according to taboos, they could neither eat, drink, nor sleep. When some of them tried to escape by swimming, they were put belowdecks; Cabral's men were imprisoned in retaliation.

All Cabral's underlying instructions had a peremptory tone. The Portuguese believed that they came by permission of the pope and the will of God to secure the commerce of India. The magnificent gifts with which Cabral presented the samudri in his audience chamber were accompanied by fulsome claims of amity to a fellow Christian king—and rigid demands. They wanted restitution for goods left behind by Gama, preferential tax tariffs and low prices for spices, a secure trading post, and exemption from the common rule that the goods of a deceased merchant became the property of the local ruler. Cabral was to get the samudri to understand that the Portuguese must wage holy war on the Muslims once they were beyond his realms, "because it comes to us by direct succession," and to ask him to expel those who were trading there altogether "because in this he would comply with his duty as a Christian king." In return he would receive "all the profit which until now he has had from them, and much more." Additionally, the party of Franciscans would correct his unfortunate doctrinal errors of faith, "as befits the service of God and the salvation of souls." There was, as yet, a complete failure to comprehend the cultural and religious realities of the Indian Ocean.

It took two and a half months of awkward negotiation, standoffs, and feinted departure by Cabral—the tactics employed by Gama—before a commercial agreement and a station could be established for the trading of goods, headed by the factor Ayres Corrêa. There was suspicion on both sides, and the inability of the Portuguese to speak directly through the medium of Malayalam remained a serious problem. Corrêa only knew Arabic, so all communication with the samudri had to be through the agency of Muslim middlemen; his confidence in relying on intermediaries hostile to the Portuguese presence might have been misjudged.

That the Portuguese had the power to inflict damage was displayed in an act of bravado that probably misfired. The samudri wanted to acquire a valuable war elephant from a merchant in the port of Cochin, farther south; his offer to purchase it had been snubbed, but when a ship carrying the animal, along with others, sailed past his coast, he asked the Portuguese to capture it. Cabral sent out a single caravel, the *São Pedro,* under Pêro de Ataíde. Initially the samudri was contemptuous of this effort—there were only seventy men on board—but Cabral had equipped the caravel with a large bombard. The Indian dhow was well armed and carried three hundred men, but Ataíde chased it up the coast. The Muslims on the dhow laughed at the tiny ship beside their overtopping craft until the caravel began to land deadly shots, severely damaging its hull and killing many on board. When the ship finally surrendered, it was sailed back to Calicut and the war elephants were handed over to the samudri with great ceremony. One beast had been killed in the attack and was eaten by the Portuguese sailors. This demonstration of what the strangers could do had a considerable impact up and down the Malabar Coast, but it might also have caused the samudri to regard them with fear: they had the power to compel.

Meanwhile, the loading of spices was proceeding slowly. After three months in Calicut, only two ships had been filled; it was apparent that the Arab merchants were in some way impeding the work, while their own ships seemed to be departing secretly with full cargoes. Cabral complained, and the samudri, caught between two rival interests, appeased his unwelcome guest by giving him permission to seize any

Muslim ship leaving in this way. When it happened again, Cabral did just that.

It is likely that he initially hesitated over such a provocation but acted on the promptings of the factor, Corrêa, who had in turn been disingenuously persuaded to this by leading Muslims. Their underlying aim was to provoke a reaction within the city. It had the desired effect. The confiscation was a flashpoint for simmering tensions. In circumstances in which the samudri's inclinations are unknowable, a mob started to gather in the city streets and surge toward the Portuguese trading post. An anonymous eyewitness recounted what happened next. There were about seventy men from the ships in the town, armed with swords and shields, trying to resist the attack against the mob, who "were innumerable, with lances and swords and shields and bows and arrows." The Portuguese were forced back inside the building, which was surrounded by a wall "as high as a man on horseback." They managed to force shut the outer gate; from the wall they fired crossbows, of which they had seven or eight, killing a fair number of people. From the building's roof they hoisted a banner as a distress signal to the ships.

Cabral, apparently too sick at that moment to attend in person, dispatched longboats armed with swivel guns to try to disperse the crowd. This had no effect. The Muslim crowd began to destroy the outer wall, "so that in the space of an hour they razed it completely." The defenders were now penned inside, firing from the windows. As the trading post was close to the sea, Corrêa decided that further resistance was useless. Their best hope was to make a break for the shore, hoping that the longboats would pull in to rescue them. Bursting out of the house, most of them managed to reach the beach. To their dismay, the boats were holding back, not daring to approach in a rough sea. The armed mob closed in; Corrêa was hacked down, "and with him fifty and more men," including Pêro Vaz de Caminha, the first chronicler of Brazil, and several Franciscans, "the first Christian martyrs in India." Twenty people made it into the water, including the anonymous narrator, "all severely wounded," and were hauled "almost drowned" into the boats—among them Corrêa's eleven-year-old son, António.

Cabral, probably groggy and unwell, expected an immediate apol-

ogy from the samudri for the failure to protect his colony. He waited
one day for a response. None came. The samudri was evidently uncertain how to react. Cabral interpreted the silence as ominous; he believed that the samudri was preparing for war. Twenty-four hours later,
Cabral moved to vengeance. He ordered the capture of ten Arab ships
in the port and the slaughter of all those aboard. The inhabitants of the
city watched with horror from the shore.

> And thus we slew to the number of five hundred or six hundred
> men, and captured twenty or thirty who were hiding in the holds of
> the ships and also merchandise; and thus we robbed the ships and
> took what they had within them. One had in it three elephants
> which we killed and ate, and we burned all nine of the unloaded
> ships.

Cabral had not finished. As night fell, he brought his ships up close
to the shore and readied his cannons. At dawn, he subjected Calicut to
ferocious bombardment; there was a popping response from a few
small cannons on the shore, but Portuguese firepower was overwhelming. All day shots tore into the town, smashing buildings, including
some belonging to the king, and killing one of his notables. The samudri hurriedly left the city, and Cabral sailed off, capturing and burning
two more ships along the way, to the city of Cochin (modern Kochi),
a hundred miles down the coast, which he had instructions to visit if
negotiations with the samudri failed. The terminal collapse of relations
with Calicut left both parties bruised and outraged. The bombardment
would never be forgiven. The massacre at the trading post demanded
revenge. It was the first shot in a long war for the trade and faith of the
Indian Ocean.

Information about the city of Cochin had probably been supplied by
Gaspar da Gama. The Portuguese knew that the raja of the city, a vassal
of the samudri, was keen to escape the yoke of Calicut and would
welcome an alliance with the new players in the game. The greeting
was cordial. Hostages were exchanged; two high-caste Hindus and the

matching Portuguese were swapped daily, as the former were forbidden to eat or sleep on the sea. In a fortnight Cabral was able to load up his ships with spices and agree to the establishment of a small permanent trading post; the Portuguese were also able to enlarge their understanding of the Malabar Coast. Messengers arrived from other ports along the coast, Cannanore (now Kannur) and Quilon (Kollam), inviting him to trade and seeking alliance against the samudri. It was here, too, that they first met authentic Indian Christians; two priests from nearby Cranganore (Kodungallur), Joseph and Mathias, came to the ships and were overjoyed by the meeting. If this was a comfort to the Portuguese, it was probably also the moment when they were finally disabused of the long-held belief in a Christian India and started to grasp the existence and nature of "pagan" Hinduism. Far from being a majority population, the priests revealed that the Christian following of St. Thomas was a small and beleaguered sect surrounded by infidels and almost all the trade of the coast was in the hands of Muslims.

In Calicut, the samudri was hankering for revenge. News reached Cabral of the imminent arrival of a fleet of eighty ships to intercept him on his return. His confidence in his artillery was sufficiently high to refuse the raja's offer of naval support, but he put to sea almost at once, abandoning the men in the trading post and carrying off the two Hindus. These sorrowful hostages would neither eat nor drink. It was three days before they could be cajoled, "and then they ate with great grief and sorrow." This act of cultural insensitivity cast a long shadow over the alliance with Cochin. Thirteen years later, the raja still recalled it in a letter of complaint to Manuel about the loyalty he had shown to the Portuguese and their lack of gratitude.

Cabral had no need for a fight. His ships were heavily laden, and the samudri's vessels, wary of Portuguese guns, only followed at a distance, then lost them in the dark. Farther up the coast, the king of Cannanore begged Cabral to put in and load up with spices. This was as much an insurance policy against Portuguese guns as a desire for alliance against Calicut. Stopping briefly, Cabral's fleet struck out across the Indian Ocean.

The ships made the long sea route back in small detachments. There was a commercial disaster at Malindi when a rash maneuver caused the

loss of a ship richly laden with spices; "nothing was saved from it except the people in their shirts." Though the wreck was burned to
prevent its cargo from being taken by the Muslims, divers from Mozambique subsequently retrieved some of the cannons, which would
later be turned on the Portuguese.

Back in Lisbon, Manuel, confident that the rich gifts to the samudri
would have ensured a peaceful resolution, was already sending off the
next expedition. In March, just as Cabral's ships were battling back
toward the Cape, a small trading fleet of just four ships under João de
Nova left the Tejo. The time between arrival and return was so long
that there was a full two-year cycle between the dispatch of one fleet
and the feedback from its voyage informing the departure of another.
Everything was determined by the rhythm of the monsoon. On their
separate tracks across the Atlantic wastes, each year's fleet blindly passed
its predecessor and proceeded under instructions based on information that was two years out of date, though some makeshift arrangements for mitigating these effects were already in place. When Nova
reached the bay of St. Brás, near the Cape, he found a shoe hanging in
a tree with a message inside informing him of the true situation at
Calicut. He bypassed the city, loaded with spices at Cannanore and
Cochin, and again came off best against the samudri's ships, thanks to
Portuguese gunnery.

    Cabral's ships returned to Lisbon in small groups in the summer of
1501. Along the way, exploratory side journeys had added new knowledge. The port of Sofala, an important center of the African gold trade,
was inspected. Diogo Dias explored the mouth of the Red Sea. Manuel was already forming strategic thoughts in that direction. It had
been tough going; the Portuguese found an arid and inhospitable
landscape, the climate hot as a furnace. Most of the sailors died, "and
thus the ship came [back] with only six men, most of them ill, and they
had nothing to drink but water which they collected in the ship when
it rained." All this information enriched the maps that the Portuguese
compiled and stored confidentially for their own future use.

    The return to Lisbon was eagerly awaited. Of the thirteen ships that had sailed, seven returned. Five of these were laden with spices; two were empty; the other six had been lost at sea. Bells were rung and processions ordered across the land. Within the Portuguese court, verdicts on Cabral's voyage were mixed. There was a strong lobby that believed the price had been too high, the distances too great. Manuel had invested heavily in the venture, and if the laden ships would provide a handsome return, the loss of life cast a pall. The discovery of land to the west was considered interesting but not significant. The failure to ensure a peaceful outcome at Calicut, the destruction of the trading post, and the now clear evidence that the majority of people and their rulers on the coast of India were not Christians added somewhat to the gloom.

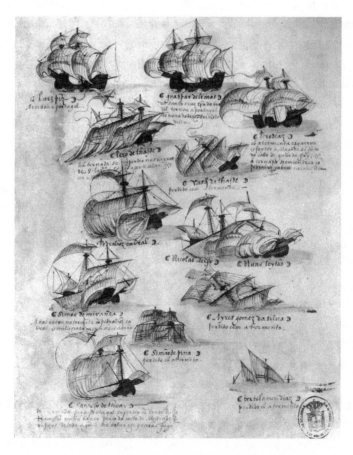

The cost of Cabral's voyage: six ships lost at sea

However, Manuel made certain that positive news was trumpeted across Europe. Nowhere was it received with greater attention than by the Venetians. For the maritime republic, the spice trade, in which they had almost a monopoly by the end of the fifteenth century, was their lifeblood. Hemmed into the eastern end of the Mediterranean, Venice worked exhaustively to maintain relations with the Mamluk dynasty in Egypt and ensure the annual loading of their vessels in Alexandria. The news of the Portuguese coup in outflanking these middlemen was stunning. It threatened the city's whole existence and called for urgent investigation. An alert Italian observer of the Lisbon scene, Alberto Cantino, wrote back to the duke of Ferrara that the king "has already told the Venetian ambassador that if his affairs do not turn out well, as it is believed, he will abandon the enterprise entirely." This may well have been hope as much as expectation in Venice. More realistic voices expressed foreboding bordering on terror. Their ambassador "Il Cretico" had been in Lisbon when the ships came in. The details were disturbing. "They took on a heavy cargo [of spices] at a price I fear to tell," he reported. "If this voyage should continue ... the King of Portugal could call himself the King of Money because all would convene to that country to obtain spices." Manuel called on Il Cretico to celebrate the spice haul, "and so I rejoiced in due form with him." The Venetian would doubtless rather have eaten sawdust.

Back in Venice, the diarist Girolamo Priuli predicted doom for his city if the Portuguese could buy spices at source and cut out the Islamic middlemen. "These new facts are of such importance to our city that I have been carried away with anxiety," he wrote. And Manuel rubbed it in. He suggested to Il Cretico "that I should write to Your Serenity that from now on you should send your ships to carry spices from here." It was the start of covert commercial war between Venice and Portugal, in which information was the key. "It is impossible to procure the map of that voyage," Venetian spies reported. "The king has placed a death penalty on anyone who gives it out."

Yet the high toll on the Cabral expedition had damaged Manuel's credibility. He was now aware of the true situation along the Malabar Coast—it contained few Christians, and the whole trade was in the hands of Muslim merchants—but he had not abandoned his ambitions. He told Il Cretico that "he would forbid the [Mamluk] sultan going for spices." He would push on.

The losses at Calicut called for a response. With the return of Cabral, the strategy for India changed. The samudri, clearly revealed as a heathen, had spurned the rich gifts, destroyed his trading post, and killed his men. In Portuguese eyes he was patently under the sway of the Muslims of Mecca. It was obvious that trade with the Indies would henceforward have to be fought for. It was clear, too, that vengeance, the default position of militant Christendom, was in the air. An Islamic lament on the Portuguese incursion into the Indian Ocean written eighty years later pinpointed Cabral's expedition as the moment when peace turned to war. It was now that "the worshippers of crucifixes" began to "trespass on the property of Mahomedans and to oppress their commerce." When Cabral declined a second posting Manuel sent for Vasco da Gama.

7

The Fate of the Miri

February–October 1502

WITH THE BELIEF THAT the commerce of the Indian Ocean required aggressive action, Manuel prepared an even larger fleet for the now yearly departure from the Tejo in the spring of 1502. Twenty ships were to go, split into two squadrons under Gama's overall command. With him went Vicente Sodré, his uncle, who had separate orders and a certain autonomy. Though Gama's written instructions have not survived, they can be deduced from what occurred: to demand reparation from the samudri of Calicut for the murder of Gama's men, to enforce his demand for the expulsion of Muslim traders, to expand trading agreements with the dissident kings on the Malabar Coast, and to enlarge the small toeholds established there through the trading posts at Cochin and Cannanore. With the confidence that the Indian Ocean contained nothing to match Portuguese artillery, it was a recipe for gunboat diplomacy, if not all-out war.

The ratcheting effect of fleet sizes and Manuel's ambitions is apparent in the instructions given to Sodré. He was to "guard the mouth of the Strait of the Red Sea, to ensure that there neither entered nor left by it the ships of the Muslims of Mecca, for it was they who had the greatest hatred for us, and who most impeded our entry into India, as they had in their hands the control of the spices which came to these parts of Europe by way of Cairo and Alexandria." It was a step forward in a geostrategic plan that was enlarging in scale. Vicente and his brother Brás, who accompanied him, although Gama's uncles, were about his age. They had grown up together and had probably cooperated in corsairing expeditions off the Moroccan coast; they certainly shared the same propensity for violence. Gama had also recruited his cousin Estêvão: it was to be a family affair.

The new expedition was prepared with the now customary rituals of departure. At the Mass in Lisbon's stern crusader cathedral, Gama was formally granted his title of admiral of the Indies and decked out with the symbols of empire and war. Dressed in a crimson satin cape and adorned with a silver chain, with a drawn sword in his right hand and the royal standard in his left, he knelt before the king, who placed a ring on his finger.

The majority of the fleet departed from Restelo on February 10, 1502, with the prayers and tears of the sailors' families fading on the wind. A second detachment of five ships under Estêvão da Gama followed on April 1. The amplified expedition included a number of observers who would write eyewitness accounts. Some were anonymous; others identified themselves. They included a Portuguese clerk, Tomé Lopes, and an Italian commercial agent, Matteo da Bergamo, both in Estêvão's squadron, who recorded the progress of an expedition that definitively tilted the Portuguese aspirations in the Indian Ocean from peaceful commerce to armed violence.

After the near annihilation of Cabral's fleet in the southern ocean, the sailors approached the voyage with considerable trepidation. Tomé Lopes, probably a landlubber without much sea experience, described the climatic changes through which they passed. From the island of Madeira, "a region with a very agreeable climate, neither hot nor cold," the ships headed for the Cape Verde Islands, then made the southwest swing into the high seas. Close to the equator, the weather started to become insufferably hot. The crew persevered "without being able to get any respite, either by day or night"; then they lost the polestar and the heat gradually drained away. Approaching the Cape, "it became extremely cold; the closer we got, the colder it became, and the less we were able to protect ourselves. To keep warm we wrapped ourselves in our clothes and ate and drank a lot." The days grew shorter; daylight shrank to eight and a half hours, night was fifteen and a half long. On June 7, Lopes's ship was suddenly struck by a violent tempest in the dark. The squadron was scattered. "Only two found themselves still together, the *Julia* and us. . . . At the third gust the wind became so strong that it shattered our lateen yard down the middle, and snapped the *Julia*'s main mast . . . great packets of sea rolled over us—it was stupefying to see." The blows of the waves sweeping over the deck started to force water into the *Julia*. While pumping furiously to keep the ships afloat, the crews made vows and drew lots as to who would undertake a pilgrimage if they survived. Freezing cold, soaked to the skin, they waited for the storm to pass. On June 9, the weather improved: "We put our clothes out to dry in the sun, but it didn't release much heat and hardly enabled us to get warm again for we had been completely drenched by the numerous hits of the sea, and we weren't helped further by the rain." Gama's men had taken to throwing relics into the sea in a bid to win safety on this stretch. This time all the ships survived, but the voyage to and from the East would always be a test of endurance, running the risk of shipwreck or foundering.

The Portuguese wanted both to trade on the eastern shores of Africa and to establish secure footholds there as way stations for replenishment and regrouping of fleets scattered by the turbulent Atlantic passage. After the tense negotiations and mutual suspicion that had dogged Gama's first visit to Mozambique and Mombasa, it is clear that he had resolved on a more muscular approach. He was impatient of the nuances and longueurs of Oriental diplomacy and confident that European cannons could command respect. He also realized that the monsoon was an inflexible taskmaster: it would not wait. If compliance was not prompt, he would simply compel.

He first visited Sofala and Mozambique, where the usual round of suspicious hostage exchanges and landings with concealed weapons allowed some gold to be purchased with reasonably good grace. But his main objective, Kilwa, the key trading port on the coast, had given Cabral a frosty welcome. Gama arrived with his whole fleet of twenty ships, flags flying and a volley of shot from his bombards to declare the magnificence and power of the Portuguese crown. He sent the sultan a brisk note requesting an audience. The reply came back that the sultan was ill and could not receive him. Gama promptly drew his ships up close to the shore in a threatening line, armed his longboats with 350 men with muskets and swivel guns, and set to shore. "He did not wish to see me," ran the admiral's own account, "but instead behaved very discourteously on account of which I armed myself with all the men I had, determined to destroy him, and went in my boats before his house, and placed the prow on dry land, and had him sent for much more discourteously than he behaved with me, and he had agreed to do so and came."

In the colorful account of the chronicler Gaspar Correia, the admiral harangued the hapless ruler through the medium of his interpreter:

> I am the slave of the king my sovereign, and all the men whom you see here and who are in that fleet will do that which I command; and know for certain, that if I choose, in one single hour your city would be reduced to embers, and if I chose to kill your people, they would all be burned in the fire.

He continued that he "would fetch [the sultan] by the ears and drag him to the beach, and that he would take him away with an iron ring round his neck, and show him throughout India, so that all might see what would be gained by not choosing to be the captive of the king of Portugal."

Gama demanded the right to trade in gold and a handsome annual tribute to the king of Portugal, in recognition of whose overlordship the sultan was also to fly the royal flag. It was an act of comprehensive humiliation. The tribute was paid in two installments. The first was handed over with due pomp, "with great noise and manifestations of joy," Tomé Lopes related, perhaps drily, while a large group of women on the beach took up the repeated refrain "Portugal! Portugal!" It was probably a call inspired more by fear than joy. The startling directness of gunboat diplomacy was beginning to be felt up and down the Swahili coast. On July 27, Gama sailed on toward Malindi, where he was received warmly, if nervously, by his old friend the sultan.

The crossing of the Indian Ocean was comparatively uneventful. By

August 20, the whole fleet was at the Anjediva islands, having raided some nearby ports, Honavar and Bharkal (Bhatkal), without any apparent justification. Gama bluntly declared to their cowering raja, in the words of Correia, that "this is the fleet of the king of Portugal my sovereign, who is lord of the sea, the world, and also of all this coast." From here it moved farther south. By early September it was at Mount Deli, a prominent headland backed by sheltering lagoons, north of Cannanore. This was the first and last port of call for merchant ships trading along the Malabar Coast, and was widely used by spice ships from the Red Sea as a stopover for water, wood, and food. Gama's twenty ships and thousand men anchored in the sheltering lagoon. Scurvy was again taking its toll, according to Tomé Lopes. They set up tents for the sick, but despite a plentiful supply of oranges, it was too late for many. Sixty or seventy died. Others were manifesting distressing symptoms of a new kind. They developed tumors between their legs, probably as a result of tropical parasites, though these were evidently not fatal.

The crest of Mount Deli, nine hundred feet above the sea, provided a wide lookout point from which to plan maritime ambush. Gama and

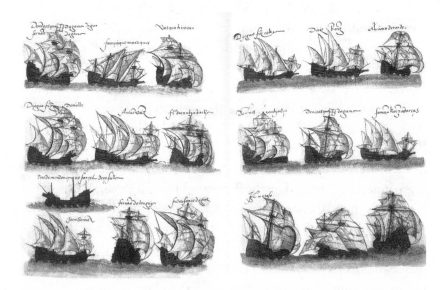

The shift to conquest: Gama's second fleet was six times the size of his first.

THE FATE OF THE MIRI

his Sodré relatives had probably carried out similar operations as young men along the coasts of Morocco. If the orders were to strangle trade with the Red Sea, there was also the matter of revenge for the massacre at Calicut, and many were doubtless interested in the chance for personal plunder. On September 29, 1502, that chance came. A large dhow was sighted coming from the north. Gama put out to sea with a detachment of ships and his bombards primed.

There are several eyewitness accounts of what happened next. The Italian commercial agent Matteo da Bergamo was too shocked to commit the details to writing in the letter he sent back to his employer. "We took no part. We were told it was none of our business," he wrote. "There are also certain details of this event which it's neither the time nor the place to disclose." The Portuguese clerk Tomé Lopes was less reticent. He was perhaps the first to cast a critical and searching glance at the methods and mentality of conquest in the Indian Ocean.

The ship was called the *Miri*. It was returning from the Red Sea with about 240 men, as well as women and children, many of whom had been on pilgrimage to Mecca. The ship evidently was armed and carried some cannons. It included a number of rich Calicut merchants, one of whom was the Mamluk sultan's factor there, Jauhar al-Faqih, an important businessman who owned several ships.

Perhaps to Gama's surprise, the *Miri* surrendered without a fight. There were well-observed rules along the Malabar Coast. It had become practice to pay a toll if intercepted by local pirates on certain stretches, and the merchants were well provided, confident that they could pay their way. Al-Faqih made his opening bid. He offered compensation for a mast cracked on one of the Portuguese ships during the approach and to provide spices for all of them at Calicut. Gama refused. The merchant tried again: he would give up himself, one of his wives, and a nephew as hostages against a full loading of spices of Gama's four largest ships—evidently a substantially improved offer. They would remain on board as prisoners. One of his nephews would be put ashore to arrange the deal. Additionally, he undertook that all Portuguese goods taken at Calicut would be returned and peaceful relations established with the city, which amounted to an open entry into the spice trade. If after fifteen or twenty days these promises had not been fulfilled, the admiral could do with him what he would. Gama was unmoved. He ordered al-Faqih to tell the merchants to hand over everything they had. The increasingly astonished man made a dignified reply: "When I commanded this ship, they did what I ordered. As you now command, tell them yourself!"

The merchants gave whatever they wanted, "without torture," according to Lopes, apparently leaving considerable wealth on the ship. There was, in some accounts, considerable gibing among the captains at Gama's stiff-necked obstinacy in neither accepting the terms nor carrying out a wholesale plunder of the ship. Lopes was plainly astonished. The refusal to profit on some strange point of principle seemed incomprehensible: "Just think of the jewels and other rich objects left on board—the jars of oil, butter, and honey and other commodities!"

Gama had other plans. To the disbelief of the *Miri*'s passengers—and probably of many in the Portuguese fleet, for different reasons—the ship was stripped of her rudder and tackle, then towed some distance away by longboats. Bombardiers boarded the ship, laid gunpowder, and ignited it. The Muslims were to be burned alive.

Now understanding the seriousness of their plight, those aboard the *Miri* responded with spirit. They somehow extinguished the fires and sought out whatever arms, missiles, and stones they could find. They decided to go down fighting. When the longboats returned to reignite the fire, they were met with a hail of missiles hurled by both women and men. They were forced to back off. They attempted to pummel the disabled ship with their gunfire, but the longboats carried cannons too light to inflict serious damage. Even from a distance they could see the women pleading for their lives, holding out jewelry and precious objects, begging the admiral for mercy. Some took their little children and held them out, "and we understood that they asked for pity," wrote Tomé Lopes, whose account becomes increasingly distraught and uncomprehending. "The men indicated by their gestures that they were willing to pay a big ransom ... there's no doubt that with this there was enough to ransom all the Christians held prisoner in Fez and there would still have been great riches for our lord the king." Gama watched all this impassively, hidden, from a spy hole. He made no response. On

the ship, the passengers started to construct barricades out of mattresses, hurdles, anything they could find. They would sell their lives at
the highest price.

For five days, the disabled *Miri* floated on the hot sea. The ship on
which Lopes sailed followed it closely, trailing a captured Muslim craft
from its stern. On the fifth day they were detailed to finish it off. "We
could see everything," wrote Lopes. "It was Monday 3 October, a date
I will remember as long as I live."

His ship closed on the *Miri* and came alongside. From point-blank
range a cannon shot blasted a hole in the *Miri*'s deck, but the Portuguese had seriously underestimated the fighting spirit of their opponents. The *Miri* grappled their ship, "so suddenly and with such fury
that we didn't have the time to throw a single stone from our fighting
top." At once the tables were turned. The Portuguese found themselves
surprised and at a disadvantage. "Many of us didn't carry weapons because we thought we were fighting unarmed people." They had to
hurriedly lock the Muslim prisoners they were holding belowdecks
and face a concerted assault. The *Miri* was higher and rained a torrent
of missiles onto their deck, so many that the bombardiers were unable
to get to the cannons. They felled a few attackers with crossbows, but
forty of their crew were out in the longboats. They were short-manned
and forced to cower: "As soon as one of us showed himself on the
open deck, we were assaulted by twenty or thirty stones and occasional
arrows."

The two ships were locked together. A furious contest raged all day.
The Muslims were maddened beyond all pain; "they hurled themselves
against us with such spirit, it was an extraordinary spectacle. We killed
and wounded many but they didn't hesitate and didn't seem to feel
their wounds." Lopes saw the situation deteriorate around him. "We
were all wounded." Fourteen or fifteen men were holed up on the
raised forecastle, which their swarming assailants were attempting to
storm. Most of the men abandoned their position and fled down the
deck. Just Lopes and the captain, Giovanni Buonagrazia, were left
there, fighting for their lives. Buonagrazia had salvaged a breastplate
from somewhere to protect himself, now battered and dented by the
volleys of stones, its straps torn away. With an attacker just in front of

him, the armor slipped right off. Buonagrazia turned amid the din of battle and shouted, "Tomé Lopes, clerk of this ship, what are we doing here, now that everyone else has gone?"

It was time to get out. The two men abandoned their position, leaving control of the forecastle to the passengers of the *Miri*. "They uttered loud shouts, as if they had already vanquished us." The Muslims were now occupying the aftercastle as well, and those who had rallied to support the captain and clerk saw that the situation was hopeless and jumped into the sea, where they were picked up by the boats. "There were few of us left on the ship, all, or nearly all, wounded." Fresh waves of men leaped across from the *Miri* to take the place of the injured, though quite a few fell into the sea and drowned. The few remaining Portuguese were hemmed in on the deck below the forecastle, sheltering from the barrage as best they could. "They killed one of us and wounded two or three more. We had difficulty in protecting ourselves from the stones, even if the sail sheltered us somewhat."

The situation was becoming terminal when quick thinking came to their aid. Another carrack, the *Joia,* sailed toward the *Miri* and feinted as if to board her. It turned the tide. Suddenly the attackers feared for their own vessel. They scrambled back onto the *Miri* and cast off, leaving the exhausted survivors to count their luck.

The spirited defense of the *Miri* had failed. It was now just a matter of time.

Gama, with six or seven of the largest ships, stalked the crippled vessel drifting rudderless on the open sea. The swell was too high to risk boarding, and the *Miri*'s death agony became horribly protracted. For another four days and nights they tracked their prey, firing shots without effect. On the fifth morning a swimmer from the *Miri* came alongside with an offer. In return for his life, he would attach a cable to the ship's rudder so that they could reel it in and burn it. He also revealed that there was no further plunder to be had; all the valuables, the goods, the food had been cast into the sea—the Portuguese should have nothing. Lopes paid a final tribute to the spirit and bravery of the Muslims: "During the battle we sometimes saw a man wounded by an arrow tear it out, hurl it back at us and continue fighting as if he hadn't noticed his wounds." "And so it was," he concluded witheringly, "after so many fights, that with great cruelty and without any pity the admiral burned the ship and all who were in it."

It is said that before it went down, Gama extracted from the vessel its hunchbacked pilot and some twenty children, whom he ordered to be converted to Christianity.

The terrible, slow-motion fate of the *Miri* shocked and puzzled many later Portuguese commentators; by Indian historians, particularly, it has been taken as signaling the start of shipborne Western imperialism. It was the first violent collision between two self-contained worlds whose terms of reference were mutually inexplicable. "It is unheard of," one Muslim ruler had said, "that anyone should be forbidden to sail the seas." Although the Portuguese were labeled pirates, Gama's motivations—an application of maritime violence that actually spurned plunder—were simply beyond explanation. He may have been extreme in his belief in exemplary terror, but he was not unique. The Portuguese came from an arena of fierce competition, rooted hatreds, and the military application of advanced technologies in navigation and artillery. They brought to the Indian Ocean a narrow view of the Islamic world glimpsed through lowered visors on the shores of Morocco. The Iberian powers who had carved up the world at Tordesillas in 1494 were conditioned to believe in monopoly trading and the obligation to crusade.

Along the Malabar Coast, the *Miri* incident was neither forgotten nor forgiven. It would be remembered for centuries: great sins cast long shadows, in the Spanish proverb. But Gama had only just started. His blood was up.

8

Fury and Vengeance

October–December 1502

Gama sailed on to Cannanore, nominally a friendly port, which contained a small Portuguese trading post. By now the prickly admiral was suspicious of all intentions and in no mood to be appeased. He refused to step ashore to meet the raja. The meeting, dressed up in displays of pomp by both parties, was awkwardly conducted, on one side from a small platform projecting out onto the sea, on the other from the poop of a ship. After the diplomatic niceties and the exchange of gifts, problems quickly arose over trading terms. The raja was unable to discuss these; spice negotiations had to be conducted with the merchants of the city—and they were Muslims.

Gama could not or would not grasp the split everywhere along the Malabar Coast between the political power of a ruling Hindu elite and the economic activities of their Muslim subjects. The merchants sent to see him demanded high prices because the Portuguese goods were too mediocre to purchase. This response cast Gama into paroxysms. Why, he demanded, had the raja sent these Muslims to him, "as he knew very well, that they had an ancient hatred of Christians and were our worst enemies?" It appeared that the king did not value his friendship. Since the raja refused to deal with him, he intended to return the few sacks of spices already loaded early the next day.

In the midst of this, the Portuguese factor in Cannanore, Pai Rodrigues, came to attempt to smooth things over. Gama ordered him to quit the town forthwith. Rodrigues faced him down: he was not answerable to the admiral and had merchandise and duties to attend to. This check only exacerbated Gama's foul mood. He left grudgingly, with a warning to the raja: if there was any harm to the Christian Portuguese, "his kaffirs would pay for it." He was in danger of alienating the whole coast. He sailed on with a fanfare of trumpets and salvos from his cannons for good measure.

He swept on down the coast toward Calicut, looking for trouble. On the way he bombarded a small port that was a tributary of Cannanore and captured a boatload of Muslims. The raja sent a mollifying letter after the furious admiral to the effect that even if they killed his "kaffirs," this would not break the peace with the king of Portugal and he would disclose everything to him. This did nothing to improve Gama's temper, as it was quite clear that the letter had been written by Pai Rodrigues.

In Calicut, however, the fate of the *Miri* was already known and causing the samudri a great deal of thought. It was apparent that the Portuguese were not chance visitors to the Malabar Coast. They were coming every year. They seized any vessels they could obtain. The danger from the unwelcome incomers would increase exponentially if they established a land base. Even the four ships sent the year before had demonstrated Portuguese invulnerability to armed resistance, and this year's fleet was immense. It was critical to find a solution to the problem of the Franks, but given their technological superiority, this would not prove easy.

The samudri did two things. He wrote a letter to Gama while he was still at Cannanore, in an attempt to establish peace. He wished the Christians nothing but friendship. He wanted to give compensation for Portuguese goods that had been left in his city. With regards to the deaths, this was something that could not be expressed in monetary terms or reimbursed, and as the Portuguese had killed even more people on the Mecca ship, as well as on others, surely they could consider themselves adequately avenged. He was proposing that they wipe the slate clean on the matter; his tone was extremely moderate.

However, he had written a rather different letter to his rebellious vassal, the raja of Cochin, stressing the urgent need for cooperation and giving a clear-eyed analysis of their joint situation: "There remained only one sure solution. If they didn't adopt it they were all lost and conquered: through the whole of [the Malabar Coast of] India not to give them any spices at any price." Unfortunately, the king of Cochin remained defiant, and it was these cracks in the local politics that would ultimately doom them all. He replied that "he was at peace with the Portuguese ... and had no intention of acting otherwise." Furthermore, he showed the letter to the Portuguese in his city, who forwarded it to Gama. The admiral was therefore in receipt of both letters. His views of Indian duplicity remained unaltered.

On October 26, as he was approaching Calicut, the admiral hanged two captured Muslims from his mast. They had been condemned on the "evidence" of the children taken from the *Miri,* who recognized them as having killed some of Cabral's men in the previous year's massacre. Another was stabbed to death with spears the following day for having stolen things from the trading post, on the same testimony. On October 29, the fleet came to anchor some way off the town. "We could only see a small part of it situated in a flat valley entirely covered by large palm trees," said Tomé Lopes. A deputation came from the samudri, repeating the terms already sent. Gama was unyielding. There must be a full restitution for loss of life and property, and all the Muslims must be expelled, "whether merchants or permanent residents, otherwise he did not wish to make peace or any agreement with him, because Muslims were enemies of Christians and vice versa since the world began ... and henceforward not to allow any ship from Mecca to come to his ports or trade." This was patently impossible, and Gama must have known that. The samudri gave the most mollifying answer he could. He wanted peace, but the Muslims had been there since ancient times. There were four or five thousand Muslim homes in the city; their people were honest and loyal and performed many valuable services.

Gama declared the reply an insult and seized the messengers. Relations deteriorated over the day, with increasingly bad-tempered notes passing to and fro. In the midst of this, some fishermen had put to sea in their boats, thinking that peace had been agreed. The Portuguese snatched the men, then seized a large dhow laden with food. The samudri's blood rose. Such actions were against the spirit of the ocean. "The Christians took more delight in theft and acts of aggression at sea than in trade ... his port had always been open," he pointed out, "and that's why the admiral mustn't hinder or chase away the Mecca Muslims." If Gama accepted these terms, the samudri "would act accordingly ... if not, he must quit his port at once and remain there no more; he wasn't authorized to stay, nor to stop at any other port in all [the Malabar Coast of] India." Gama responded with some cultural sneers: his own master could create as good a king out of a palm tree. The order to leave would have no other effect than to ensure that he didn't get to enjoy chewing his betel leaf that day. He demanded a fitting reply by noon the following day. Or else.

That evening he ordered all his ships toward the city; they were firmly anchored bows forward to minimize the target for the samudri's guns. As darkness fell, the crews saw a large number of people on the beach with lanterns. They worked all night digging trenches and emplacements for their own artillery. "At dawn," Lopes remembered, "we saw many more people come to the beach." Gama ordered his ships to draw nearer and to be ready. Then he gave further orders. At one in the afternoon, if there was no further reply, they were to hang the captured Muslims from the masts, and many of the Hindu fishermen from the yards, "hoisting them up very high so that they could be more clearly seen." No reply came. "And thirty-four were hanged."

There was soon a large crowd on the beach, looking aghast at the sight—and doubtless trying to identify their relatives. While they gazed up in horror, the ships fired two shots into the crowd from their heavy guns, scattering the people. All the other cannons opened up, hurling "a continuous storm and rain of iron balls and stones that created enormous destruction and killed many people." Lopes watched as the people threw themselves on the sand, then fled, or crawled away on their stomachs "like serpents; and seeing them cry we jeered at them loudly and the beach was soon cleared." There were attempts to return fire, but the Indian bombards were ineffectual—"they fired badly and took a long time to load"—and were abandoned as heavy shots started to land nearby. The firing continued until evening without a pause,

The power of Portuguese artillery, unmatched in the Indian Ocean

tearing holes in the wooden houses and felling palm trees, with "such a crash that it seemed like they were being chopped down by axes. Sometimes we saw people fleeing from the town in places hit by shot."

But Gama had not finished. Late in the evening, to speed things up and to increase the terror, he ordered all the bodies hanging from the yards to be hauled down. Their heads, hands, and feet were cut off and the truncated corpses thrown into the sea. The decapitated body parts were stowed in one of the fishing craft. A letter was drafted, translated into Malayalam, and fixed by an arrow to the prow; the boat was then towed toward the beach. The letter read:

I have come to this port to buy and sell and pay for your produce. And here is the produce of this country. I am sending you this present now. It is also for your king. If you want our friendship you must pay for everything that you have taken in this port under your guarantee. Furthermore you will pay for the powder and the cannon balls that you have made us spend. If you do that, we will immediately be friends.

The corpses washed up on the shore. Cautiously, people came to inspect the boat and the prominent letter. Gama ordered the firing to stop so that those on the beach could absorb the impact of his offering. Lopes watched what happened next. When they saw the contents of the boat

their faces changed, betraying the seriousness of the matter. They were utterly distraught, they couldn't believe their eyes. Some of them came at the run, and when they saw the heads they always took off again at a run. Others took some of the heads and carried them away, holding them at arm's length. We were very close and could see it all well. We all stayed awake that night, because of the great wailing from the shore, and the chanting over the bodies that the sea had thrown up. And all night they didn't stop repairing their trenches by the light of candles and lanterns, out of fear that we were going to set fire to the town.

At dawn, the artillery from all eighteen ships opened up again. The houses close to the water had already been ruined. This time the aim was higher, targeting the grand mansions of the wealthy and important farther back. The town seemed almost deserted; Gama could probably have sacked it if he had wished. Maybe he was still hoping to pummel the samudri into submission. The firing continued all morning. Four hundred shots from the heavy bombards tore into the town. There was a belated attempt by some craft to rescue a dhow the Portuguese had taken, but they were forced into hasty retreat.

The next day Gama set sail for Cochin, trailing bloody vengeance behind him and leaving six carracks and a caravel, under the command of Vicente Sodré, to blockade Calicut by sea. At least the Portuguese could rely on some support at Cochin. Its raja proved to be Portugal's most durable ally, whose loyalty in the long run largely went unrewarded, but his desire to escape the yoke of Calicut ensured a warm welcome.

The whole Malabar Coast, however, was disturbed by the turbulent visitations of the Portuguese, and the growing tension between the Hindu kings and their Muslim trading subjects caused frictions even in Cochin. The loading of spices was a stop-and-start affair, with prices not agreed—and the merchants performing a tactical slowdown at strategic moments. "Sometimes they asked more for the spices," according to Lopes, "at others they wouldn't take our merchandise. Because of these new demands they made every day they would suddenly stop loading our ships. They thus compelled the admiral to go ashore every day." Lopes noted, "When they had settled with him on one point they commenced loading again, and then suddenly they stopped." Gama perhaps realized the limits to irascibility—it was crucial not to alienate his one true ally—and trading at Cochin at least provided some temperate local advice. In this interval, the Portuguese were able to widen their knowledge of the Indian subcontinent. They heard tales of Ceylon, "a rich and very large island three hundred leagues long, with great mountains, cinnamon grows in enormous quantities, precious stones, a great profusion of pearls." It was an enticing prospect—to be added to the avid list of places for future investigation. Interested groups of Christians, followers of St. Thomas, came to see them from neighboring ports and offered both submission to King Manuel and help loading spices.

In Calicut, the blockade of the Sodrés was causing hardship and the samudri was still working to find a solution to the Portuguese problem. He was attempting to construct a united front against the incomers by direct and indirect means, in the face of their terrifying firepower and aggression. His strategy was attritional: to attempt to slow down spice negotiations with Gama's factors so that the Portuguese would stay too long and be trapped by the monsoon. This accounted for the stop-and-start tactics of the Muslim merchants at Cochin, but a blockade of its port from other trade forced them to come round.

The samudri tried one more tack. He sent a Brahman to Gama with a fresh peace offer. Gama was impressed: the Brahmans, the high priests of India, were men of eminent caste. Through this emissary, the samudri offered payment for damages and a new treaty of friendship. Gama was inclined to take this visitor seriously, despite some discordant details in his story. He personally wanted to come to Portugal and asked to have his spices loaded on the ships. The Brahman and some other hostages departed with Gama back to Calicut. At Calicut the Brahman was let ashore, leaving his sons on board, promising to return. He failed to do so; another man came instead, asking Gama to send "a gentleman" ashore to receive what was owed. On hearing the word "gentleman," Gama exploded. He demanded to make known to the king that he wouldn't send even the least of his ship's boys. He owed the king nothing; if the samudri had something to give him, he must bring it to the ship himself. Mollifying words were given in reply. It would all be sorted out by the end of the following day, but by evening the admiral's patience had been exhausted.

Tropical night fell over Calicut.

In the dark hours before dawn, the lookouts of Gama's ship saw a fishing boat leaving the harbor. As it came closer, they realized that it was actually two boats tied together. Gama was roused from his cabin. Dressing quickly, he came out on deck, thinking that the king was delivering on his promise. It was soon clear that something different was in train. They could discern seventy to eighty boats silently putting to sea. For a while those on watch persisted in believing they were a fishing fleet. It was when the first shots rang out that they realized their mistake.

The fireballs from the attackers' bombards skimmed the water and thwacked holes in the flagship. Soon the boats had surrounded the ship. Showers of arrows hit anyone who appeared on deck. Rocks were hurled from the top masts, but the attackers were now too close and delivering too much fire for the Portuguese gunners to operate their own guns. A captured dhow attached to the carrack's stern was set on fire in the hope that the flames would spread to the ship itself. It was cut loose. More boats swarmed around, armed with light bombards and bows and arrows. There was nothing for it but to cut the anchor cables, abandon the anchors, and cast off, but Gama's flagship had been secured with a stout chain precisely to prevent someone from cutting its cable in the dark. The crew had to hack away labori-

ously at this with axes, under steady fire, before the ship could be released. When it was finally freed, the sea was so calm that the vessel sat
motionless on the dawn water, being subjected to a storm of missiles.

It was chance that saved Gama's ship. Vicente Sodré's flotilla—a carrack and two caravels—unexpectedly appeared from Cannanore. The
sea was flat calm, and the ships had to be laboriously rowed forward
against the armada of small boats, firing their guns. The attackers finally drew off, "some without arms or legs, others killed outright by
the cannons."

The deeply suspicious Gama was doubly furious: both at the trap
and at having allowed himself to be lured into it. Again the suspended
bodies of the hostages were paraded along the seafront from the yardarms of his caravels, then dumped in a native boat and floated to the
shore with an even more sulfurous message: "O miserable man, you
had me called and I came at your request. You have done all that you
could, and you would have done more if you could. You have had the
punishment that you deserve: when I return here I will pay your
due—and it won't be in money."

Signature of Vasco da Gama

9

Toeholds

December 1502–1505

GAMA SET SAIL FOR Lisbon in February 1503, leaving behind two fragile toeholds on the Indian coast—the trading posts at Cannanore and Cochin—and a furious and humiliated samudri in Calicut, additionally enraged with the sultan of Cochin for defying his attempts to uproot the Portuguese pirates. It was clear that there could be no peaceful negotiations with these intruders, whose visitations were assuming an ominous regularity. With the dying of each monsoon, their ships returned, sometimes in small squadrons, sometimes in major shows of force. They announced themselves with displays of flags and volleys of cannon fire. They came with intemperate demands for spices and for the expulsion of the deep-rooted Muslim community; they flouted the taboos of Hindu culture and backed up their threats with traumatic acts of violence beyond the acceptable rules of war.

The Portuguese now started trying to introduce a toll system for shipping along the shores of the Malabar Coast; they issued safe-conduct passes, called *cartazes,* that ensured protection for the vessels of friendly powers. This was effectively a tax on commerce. In time it would require merchant shipping to trade in Portuguese-controlled ports and, additionally, pay substantial import and export duties. The *cartazes,* stamped with the image of the Virgin Mary and Jesus, marked a radical shift in the Indian Ocean. With the coming of the Europeans, the sea was no longer a free-trade zone. The *cartaz* system introduced the alien concept of territorial waters, a politicized space controlled by armed force and the Portuguese ambition to dominate the sea.

The full implications of these threats to Indian Ocean trade were now echoing across the wider world. In December 1502, the worried Venetians established a Calicut committee with the express purpose of soliciting action from the sultan in Cairo; this was to be undertaken by their ambassador, Benedetto Sanuto, "to find rapid and secret remedies." The utmost discretion was essential. The potential scandal of aiding Muslims against their Christian brethren made Venetian overtures extremely delicate, but Sanuto's mission was clear: to highlight to the sultan the threat posed by a Portuguese blockade of his spice route, to urge him to put pressure on the samudri to expel the intruders, and, to the obvious advantage of the Venetians themselves, to lower tariffs on spices traded through Egypt to compete with the Portuguese.

In Cairo itself, the sultan, Al-Ashraf Qansuh al-Ghawri, had other things to concern himself with—outbreaks of sedition, threats to the pilgrim routes to Mecca and Medina from Bedouin tribesmen, an empty treasury—but the sudden appearance of the Portuguese in the Indian Ocean was as disconcerting as it was inexplicable. "The audacity of the Franks knows no limit," reported the chronicler Ibn Iyas of their growing incursions.

> They say that the Franks have succeeded in effecting a breach in the dyke constructed by Alexander [the Great] . . . this breach has been made in a mountain that separates the China Sea [the Indian Ocean] from the Mediterranean. The Franks have been striving to enlarge this cutting to allow their ships to pass into the Red Sea. Such is the origin of this piracy.

In the *Arabian Nights* world of Mamluk Cairo, such fantasies circulated. The sultan turned a deaf ear to the Venetian suit: the notion of cutting his tax revenues held little appeal, but the echo of Portuguese outrages continued to amplify. The sultan was guardian of the holy places of Mecca and Medina and, according to his title, "Defender of the Faithful." While a blockade of the Red Sea would affect his purse, freedom for hajj pilgrims and the wider protection of Muslims touched his very legitimacy. The fate of the *Miri* had made a deep impression. A second event in the winter of 1502, while Gama was still in Cochin, ensured that, sooner or later, the Portuguese problem would have to be addressed.

Vicente Sodré, Gama's uncle, had left to patrol the Malabar Coast farther north and was off the coast of Cannanore, where the Portuguese were on friendly terms, when he received a request from its raja to apprehend ships belonging to a wealthy Muslim merchant that had just departed without paying their taxes. Sodré, whose taste for violence was equal to that of his nephew, would have burned the ships if the raja wished. The raja did not—paying the taxes would be quite sufficient. The merchant, known as Mayimama Marakkar, returned to port and paid grudgingly, then left again with curses on the raja and the king of Portugal.

On the raja's complaint, Sodré took the law into his own hands. He had the merchant stripped naked and tied to the mast, where he was savagely beaten and subjected to one of the unpleasant outrages that the Portuguese were prone to inflict on the Muslims of Morocco, that of *merdimboca*—"shit in the mouth"—to which Sodré added a further ingredient. He was gagged with a short stick and, with his hands tied behind him, a piece of bacon fat was also inserted into his mouth. The abused man offered a huge sum of money to be spared these humiliations. Sodré's reply was akin to that of Gama when the *Miri* tried to buy its freedom: "goods could be paid for with money, but not the honor of kings and great lords." Marakkar was a powerful figure within the trading world of the Indian Ocean, and this traumatic ordeal left him burning for revenge. In 1504 he went in person to Cairo to report this blasphemy to the sultan, Defender of the Faithful, and request action against the cursed infidels.

Back on the Malabar Coast, the samudri was also hankering for vengeance. He fully understood the danger the Portuguese would pose if they secured a permanent foothold within the spice kingdoms. It was almost common knowledge that when Gama sailed away on the inevitable winds, the samudri would fall on Cochin to punish its sultan and destroy the nascent Portuguese trading post. To this end, the squadron of Vicente Sodré was tasked with protecting the colony and supporting Cochin's ruler. Sodré, however, had also been commissioned to blockade the Red Sea and destroy Muslim ships traveling to and from Calicut, and this latter task, which promised rich plunder, was more to his liking. Aided and abetted by his brother Brás, Sodré ignored all the pleas of the king of Cochin and the Portuguese trading post and set sail north to line his pockets. This flagrant desertion of his countrymen did not go unprotested. Two captains gave up their commands to stay with the beleaguered colony.

With the Sodrés' departure, the samudri acted promptly. He advanced with a large army toward Cochin and dispatched a peremptory letter to its raja, pointing out the evil consequences of offering "a place to the Christians, from whom we have received so much harm," and demanding that he hand them over. Otherwise the samudri was "determined to enter your land and to destroy it, and to seize the Christians with all their things."

This thunderous message was met with a refusal. The raja had thrown in his lot with the Christians and would live or die by his decision. The Portuguese interpreted this steadfastness as an act of high chivalry, for which, in the long run, he would receive scant reward. The samudri had probably assessed the consequences of siding with the incomers more realistically, but the raja stood firm. He sent out his troops to do or die under his nephew and heir, Narayan. After some initial success, the samudri bribed Narayan's men into disaffection and their leader was killed; the territory of Cochin was overrun. According to the laws of the Hindu military caste, the two hundred survivors swore themselves to ritual death. They shaved off all their hair and advanced toward Calicut, killing everyone they met until they had been hacked down to the last man.

But Narayan had bought the king and the Portuguese time. They retreated from Cochin to the offshore island of Vypin. The samudri burned the town but was unable to reach the island as the monsoon weather set in; he fell back on Calicut as rain and rough seas started to batter the Malabar Coast, leaving a small garrison. He swore to return in August and destroy all who resisted. The Portuguese presence in India was hanging on by its fingertips, but the raja had confidence that their ships would return with the regular rhythm of the sailing season. Meanwhile, the Sodrés, intent on plundering Muslim shipping from the Red Sea, had been shipwrecked on a small island. Vicente was drowned; his brother Brás, deeply loathed for his greed, survived but was then probably killed by his own men. To pious chroniclers it was a just comeuppance: "It seems clear that the loss of the two brothers, because of the sins they committed, is the result of their not helping the king of Cochin, and leaving [their fellow] Portuguese in such great danger."

With the Sodrés now unable to help, the small Portuguese colony and the king of Cochin, along with his immediate followers, remained holed up on Vypin, awaiting rescue. At the start of September 1503, their faith was rewarded by the arrival of two ships from Lisbon, the first installment of the year's spice convoy, commanded by Francisco de Albuquerque. Hard on his heels a fortnight later, four more ships reached the island. They carried two of the most talented commanders Portugal was ever to produce.

The captain of this second squadron was Francisco's cousin Afonso de Albuquerque, the man destined to irreversibly alter the course of events in the Indian Ocean, to shape and shock the world. He was probably over forty in 1503 and had behind him a lifetime of military experience in the service of the crown. Of striking appearance—lean and hawk-nosed, with shrewd eyes and a waist-length beard that was already turning white—he had fought the Ottoman Turks in Italy, the Arabs in North Africa, and the Castilians in Portugal; he had seen his brother cut down beside him in Morocco and campaigned alongside João II as a young prince. Like Gama, he had imbibed the honor code of the *fidalgos,* with its rooted hatred of Islam and its unbending ethic of retribution and punitive revenge. He was unmarried, though with an illegitimate son, fiercely loyal to the crown, incorruptibly honest, and utterly sure of his abilities: to sail ships, command fleets and armies, build fortresses, and rule empires. "I am a man who, if you entrusted me with a dozen kingdoms, would know how to govern them with great prudence, discretion and knowledge," he once wrote to Manuel, who was initially wary of him. "This is not because of any special merits of my own but because I am very experienced in such matters and of an age to tell good from bad." He was a man in a hurry, possessed of demonic energy, and he did not suffer fools. Afonso divided people, but he shared Manuel's sense of charismatic mission and world empire. He evidently believed that his moment had come.

Afonso de Albuquerque

With him, as captain of one of the ships, came the equally talented Duarte Pacheco Pereira; seaman, leader, and tactical genius, geographer and experimental scientist, savant and mathematician. Pereira had been one of the cosmographers tasked with hammering out the treaty of Tordesillas in 1494; a man who may have secretly been to Brazil before it was officially discovered; who produced the first written account of the chimpanzee's ability to use tools; who calculated the degree of the meridian arc to a level of accuracy unrivaled at the time; who recorded the tides of the Indian Ocean and was able to put this knowledge to good use; a man whom the epic poet Camões later came to laud as the Portuguese Achilles—"with a pen in one hand, a sword in the other."

King Manuel had given neither of the Albuquerques overall command, and relations between the two quickly deteriorated. The highly competitive Afonso had hurried to depart from Lisbon first, but his fleet had been hit by a storm and lost a merchant ship. He arrived in a foul mood to find Francisco already in place and basking in the glory of having put the samudri's garrison in Cochin to flight and restored the raja to his throne. He had also bought up the available stocks of pepper in the city.

Strained relations were made worse by the unexpectedness of the situation. Their orders from Manuel were simply to buy spices and return. Instead they found their trading post under threat; the Sodrés, charged with protecting it, dead; and the certainty that the samudri would return in due course to destroy it. The resident agent and his companions gave due notice that they would not stay unless provided with a secure fortress and a garrison. It was therefore necessary to deviate from the king's written instructions, and Francisco had already persuaded the reluctant king of Cochin to grant them a site and provide both wood and manpower for the task. The fort was to be built at the tip of Cochin's long peninsula, guarding the mouth of a large inner lagoon and a network of rivers and towns in the hinterland.

The construction of a wooden fort was hurried forward. "Every ship contributed to the outfitting," according to Giovanni da Empoli, a young Tuscan who accompanied the voyage as a commercial agent. The primitive fort, square in shape, with a stockade of earth and wood and a rough stone keep, took little more than a month to construct. It was, according to Empoli, "very strong . . . with deep ditches and moats around it, and well garrisoned and fortified." It marked a significant milestone in the Portuguese imperial adventure. This was the first solid

foothold on Indian soil, and its completion was auspiciously celebrated
with all the ceremony that could be mustered on All Saints' Day, November 1, 1503. Dressed in their finest clothes, with flags flying from
the walls, they attended a solemn Mass. The raja came, splendidly ar-
rayed on his elephant and attended by his warriors, to view the finished edifice.

Although they had been careful to keep any internal disagreements
hidden from their Hindu allies, the atmosphere between the two Albuquerques was poisonous. They quarreled about everything—the
share of spices, the speed of the building work, even the fort's name.
One of the friars, horrified by these rifts, was brought in to arbitrate.
Francisco wanted the fort to be called Albuquerque Castle; Afonso,
tied into messianic ideas of Manuel's kingship, wanted to name it after
him. Eventually Afonso prevailed, but his intemperance, competitive-
ness, and impatience, which sometimes compromised his judgment,
were already a hallmark of his leadership.

Hostilities with the samudri guttered and flared; the two sides
agreed to a cynical truce, the Portuguese to make up their loads of
pepper along the Malabar Coast for the Lisbon return, the samudri to
plan a fresh strike. The peace was quickly broken by the Portuguese,
who attacked a spice consignment without justification, and the war
restarted. The samudri, however, was biding his time. He knew, as certain as the seasonal rhythm of the winds, that early in 1504 the bulk of
their laden spice fleet must sail home. The Portuguese knew this, too.
In Calicut, the samudri began to assemble a new army to finally drive
the Portuguese out.

As January 1504 advanced, the need for the Albuquerques' departure was pressing. The easterly winds would soon fail. Manuel had
ordered that the whole fleet should sail together, but in the event this
did not happen. In Cannanore, Francisco was still loading spices at a
leisurely pace, and Afonso would wait no longer. On January 27 he set
sail, leaving his cousin dallying. Francisco finally departed on February 5. They left behind just a tiny force to guard Fort Manuel and the
kingdom of Cochin: ninety men and three small ships under the command of Duarte Pacheco Pereira. All had volunteered. It seemed to
those sailing away to be a sure assignation with death. "God rest the

souls of Duarte Pacheco and his men" was the word on their lips, and they crossed themselves as the Malabar Coast vanished from sight. The king of Cochin looked aghast at the fragile promises of his allies. It would be eight months before further reinforcements could reach him from the ends of the earth.

The return voyage of Afonso's ships was typical of the enduring hardships of the India venture: storms, contrary winds, shortages of supplies, huge swings of fortune. The Tuscan Giovanni da Empoli left a vivid account of a nightmare voyage, becalmed for fifty-four days off the Guinea coast:

> with little water . . . and no wine or other ship's stores; the sails and everything else were worn out, so that people began to fall ill, and in five days we threw overboard from our ship seventy-six people, and there were only nine, and no more of us, who remained on the ship . . . we were in complete despair. The ship was sinking because of the ship-worm which consumed it; there was no hope of salvation except with the help of God . . . it was so bad I cannot find words to describe it.

Somehow they made it back to Lisbon at the last gasp.

> The wind was against us, and the black people we had brought, as soon as they felt the cold, began to die, and once again, on the brink of entering port, with a contrary wind we were on the point of sinking. We were in such a bad state that, if we had had to stay half a day more, we would have gone to the bottom at the mouth of the river.

They were luckier than they knew. Francisco's flotilla departed from Cannanore on February 5. He was never seen again, his ships swallowed up somewhere in the Southern Ocean. It was Afonso's account of deeds done that reached the king's ears.

Back in India, the samudri started his advance on Cochin in March 1504. He had assembled a vast army, some fifty thousand men, com-

posed of troops drawn from his own territories and those of his vassal
cities, comprising a large contingent of Nayars, the military caste of the
Malabar Coast, supported by the Muslim community of Calicut, along
with the baggage and paraphernalia required: three hundred war elephants, artillery, and a force of some two hundred ships to close the
port of Cochin. The raja judged the situation hopeless. He begged the
Portuguese to catch the winds and winter on the coast of Arabia, rather
than die pointlessly, presumably leaving him to make a humble submission to the lord of Calicut.

Duarte Pacheco Pereira, however, had come for the fight. He understood perfectly what was at stake: lose Cochin, and the other
friendly ports would submit to Calicut. The whole Portuguese venture
would be over. He had already spent some months fighting the samudri's forces during the Albuquerques' stay and had had time to study
the terrain. Cochin was situated on a long tongue of land on the rim
of the ocean, backed by a lagoon. The region, peppered with mudflats,
islands, and tidal fords fringed with palm trees, was a complex laby-
rinth, ideal terrain for ambush. Pereira would not back off.

His response was forthright. He told the king that he would defeat
the samudri or "we will die serving you if necessary." Cochin was to
be a last stand—a Portuguese Thermopylae. Pereira had at best 150
men and five ships—one carrack, two caravels, and two sizable ship's
boats. The Cochinese could nominally call on eight thousand men,
though it was doubtful how many would actually fight for an unpopular cause. The raja thought that Pereira had taken leave of his
senses. Yet when a large relief fleet reached Cochin in the autumn of
1504, they found the Portuguese commander and nearly all his men
alive and the samudri in ignominious retreat.

In between, Pereira had pulled off a brilliant strategic victory. He
had realized that access to Cochin, situated on its peninsula surrounded
by saltwater creeks and channels, depended on the crossing of a few
narrow fords, according to the tides. By close observation, Pereira,
probably the first man to scientifically study the relationship between
tides and lunar phases, was able to predict when each ford would be
passable and to shuttle his few ships and men accordingly to meet
points of attack. The fords were stockaded with lines of sharpened

stakes chained together and protruding from the water, and his ships were heavily planked with defensive wooden screens. The samudri's military operations were tactically inflexible and heavily leaked. At each attack across a narrow ford, Portuguese firepower shredded the wading Nayars as they attempted to hack their way through the stockades. So successful was Pereira in restoring local morale that when the Nayars encountered low-caste peasants working in the paddy fields, they were attacked with hoes and spades and fled in terror of ritual contamination. Over four months the samudri mounted seven major assaults; they all failed. As casualties from battle and cholera mounted, he lost heart. In July 1504 he finally withdrew, with massive loss of prestige, abdicated his throne, and retired into the religious life. His nephew succeeded him.

The fleet that relieved Cochin in the autumn of 1504 was substantial: fourteen carracks, including five large and newly built ones, carrying a substantial complement of soldiers and sailors and great firepower. With news of the samudri's abject defeat resounding along the Malabar Coast, the new arrivals made a powerful impression on the trading cities and their rulers. The Portuguese were evidently invincible. Defections to their cause grew; another of the samudri's vassals, the king of Tanur, pledged his allegiance to the Portuguese when the fleet reached Cochin. The mood among the Muslims of Mecca darkened. One by one, the trading ports were being closed to their business.

The implacable opposition of the Portuguese, the ferocity of their actions, the mobility of their fleets, the superiority of their firepower, and their relish for the fight seemed an irresistible force. Not just down the Malabar Coast but along the palm-fringed sands of East Africa, a dejection came upon the traveling merchants of Cairo and Jeddah. Toward the end of 1504, dispirited by the turn of events, a large number decided to take their families, their goods, and their wares and return to Egypt. On the last day of the year, Lopes's fleet caught and burned this convoy and killed possibly two thousand Muslims. It was a final blow to the samudri's alliance with his commercial allies from the Arab world. "And with this defeat the king felt himself to be ruined; henceforward the good times could not be restored, because he had lost so much, and the Moors were all going away from Calicut;

because there was such great hunger there that the city was being de-populated." The great days for Calicut were drawing to a close. The Portuguese entered the new year of 1505 with the confident expectation of a permanent occupation of the Malabar Coast. Manuel was already planning the next voyage with just this in mind.

The repercussions of this rupture in the traditional trading system were being felt in ever-widening circles. The Venetians had hoped that distance, disease, and shipwreck would defeat the Portuguese spice route. The twenty-four-thousand-mile round-trip, with convoys now sailing out of the Tejo in March each year, was an extraordinary feat of seamanship. It was also highly attritional. It was not for nothing that people stood on the beach at Restelo, weeping and watching the de-parting sails until they vanished. Of the 5,500 men who went to India between 1497, on Gama's first voyage, and 1504, some 1,800—35 percent—had not returned. The majority of these had gone down in shipwrecks. Yet the rewards were excellent. Vasco da Gama's first voyage had covered the capital investment sixty times over. It was calculated that the crown was making a million cruzados a year after costs—a vast sum—and the smell of spices on the quays of Lisbon at-

Shipwreck losses haunted the Portuguese imagination.

tracted avid recruits to the boats. Many had nothing to lose. Portugal was poor in natural resources, peripheral to the political and economic hubs of Europe; the lure of the East was irresistible. The French king Francis I came to dub Manuel "the Grocer King," an envious gibe at the vulgar pretensions of a petty monarch who lived on trade, yet this aspect of the Portuguese monarchy was as innovative within medieval Europe as the voyages themselves. The kings of Portugal were royal merchant capitalists, sucking in large monopolistic profits.

This fountain of money enabled Manuel to remake central Lisbon in a new image. In 1500, space was cleared on the banks of the Tejo for a vast new royal palace that overlooked the river, and from which the king could watch the wealth of the Indies sail in. The Riverside Palace was both a statement of imperial splendor and a center of commercial activity—the two were linked in royal identity. Attached to it were the administrative infrastructure departments: the India House, the Customs House, the departments that dealt with the import of wood and slaves and trade with Flanders, the royal mint, and the arsenal. In the early years of the new century Lisbon had become a world on the move, one of the most dynamic centers of Europe, electric with money and energy, and run as a price-fixing venture by the crown itself. Much of the commercial and technological infrastructure was purchased from abroad. Portuguese sailing skills were unrivaled, but the country lacked an entrepreneurial middle class. As well as cannon founders and gunners, it required knowledgeable resident agents in the Indies to buy and sell, and in Lisbon and across Europe it needed distributors, retailers, bankers, and investors with business acumen. It attracted an influx of human capital from Florence, Genoa, Bologna, Antwerp, Nuremberg, and Bruges.

When the powerful bank of the Fuggers set up in the city in 1503–04, it was taken as a sign that Venice's reputation as the spice hub of Europe was under serious threat, to the malicious delight of the city's rivals across Italy and beyond. Priuli's pious hope that Portuguese trade would founder on the rocks of the Cape proved overly optimistic. In February 1504, the Venetian senate listened somberly to a report on the spices that had flowed in from Gama's second voyage. In contrast, spices had been in extremely short supply for Venetian merchants in

LISBONA

Lisbon and the Tejo in the sixteenth century

Alexandria, for reasons that, unknown to Venice, had as yet little to do with the Portuguese, everything to do with the internal troubles of the Mamluks.

In the spring of 1504, the Calicut committee decided to renew its secret operations to undermine Portugal's position. The Venetians commissioned two agents: Leonardo da Ca'Masser was sent to Portugal to investigate further the state of its spice trade. He was to pose as a merchant, to report back in code, and to garner as much information as he could on the whole operation. Meanwhile, Francesco Teldi was to assume the role of a dealer in jewels and go to Cairo, to urge the sultan again, and in utmost secrecy, to break the Portuguese operation in the Indies. The Calicut committee, in conclave within the doge's palace, entertained wilder schemes. Could the sultan be persuaded to dig a canal at Suez, which might lower the transport costs to Europe? There is no evidence that this idea was ever put to al-Ghawri, but Teldi was instructed to suggest to him that many Venetian merchants were anxious to buy spices in Lisbon, and Manuel had cheekily invited them to do so; that the *signoria,* of course, wanted to stand by its old trading alliances but if, alas ... Implications were to be left hanging in the air, hints and suggestions that other courses might have to be pursued. The truth was that both sides had a common interest but they could approach each other only tangentially, across a frontier of mutual suspicion.

Even before these men could depart, the growing cries of outrage from the Indian Ocean had compelled the sultan in Cairo to act. He decided on a more muscular approach to test Venetian support and Christian resolve. In March he dispatched a Franciscan monk, Brother Mauro, with a blunt threat: get the Portuguese to withdraw from the Indian Ocean or see the holy places of Jerusalem destroyed. In April, when the Venetians received the monk, they played it ambiguously. They dared not support the sultan's position; they made a show of asking the sultan not to act but intimated sympathy by hints and circuitous phrasing. Teldi was to inform the sultan that they had not felt able to openly side with him, but also that the Christian powers would be unlikely to defend Jerusalem. They quickly passed the unwelcome visitor on to the pope, like a hot potato. Julius II, in his turn, hurriedly referred the horrifying threat on to Manuel, first by letter, then by forwarding its human agent, Brother Mauro, in person to the Portuguese court. As the monk did not reach Lisbon until the following summer, in June 1505, Manuel had plenty of time to prepare his response. And when the message did arrive, it would have a decisive effect on the Portuguese, though not the one the sultan intended.

Ca'Masser's spying mission to Portugal started badly. By the time he reached the capital he had been unmasked, betrayed by Venice's Florentine rivals there, and thrown into a "horrible prison," as he later put it. Brought before the king, he somehow managed to talk his way out and spent two years collecting invaluable intelligence for the Venetian state. But Manuel was becoming increasingly wary of foreign snooping. A month after Ca'Masser's arrival, he issued an edict banning the construction of globes and the reproduction of charts, in an attempt to hoard Portugal's hard-won advantages against inquisitive interlopers.

The Portuguese certainly came to think the worst of the Venetians in an increasingly acrimonious commercial contest. They believed, probably erroneously, that two cannon founders who had aided the samudri in 1504 had been sent from Venice. The maritime republic seems to have stopped short of supplying Cairo with technical aid at state level, but there were certainly merchants willing to ship copper bars to Alexandria for the purpose, and they stiffened Arab resolve. There was a floating pool of seamen, artificers, gunners, and technical experts, outcasts and criminals from the Mediterranean basin, some of them probably from the Venetian colonies close to the African shore—Crete and Cyprus—willing to sell their skills to whoever would employ them, and by 1505 some of these men were finding their way to Cairo. The slow buildup of pressure within the Arab world would soon demand decisive action.

10

The Kingdom of India

February–August 1505

LISBON, FEBRUARY 27, 1505. The orotund phrases of an imperial edict. An address to all those involved in the business of India:

Dom Manuel, by the grace of God king of Portugal and of the Algarves of this sea and the sea beyond in Africa, lord of Guinea and of the conquest, navigation and commerce of Ethiopia, Arabia, Persia, and India, we declare to you captains of the forts that we order to have built in India, judges, factors . . . the captains of ships, that we send there in this squadron and fleet, noblemen, knights, squires, ship's masters, pilots, administrators, seamen, gunners, men at arms, officers and platoons, and all other persons . . .

The list ran down the hierarchy of rank. Then came the substance: "that through this our letter of authorization as proof, that we, through the great confidence that we have in Dom Francisco d'Almeida . . . we give him charge as captain-major of all the said fleet and armada and the aforesaid India and to remain in possession of it for three years."

There had been repeated debates and fierce opposition voiced within the court about the wisdom of the India venture. The high loss of life, the stubborn resistance of the samudri, the massacre at Calicut, the noble preference for local crusading in nearby Morocco, the fear of the jealousy of rival princes—all these had led to strong resistance to Manuel's plans. But by 1505 the king, supported by an inner circle of ideologues and advisers, was sure that it was his destiny to pursue the India project. What was wrapped up in the proclamation of February 27 was an entirely new strategy, a bold long-term plan resting on ambitions of breathtaking scale: to establish a permanent empire in India backed up by military force and to gain control of all the trade of the Indian Ocean. The timing was not incidental. Manuel, aware that Brother Mauro was on his way from the pope to express his fears for Jerusalem, probably wanted to act before the unwelcome messenger arrived in person. On a larger scale, the conjunction of international events was highly favorable: Italy was convulsed by war; the Venetians were distracted by their Ottoman campaigns; the Mamluk regime seemed to be in decline; Spain was embroiled in Europe. A window of opportunity existed, a moment of destiny. Manuel realized, too, that the time lags in communication made control from Lisbon impractical. Congenitally insecure and suspicious as he was, Manuel had to delegate to a chosen representative and hand over the baton of command long enough for effective plans to be implemented.

Francisco de Almeida

The man to whom this was to be entrusted, Dom Francisco de Almeida, was only the king's second choice. Tristão da Cunha had been his initial nomination, but the experienced seaman had suddenly been struck down by blindness, probably the result of a vitamin deficiency. Though he later recovered, the incident was taken as a sign from God. Almeida was to be the first member of the high nobility to lead an India expedition. He was about fifty-five years old, with wide military, diplomatic, and nautical experience, but he also possessed the personal qualities that Manuel hoped for in a man to whom he might entrust high affairs of state. Almeida was incorruptible, unmoved by the lure of riches, benevolent, a widower without home ties, pious, and mature in his judgments. For many, the attraction of India was the prospect of personal gain; Almeida was untarnished by the appetites of the Sodrés. He valued titles above bales of spices, and he knew how to fight.

Almeida was not just to be the captain-major. He was also granted the elevated title of viceroy, nominally with executive power to act in the king's place. What this meant in practice was spelled out a week later in the *regimento,* the instructions given to him by the king. They ran to 101 closely written pages, containing 143 different items divided into chapters and subchapters that revealed both the microscopic level of detail at which the king wished to direct his appointee and the breathtaking scale of his ambition.

After sailing around the Cape, Almeida was ordered to get control of the Swahili coast. His targets were to be the ports of Sofala, key to the gold trade, and Kilwa. The recommended method was to arrive in the guise of friendship, then attack the towns by surprise, imprison all the Muslim merchants, and seize their riches. Forts were to be constructed and control then exercised over the sources of gold, necessary for trading on the Malabar Coast in exchange for spices. It was to be a mission of war, disguised as peace. Then, wasting no time, he was to proceed directly across the Indian Ocean and build four more forts: at the stopover island, Anjediva, as a support and provisioning hub, and in the friendly cities of Cannanore, Quilon, and Cochin.

Moving north, another fort was to be built at or near the mouth of the Red Sea and close to the kingdom of Prester John, to choke off the sultan's spice trade and ensure that "all India should be stripped of the illusion of being able to trade with anyone but ourselves." Two ships were to be on permanent patrol along the African coast as far as the Horn of Africa.

The *regimento* then turned its attention to the intractable Calicut problem. One way or another, the new samudri, as hostile as his predecessor, was to be dealt with. Almeida was to establish peace if the samudri agreed to expel all the Muslims; if not, "wage war and total destruction on him, by all the means you best can by land and sea so that everything possible is destroyed."

No strategic point was to be overlooked. After locking up the Red Sea, a fleet was to be sent to other Islamic city-states and kingdoms: Chaul and Cambay, and Ormuz, at the mouth of the Persian Gulf. Almeida was to demand annual tribute to the king of Portugal; to

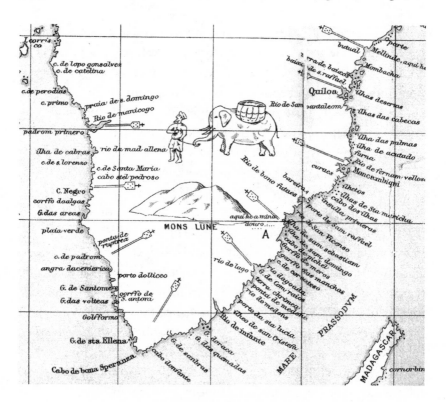

Portuguese map of southern Africa from 1502,
the coastline marked with pillars

order these states to break off all commercial relations with the Arab merchants of Cairo and the Red Sea; to capture all Muslim shipping along the way. To pay for all this, he was to ensure the full loading and prompt sailing of the annual spice fleets.

Manuel's ambition did not end there. After seeing to the spice ships, the viceroy was ordered to open up new frontiers by "discovering" Ceylon, China, Malacca, and "whatever other parts have still not been known." Pillars were to be planted on this new soil as markers of possession. It was an exhaustive list.

Though the instructions also claimed to allow Almeida a certain freedom of action in the case of unseen eventualities, in practice they imposed a rigid agenda. Manuel never had seen and never would see the world whose conquest he was demanding, but the *regimento* revealed an astonishing grasp of the choke points of the Indian Ocean and an authoritative geostrategic vision for controlling them and constructing his own empire. This knowledge had been acquired at breathtaking speed. Within seven years of bursting into the new world, the Portuguese understood, with a fair degree of accuracy, how the twenty-eight million square miles of the Indian Ocean worked, its major ports, its winds, the rhythm of its monsoons, its navigational possibilities and communication corridors—and they were already eyeing farther horizons. The methodology of knowledge acquisition had been developed over the years of slogging round the coast of Africa, during which the Portuguese had become expert observers and collectors of geographical and cultural information. They garnered this with great efficiency, scooping up local informants and pilots, employing interpreters, learning languages, observing with dispassionate scientific interest, drawing the best maps they could. Astronomers were sent on voyages; the collection of latitudes became a state enterprise. Men such as Duarte Pacheco Pereira, substituting firsthand observation for the received wisdom of the ancients, operated within the parameters of Renaissance inquiry. Information about the new world was fed back into a central hub, the India House in Lisbon, where everything was stored under the crown's direct control to inform the next cycle of voyages. This system of feedback and adaptation was rapid and effective.

Manuel had drawn on a small coterie of advisers to construct the
regimento for Almeida. Influential among them was Gaspar, the Polish
Jew posing as a Venetian whom Vasco da Gama had kidnapped on his
first voyage. He is woven into the first decade of Portuguese exploration, invaluable as an expert and an interpreter, an elusive figure,
changing his identity and name to suit the patron of the moment and
the needs of the situation. First Gaspar da Gama, to Manuel probably
Gaspar da India, on the forthcoming voyage he would call himself
Gaspar de Almeida "out of love for the viceroy." He had a propensity
to tell his new employers what they wanted to hear, but he was well
informed. He seems to have had a good knowledge of the Indian
Ocean and to have traveled widely. It was he who suggested the first
overture to Cochin, and he had probably made voyages to Ceylon,
Malacca, and Sumatra. He also understood the strategic importance of
the Red Sea. It was this information that seeped into Manuel's grand
plan of 1505.

Gaspar had advocated that the Portuguese should go straight for the
Muslim jugular—attack Aden, close the Red Sea, and suffocate Mam-
luk trade first; then the samudri would be compelled to become a
Portuguese client—rather than laboriously constructing forts on the
Malabar Coast that would cost money and lives. The wisdom of the
forts strategy would become a hotly debated issue in the years ahead.
Manuel had absorbed the plan but not the sequence: he preferred first
to establish secure bases on Indian soil as a platform for snuffing out
Muslim trade.

Other figures in the group that surrounded the king were encouraging him in an increasingly grandiose interpretation of the astonishing events unfolding in the Indian Ocean. Among them his second
wife, Maria of Aragon, believed deeply that Manuel's destiny was directed by heaven; so did one of his key advisers, Duarte Galvão, and
the man who would become the executive architect of the Manueline
dream: Afonso de Albuquerque.

It was with the advice of this tight circle that Almeida's instructions
were drawn up and the expedition fitted out. The fleet was huge:
twenty-one ships, seven times the number that had sailed with Gama
just eight years earlier, captained by an illustrious generation of expe-

rienced seamen—including João de Nova and Fernão de Magalhães, the Magellan who would circumnavigate the world in the following decade. Almeida's son also went, the dashing Lourenço, "a noble gentleman ... physically stronger than anyone else, expert in the use of all weapons."

In all, fifteen hundred men were enrolled, comprising a microcosm of society sent to create a Portuguese state beyond the sea. They ranged in tiers from noble gentlemen to the outcasts and the lowest rungs of society—converted Jews, blacks, slaves, convicts—as well as a component of foreign adventurers and merchants. All had volunteered. They had been chosen to provide the skills not only to sail and fight but also to establish a new state. They included shoemakers, carpenters, priests, administrators, judges, and physicians. There was a substantial contingent of German and Flemish gunners, as well as three privately financed ships, got up by German and Florentine bankers and merchant capitalists, a huge investment. Gaspar went along with another Venetian interpreter. Even a few women smuggled themselves aboard, disguised as men; their names appeared in the registers soon after: Isabella Pereira, Lianor, Branda, and Ines Rodrigues.

This was, to all intents and purposes, the Portuguese *Mayflower*, departing to settle a new world. It carried cannons for forts as well as cannons for ships; goods to trade (lead, copper, silver, wax, coral); prefabricated components for fortresses, such as window frames and dressed stone; wood for the construction of small ships; and a host of other building materials and tools. They had come to stay.

The charged significance of this particular expedition was reflected in the ritual Mass, on March 23, 1505, in Lisbon Cathedral. The chronicler Gaspar Correia left a bravura account of this theatrical event. After the service the ceremonial bestowal of the banner, "of white damask emblazoned with the cross of Christ in red satin, outlined in gold and fringed with gold tassels and a gold star"; the king appeared through a curtain to present this talisman, which carried "the sign of the true cross," to his viceroy, accompanying it with a long speech of benediction and an exhortation to perform great deeds and "the converting of many infidels and peoples." Almeida and all the nobles and captains knelt to kiss the king's hand. Then the sumptuous procession to the waterfront, with "Dom Francisco de Almeida, governor and viceroy of India," and his captains riding, the retinue on foot. Almeida himself cut a distinguished figure, dressed in a fine tabard and a hat of black satin and mounted on a richly caparisoned mule, a man "of medium height and dignified presence, a little bald but of great authority, preceded and followed by eighty men of arms carrying gilded halberds." They wore gray shoes, jackets of black velvet, and white leggings, outfitted with gilded swords, in their hands caps of red satin; the captain of the guard, on horseback, carried the baton of his authority. This was how Manuel projected his mission and destiny.

And so this pageant proceeded solemnly down the winding streets to the waterfront, with Correia no doubt adding extravagant details to a scene that he almost certainly could not have witnessed with his own eyes: Almeida's son Lourenço, also spectacularly dressed and carrying the banner, and the captains and nobles similarly richly costumed; the king, the queen, and all the other ladies of the court watching from the windows as they passed. The viceroy was the first to step onto his ship, decked out with flags and standards. With a thunderous artillery salvo, the anchors were raised and the ships made their way down to Restelo for a further ceremonial blessing at the sacred shrine of Santa Maria de Belém. They finally departed on March 25, the auspicious day of the Annunciation of the Virgin.

The expedition endured the now customary losses and hardships. One carrack, the *Bela,* sprung a leak and sank, slowly enough for the crew to transfer themselves and their valuables. Passing Brazil, at about forty degrees south the fleet was hit by violent thunderstorms and volleys of snow. Almeida's flagship lost two men overboard; ships got separated. Rounding the Cape in late June, Almeida fell upon the Swahili coast with the ferocity and cunning stipulated in the *regimento.* They reached their first objective, the island of Kilwa, on July 22. It was a welcome sight after three months at sea: whitewashed houses with thatched roofs visible among brilliantly green palm trees. To Hans Mayr, the German clerk of the *São Rafael,* it was a place of luxuriant ease and plenty. The red earth was "very fertile, with a lot of maize as in Guinea," and the grass grew as tall as a man in neatly fenced gardens that produced an abundance of food: "butter, honey and beeswax ...

honeycombs in the trees ... sweet oranges, limes, radishes, small onions." The citrus fruits would have been particularly welcome to the
scurvy-struck sailors. The place was not insufferably hot; plentiful fodder nurtured fat livestock; fish teemed and whales sported around the
arriving ships. Kilwa was a small and prosperous city of some four
thousand inhabitants, with many vaulted mosques, "one like that of
Cordoba," whose Muslim merchants, "well fed and heavily bearded,
[were] an intimidating sight," according to Mayr. Dhows as large as
fifty tons—the size of a caravel—held together by coir ropes, lay
beached in the harbor. The fields were worked by black slaves. Kilwa
traded all along the Swahili coast, to the Arabian Peninsula and the
Gujarati states of India, and with Sofala, in gold, cotton cloth, costly
perfumes, incense, silver, and gems. It was a key link in the self-sufficient
trading network of the Indian Ocean, whose development stretched
back centuries. It was about to feel the full force of an intervening
world.

In fact, the present sultan was an unpopular usurper who had already experienced the blunt methods of Portuguese diplomacy. In
1502, Vasco da Gama had threatened to drag him round India like a
dog on a chain. He had been forced to submit to the Portuguese
crown, fly its flag, and deliver an annual tribute. When Almeida arrived,
the tribute had gone unpaid for two years. There was no sign of the
flag. On Gama's visit, the sultan had tried to excuse himself from the
unwelcome visitors by claiming illness; this time, he had guests. He
sent out gifts of food in a vain attempt to placate Almeida.

Unappeased, the viceroy lined up his ships the following morning
with bombards loaded, stepped ashore in full finery, and demanded an
audience. The sultan sent five of his leading men and a promise to pay
the tribute. Almeida's patience snapped. He impounded the ambassadors and prepared to storm the town. At dawn on July 24, he launched
an attack. The viceroy was the first ashore, planting the Portuguese flag
on the beach—an instinct for leading from the front that revealed a
hint of recklessness. The prospect of plundering this fat town ensured
a keen assault from the rank and file. In the event, it proved surprisingly easy. At the first show of force, the sultan fled with many of the
inhabitants. When the attackers reached his palace, they were met only

by a man leaning from a window, waving the missing Portuguese flag as a safe-conduct and shouting, "Portugal! Portugal!" The doors were smashed open with axes, but the sultan and all his wealth had gone. Franciscan friars erected a cross on a prominent building and began to sing the Te Deum.

Elsewhere there followed a wholesale sack of the town; large quantities of booty were collected, though not distributed according to instructions: men were out for personal gain rather than to enrich their king. Manuel would later declare himself dissatisfied with the haul. The following day, July 25, the feast of St. James, patron saint of the holy war against Islam, they began building their first stone fort on the Indian Ocean, constructed from demolished houses. It took just fifteen days. A garrison was detailed, and the sultan's rival, a rich merchant, was installed on the throne with a fitting display of pomp. A gold crown destined for the king of Cochin was briefly placed on his head; he swore eternal loyalty and—equally important—annual tributes to the Portuguese king. Then, splendidly dressed in a scarlet robe stitched with gold thread and mounted on a horse "saddled in the Portuguese fashion, and accompanied by many richly dressed Muslims, he was carried throughout the city."

Gaspar the interpreter preceded him as crier, explaining to those who might have missed the point, "This is your king, obey him and kiss his feet. He will always be loyal to our lord the king of Portugal." Almeida was writing back to the king in jubilant tones: "Sire, Kilwa has the best port of any place I know of in the world, and the fairest land that can be . . . we are constructing there a fortress . . . as strong as the king of France could ever hope for." And he suggested that "in my time you will be emperor of this world in the East, which is so much greater than that in the West."

Puppet ruler installed, it was time for the zealous viceroy to hurry on with the next in his long list of objectives. Two ships were sent up the coast to patrol the Horn of Africa, and arrangements were made to blockade Sofala until a follow-up flotilla from Lisbon could compel its submission and the building of a second fort.

At this point Almeida had been ordered to run directly across the Indian Ocean, but he was already showing signs of using the authority with which he had been invested at his own discretion. He decided to increase the number of tributary towns along the coast with an attack on Mombasa Island. Its sultan had so far been resistant to the Portuguese, and the city was a powerful center of Arab trade; its two harbors, sheltered by the island, were superior to any others along the Swahili coast and formed a difficult target. The sultan, aware of the now regular and unwelcome return of the Portuguese, had fortified his defenses with a bastion and a number of cannons, salvaged by divers from the wreck of a ship lost on Cabral's expedition four years earlier. The know-how to operate them was being provided by a renegade sailor who had converted to Islam.

As Almeida's fleet approached the island, these cannons opened up and hit one of the ships. It was a short-lived success. Returning fire, a lucky shot hit the bastion's powder magazine. The Muslim gunners fled from the wrecked battery. Almeida put a party ashore to request that the sultan submit peacefully to the king of Portugal. In reply they

Mombasa

got a torrent of abuse in Portuguese to the effect that they were dogs, curs, pork eaters ... Mombasa was not like Kilwa, full of chickens waiting to have their necks wrung. Warming to his theme, the renegade listed the formidable opposition confronting them: four thousand fighting men, including five hundred utterly loyal black archers, further artillery in the city, two thousand more men on their way. The sultan was prepared for an all-out fight for Mombasa, Almeida even more determined to take it.

The city was similar to Kilwa but bigger and grander. Its tightly clenched nucleus, typical of Arab souks, consisted of narrow warrens of streets, a labyrinth of blind alleys and passages. There were grand stone houses, some of three stories, but many others were wooden with reed roofs, and in this Almeida saw an opportunity. He decided to fire the city first, then sack it. A landing party threw pots of gunpowder into the houses; the flames spread quickly. Soon a large portion of the city was ablaze. According to the chronicles,

the fire that ran through the city burned all that afternoon and the night that followed. It was terrifying to see. It seemed as if the whole city was on fire. There was enormous destruction both in the wooden houses, which burned to the ground, and to those of stone and mortar, which caught fire and crashed down. And in them great riches were destroyed.

The following morning before dawn, with the fires still burning, Almeida's troops launched a four-pronged attack. They met spirited resistance and quickly found themselves embroiled in fierce fighting in lanes so narrow that two men couldn't pass abreast. Both men and women rained rocks and tiles down on them from balconies and rooftops, with hails of arrows and javelins, so fast "that our men did not have time to fire our muskets." They were forced to duck behind walls, moving from cover to cover.

Almeida had already identified the palace, and his men fought their way toward it, street by street. In desperate defense, the Swahilis drove wild elephants into their midst, but to no avail. As the attackers drew near, they glimpsed a large group of richly dressed men hurrying away;

it was the fleeing sultan and his followers. Bursting into his palace, the attackers found it empty. Again the Franciscan friars raised their cross, the flag hoisted high to shouts of "Portugal!"

Then the looting began. One by one, house doors were smashed in, the contents and their occupants carried off to the ships. Mombasa was the chief trading center on the Swahili coast, and the prizes were considerable, including "a great number of very rich cloths, of silks and gold, carpets and saddle-cloths, especially one carpet that cannot be bettered anywhere and was sent to the king of Portugal with many other articles of great value." To prevent private theft, Almeida had tried to make this operation systematic. Each captain was assigned an area to plunder; everything was to be taken away and sorted and rewards assigned according to orders set out in the *regimento:* the finder was to receive a twentieth part of the value. In practice there were widespread abuses. Men came to the Indies less to spread the faith or out of loyalty to their king than to become rich. Later Manuel was told that if those who had stolen booty at Mombasa were to be punished, Almeida would have had to destroy the majority of his forces. The tension between the private desires of both the ordinary soldiers and the *fidalgos* and the viceroy's responsibility to fulfill the royal mandate remained acute through all the centuries of the Portuguese adventure. The upright, incorruptible Almeida was disgusted by the flagrant breaches he was incapable of preventing.

From the shelter of a group of palm trees a gunshot back from the city, the sultan and his retinue watched Mombasa being sacked and burned. The Portuguese were too exhausted for pursuit. The casualties were, as ever, asymmetrical. Seven hundred Muslim dead lay in the streets and houses. Five Portuguese died, though many more were wounded. Two hundred prisoners were taken, "of whom many were light-skinned women of good appearance, and many young girls of fifteen and below."

The next day the sultan, realizing that resistance was useless and keen to avoid the fate of Kilwa's ruler, sent an enormous silver plate as a sign of peace and surrendered his city. As a gesture of goodwill, Almeida freed many captives and promised to protect the life and property of all who returned. The sultan paid a large tribute, which was to be annual, and signed a peace treaty to last "as long as the sun and the moon endured." On August 23, Almeida departed from the Swahili coast, leaving trails of blood. A trading system that had endured for centuries was being bombed into submission.

The traumatized sultan wrote a plaintive account to his old rival the king of Malindi:

> God keep you, Said Ali. I would have you know that a great lord passed here, burning with fire. He entered this city so forcefully and cruelly that he spared the life of none, man or woman, young or old or children no matter how small. . . . Not only men were killed and burned, but the birds of heaven fell to the earth. In this city the stench of death is such that I dare not enter it, and none could give account of or assess the infinite wealth that they took.

11

The Great Whore of Babylon

June–December 1505

Almeida's mission was already ambitious, but back in Lisbon Manuel's strategic thinking about the Indian Ocean was undergoing continuous development. The strong messianic streak that tinged his court was growing more pronounced. His close counselors encouraged him to believe that he had been chosen by God to perform great deeds. Signs were read—in his name, in the extraordinary circumstances of his kingship, through the deaths of six better-placed candidates, in the tide of wealth flowing into the wharves of Lisbon, in the rapid advances in exploration. That Manuel had succeeded in reaching the promised land of India at a first attempt, whereas it had taken his predecessors three-quarters of a century to round Africa— this was seen as a miracle of God, an indication of a new age of peace and Christian triumph, perhaps even an acceleration toward the end of time. The five dots of the Portuguese coat of arms, patterned like the five wounds of Christ, and the persecution of the Jews, whose forced conversion or expulsion was justified as a purification of the nation— all were indications of a febrile belief that the Portuguese were the new chosen people, tasked with great work in God's name. With each successive haul from the Indies, the objective became amplified.

Specifically, this was now to be the collapse of the Muslim world, for which Manuel's inner circle found encrypted references in the biblical Apocalypse of St. John. The Mamluk dynasty in Cairo was identified with the Great Whore of Babylon, to be brought down low. The deeply rooted idea of holy war as a Portuguese vocation—"the sanctity of the House of the Portuguese Crown, founded on the blood of martyrs and by them extended to the ends of the earth"—was now to be advanced on a huge front. Manuel was being encouraged by his inner circle to assume the title of emperor. "Caesar Manuel" was how Duarte Pacheco Pereira addressed him in his book on the Portuguese discoveries.

The messianic tone and reach of Portuguese ambitions, as well as hints of Manuel's strategy, were evident in an address made to Pope Julius II in early June 1505:

> Christians may therefore hope that shortly all the treachery and heresy of Islam will be abolished and the Holy Sepulchre of Christ ... which has for a long time been trampled and ruined by these dogs ... will be returned to its former liberty and in this way the Christian faith will be spread throughout the whole world. And so that this might come to pass more easily, we are already striving and hoping to ally ourselves with the most important and powerful of Christians [Prester John], sending ambassadors to him and offering the greatest help by contacting him.

Warming to his themes, Manuel's ambassador finished with a grandiose rhetorical flourish—the invitation to the pope to grasp the world:

> Receive your Portugal, not only Portugal but also a great part of Africa. Receive Ethiopia and the immense vastness of India. Receive the Indian Ocean itself. Receive the obedience of the Orient, unknown to your predecessors, but reserved for you, and that being already great will be, through God's mercy, each time greater.

The pope was to have religious authority over a huge area designated as the State of India, which Almeida had been sent to construct, but Manuel's ambitions were advancing even further beyond the *regimento*. The drift of this started to become apparent just a week after the papal address, when the sultan's threat to destroy these holy places finally reached Lisbon, in the person of the monk Brother Mauro. Its effect was the diametric opposite of that intended. Manuel faced down the sultan's blackmail. He sent Mauro back to Rome with an intransigent counter to the sultan, threatening a crusade of his own if the holy places were harmed. He drew on the memory of Portugal's crusading history; he would utterly destroy the infidel. He claimed the sanction of God. The threat seems to have crystallized a definitive plan in Lisbon: not only to destroy the Mamluks but also to recapture the holy places for Christendom. In secret, Manuel dispatched ambassadors to Henry VII in England, to King Ferdinand in Spain, to Julius II, to Louis XII in France, and to Maximilian the Holy Roman Emperor, inviting participation in a ship-borne crusade across the Mediterranean to the Holy Land. There was no response—though Maximilian was supportive—but Manuel remained undaunted.

After 1505, this amplified project dominated Portuguese thinking for fifteen years. Its architects were a closed cabal within the Portuguese court who kept their plans well guarded in the face of much commercial opposition, the jealousy of rival monarchs, and the antagonism of the Mamluk sultan. If its inspiration was medieval eschatology about divine providence and the end of the world, its strategy was drawn from the most contemporary grasp of the known world, and its scale was planetary. Some of it was already implicit in Almeida's instructions: first to suffocate the Mamluks economically, then to attack them directly from the Red Sea. The grandiose new dimensions involved a pincer movement. Manuel was proposing a simultaneous Mediterranean ship-borne crusade to the Holy Land and concerted strikes at Muslim power in Morocco.

The destruction of the Islamic bloc was now the clear cornerstone of the policy, to the extent that India could be a platform for attack rather than an end in itself; even the sea route might in time be abandoned after Islam had been destroyed. Trade could resort to the safer and shorter Red Sea once that was in Christian hands. The inflationary bubble of wealth encouraged the king to dream. In July, the pope granted Manuel a crusading tax for two years and remission of sins for all those thus engaged. Though the public expressions of these ideas were strictly limited, Manuel seems to have aspired to the title of emperor of a messianic Christian realm. Its builder was to be Afonso de Albuquerque.

Meanwhile, Ca'Masser, Venice's spy, was assiduously gathering hard data on the fortunes of the Portuguese voyages along the Lisbon waterfront as each fleet departed and returned. Despite Manuel's embargo on information, he was alarmingly well informed. "I have seen the sailing charts of the route to India," he reported back, "and how this shows all the places these Portuguese trade and deal in and have discovered." He soberly recorded the composition of fleets, tonnages, cargoes out, captains, setbacks and shipwrecks, journey times, quantities of spices bought, arrangements for their sale and selling prices, and a mine of other information on the infrastructure of trade and government. He was there on July 22, 1505, when the annual spice fleet pulled into Lisbon with ten ships, carefully noting the quantities of mace, camphor, ginger, and cinnamon and "pearls to the value of 4000 ducats." He heard of a crushing victory at Panthalayini in December of the previous year, when seventeen Muslim merchant ships were destroyed, "all burned with the spices which were the cargo destined for Mecca ... an incredible loss ... 22 Portuguese dead, 70–80 wounded," and added confused accounts of the dimensions of the expedition: "the voyage lasted 18 months, 5 going out, loading 3½, return 6½—they would have returned sooner but were delayed for twelve days in Mozambique due to the poor condition of the ships.... The first ship made the journey in 24 months and 8 days."

The commercially minded Venetians were only too well able to appreciate the vast quantities of spices being unloaded at Lisbon. They had fervently hoped that the long route to India would prove impractical, yet the rhythm of Portuguese voyaging was remorseless. Metronomically, year after year, fleets were dispatched and returned. Ca'Masser was under no illusions of the threat to Venetian interests:

I see that this enterprise can't be destroyed by the inability to sail there. It goes on as a regular and stable business, and without doubt the king will dominate the sea completely, because it's patently obvious that the Indians can't protect the maritime trade, nor resist the shipping or artillery of this Most Serene King. The ships of the Indians are weak … without artillery because at present they don't carry any.

For Venice, the only recourse was to try, yet again, secretly to prod the Mamluk sultan into action. In August 1505, while Almeida was sacking Mombasa, they briefed yet another ambassador to Cairo, Alvise Sagudino: "Speak to the sultan without witnesses … we have a very strong desire to ascertain that the sultan has taken firm measures.… In the matter of Calicut we give you freedom to speak and put forward whatever seems appropriate." To impress on the sultan the urgency of their joint predicament, he was to show him "a copy of a letter just received from Portugal, on the arrival of a large quantity of spices," doubtless written by Ca'Masser.

The Venetians were just one of a growing hubbub of voices being raised against the Portuguese in Cairo. The burning of ships, the violence against Muslim merchants, the hindrances to the hajj pilgrimage, the fear for Mecca itself—the sense of Islamic outrage was ever rising. The Arab chronicles are exhaustive on the Portuguese affronts to Muslims in the Indian Ocean:

hindering them on their journeys, particularly to Mecca; destroying their property; burning their dwellings and mosques; seizing their ships; defacing and treading under foot their archives and writings … slaying also the pilgrims to Mecca … openly uttering execrations upon the Prophet of God … binding them with ponderous shackles … beating them with slippers, torturing them with fire … in short, in their whole treatment of the Mahommedans, they proved themselves to be devoid of all compassion!

Aside from the aggression against Islam, the threat to his tax revenues ensured that a collision with the Mamluk sultanate was inevitable.

Within the perfumed pleasure gardens and elaborate ceremonial life of Cairo, the Indian Ocean seemed far away. In July the sultan was overseeing the installation of a new wife in the city. "Her arrival occasioned a grandiose display," according to the chronicler.

She was carried on a palanquin embroidered with gold; the parasol
and the bird were hoisted above her; small gold and silver coins were
strewn in her way and silk carpets were spread out before the door
of the bridal suite as far as the hall of the columns; the princesses
processed before her until she was seated on her dais. The sultan had
had the hall of the columns restored for her use and decorated in an
original way.

In August the ceremonial opening of an irrigation channel took place,
"according to custom," to accommodate the annual flooding of the
"blessed Nile," and the sultan celebrated the birth of the Prophet,
"magnificently, as he always did."

Yet the murmurings of distant trouble could no longer be suppressed. The following month he reviewed the army in preparation for
the forming of three expeditionary corps. Two were to suppress internal revolts in the Arabian Peninsula, the third "to oppose the incursions
of the Franks on the shores of India. A large number of soldiers were
mobilized and the preparation of equipment actively pushed forward."
On November 4, the troops were ready to depart; they were given
their provisions and four months' pay in advance. The majority of the
men were from North Africa, along with Turkomans from Anatolia
and companies of black archers—a mixed force of Islamic mercenaries
whom the Portuguese called Rumes. Masons, carpenters, and other
workmen also accompanied the force, with the aim of fortifying Jeddah and surrounding it with a wall—there was already fear of a strike
on Mecca and the heartlands of the Islamic world. They started their
march to the Red Sea port of Suez.

The technical preparations for this expedition remain shrouded in
mystery. The Mamluks were not a maritime power; the dynasty lived
parasitically by taxing the private trade of the Muslim merchants of the
Indian Ocean. They had no war fleet and suffered from a chronic
shortage of wood for shipbuilding. Timber had to be laboriously imported from the Mediterranean shores of Lebanon, floated down the
Nile to Cairo, then transported by camel or cart the eighty miles over
the desert to Suez. The acquisition of metal for cannon construction
was a similar conundrum. But the materials for both were being as-

sembled for a concerted campaign. Manuel received warning of this during the course of the year via the island of Rhodes, where one of the Knights of St. John, the Portuguese André do Amaral, fed information on the Mamluks back to Lisbon.

The Portuguese would later claim that the ships in the dockyards of Suez were built with timber cut, dressed, and supplied by the Venetians, and their construction overseen by Venetian officials. When the Portuguese ambassador at the court of Henry VIII in England put such charges to his Venetian opposite number in 1517, this was flatly denied. The Serene Republic had enough trouble elsewhere. Venice saw price as a better weapon than warfare: "the most certain and swift way of getting the Portuguese to give up their India voyages," it was later reported to the city's Committee of the Ten, "will be to lower the price of spices so that they become cheaper in Venice than Lisbon." It was a tack they tried repeatedly, though unsuccessfully, with the sultan. But it was likely that private Venetian merchants were supplying the copper bars for cannon founding—they always had—and freelance technical mercenaries from the Venetian commonwealth, such as shipwrights and cannon founders, were building vessels to European designs in Suez and cannons in Cairo.

The force the sultan had assembled was believed to be adequate to the task: eleven hundred men marched to Suez in the winter of 1505 under the experienced naval commander Hussain Musrif, a Kurd. They boarded the assembled fleet, which consisted of six European-designed carracks and six galleys, and started the voyage down the strait to Jeddah. The latest intelligence they had was that the Portuguese had four ships in the Indian Ocean and command of just one fort, at Cochin. This had been approximately true in the summer of 1505, before Almeida's arrival. Very soon it was not.

On August 27, Almeida caught sight of the Malabar Coast for the first time: "very high with great peaks and very tall trees of an incredible green," according to Hans Mayr. The Portuguese still had the merest toehold on the Indian coast—just some trading posts granted with the permission of Hindu potentates in the face of strong opposition from

the Muslim trading elites, plus the wooden fort at Cochin, which had
survived, by the skin of its teeth, solely through the genius of Duarte
Pacheco Pereira. Almeida's seat of government was effectively the deck
of his ship. His orders were to consolidate this position at lightning
speed by constructing a series of fortified bases, through peaceful alliances if at all possible; if not, by all-out war.

Following instructions, he landed first on the uninhabited island of
Anjediva, considered valuable as a fallback point for the Portuguese
and a lookout post for ambushing Muslim ships. The outlines of a fort
were constructed within a month. Then, working his way south, he
made an unscheduled visit to the port of Honavar. A dispute with its
raja over a cargo of horses led to a major assault. In one of those short,
sharp fights that characterized Almeida's progress, part of the city was
destroyed and a number of ships burned, belonging to Timoji, the notorious pirate of the Malabar Coast whom Vasco da Gama had encountered seven years earlier. The attack had been led by Almeida's son
Lourenço, who soon earned the nickname of "the Devil" for the ferocity of his assaults. On this occasion he came close to being cut off
and killed. Almeida himself received an arrow in the foot. The wound
caused him "more indignation than pain," but the honor code of reckless bravery created risks that would have consequences for the whole
Portuguese enterprise. In the aftermath, the raja sued for peace, promising an annual tribute, and Timoji pledged himself to the Portuguese
cause—a development that would be significant. The trail of smoldering cities and ships sunk, the news of which was spread on the monsoon winds, was commanding obedience across the whole ocean.

Manuel had urged Almeida to hurry directly to Cochin to secure
the loading of spices for the winter return and, specifically, not to lose
time on the way at the city of Cannanore, where the Portuguese had
a trading post. The viceroy disobeyed, probably because he had received word that the commercial position was under threat from Muslim merchants fearing for their trade. In a whirlwind eight days there,
he received ambassadors from the powerful Hindu king of Narsingha,
who offered him the use of coastal ports and the hand of a sister in
marriage to Manuel, then a welcome from the king of Cannanore.

Hans Mayr was bemused by the spectacle of Hindu ceremonial, as well as the populousness of India.

> [The king] ordered hangings to be set up under a palm tree, and he came accompanied by columns of men. He brought three thousand warriors with swords and daggers and spears, and archers, trumpets and flutes. It's two leagues from Cannanore to the king's palace and the way is lined with a village like a street so that by the time he arrived at the tent he was followed by more than six thousand people. In the tent was a couch with two cushions. He wore a robe of fine cotton to the knees that was fastened at the waist with a sash and on his head a silk hat like a Galician cap; and in that fashion his page carried a gold crown that must have weighed eight marks [of gold].

The king, perhaps aware of the scorched trail that the Westerners were leaving in their wake, decided to withstand the pressure of the

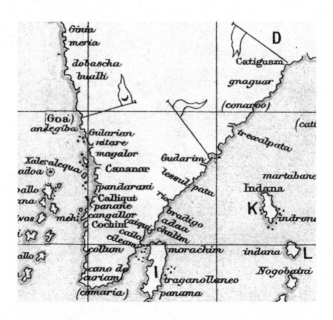

Map of India from 1502. Sri Lanka is included along with a scattering of semi-mythical islands.

Muslim community. He both granted leave for the trading post to be fortified and provided the stone to construct it. Almeida stayed just long enough to lay the foundations and sailed on, leaving 150 men and artillery to consolidate and construct a redoubtable structure—one that would quickly be tested by siege.

By All Saints' Day—November 1—Almeida was in Cochin. The city was the key to all of Manuel's India plans. It was the only reliable ally the Portuguese had. When Almeida arrived, he discovered that Trimumpara, the old king, had retired into the religious life and that under the laws of succession the throne had passed to his nephew, Nambeadora, though this was contested by rivals. In what might pass for colonial sleight of hand, Almeida conferred legitimate sovereignty over his own kingdom on Nambeadora at a magnificent ceremony involving elephants, trumpets, processions, and the presentation of a gold crown and valuable presents; Nambeadora "accepted these things from the hand of the king Dom Manuel, as the greatest king of the West and king of the seas of the East, and the lord of his coronation, and of all those who ruled in Cochin." The Portuguese had been finessing such strategies along the African coast for fifty years. Following up quickly, Almeida requested, rather disingenuously, that the present wooden fort be replaced with a stone one "that would be the headquarters and seat of the governor and others from then on who would come to organize the conquest and trade of these parts so that the ships of the kingdom might come there to load cargo and not to any other port of the Malabar Coast." With some reluctance—stone buildings were, by tradition, the prerogative of kings and Brahmans—the king granted it. Persuasion included Almeida's promise that he would hand over the keys, as a sign that it belonged to the king. Yet rulers up and down the Malabar Coast were to find that once the Franks were ensconced behind solid ramparts, with artillery mounted on stout gun platforms, they proved almost impossible to dislodge.

However, the persuasive speech of Almeida, as reported by the historian Barros, contained another, perhaps more far-sighted, strand. He declared that "the principal intention of his king Don Manuel in making these discoveries was the desire to communicate with the royal families of these parts, so that trade might develop, an activity that results from human needs, and that depends on a ring of friendship through communicating with one another." It was a prescient awareness of the origins and benefits of long-distance trade: the runaway train of globalization that had started with Vasco da Gama.

During the final months of 1505 and into 1506, Almeida was furiously busy, as if the window of opportunity that had opened to him might be slammed shut by a change of heart among the potentates of the Malabar Coast, and he had the pressing demands of his *regimento* to fulfill. Of all the simultaneous edicts Manuel had imposed upon him, he set himself two priorities: wealth and security—the loading up of the spice fleets from Cochin and the construction of the fortresses there and at Cannanore. He worked with exemplary diligence and energy. According to his secretary, when a ship was to be loaded, "the viceroy continuously took great care over this. He was always there in person overseeing the weighing, even at night." His aim was to curb the ever-present temptation to fraud, committed either by underweighing or "accidentally" bursting the spice sacks and filching some of the contents. With the construction of the Cochin fortress, he was equally assiduous: "every day he got up, and gets up, two and sometimes three hours before morning and was then at work with the masons . . . and thus he went on until two hours after sunset."

Almeida was busy everywhere, with repair of the ships, establishing a hospital, building the infrastructure of an imperial administration. At his side an overseer of the treasury, a secretary of the administration, an ombudsman to administer justice, factors, and captains; within his own small court, a working team—chaplain, torchbearers, trumpeters, bodyguards, servants. Each fort had its own captain, as well as a factor experienced in commercial transactions and a body of supporting functionaries: storekeepers, scribes, secretary-general, chief of police and court officials, tax collectors, an overseer of funeral arrangements and probate. Hospitals, houses, chapels, and churches were constructed. Maritime security was maintained by a permanent naval force under his son, Lourenço.

Almeida was an excellent administrator and an incorruptible guardian of the royal interests, obsessive about honesty, discipline, and fair dealing. With the returning spice fleets he sent scrupulous ledgers detailing the management of the imperial system. "Believe me Your Highness," he wrote to the king, probably not without some exaggeration, "no one comes to the town [of Cochin] without my permission and my knowledge, not a *real* is stolen ... here everything is as secure and as well taken care of as in Portugal." He battled continuously against individual corruption. When Kilwa was taken, with a rich haul of merchandise, gold, and silver, he kept for himself just one arrow as a memento of his victory, writing to the king that "my reward is to serve you in such a way that my deeds will bear witness." He never claimed more than a small fraction of the pepper that was due to him as viceroy, and he stoutly championed the cause of the rank and file, suffering and dying to construct the Indian empire, whose back pay was always late.

The annual spice ships were promptly loaded in Cochin and sent off in successive squadrons during the winter of 1505. Nine vessels made it back to Lisbon; just one, the enormous but now aging *Frol de la Mar* ("Flower of the Sea"), sprang a leak and had to overwinter in Mozambique. The rewards bore witness to the efficiency and good order of the commercial functioning of the Indies venture, which Almeida had always perceived to be at the heart of the enterprise. The Venetian Ca'Masser watched the ships return in volleys and could report in detail on the cargoes, "as seen in the books of the [ship's] scrivener," and on the increasingly sophisticated arrangements for managing the goods in Lisbon: "everything is unloaded in the India House, which is the new customs house recently created for this purpose, and each ship has its own storage room. There are twenty such rooms in the customs house, where all the pepper is stored in an orderly fashion." Ca'Masser could estimate that the value of the cargoes dispatched by Almeida in the winter of 1505–06 was "certainly a very great sum"—the figure of thirty-five thousand quintals of spices (according to his calculations) was an unprecedented haul in global trade and a figure not surpassed until 1517.

When he wrote to Manuel in December 1505, Almeida could look back on a list of solid achievements. In a four-month period of intense activity, the viceroy had built the durable foundations of a permanent Portuguese presence. He now suggested that Manuel should take not just the title of Lord of the Navigation but an even grander acclamation:

> It seems to me that Your Highness should strive to be addressed as
> Emperor of the Indies ... because the kings of Kilwa and Mombasa ... and Malindi and Mogadishu ... are calling you their lord
> and they your vassal ... and on the other coast [of India] you have
> royal and peaceful forts and nothing goes across the sea except under
> your protection; Batecala [Bharkal] and Honnevar [Honavar] have
> promised me that they will be your vassals and pay you ... so nothing could be more just or more rightfully earned than that Your
> Highness should take the title.

At the same time, Almeida was aware of his inability to fulfill all the
instructions given in the *regimento*. Having prioritized the construction
of fortresses and the dispatch of spices, he wrote to Manuel, "I have
decided, My Lord, not to go to the Red Sea this year, although it's the
thing I most desire in the world," citing the need to get the forts securely in place and the required timely loading of the spice fleets
completed before proceeding further. Meanwhile, the samudri remained an unsolved problem.

When the letter reached Lisbon, in the middle of the following year,
the king ordered Masses to be said and ceremonial processions
throughout the land, and contemplated the construction of a series of
monumental tapestries to celebrate the great events that sealed the
creation of the State of India—the coronation of the king of Kilwa,
the taking of Mombasa, the fort construction along the Malabar
Coast—grandiose forms of self-promotion. The pope considered
granting him the title of Most Christian King. In the interim Manuel's
ambitions had vaulted on; and in May 1506, Christopher Columbus,
the agent of Spain's rivalry with Portugal, died in Valladolid still convinced that he had reached the Indies.

12

"The Terrible"

January 1506–January 1508

W HILE FRANCISCO DE ALMEIDA worked to stabilize a profitable Indian empire, in Lisbon King Manuel had been
changing his mind about the command structure. The king's management of affairs on the other side of the world, which he could hardly
envisage and which involved long delays of communication, was riddled with contradictions. His orders to Almeida had been querulously
detailed, but the king was prey to doubt and the pressures of his envious cabal of courtiers. Manuel was incapable of distinguishing men of
true merit from the inept, the corrupt, and the self-interested. Duarte
Pacheco Pereira, whose exploits in Cochin had single-handedly saved
the whole Portuguese enterprise over the winter of 1503, sank into
obscurity on his return. Even before he'd received Almeida's first account of his work, Manuel had decided on the new man to replace
him. Afonso de Albuquerque shared and magnified Manuel's belief
that he was destined by God to sweep Islam out of the Indian Ocean
and to regain Jerusalem. Albuquerque was now to become his chosen
instrument.

On February 27, 1506—an exact year after Manuel had publicly
expressed total confidence in Almeida—the new man signed a secret
document:

I, Afonso de Albuquerque, declare that I have taken my oath to our lord the king, in his presence, that I will divulge to none the provision made regarding the captaincy of India, now held by D. Francisco [de Almeida], against the latter's return to these realms or in case of his death—which document I hold and may reveal to no man until such time as it should take effect and I remain in tenure of his office.

Manuel was already appointing him to take over from Almeida almost three years later with the title of governor, a lesser power than viceroy, but this information was to be kept secret until the appointed time. In the meantime, he wrote to Almeida to notify him that Albuquerque was empowered to impinge on regions and activities that he had previously given to the viceroy's sole charge in the western half of the Indian Ocean. This overlapping of authority was destined to create confusion and antagonisms in the years ahead. Meanwhile Manuel's tone toward Almeida, influenced by the snide tittle-tattle of returning captains and the malevolence of court rivals, was becoming increasingly sharp.

The spice fleet being prepared for the spring of 1506 was to consist of fifteen ships, under the overall command of Tristão da Cunha. Nine of those were under his direct authority, accompanied by Albuquerque with six more. The whole fleet was intended to enter the Indian Ocean and establish a presence on Socotra, a small island near the mouth of the Red Sea that was believed to be controlled by Christians and, thus, an ideal base for stamping out Islamic traffic bound for the Muslim markets of Egypt and the Middle East.

Lisbon was a dynamic, brawling, and turbulent place in the early years of the century. With the wealth of the Indies pouring into the wharves on the banks of the Tejo, entrepreneurial merchants, tradesmen, sailors, and chancers came to the "New Venice," attracted by the smell of spices and the demand for luxury items. If much of the waterfront was being laid out in a grand imperial style to reflect the aspirations of the Grocer King, it was also a city of squalor and hysterical passions. In January 1506, plague broke out, probably brought up the

Tejo on ships. Soon it was carrying off a hundred a day, and the king considered evacuating the city; by April he had removed his court to Abrantes, ninety miles away. The mood was fraught; Masses were said for deliverance from plague; hooded penitents stalked the streets. It became difficult to fill the ships of the fleet. No one wanted to sail with men from Lisbon.

The Lisbon waterfront

As April 5, the date set for departure, approached, the fleet was at Belém as usual, undertaking the rituals of departure. Albuquerque was compelled to sweep the prisons to make up the numbers, which added an additional combustible element to the expedition. The crews were unruly and violent. Albuquerque was to declare that there were more scuffles and knife fights on board his ships than in the whole of Salamanca. A ruffian crew that combined a deep hatred of Muslims with experience of violent piracy would prove hard to contain. On the intended day of departure, Albuquerque had another problem. His pilot, an experienced navigator named João Dias de Solis, failed to turn up. Solis had chosen that moment to murder his wife and flee over the border to Spain. Albuquerque, never one to underestimate his own talents, decided to steer the ship himself. "I presumed I could take my ship to India as well as the best pilot in the fleet." A fortnight after they had sailed, Lisbon reached a flashpoint. The New Christians, recently converted Jews who had been allowed to stay in the city, were accused of heresy and of spreading the plague. A hysterical mob led by Franciscan monks turned on them in the streets. Two thousand died in the pogrom before order could be restored.

Cunha and Albuquerque were related, but the expedition was no more harmonious than that which Albuquerque had shared with his cousin Francisco in 1503. The two men chafed against each other. Albuquerque, who was subordinate to the appointed commander but whose confidence in his own abilities had been further increased by his secret appointment, was temperamentally incapable of bowing to anyone. From the larger Portuguese point of view, their mission was a commercial disaster. The fleet was hit by storms, almost doubled back to the African coast, delayed by Cunha's impetuous desire to explore the newly discovered island of Madagascar, sidetracked by plundering the Somali coast. It took sixteen months to accomplish a task that should have taken six. Socotra, the first stated objective, nominally Christian, was in fact a Muslim stronghold and had to be stormed. It turned out to be strategically useless for patrolling the mouth of the Red Sea and barren of supplies to support its new garrison. In the process, Cunha missed the 1506 sailing season to the coast of India and the loading of spices.

Elsewhere, the Mamluk naval expedition that had set out in 1505 was moving at a similarly leisurely pace. The commander, Hussain Musrif, was evidently in no hurry to confront the Franks, and his expedition had multiple tasks to perform along the way. The fortification of Jeddah, of which he was also the governor, was his first priority—in particular, overseeing the construction of robust defenses against the possibility of Portuguese attack. The danger of a strike against Mecca, at that moment being proposed in Lisbon, was sufficiently alarming to ensure that the whole of 1506 was spent in the Red Sea. There were also revolts among the Bedouin to be crushed. It was not until May the following year that the Jeddah defenses were complete.

The effects of this initial campaign had been attritional. Desertions and combat losses had reduced the original twelve ships to six by the time they reached Aden, in August 1507. Bad news from the Indian Ocean continued to filter back to Cairo. "Latterly the audacity of the Franks knows no bounds," wrote the chronicler Ibn Iyas. "More than twenty of their ships dare to plow the Red Sea, attacking merchant vessels from India, waiting in ambush to attack convoys, seizing cargoes, so that a lot of imports are stopped. It's extremely difficult to acquire turbans and muslin in Egypt." But there was full confidence that a pan-Islamic alliance fired by the spirit of jihad and additional help from the samudri would be sufficient to crush the intruders.

Meanwhile, as Almeida's fleet continued to damage Muslim commerce along the Malabar Coast, the merchants of Arabia were diverting their ships to other spice markets. An increasing number were striking south to the low-lying atolls of the Maldives, where they could take on food and fresh water before sailing on to Ceylon. Almeida sent his son to cut off the Maldives route, but the navigators missed their way; currents carried Lourenço's ships south to Ceylon, where they made the first Portuguese landing, established a treaty, and planted a cross.

For the viceroy, however, the picture was darkening. All of Manuel's expansionist plans depended on maintaining a stable base on the Malabar Coast, and this rested not only on a disciplined naval force, with its unanswerable bronze cannons, but also on prestige. It was essential that the perceived advantages of trading with the Franks remained high among the network of city-states. During 1506, confidence in the Portuguese was starting to falter.

Within a couple of months of its construction, the Anjediva fortress was found to have been a mistake. Wherever they went, the incomers were intruding on a vested interest. Here it was the preserve of the sultan of Bijapur, whose ships forced passing traffic into his own port of Dabul to pay customs dues. He was not about to tolerate an interloper. At the start of the monsoon season a carefully timed attack, led by a Portuguese renegade, put the fort under siege. Three ships were

burned before the news of Lourenço's imminent arrival forced a withdrawal, but it was clear that the fort was unsustainable: too close to
hostile Bijapur, too short of natural resources. At the end of the year,
Almeida took the decision, without reference to Manuel, to abandon
and dismantle the structure. It was a riposte to the wisdom of the
grand plan, and it did not go down well. At the same time, it gave hope
to Muslim merchants that the Portuguese could be dislodged.

Two more serious blows followed. The Portuguese had brought an
unprecedented level of polarization and militarization to the affairs of
the sea. To those loyal to the newcomers, who in time included some
of the Mappila merchants—the indigenous Muslims of the Malabar
Coast, particularly in Cochin and Cannanore—they pledged protection to shipping and issued safe-conduct passes, on the presumption
that the Indian Ocean was to be a Portuguese monopoly. It was in the
fulfillment of this duty that Lourenço was convoying ships north
toward the port of Chaul at the end of 1506. Stopping along the way
to dismantle the Anjediva fort, he had anchored near hostile Dabul
when some Muslim merchants, identifying themselves as natives of
friendly ports, came aboard to plead for help. Their richly laden ships
from Cochin and Cannanore had been in Dabul's port, where a larger
contingent of Mecca ships had subsequently docked. These were now
planning to sack the ships of Portugal's allies. The visiting merchants
begged for Lourenço to lose no time in launching an attack.

Lourenço was determined to fight but was bound by instructions
from his father to convene a captains' committee before deciding on
battle. That evening at table, they voted by a majority of six to four
against action: they were concerned that the request might be a trap,
that the river mouth in which Dabul lay was unknown to them, that
they might not be able to retreat, and that, anyway, they had been ordered to convoy ships to Chaul. It might have been prudence or it
might have been spite; there were experienced captains ill-pleased to
obey the viceroy's twenty-five-year-old son. Lourenço listened in
stunned silence. He accepted the verdict and withdrew, but not before
he had prudently extracted signed statements from the dissenters as to
their votes. Elsewhere on the vessels there was fury from the knights
and seamen itching for a fight and the chance to win booty.

The inevitable happened. The friendly merchantmen were sacked and their crews killed. Calicut ships fired mocking shots as they sailed past the fort at Cannanore. For the first time, the Portuguese had flunked a fight. The refusal to protect their ships was taken badly in friendly Malabar ports. Almeida was appalled by the news. He court-martialed all the captains, including his son. Those who had voted against were imprisoned, demoted, and returned to Portugal. A question mark remained against Lourenço's name.

The Dabul incident cast a long shadow. The historian João de Barros summarized its consequences for captains and commanders: "that in decisions about whether to fight . . . so that honorable deeds may be done, even if dangerous, they must not raise objections based on the personal safety of their lives." Henceforward prudence was impossible. No one felt able to refuse an engagement, however rash, without accusations of cowardice. Only bravery of the most explicit kind would suffice. The honor code of the *fidalgos* was accentuated to the extent of an emphasis on hand-to-hand combat over the distant destruction of cannon fire.

An even more serious loss than the Dabul incident befell loyal local merchants over the winter of 1506. Tristão da Cunha's fleet failed to arrive. For the first time since Vasco da Gama's first visit in 1498, no fleet came from Lisbon to buy spices. The ports of Cannanore and Cochin were well stocked with merchandise they were unable to sell. Merchants began to rue the monopoly pact with the Franks and yearn for a return to the reliable Mecca trade.

Cannanore was particularly disaffected. Its Muslim community was dismayed by the growth of the Portuguese fort and well understood its implications. Merchants feared that their profitable horse trade with the Persian Gulf might be about to vanish. The Portuguese had started to seize boatloads from Ormuz, and the merchants had lost a valuable cargo of elephants, destroyed by Lourenço during an attack on hostile Quilon. Lourenço's probe in the direction of the Maldives and Ceylon only increased their disquiet. There was apparently no limit to the incomers' ambitions. They began to fear for all their markets. Within the city itself, the Portuguese were starting to disrupt the social hierarchy and to flout its mores. Women of low caste were consorting with the men of the garrison; the development of mixed communities, in which people were being converted to Christianity, fueled Muslim resentment, and the temptation for the incomers, craving red meat, to kill the occasional cow only increased tensions with the Hindus. The ruler of Cannanore wrote to Manuel more than once about his disquiet that "the sugar of the Portuguese friendship would turn to poison."

When the ruler of Cannanore died, in April 1507, the samudri used his influence to place a more sympathetic candidate on the throne. It was just at this moment that a number of bodies washed up on the city's beach, among them that of the nephew of a prominent Muslim merchant. The finger of blame pointed directly at a Portuguese captain who had intercepted a local merchant ship, declared its safe-conduct pass to be a forgery, even though signed by Almeida's garrison commander, and killed the crew. Before dumping them in the sea he had wrapped the bodies in sails to ensure that they sank, only for the current to work them loose and present them to their grieving relatives.

It was the signal for a wide-ranging Malabar revolt. Eighteen thousand warriors converged on the city; the samudri sent twenty-four cannons. The fort, positioned on a headland, was cut off from any relief from land—and provision from the sea was becoming difficult.

In the Indian Ocean, the monsoon dictated the rhythm of everything: when ships could sail, when wars could be fought, when the spice fleets could arrive and when they must depart—missing a critical moment could cost months. Opponents of the Portuguese quickly worked out that an enemy dependent on sea power was vulnerable once storms came. They timed their attacks accordingly. During April, the weather started to worsen.

It was Good Friday when the news of the attack on Cannanore reached Cochin. Almeida, realizing that time was now tight, wasted not a moment. He went from house to house calling for people to bring out food and arms. A mystery play was in performance in the church; men dressed as Roman centurions guarding Christ's tomb had to give up their greaves and breastplates on the spot. With rising seas, Lourenço took what could be found and set sail to Cannanore. He had time to unload men and materials before the winds mounted and he was forced to sail back to Cochin, leaving the fortress captain, Lourenço de Brito, and some four hundred men cut off by the monsoon weather to withstand a furious siege. It was still under siege in August when Cunha and Albuquerque, having taken and garrisoned the forlorn island of Socotra, went their separate ways: Cunha to India, a year late with the spice fleet, Albuquerque to patrol the Arabian Sea. It was Cunha's ships that relieved the starving Cannanore garrison at the end of the month, finally breaking the anti-Portuguese coalition there.

Cunha and Albuquerque had hardly been on speaking terms when they parted at Socotra. Albuquerque was impatient and furious. He was left with six worm-eaten ships, rotting equipment, short supplies, and just four hundred men. As a final snub, Cunha had sailed off with all the trumpets, essential for staging displays of prestige and power in foreign ports and for rallying troops in battle. Albuquerque had not only to provide food for his crews but also to return supplies for the undernourished garrison left on Socotra.

His brief, as explained by Manuel in a letter to Almeida, was to "guard the mouth of the Red Sea, capture Muslim cargo ships, secure all the prize cargoes that can be found in them, establish treaties in places that seem useful, such as Zeila, Barbara and Aden, also to go to Ormuz, and to learn everything about these parts." It provided Albuquerque with a huge field of operations, from the Red Sea, along the Arabian Peninsula, and across the Persian Gulf to the shores of northwest India. He chose to interpret these instructions loosely, in his own fashion.

Despite a shortage of men and materials, shoddy ships, and inadequate weapons—and orders that seemed pacific in relation to the places mentioned in Manuel's letters—Albuquerque took his cutthroat crews on a thunderous blitz along the Arabian coast. The small ports on the barren shores of what is modern Oman, backed by the irreducible deserts of Arabia, were surprisingly prosperous. They lived by exporting dates, salt, and fish and by the valuable trade in horses to the warlords of continental India.

It was here, in a few short weeks, that Albuquerque founded a reputation that was exceptional within the ranks of Portuguese conquistadors, and that would be cemented in its history with the singular title

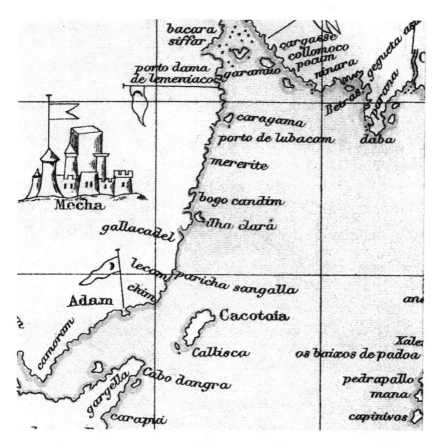

Albuquerque's field of operations on a contemporary map, showing Socotra (Cacotoia) near the mouth of the Red Sea, the coast of the Arabian peninsula east of Aden (Adam), and the island of Ormuz (unlabeled) at the entrance to the Persian Gulf.

of "the Terrible." His fleet of tattered ships, adorned with all their flags, sailed into the trading ports of Oman, one after another, demanding submission to the Portuguese crown. Instead of the absent trumpets, the crews were ordered to raise a clamor of warlike noise as their vessels rode boldly into view. Albuquerque would demand an audience on his quarterdeck that was designed to impress and unnerve. The hapless emissaries of the local sheikh would step aboard into a carefully framed tableau: the captain-major dressed in gray velvet and cap, a gold chain around his neck, a scarlet cloak around his shoulders, sat in an ornately carved chair, surrounded by his captains got up as brightly as they could manage, in a setting decked with finely worked hangings. Each commander carried an unsheathed sword that implied a clear message: submission or war. Albuquerque had little time for the pleasantries of Oriental diplomacy. Gifts were refused. The messengers would be routinely informed that he did not accept presents from those he might soon have to fight. With his long beard and unflinching demeanor, he aimed to frighten. There was a great deal of psychological bluff in these choreographed shows. Vastly outnumbered and thousands of miles from home, he used his intimidating presence to great effect. Sometimes he would insist that his men dress in different outfits each day to deceive visitors about the numbers at his disposal.

Some of the ports along the Omani coast submitted meekly. Others resisted and were sacked. Swarms of criminalized seamen from the Lisbon jails looted, murdered, and burned. Exemplary terror was a weapon of war, intended to soften up resistance farther down the coast. In this fashion, a string of small ports went up in flames. In each one the mosque would be routinely destroyed; the destruction of Muscat, the trading hub of the coast and "a very elegant town with very fine houses," was particularly savage. When the ships' gunners set about cutting away the pillars that supported its mosque, "a very large and beautiful edifice, the greater part of it being built of timber finely carved, and the upper part of stucco," the building collapsed on top of them. Albuquerque gave the men up for dead, but, "thanks to Our Lord," went on the chronicler, "they came out alive and sound, without a wound or a bruise. . . . Our people were frightened, and when they saw them gave many thanks to Our Lord for that miracle which he had done for them, and set fire to the mosque, which was burned so that nothing remained of it." Such providential acts inflamed Albuquerque's sense of divine mission. At the port of Qurayat, having collected all the useful supplies he could, "he ordered the place to be set on fire . . . and the fire was so fierce that not a house, not a building, nor the mosque, one of the most beautiful ever seen, was left standing." Albuquerque was intent on transmitting terror ahead of him: "he ordered the ears and noses of the captured Muslims to be cut off, and sent them to Ormuz as a testimony to their disgrace."

That Albuquerque possessed an intemperate streak was becoming increasingly apparent, not just to the hapless Omanis but also to his own captains. It was usual for the captain-major to consult with his ship commanders and, often, to be subject to a vote of the whole group. Albuquerque, intelligent, impatient, and possessed of an unshakable belief in his own abilities, had no such tact or cooperative spirit. The captains had been nominally informed at the start of the Omani expedition, but as the weeks wore on the relationship became strained. By mid-September they were inside the mouth of the Persian Gulf, increasingly distant from the key task to which they had been assigned: blocking the mouth of the Red Sea. The drive up the Arabian coast had one clear destination in Albuquerque's mind: the island city of Ormuz, a small nugget of parched rock anchored offshore that was the axis of all Gulf traffic between Persia and the Indian Ocean. It was an immensely wealthy trading place—the great Arab traveler Ibn Battuta had found it "a fine large city with magnificent bazaars" and tall handsome houses. When the Chinese star fleet had called, they'd declared "the people of the country . . . very rich. . . . There are no poor families." It controlled the famed pearl fisheries of the Persian Gulf and dispatched large numbers of Arabian horses to meet an insatiable demand among the warring empires of continental India. "If the world were a ring, then Ormuz would be the jewel in it," ran the Persian proverb. Albuquerque was well aware of the city's reputation and strategic worth.

Aggressive action against Ormuz seems to have formed no part of his instructions from King Manuel to "establish treaties." The harbor was thronged with merchant ships when Albuquerque arrived, but he proceeded in customary style. He refused all gifts from the king's messengers; his reply was simple: become vassals of the Portuguese crown or see your city destroyed. The chief vizier, Hwaga Ata, concluded that Albuquerque, with just six ships, was a seriously deluded man, but on the morning of September 27, 1507, in a hubbub of noise, Portuguese bronze cannons again outgunned a far larger Muslim fleet. The vizier quickly sued for peace, accepted Manuel as his lord, and agreed to payment of a hefty annual tribute.

Albuquerque saw the hand of the Christian God at work in the victory. In the aftermath he wrote to Manuel about "the great miracle Our Lord performed . . . which was seen by all of us who were there three days after the battle. . . .

> A considerable number of dead Muslims, more than nine hundred, floated on the water, and most of them had many arrows sticking in their bodies, legs and arms, despite the fact that I had brought with me neither archers nor arrows. A great deal of gold, swords chased with silver and jewels belonging to the nobles were found on them. The gathering of this booty by our men working in boats took eight days, during which some gained considerable wealth from what they found.

This miracle of friendly fire seemed like a confirmation of Manuel's divine mission in the Indian Ocean that delivered both victory and profit.

Albuquerque had not finished with Ormuz. He insisted on the right to build a fort. At this juncture, relations with his captains reached a crisis. The ship commanders could see no point in this activity: it was not in their orders, the blockade of the Red Sea was being neglected, Socotra needed to be resupplied with food, Ormuz had already submitted to the crown, and in any case, there would be insufficient men left to garrison a new stronghold. These men, and their crews, also had vested interests in returning to the mouth of the Red Sea, where they believed there were valuable prizes to be seized, but Albuquerque brushed aside their complaints. He even insisted that the captains should participate in the manual labor. It was to be a team effort. As this work was undertaken in full view of the watching population, it was considered a personal insult by the high-ranking captains and *fidalgos*.

The four captains came to see the captain-major as an intractable martinet who refused to listen to legitimate grievances. If he was constructing a huge strategic plan on behalf of Manuel for control of the Indian Ocean, this was not apparent in the written orders, and he failed to carry his commanders with him. In person he was physically intimidating; his rages cowed people. It seemed that by sheer force of

personality he was intent on subduing the Muslim sea. The four leading captains, including the experienced João de Nova, came to the
conclusion that Albuquerque was dangerous and possibly mad. Finding themselves verbally abused, they committed their complaints to
paper:

> Sir, we do this in writing, because by word of mouth we dare not, as
> you always answer us so passionately; and for all that you sir have
> frequently told us that the king gives you no orders to take counsel
> with us, yet this business is of so great an importance, that we con-
> sider ourselves obliged to offer you advice; did we not do so we
> would be worthy of punishment.

A first written deposition in November 1507 was torn to pieces. When
they presented a second, he folded it up without a glance and placed
it beneath a stone doorway being constructed in the fort.

When four men defected to Ormuz, converted to Islam, and the
vizier, Hwaga Ata, refused to hand them back, Albuquerque's rage
knew no bounds. "I was out of control," he later confided to Almeida.
He ordered his captains ashore to "kill every living thing. They obeyed
their commander against their will, being extremely unhappy at having to do this. They went ashore . . . and killed just two old men but
couldn't bring themselves to do it. Killing four or five animals, they
came across some more people and told them to run away." According
to the chronicler, they believed that their commander "was damned
and had the Devil in him."

Albuquerque pressed ahead with full-scale war against Ormuz in
the face of these objections. He poisoned the wells and began to bombard its walls. "The captains were driven to despair . . . and didn't stop
petitioning . . . to which [Albuquerque] took no heed. They didn't
want to obey a captain-major who was mad and who wasn't fit to
command a rowing boat, let alone a fleet." Furious at this insubordina-
tion, Albuquerque on one occasion "seized [João de Nova] by the
chest and grappled with him and João began to shout that he was
hurting and assaulting him for no good reason. All the captains were
witness that [Albuquerque] grabbed his beard and pulled it out." Ac-

cording to the chronicler, "when they saw that their complaints made so little impression on the captain-major . . . they took counsel to depart for India." In mid-January 1508 they deserted, sailing off to Cochin to tell their side of the story to the viceroy. Albuquerque was furious. He had now but two ships, and the siege of Ormuz had to be lifted. He sailed back to Socotra to relieve the famished garrison.

The failure to patrol the Red Sea was to prove costly. The slowly advancing Mamluk fleet reached Aden in August 1507. While Albuquerque was blitzing the Omani coast in September, it slipped across the Arabian Sea behind his back to the Gujarati port of Diu. The Portuguese had no idea that it was there.

13

Three Days at Chaul

March 1508

Along the west coast of India, Lourenço de Almeida remained unceasingly busy with naval operations. After the dispatch of the annual spice fleet at the end of December 1507, he was again tasked with convoy duties. In January he set off up the Malabar Coast, escorting a merchant fleet from Cochin. Along the way he took opportunities to burn the ships of Arab traders and damage ports friendly to the samudri. A warlike approach to Dabul, still a haunted place for the young commander, brought a rapid capitulation and the immediate payment of tribute. By February the fleet of merchant ships and their accompanying Portuguese carracks, galleys, and caravels had reached its final destination, the trading terminus at Chaul, nestling in the curved mouth of a river.

It was near the end of the sailing season. Soon monsoon weather would close the sea to shipping and the Portuguese could expect to hole up in Cochin, recuperating and repairing their vessels during months of enforced idleness. The men were tired; Lourenço was still recovering from wounds received earlier; the holds were full of booty collected along the coast; the heat was rising. Meanwhile, the Cochin merchants, whom they were escorting, were conducting their trade with interminable sloth. A month passed. February slipped into March. Low-lying Chaul was becoming insufferably humid. The men had nothing to do but spend their money on wine and dancing girls and sink into indolence. Lourenço was kicking his heels in frustration. There was an expectation that Afonso de Albuquerque's squadron would join them soon.

As they waited for the Cochin merchants to conclude their loading, other, more muffled rumors reached Lourenço's ears: that an Egyptian fleet was on its way; that it had docked at one of the key ports of Gujarati trade, Diu, two hundred miles away across the Gulf of Cambay; that it was coming to wage holy war on the Franks; that its troops were "white" men (probably Turks) and highly committed, well armed and with artillery. These rumors came variously: from the local people in Chaul, from a venerated Brahman who came to see Lourenço from Diu, and finally from the viceroy himself. But Francisco de Almeida evidently believed that there was no threat worthy of serious consideration. He sent just one ship. There was no evidence that any fleet yet encountered had the ability to match Portuguese gunnery, even when hopelessly outnumbered. Lourenço paid little heed to the reports.

In fact, the tardy Egyptian fleet had finally reached Diu six months earlier, after a long and wandering voyage during which it had suffered considerable attrition. Men had deserted for lack of pay; two ships had mutinied; a quarter of the men had been killed in the Arabian campaign along the way; and at Diu, Hussain Musrif, the fleet commander, was receiving a somewhat cautious reception from its governor. Malik Ayaz was a self-made man, a former military slave from the Caucasus who had risen to a position of power under the Muslim sultan of Gujarat and held Diu almost as a personal fiefdom, with its own fleet of fustas—small galleys. Shrewd, pragmatic, and extremely cunning, Ayaz had a realistic idea of the balance of power at sea. His trade with the outside world, which included the export of the cotton and turbans that were no longer reaching Egypt, was being paralyzed by Portuguese blockades. His independence at Diu required room for maneuvering between two implacable forces: growing Portuguese supremacy in the Indian Ocean and Muslim determination to destroy it. He now found himself in a difficult situation, knowing that sooner or later he would receive a "visit" from the Franks, yet aware that failure to embrace holy war could invite destruction at the hands of his powerful overlord, the Gujarati sultan. He had already attempted secret negotiations with the viceroy but knew how carefully he had to play his hand.

Hussain had entered the arena with a clear strategic plan and a rallying call to jihad. Among those who responded was Mayimama Marakkar, the Arab merchant who had been abused by Vicente Sodré in 1503. Marakkar had been vocal in Cairo on behalf of the samudri in trying to prompt the sultan into constructing a pan-Islamic front against the detested Christian interlopers. He came to Diu with a sizable ship got up at his own expense and with three hundred armed men, many of whom were skilled archers drawn from his own tribe. They had sworn to die for vengeance and the faith, and their ship was well equipped with artillery and munitions.

The Egyptians had their spies in Chaul, and they were infinitely better informed than the Portuguese languishing there in the heat. They knew how small Lourenço's force was. He had three small carracks, three caravels, and two galleys—about five hundred men in all. Hussain's aim was to fall on them suddenly and wipe them out, then tackle the Portuguese caravels blockading Calicut and cut off the forts at Cochin and Cannanore before the monsoon. He now called on the support of Ayaz. There was no alternative but a show of enthusiasm from Diu's governor. With the addition of his small fleet, Hussain led a fleet of forty-five vessels: forty fustas and galleys, one galleon, and four carracks that had been constructed by European shipwrights at Suez. It was to be a definitive showdown for power and the trade of the Indian Ocean.

A Friday in March—the chosen day of the week for the start of Islamic campaigns. At Chaul, the Portuguese were whiling away their time on the banks of the Kundalika River. The Cochin merchants' ships were still concluding their loading operations beside Chaul town on the northern bank. The Portuguese ships were drawn up across the water in haphazard order. Lourenço's ship, the *São Miguel,* and that of his experienced vice-captain, Pêro Barreto, the *São António,* were anchored in midstream. The others were closer to the southern shore with their prows to land. Many of the men were ashore, and Lourenço was amusing himself by throwing spears with other noblemen.

Toward the middle of the day, with the breeze coming in, lookouts

For naval operations along the Indian coast the Portuguese
employed oared galleys as well as sailing ships.

sighted five European carracks out to sea. The long-awaited arrival of
Albuquerque's squadron was greeted with joy. Men stopped to watch
their approach with relaxed interest, but one old soldier was scrutinizing the rigging more intently. Then he shouted to his squire, "I want
to arm myself now, we all need to!" He called for his breastplate and
started rapidly to buckle it on—to the mocking amusement of others
standing about. "These Albuquerques coming in," he snapped, "they
haven't got crosses on their sails. They're flying the banners of Ma-
homed. . . . Sirs, I pray to God that I alone will be the fool today and
that you'll still be laughing at nightfall."

The ships sailed into the mouth of the river; behind the carracks, six
galleys rowing in good order. Everyone could now see that the vessels
were decked with red-and-white flags and pennants emblazoned with
black crescent moons. They made an impressive show, their warriors in
magnificent turbans and brilliantly colored silks over their armor,
which glittered in the sun, "and entering the river decked out like this,
sounding many war trumpets, that together with the gleaming of their
weapons made the fleet more terrifying. Advancing like this, our men

finally realized that they were the Rumes." Their main sails were furled and their sides were covered with nets to impede projectiles. They were stripped for action.

There was panic in the Portuguese fleet: men hurrying to rowboats to be ferried out to the offshore ships; buckling on armor; snatching up swords and helmets and muskets; unprimed cannons being rolled out; oarsmen frantically trying to spin the galleys so that they could deploy their forward guns; shouting and uproar, orders and counterorders. There was time to establish some semblance of discipline because Hussain had paused in the river mouth, waiting for Ayaz's fustas, which seemed to be dawdling. The governor of Diu had in fact feigned some difficulties and anchored outside with the aim of watching to see who would win the contest—and then acting accordingly. Undeterred, Hussain swept on, passing the vulnerable Cochin merchant galleys without a shot fired, on toward the *São Miguel* and *São António,* perilously isolated in midstream from the rest of the fleet. His intention was to shatter Lourenço's flagship at a first strike.

As the distance closed, two of the Muslim cannons opened up broadside. An iron ball passed clean through the *São Miguel* but killed no one; the ship juddered from stem to stern. For the first time, the Portuguese were on the receiving end of artillery bombardment in the Indian Ocean. The Muslim archers, with their short, whippy Turkish bows, fired off a buzzing shower of arrows "that seemed like rain," loosed at a rate of twenty a minute. The *São Miguel*'s mast was studded with arrow shafts; out of a hundred men, thirty were hit and wounded. But the men-at-arms fought back with their own torrent of crossbow bolts and shot from muskets, and the ship's gunners had had sufficient time to prime their cannons and loose off their own counterblast. In the shattering roar of the guns, both ships vanished in the smoke and reappeared. Eight shots from the *São Miguel* hit the Muslim ship, crowded with four hundred fighting men. Netting was useless against this salvo; the cannonballs ripped through the closely packed ranks, shattering armor, dismembering bodies; splinters of wooden shrapnel increased the carnage. The deck was a scene of chaos. Hussain changed his mind about attempting to board. On the inshore breeze and the tide, he swept on past the Portuguese carracks, now supported by the two galleys, and anchored upstream on the opposite shore, followed by his other vessels.

Lourenço, sensing the damage inflicted on Hussain's flagship, was determined to press home the advantage. This required the leading carracks to be towed toward the enemy by their oared boats, but the execution was inept, as he failed to provide any support from his galleys. Hussain simply sent forward his own galleys, which put the fragile towboats under such a hail of fire that they were forced to withdraw. The attack had to be abandoned.

It was the end of a tense day. The two fleets were locked into a small arena, anchored on opposite banks and separated by a mere five hundred yards. The Cochin merchant ships lay at anchor before the town, unmolested. Each side tended to its wounded and counted the costs. Hussain's ships had been badly mauled; casualties were frighteningly high, and his supplies of gunpowder were running low. As night fell, the Portuguese captains were ferried to the *São Miguel* for a council of war. Without information, they were uncertain how to proceed. They decided to put ashore Balthazar, the son of the interpreter Gaspar de Almeida and also fluent in languages, to seek information in Chaul. He learned that Hussain was awaiting the arrival of Malik Ayaz before launching a further attack; in the meanwhile he was working to win the townspeople over to his side. For the moment they were also maintaining a cautious neutrality, watching to see how events turned out.

With the return of day, Lourenço could see that Hussain had arranged his ships in a tight defensive formation. They were drawn up along the shore, chained together, prows to the river, and connected one to another by gangplanks, so that men could be moved from one ship to the next in the event of attack. This was tactical suicide. His carracks were no longer capable of using their broadside bombards; nor could they escape. Hussain had transformed his fleet from an attack force into a huddled encampment waiting for Ayaz to come. And Ayaz was still loitering offshore. In the interim, the fleet was a sitting duck.

What Hussain did not know was that his opponent's thinking had been similarly warped. When the council of war reconvened on the *São Miguel* the next morning, with the attitude of the enemy fleet now clear, the decision was taken to attack. This required an onshore wind, which would not arise until midday. There were two strategic options: either to bombard the Egyptian ships or to take them by storm.

In a speech probably fabricated by a chronicler, Lourenço's master gunner, the German Michel Arnau, proposed a simple solution. "Don't put yourself and your men at risk, because what you want can be done without any danger, except to me and my companions." If Lourenço would allow the carracks to be positioned where he indicated, all his men could disembark and his gun crews could sink the entire fleet by nightfall, "and if not . . . you may order my hands to be cut off."

The shadow of the flunked engagement at Dabul hung over the group of men assembled in the cabin. Lourenço needed to reestablish honor and the credibility of prizes. Cannon fire, the simple and deadly solution, had almost come to be associated with cowardice in the honor code of the *fidalgos*. Glory came from individual courage, hand-to-hand fighting, and the winning of booty. And so, as Correia put it with the benefit of hindsight, "avid to gain honor and wealth . . . the German's advice went unheeded. They decided to board, so that they might win glory at the point of the sword." It is possible that Pêro Barreto, the second-in-command and a cooler head, backed Arnau up. They were overruled. The council chose to fight on Hussain's terms.

Despite the damage inflicted on the Rumes' fleet, the task was not straightforward. Their carracks were considerably larger and higher than Lourenço's. They could rain missiles down on his decks, and maneuvering the sailing ships into a boarding position promised to be tricky, given the shifting winds, tidal pulls, and cross-currents. A plan of attack was drawn up. The *São Miguel* and *São António* would tackle Hussain's flagship fore and aft. The other ships would engage the rest of the line to prevent men from being transferred to help, with the light caravels and galleys falling on the opposing galleys.

Early on Saturday afternoon, on the surge of the tide and the breeze off the sea, the ships weighed anchor and started to move up the river. As the *São Miguel,* leading the line, approached the target, it was again met with a torrent of arrows. The Portuguese limited their cannon shots with a desire not to damage the potentially valuable prizes. Despite the whip and buzz of missiles from Hussain's higher vessel, the *São Miguel* was closing in, only ten or fifteen yards away, when the plan of attack started to unravel. The wind shifted, then died. The ship was drifting on the current; forward momentum was sufficient to bring the *São Miguel* in to grapple with the enemy flagship, with the *São António* following behind, but Hussain, seeing the moment, managed to effect an extraordinary maneuver. By slackening the forward anchor cables and hauling in the stern cables tied to the bank, his sailors managed to pull the ships back to the shore—out of the path of the oncoming attack. The rudder of the *São Miguel* was unable to correct its course. It began to drift past its target.

Instinctively, the boatswain's mate decided to drop anchor to prevent the ship from overshooting, and the vessels behind were similarly forced to pay off and anchor to avoid colliding. The attack ground to a halt. The squadron hung motionless in the river, in disarray. Lourenço, furious at this sudden disruption, advanced down the deck, sword in hand, to kill the man responsible for botching the attack. The boatswain's mate, weighing his options, leaped overboard and swam to the shore—where he was killed anyway.

For Lourenço's crew, the situation was now perilous. The *São Miguel* was swinging idly on its anchor in the current close to the enemy ship, which was able to shower missiles on the deck from its higher vantage point. It became unwise to expose oneself without good armor. Ducking the field of fire, Michel Arnau, the master gunner, again came to propose that if the ship were swung broadside on its cables he could blast the Egyptians out of the water at point-blank range. Lourenço would not countenance the idea of leaving the battlefield without trophies and honor. The missiles continued to sweep the deck. Conditions on the *São Miguel* were becoming uncomfortable. The men were completely exposed, and Lourenço, heedlessly brave, insisted on barking orders from the open deck. He became an obvious target. A first arrow merely grazed him; a second hit him full in the face. Streaming with blood, he finally gave the order to raise anchor and escape the blizzard of projectiles. The *São Miguel* and *São António* passed downstream and anchored out of bowshot.

Meanwhile, the two Portuguese galleys and the light caravel, able to maneuver in the slackening wind, had fared better. They bypassed their immobilized carracks and bore down on the Egyptian galleys anchored a little farther down the line. Again as they closed to board, they rowed through the buzz and sting of the arrows; the unprotected galley slaves were hit repeatedly until they fell on their oars, but the assault was unstoppable. They crashed into the moored ships. The men-at-arms, well protected by chain mail, steel breastplates, and helmets, smashed their way on board and swept down the decks, trampling the chained oarsmen underfoot, scything and hacking armed men down, butting them into the sea with lances, halberds, and huge two-handed swords. The onrush of this highly trained and armored phalanx was irresistible; each ship was reduced to a shambles, the decks slippery with blood. Men died where they stood, or threw themselves overboard, or fled to the adjoining galleys along the connecting gangplanks. As each vessel was swept clean, the Portuguese pursued the fleeing enemy, hammering up the gangplanks after them. Those who leaped into the sea were hunted by other Portuguese in rowboats; then their route to the shore was cut off by one of the caravels. Boxed in, like tuna in a fish trap, they were mercilessly harpooned from the boats. It was a massacre.

Four of the abandoned galleys were towed away as prizes, while the *São Miguel* and the *São António* took to firing at the Egyptian carracks from a distance, aiming at their rigging. A lucky shot brought down the crow's nest from one ship, killing all the men. The other masthead battle stations were abandoned. Among those killed in the cause of holy war was Mayimama Marakkar, standing on his poop deck spurring his men on with verses from the Koran.

With the massacre on the galleys and the crews of the carracks cowering from the Portuguese bombardment and shocked by the catastrophe that had befallen their comrades, the advantage seemed to swing back to Lourenço. This encouraged him to think again of attacking Hussain's flagship and making a clean sweep of the day. Aboard the *São Miguel,* a further heated debate about how to proceed ensued. There was no wind; Lourenço wanted the ship's boats to tow his sailing vessels in for a second attempt. Lourenço met considerable reluctance from the captains: the men were physically exhausted; many were wounded, including Lourenço himself; it was late in the day; any spirited resistance could lead to disaster. Again Arnau offered to sink the ships from a safe distance. Lourenço remained obdurate—he wanted, needed, the trophies of war to lay before his father, rather than see the ships sunk. Although the commander could be outvoted, the captains were probably unwilling to do so after Dabul. The matter was still unresolved when events took a fresh turn.

It was almost twilight. Looking back toward the open sea, they could make out a line of light galleys entering the mouth of the river. It was Malik Ayaz with his thirty-four fustas. After a day of agonized waiting to see the outcome of battle, the governor of Diu had come to the conclusion that he could delay no longer: to be accused of foot-dragging or cowardice in the Islamic cause was perilous to his own position. In the Rume fleet there were shouts of joy. They mimed hanging the Portuguese by the neck, and the largely Muslim community of Chaul, who had also been adopting a wait-and-see approach to events, began to openly demonstrate their fervent desire for an Islamic victory. They came down onto the beach and loosed off their bows at the exhausted enemy. The council on the *São Miguel* was forced to rethink its options yet again. They were now facing three opponents within the river mouth—and the Cochin galleys near the town, forgotten during the events of the day and for which they had responsibility, were in increasingly grave danger.

Ayaz's approach was tentative. Instead of coming forward in line of battle to support Hussain, he drew his ships up near the southern bank of the river, in the position occupied by the Portuguese that morning. He was still maintaining a cautious attitude to the unfolding events. He tried to send three ships to establish contact, but Lourenço drove them back. It was not until darkness fell that he was able to make it across to meet Hussain. The admiral wanted gunpowder and cannonballs, of which he was in short supply. He also wanted to give Ayaz a piece of his mind for turning up after the day's fighting and the loss of some two hundred men.

In the Portuguese fleet, the mood was sober. After the twists and turns of the day, the attacks and retreats, the men were spent, and stocks of gunpowder were also running short. The triumphant shouts of the Muslims rang out across the water in the dark. The wounded Lourenço had been confined to bed with a fever; the doctor in attendance was bleeding him.

On the *São Miguel,* the debate among the captains raged on. It was certain that with the return of day the Cochin galleys, at last fully loaded, would be in grave danger. Their destruction would mean an unacceptable loss of face and a further erosion of Portuguese credibility. The practical solution was to slip away under cover of darkness, catching the night wind. There was furious opposition to this from the interim commander, Pêro Barreto, supported by another captain, Pêro Cão, who said "that because their sins demanded that they flee, at least let them not show that they were doing so, that the Portuguese might not lose their reputation in India. If the Malabar ships left first and they then departed in the morning light, the enemy couldn't then claim that they were leaving the field of battle out of fear." It was again a question of honor. They cajoled the others into agreeing to sail out at daybreak, towing the captured galleys behind them as a calculated snub.

At midnight under the light of the moon, the Cochin merchant ships began silently to slip their moorings and push out to sea on the wind. Toward dawn the Portuguese stealthily followed suit. No whistles. No shouts. They started to hoist their anchors, or in some cases cut the cables, leaving the anchors on the seabed. This strategy was undone by the obdurate Barreto, who refused to cooperate with such a demeaning retreat. He climbed into the ship's boat with the greatest ostentation and hauled in his anchor. He was immediately spotted by the enemy and fired on. With the anchor retrieved, he boarded the ship again. Lourenço had by this time recovered somewhat. He had demanded that the *São Miguel* should be the last to depart, and he resolved to follow Barreto's daredevil attitude and personally supervise the lifting of his anchor.

By this time Hussain had also quietly raised the anchors of his two remaining undamaged carracks, and Ayaz, concluding that the Portuguese were fleeing the scene of battle, finally decided that it was time for a "brave" show of force and similarly prepared his fustas for action.

Lourenço was in the ship's boat, in the process of raising anchor, when behind him the ship's master, seeing the growing daylight and the enemy preparations, lost his nerve. He cut the anchor cable, leaving Lourenço stranded for a while outside his own vessel.

The Muslims were now pursuing their enemy downriver on an ebb tide. Most of the Portuguese ships were able to fight off their assailants and make it out of the river mouth; the *São Miguel,* however, was the laggard, and also slowed by towing one of the captured galleys. It was the most attainable and attractive target. The incentive to down the flagship immediately made it the focus of all Hussain's efforts, and the captain of the *São Miguel,* instead of following the line of the departing ships, swung his vessel toward the further bank to distance it from the enemy fleet.

The light bombards of Ayaz's fustas tried to disable the ship by hitting its rudder. One stone ball struck the stern close to the waterline and stove in a plank. No one on the Portuguese ship was aware of this. Their attention was fixed on fighting off the snapping fustas and Hussain's two carracks. The ship sailed on with water starting to seep slowly into the rice store in the hold. Still as yet unnoticed, it was gradually getting heavier, more sluggish to respond. And then the wind dropped. At once the *São Miguel* was at the mercy of the current, which was pushing it toward the southern shore, where fishermen had planted rows of stakes in the water for mooring their boats. Drifting on the current, the ship became entangled among these obstacles, paralyzed by the increasing weight of the water. Attempts to shift it were useless. One of the Portuguese galleys, captained by Payo de Sousa, tried to take it in tow, to no avail. Men were sent overboard to hack away the stakes with axes. Each time, the weight of water in the hold settled the *São Miguel* more securely on the stakes; there was now a discernible list, the deck sloping and the bows tilting upward.

For a time it was impossible to understand the problem. Only when the tilt on the ship became pronounced was it clear that its stern was dragging. Lourenço sent the pilot down into the hold to investigate. In the gloom, the man saw with horror the truth of the situation: the hold was filling with a sloshing soup of water and rice. He came back to report, ashen-faced. It was impossible to bail out; the water was too deep, and the rice would impede the operation of the pumps—and there were too few able-bodied men left to work them. The ship was effectively lost. And having delivered his report, the pilot "went back down into the hold and they say that he died of fright." The order was given to cut loose the prize galley in tow. Ayaz, realizing that the *São Miguel* was wounded prey, started to encircle it with his fustas, while Hussain's two carracks moved closer.

Payo de Sousa was still intent on using his galley to free his commander's ship. It was now that fear began to infect the fleet, dividing its sailors into those who would fight and those who would run away, and coloring the accounts they would give later. Many of those in the galley were wounded, the *São Miguel* would not budge, and the enemy was closing in. Some claimed afterward that the tow rope just snapped as the oarsmen attempted to heave the sinking *São Miguel* away; more likely, it was cut. The galley was swept downriver on the current; Sousa tried to spin it back for another attempt, but the men could not or would not do so. Frantic efforts were made by other ships to reverse and aid the stricken flagship, but they were too far downstream to help.

Ayaz and Hussain sensed that it was time for the kill. The growing weight of water settled the tilting *São Miguel* lower and lower. The busy fustas and the carracks rained shots in. To the *fidalgos,* the imperative was to get Dom Lourenço away alive because "whether he survived or not was for the honor of Portugal." They ordered the boatswain to prepare the ship's boat with a complement of men still able to row. But Lourenço was not to be moved. He would fight and die. When his men became insistent, he threatened them with his halberd.

Water was continuing to drain into the ship; there were only some thirty able-bodied men left aboard. Lourenço split those who could still stand into three groups, each under a captain, to attempt to defend the *São Miguel:* at the stern, the mainmast, and the forecastle, respectively. The boatswain's nerve cracked. He untied the ship's boat and made off on the current to the *São António,* where he lied to the faithful Pêro Barreto that he had been sent to ask for help. Barreto's sailing ship was powerless against the current and the tide; climbing into the boat, he ordered the boatswain to the nearest galley, the *São Cristóvão,* which might have at least some chance of rowing back toward the stricken flagship. He begged the captain, Diogo Pirez, to do all he could, telling him "the survival of Dom Lourenço lay in his hands." Pirez set about attempting to rouse his galley slaves into action. They were exhausted and refused to budge. Desperate and furious, Barreto began to belabor them with his sword. He killed seven before conceding the futility; turning to the free Portuguese, who similarly "wanted to row as little as possible," he tried to force them into the rowing benches. It was hopeless. There was nothing more he could do but retire to his ship and hope that a shift in the wind might still push the São Miguel away. It was becoming more obvious by the minute that this would require a miracle.

It was mayhem aboard the São Miguel. Shots from the fustas were smacking into the immobilized vessel; clouds of arrows buzzed and whined through the air. Thick gun smoke obscured the increasingly defenseless ship. The deck sloped at a steepening angle; some of the cannons were submerged; the powder supplies lay spoiled with the steady seep of the water. The defenders beat off one, two attempts to board. They "fought like men who wanted revenge before they died," but the ship was being destroyed around them. The deck was a shambles, littered with dead and dying men, dismembered heads and legs, blood running down the planks, jagged timber splinters, ropes, discarded weapons, shouting and screaming.

Lourenço, tall and conspicuous in bright armor, was an unmissable target. The ball from a light cannon severed his leg at the thigh. He started to hemorrhage uncontrollably. Still conscious, but with his life draining away, he asked to be sat in a chair at the foot of the mast. Shortly after, another shot smashed his chest and killed him. His servant Lourenço Freire, bending over his fallen captain and weeping, was shot down by his side. It was apparent to those left alive that the ship must fall. Desperate to prevent Lourenço's body from being seized as a trophy of war, skinned, stuffed with straw, and paraded around the Islamic world—an unendurable coup—they dragged him down into the flooded hold, along with the body of his faithful servant.

The Portuguese fought on. Men who could no longer walk propped themselves up and resolutely clasped their swords. The Muslims had pounded the *São Miguel* from a distance; now they closed in. A third, fourth, and fifth attempt to board were seen off. Many of Ayaz's men were killed. By the sixth the ship had been reduced to a tableau of destruction. There was no answering fire. With shouts of triumph, the Muslims leaped aboard and rounded up the survivors. Conquest quickly turned to thoughts of plunder. The victors were eager to see what they could salvage from the sinking ship. Marching some of their captives forward at sword point, a hundred men descended into the flooded hold in search of booty. The vast throng of people caused the lower decks to collapse; pitched into the water in the dark, they all drowned.

Eighteen remaining men, nearly all wounded, were taken prisoner. There was one final act of resistance. André Fernandez, a sailor from Porto, climbed up into the crow's nest and defied all attempts to dislodge him from the top of the foundered vessel. He stayed there for two days, hurling stones and insults on those below. Finally Ayaz had to grant the gallant seaman a safe-conduct before he could be coaxed down.

Hussain's two carracks detached themselves from the wreck of the *São Miguel* and set out to pursue the other ships, anchored and watching from within and without the mouth of the river. Some of these cut their cables and fled ignominiously, south toward Cochin. Pêro Barreto, however, stood his ground, furled his sails, and prepared to fight. The Egyptian ships backed off.

Ayaz was disappointed at being denied the prestige of taking Lourenço alive; he still hoped that the body might be retrieved. But the illustrious corpse, weighted down with its plate armor, had vanished, probably dragged out of one of the holes in the bottom of the ship into the Chaul River, and was never recovered. "And so ended Dom Lourenço," wrote the chronicler Castanheda, "and the eighty Portuguese who died with him, among whom were João Rodrigues Pacanha, Jorge Pacanha, António de São Payo, Diogo Velho the fleet factor, and a brother of Pêro Barreto—and others whose names are not known."

Honor, glory, fear, a greed for booty, and bad luck had inflicted this wound. The Portuguese could have destroyed the entire Egyptian fleet at a distance if they had followed the advice of their master gunner. But this was not the Portuguese way. As it was they sailed away, badly scarred. They had lost probably two hundred men at Chaul. The killing of the viceroy's son conferred immense prestige on the sultan in Cairo, and on the valor of the Muslim world. When word of the victory over "the Europeans who infest the Indian Ocean" reached Cairo several months later, it was greeted ecstatically. "The sultan, enchanted with the news, ordered drums to be beaten for three whole days," reported Ibn Iyas. "Hussain called for reinforcements to put an end to the remaining European forces."

Hussain certainly needed fresh manpower. The victory at Chaul had been largely pyrrhic. He had lost somewhere between six hundred and seven hundred men out of a total hardly exceeding eight hundred, and his fighters had come to fear the power of European gunnery. As for Ayaz, he refused to hand over the nineteen Portuguese prisoners to the Egyptian commander; he treated them well, ensured that their wounds were cared for, and showed them off to important visitors. He was wise and cautious enough to know that there would be further consequences of this battle. The prisoners were bargaining chips.

The Portuguese ships fled toward Cochin to face the wrath and grief of the viceroy. They were thrown into further confusion by the appearance of three large vessels trailing in their wake. It was only as these ships closed that the seamen saw the Portuguese flags flying from their mastheads. These were the vessels of the captains who had mutinied against the command of Afonso de Albuquerque and were making their way to Cochin with their tale of complaint.

14

"The Wrath of the Franks"

March–December 1508

THE MUTINEERS WHO ACCOMPANIED the Chaul survivors back to Cochin had left a furious Albuquerque in Ormuz. He had only two ships; he was forced to abandon the siege ignominiously and sail back to Socotra to relieve the famished garrison. He returned to Ormuz in August in the hope of finally taking the city, but he found his unfinished fort armed against him and the streets barred. He was compelled to withdraw for a second time.

During the middle of 1508, letters were flying back and forth across the Indian Ocean, as well as reports back to Lisbon. Albuquerque wrote angrily to Almeida, still his superior until the end of 1508:

> If these men had not deserted me, in fifteen days Ormuz would have surrendered. . . . I cannot imagine what grievances made them go! If they say I have ill-treated them I beg your lordship to have set down in writing what they say I did. . . . Nevertheless, sir, [nothing] could absolve them from the crime and evil they have committed, deserting me in time of war . . . whatever punishment your lordship may give them—they deserve it!

Almeida's rebuke, in a letter that was never dispatched, probably expressed the bitterness at Lourenço's death and the culpability of Albuquerque in failing to intercept the Mamluks: "Sir, I remind you that the principal end to which His Highness sent you was to guard the mouth of the Straits [of the Red Sea], so that spices from India couldn't enter there, and that was totally changed by your sojourn in Ormuz and the Straits were abandoned."

Albuquerque was intelligent, fearless, incorruptible, and strategically brilliant—in all senses the king's most loyal servant—but Manuel would prove too obtuse to fully appreciate him. His aloof, arrogant, obsessive, and somewhat egocentric character alienated many. In the second half of 1508, the desertion from Ormuz split opinion across the Portuguese ocean, as it has divided the subsequent judgments of history, and it led to factional infighting. The episode revealed Albuquerque often to be maladroit and isolated as a leader of men. As a conqueror, he had already proved himself formidable, but events at Ormuz had wounded him. He vowed never to trim his beard until the city should be taken back. It remained in his tally of scores to be settled.

Beards were an issue in Cochin, too. Among the *fidalgos,* a man's beard was a sacrosanct symbol of his manhood, status, and martial prowess. Paintings of the great Portuguese conquistadors portray these men standing proudly in almost identical postures: arms akimbo, dressed in black velvet and sleeves slashed with colored silk, their coats of arms and attributed titles painted in the backdrop, looking stern beneath long black beards like Mars, the Roman god of war. João de Nova, outraged at Albuquerque's attack on his beard, solemnly preserved the ripped-out hairs in a piece of paper and carried them back to the viceroy as evidence of the insult. These relics made a powerful impression on a sympathetic noble audience.

Almeida issued no punishment to the deserting captains. Instead he co-opted them into his fleet. Worse than that, he wrote a letter to Hwaga Ata, in Ormuz, apologizing for Albuquerque's behavior, which the vizier gleefully showed to a stunned Albuquerque. But during 1508, Almeida had other things on his mind. The catastrophe at Chaul and the death of his son had marked the viceroy deeply. Strategically, he realized that the continued Rume presence in the sea threatened the very existence of the Portuguese project; personally, he had Lourenço to avenge. In his reported words: "he who eats the chicken also has to eat the cockerel, or pay the price."

It took almost nine months to prepare a new campaign. First the monsoon, then the overriding requirement to load and dispatch the annual spice fleet delayed his plans. If Almeida was wounded by the news from Chaul, he was doubly hurt by the growing frostiness of Manuel's tone. The viceroy had lost his master's confidence. The king's letter of 1507 contained a long list of grievances and peremptory commands, based on the seeping complaints of dissident captains and envious courtiers. Almeida was accused of acting beyond his authority, of maladministration, of failing to secure Malacca, of failing to keep the king informed. Albuquerque's parallel mission within his area of jurisdiction had been a heavy blow for the viceroy. In 1508, he also learned that this was the man due to replace him at the year's end. The expansion of Manuel's strategic dreams and the time and distance lags had created a widening gap between the king's priorities in Lisbon and Almeida's interpretation of them in India.

By the end of 1508, it was clear to the viceroy that the destruction of the Rume fleet was his overriding priority and his last opportunity before his term of office expired. By December he had gathered a formidable war fleet in Cochin of eighteen ships and twelve hundred men. These included the dissident captains Albuquerque had requested him to punish.

On the eve of departure, Almeida wrote a lengthy letter to his king. The viceroy believed he was possibly composing his last will and testament, at once an expression of personal grief, a justification for his actions, a point-by-point rebuttal of the accusations leveled against him, an apology, and a preparation for death. It is the testament of a man worn down by work and duty. India used men up: the climate, the corruption, the distance from home, the hostility of surrounding enemies—all these were attritional factors of the Portuguese colonial experience:

To the very high and mighty king, My Lord,

I have a great desire to write to Your Highness because I cannot
forbear to touch on matters that wound my soul and of which I
have determined to leave a memory, whatever happens to me....
My son is dead, as God willed and my sins deserve. The Venetians
and the sultan's Muslims killed him ... as a result of this the Muslims
in these parts are hopeful of great help. It seems to me that this year
we cannot avoid a trial of strength with them, which is the thing I
most desire, because it seems to me that with God's help we have to
remove them totally from the sea, so that they do not return to this
land. And if Our Lord is served by my ending my days in this way, I
will have obtained the rest I seek—to see my son in glory, where
Our Lord has taken him in his mercy, then we die for him and for
you.

Signature of Francisco de Almeida

There was a dire warning in the rationale for this venture: "there are
more Muslims from Malacca to Ormuz than in the kingdom of Fez
and Tunis—and all of them damaging to us." He completed the letter
in his cabin on December 5, 1508. Almeida was clear in his mind. He
was ready for the final battle, which would decide the fate of the Portuguese in India, and he was prepared to die.

The letter was ready for sealing when ships were spotted approaching the coast. Almeida's fleet sailed out to fight. It was only as they
drew near that they could pick out the Portuguese flags. It was Albuquerque finally coming to Cochin to claim his governorship. He had
been at sea almost continuously for nearly two and a half years. His
ship, the *Cirne,* was so rotten with worms that fish were swimming in

the hold. It took thirty men working at the pumps day and night to keep it afloat.

There followed an uncomfortable meeting between the two commanders. Initially it was friendly. Albuquerque had come politely to claim governorship of the Indies. Almeida pointed out that his term of office did not end until January and that he was preparing to sail for war. In some accounts Albuquerque offered to take the fleet and finish the job for him; in others he excused himself from Almeida's offer to join the expedition: he was exhausted and would prefer to remain in Cochin. Probably he had no taste for accompanying the captains who had deserted him at Ormuz. The following morning, Almeida's ships slipped anchor and set sail to hunt the Egyptian fleet.

Terror and vengeance, a trial of strength. Almeida sailed up the west coast of India impelled by powerful forces both personal and strategic, and aware that a final confrontation with the forces of Islam was inevitable and pressing. The viceroy had been accused of being overly cautious in his interpretation of Manuel's orders. In refusing to cede the governorship of India to Albuquerque, he was now openly disobeying them. He was convinced that a showdown with the Egyptian fleet was necessary for the security of the Portuguese enterprise. At the same time, he sought revenge. He had decided to take the law into his own hands, whatever the consequences for himself if he made it back to Lisbon.

The Muslim "victory" at Chaul had inspired a new heart and hope that the Portuguese could be expelled from the Indian Ocean. The samudri was preparing to send ships to join up with the fleet at Diu to finally uproot the cursed intruders. Yet up close, the Egyptian-led coalition was divided and uneasy. Hussain knew that it was only a matter of time before the Portuguese came again, and he was not sanguine. He had experienced European cannon fire at close quarters. His fleet had been severely damaged at Chaul; he was short of men and short of the money to pay them, and his alliance with Malik Ayaz was fractious. Retreat, and facing the sultan's wrath, was not an option. All Hussain could do was hope for reinforcements. He ardently desired to kill the Portuguese captives being held by Ayaz and send their flayed corpses, stuffed with straw, to Cairo as firsthand proof of his successes. But Ayaz was not cooperating. He kept the prisoners carefully guarded and pondered how to manage the situation, caught between the fervor of the Islamic world and the ferocity of its enemies.

A demonstration of their power was not long in coming. With the reinforcements recently arrived from Lisbon, Almeida had the best fleet seen in the Indian Ocean since the withdrawal of the Chinese. And the viceroy was in a grim mood, raiding the coast as he sailed north, demanding submission from the tiny trading states as he passed, and food for his crews. By the end of December 1508, he had reached Dabul, which Lourenço had disastrously failed to attack two years earlier, and which he suspected of being in league with the Egyptian fleet. On the last day of the year, he brought his ships into the mouth of the river, carefully sounding his way, intent on retribution.

Dabul was a wealthy Muslim trading port—and well protected by a double wooden wall, fronted by a ditch, and equipped with reasonable artillery. There were four Gujarati merchant ships in the harbor at the time, doubling Almeida's ire. On the eve of attack, the viceroy gathered his captains and delivered an incendiary message. The asymmetry of numbers between the Portuguese and their perceived enemies justified extreme methods. Almeida reminded his captains that they needed not just to take the city but to "instill terror in the enemy that you're going after so that they remain completely traumatized—you know that they're presently puffed up and haughty at the death of my son and the others."

They obeyed these instructions to the letter. On December 31, at dawn, the ships launched a heavy bombardment, then simultaneous amphibious landings from both sides of the stockade. The resistance in front of the ditch was smashed by this pincer movement. The wooden wall fell. As the troops fled in disarray, the Portuguese pursued them. Heavily armed and protected by plate armor from the annoyance of arrows, they slammed into the town. What followed was a black day in the history of European conquest that would leave the Portuguese cursed on Indian soil.

Taken by surprise, people fled in all directions. The slaughter was indiscriminate, with the aim of leaving nothing alive. A noblewoman being carried away in a litter was tipped to the ground and slaughtered along with all her bearers; little children were ripped from the grasp of their terrified mothers, dangled by their feet, and dashed against walls. Women and men, young and old, wandering holy cows and stray dogs—all went down before the sword: "finally no living thing was left alive." The ships of the Gujaratis were burned. In places, resistance was valiant, but futile. At the day's end, Almeida regrouped his men at a mosque and secured the streets. The next morning, he permitted a free sack of the town. Men were sent out in groups of twenty, then returned to the shore with their plunder. As the day wore on, however, Almeida became concerned that the disorderly looting and drunkenness of the men would be a liability should the inhabitants regroup. Secretly he had the city set on fire. People hiding in cellars were burned alive, along with animals tethered in their stalls; women and children ran screaming from the burning buildings, but the viceroy had detailed detachments to cut them down. Throughout the city there was pandemonium: the bellowing of cows, the neighing of horses torched in the royal stables, the cries of human beings, the smell of burning flesh, the destruction of much of the city's wealth. When the fires died down, the looters raked through the ashes, poking into cellars, still with their human corpses, and investigated wells in the hope that something of value might yet be retrieved.

Stopping just to destroy settlements along the shore, Almeida reembarked his army and departed on January 5, 1509. The number of Muslim deaths had been uncounted but huge, the Portuguese negligible. When they reached Chaul, Almeida sent a peremptory message to demand tribute, which he would expect to collect on his return from victory against the Muslim fleet. The island of Mahim (near Mumbai) they found deserted. The people had fled; the news of Dabul had traveled along the whole coast with the speed of the wind. This massacre stood beside Gama's destruction of the *Miri* as an unforgiven act that lingered long in the memory. Along the scarred coast, a man would curse with a new oath: "May the wrath of the Franks fall upon you."

Almeida sailed on toward Diu, intent on finding and destroying the Egyptian fleet. In his possession was a letter from Malik Ayaz, who was halfheartedly preparing with Hussain for the expected battle. It sought the friendship of the viceroy and assured him that the prisoners taken at Chaul were in his care and being well treated. And it provided useful information on the disposition of the Mamluk fleet. Ayaz was again hedging his bets.

If Ayaz had any doubts about what was coming his way, in addition to swift news about the fate of Dabul, he received Almeida's reply. It was politely formal and deeply threatening:

> I, the viceroy, address you, most honorable Malik Ayaz, to let you know that I am on my way to your city with my knights, to seek out the men sheltering there after fighting with mine at Chaul and killing a man known to be my son. And I am coming with the hope of God on High to wreak vengeance on them and on those who help them. And if I don't find them your city will not escape me. It will repay me for everything and so will you, who gave them such great help at Chaul. I am informing you of all this so that you are fully aware of it when I arrive. I am on my way. I am presently at the island of Bombaim [Mumbai], as the man who is bearing this letter will testify.

15

February 1509

WHEN THE PORTUGUESE FLEET hove into view on February 2, 1509, the Muslim tactical discussion was riddled with hesitation and distrust. The Muslim fleet consisted of six Mamluk carracks and six galleys, four Gujarati carracks, Ayaz's fustas, now reduced to thirty, and possibly seventy light vessels from Calicut. They had some four to five thousand men. The ships were nestled inside the mouth of the river on which Diu lay, in a situation analogous to that at Chaul. There was strong disagreement about how to proceed.

Hussain wanted to take the fight to the enemy early, while the Portuguese were still unprepared after a long voyage, and to engage them out at sea. Ayaz saw this as an excuse for the Egyptians to cut and run if the fight went badly, which he was certain it would, leaving him to face the consequences alone. He insisted that they fight within the river, protected by shore guns and potentially with the help of the townspeople—which would give him the chance to escape overland. He refused to allow his ships or those of Calicut to sail out. With Almeida's threatening message ringing in his ears, he judged it best not to attend the battle at all, citing urgent business elsewhere. Hussain promptly called his bluff by sailing out and ordering Ayaz's carracks out as well. Ayaz, summoned back to the city by messenger, then countermanded the order. There was a stalemate. The two commanders were to be shackled together and hobbled by mutual mistrust. Hussain, after a fruitless long-range artillery duel out at sea, was forced to accept the inevitable and fight inside the river. Ayaz was compelled to participate, again hoping to make just a show of battle while minimizing both his involvement and his losses. He could have barred the Portuguese altogether by raising a chain that closed the harbor; they would have been forced to turn back. The fact that he did not was probably a fine reckoning: he calculated that doing so would be perceived as a hostile action by Almeida for which he would pay sooner or later; he may have also calculated that the destruction of the embarrassing Mamluk fleet would be to his advantage and that he could one way or another strike a peace deal with the viceroy.

These suspicious cross-purposes left the Muslim fleet again adopting a defensive position, similar to that at Chaul. The carracks were anchored in pairs close to the shore in line, bow forward; first Hussain's six carracks, then the galleys, then the Gujarati carracks. The fustas and light-oared ships from Calicut stayed farther upstream, with the aim of falling on the Portuguese from behind once they were engaged with their big ships. The shore guns would provide further covering fire. It was assumed that the enemy would repeat the tactics from Chaul; hungry for honor, they would grapple their opponents rather than blast them from afar.

Matching tactical discussions were taking place on Almeida's ship. The viceroy was emphatic that this battle was the critical moment for Portuguese fortunes—"be certain that in conquering this fleet we will conquer all of India"—and that their whole presence there was hanging in the balance. He wanted the honor of leading the attack on Hussain's flagship in person. However, the captains objected to this. Given the death of Lourenço, they firmly resisted Almeida's desire to endanger his own life in this way. It would be better for him to control the battle from his flagship, the *Frol de la Mar,* and to leave others to take the initial hits. It was the first sign that they had learned from the debacle at Chaul. They refined their tactical sense in other ways. Cannon fire was to play a part in the battle. They would place their best archers and sharpshooters in the crow's nests, insure against contingencies—materials to plug holes and water to put out fires would be prepared, and men on hand to do so—then attack as before: carracks would tackle the Muslims carracks, galleys their galleys. The powerful *Frol de la Mar* was to be a floating gun platform, stripped of soldiers. Its skeleton crew of sailors and gunners would pulverize the ships and specifically block a counterattack from the rear by the Muslim oared vessels. Some of the lessons of the German master gunner at Chaul had been absorbed.

Portuguese carracks: heavily gunned with large fighting tops

Dawn. February 3, 1509. The ships waiting for the breeze and the tide to enter the shallow channel of the river. The viceroy sent each captain a message:

Sirs, the Rumes will not come out, since so far they have not done so. Therefore recalling the Passion of Christ, keep a sharp lookout for the signal that I will make when the sea breeze starts blowing, and we will go and serve lunch to them; and above all, I recommend that you take great care ... that you escape from fire, should the Muslims set it to their own ships to burn them with yours or to drag you to the shore cutting their anchor cables.

Two hours later, the breeze began to rise. A light frigate passed down the line of ships. At each one, a man stepped aboard and read the viceroy's proclamation to the assembled company. Almeida had composed for a rapt audience a rhetorical and heart-stirring message, gravid with a sense of destiny and holy war:

Dom Francisco d'Almeida, viceroy of India by the most high and excellent king Dom Manuel, my lord. I announce to all who see my letter, that ... on this day and at this hour I am at the bar of Diu, with all the forces that I have to give battle to a fleet of the Great Turk that he has ordered, which has come from Mecca to fight and damage the faith of Christ and against the kingdom of the king my lord.

He went on to outline in ringing terms the death of his son at Chaul, the attacks on Cannanore and Cochin, the enmity of the king of Calicut "with the great armada which he has ordered to be sent." He emphasized the peril and the need "to prevent the massive danger that will follow if these enemies are not punished and wiped out." It was not just victory, it was annihilation that Almeida was seeking to inflict, in the course of which those who died on the Portuguese side would be martyrs. Though there are no records of the preparations on the Muslim ships, it is highly likely that similar calls to martyrdom in the name of God were being made.

As the herald passed down the line, he was also instructed to read out to the men on each ship a list of promises and rewards that would follow a victory—from the knights who would be elevated to the higher nobility, to the convicts whose sentences would be wiped clean.

In the name of slaves who died in the battle, payments would be made to their owners; if they lived, their reward would be freedom. All were granted permission to loot when the battle was won.

With the breeze rising, the men were fired up for battle. The *Frol de la Mar* fired a shot to signal the advance. In the Muslim camp, they had also made their preparations. The ships were draped with nets to hamper boarding and allow men to throw missiles down on their attackers; their sides were fitted with thick boards to provide further protection, and their hulls above the waterline were draped with wet bags of thick cotton stuffing to hinder the operation of fire.

With their traditional war cry of "Santiago!" the Portuguese unfurled their flags. The ships moved into the channel to the blare of trumpets and the thunder of drums. The Muslim guns were readied on the shore and an island across the channel as the fleet passed through. Almeida had chosen his oldest vessel, the *Santo Espirito,* to lead the way, sounding as it went, and to take the first hit. Caught in the cross fire from both sides, "over everything a rain of shots, falling like a rain of stones," the deck of the *Santo Espirito* was swept clean. Ten men were killed, but the fleet passed on through the neck of the channel and turned one by one to bear down on their chosen targets.

The prime objective for the lead carracks was the enemy flagship, always the key to a battle. This time the Portuguese intended to make wiser use of their artillery. The *Santo Espirito* steadied itself as it approached and fired at the anchored carracks at close range. A direct hit on the ship beside Hussain's tore a hole in its flank; the listing vessel keeled over and sank, drowning most of the crew, to the cheers of the attackers. Rapidly the Portuguese closed on the flagship in groups of two. Farther down the line, battle was also being joined—carracks against carracks, galleys against galleys. Upstream Ayaz's light fustas waited to advance on their enemies from behind.

There was a confused roar as the ships converged: the Muslim vessels anchored, waiting for the hit; the Portuguese turning broadside to fire at close range before tackling their foes; the Egyptians replying as best they could. The sun was blotted out, "the smoke and fire so thick that no one could see anything." In the accounts of the chroniclers, it was a scene from the end of the world: the roar of the guns "so fright-

Diu

ening that it seemed to be the work of devils rather than men"; "an
infinity of arrows" ticking through the thick smoke; the battle cries of
encouragement calling out the names of their gods, Christian and
Muslim, the names of saints; the screams of the wounded and the
dying "so loud that it seemed to be the day of judgment." Closing accurately on targets was made difficult by the velocity of the current
and the stiff breeze; some vessels smashed directly into their chosen
opponents with a juddering impact; some only hit glancing blows and
were swept on; others overshot their targets altogether and were carried upstream, temporarily out of the fight. It was clear that Hussain
had skilled gunners and good cannons on his carracks—many of
whom were European renegades—but their field of fire was hampered
by their static forward-facing position, and he had far fewer experienced fighting men.

Boarding parties on the forecastles of Almeida's ships were readied
to leap at the first impact, when grappling hooks were flung across to
tether the ships together, then reeled in by the slaves. The shock of the
collisions was explosive. The *Santo Espirito,* despite being hit in the
channel, advanced on Hussain's flagship, the key prize and the eye of
the battle. Men jumped across almost before the ship was secured and
battled their way up the deck. Above them, clinging to the net, Mamluk archers rained down missiles; then the captain of the *Santo Espirito,*
Nuno Vaz Pereira, led a second force across. It looked as if Hussain's
ship must fall, but in the smoke and confusion reversals of fortune

were sudden. One of the other Egyptian carracks, maneuvering on its anchor cables, attacked the *Santo Espirito* from the other side, leaving it sandwiched between two Egyptian ships. At once attack switched to defense; the Portuguese were forced to abandon their prize and protect their own vessel. In the heat of the battle, Nuno Vaz, insufferably hot in his plate armor, lifted his throat guard to take a breath of air and was hit by an arrow. He was carried below, mortally wounded. It was a critical moment for the flagship fight; the Portuguese wavered. Then a second ship, the *Rei Grande,* slammed into the flagship from the other side and a fresh wave of men stormed aboard and managed to pull down the scrambling net, trapping those clinging to it inside. The initiative shifted once more.

Similar fights were in progress all down the line of carracks; having fired off their cannons, the Portuguese fell upon their foes with reckless bravery. The small *Conceicão* attempted to board another high-sided carrack; twenty-two men leaped aboard, including Pêro Cão, its captain, but the *Conceicão* was swept on past, isolating the men on the enemy ship, where they were heavily outnumbered. Cão tried to out-flank their attackers by crawling through a porthole and was promptly decapitated as his head emerged. The remaining men holed up on the forecastle and resisted until they were rescued in a further assault by other ships. On the *São João,* heading for another Mamluk vessel, a dozen men waiting for the strike had sworn an oath to leap across together and do or die. The *São João* smacked into its target so hard that it bounced back and was deflected. At the moment of the leap, only five made it across and were immediately outnumbered; three were shot dead by archers, but the other two secured themselves in the hold behind screens and could not be winkled out. Despite losing blood from arrow wounds and wooden shrapnel, they fought on, killing eight men who tried to pry them out and finally being rescued more dead than alive when the ship was taken.

Along with many of the Portuguese who took part in the battle, the names of these two stalwart men were recorded—António Carvalho and Gomes "Cheira Dinheiro"—yet their opponents remain almost completely anonymous. The trained fighting men, the Mamluk infantry, in flexible chain mail and open helmets with red plumes and neck and nose guards, were more agile than the heavily armored Europeans. They fought bravely but were outnumbered, hobbled by the ill intent of Ayaz, who devoutly wished them off his territory either dead or alive, and their ships were pinioned by Hussain's tactics and outgunned by the superior firepower of the Portuguese. Alongside them fought black Nubians and Abyssinian and Turkoman archers, "highly skilled and extremely accurate." In the aerial battle in the fighting tops, the ability of these bowmen daunted their opponents. The Portuguese were forced to take cover behind wooden screens from the hissing flight of the shafts, whipping through the air, studding the masts until they bristled, hitting their human targets again and again. By the end of the day, a third of all Almeida's men had sustained arrow wounds. In their crow's nests, the best the Portuguese could do was dash out from behind their screens, hurl rocks down onto the decks of the rival ships, and rapidly take cover.

But the spirit of the Mamluks and the skill of their archers were not enough. Many of Ayaz's men were not professionals, and the tempting safety of their city gates was close at hand. While Hussain tried valiantly to save his flagship, Ayaz remained ashore, watching from a prudent distance. Even the smoke that obscured and revealed the battle in alternate glimpses was to the advantage of the enemy: the wind blew it into the faces of the Muslims, affording moments of advantage to their assailants.

Upstream, there was fierce fighting between the rival galleys. The weight of gunfire cleared two Muslim galleys; once these were boarded, the Portuguese managed to turn their cannons on the remainder. Eventually the shots pouring into the flanks of the low-slung Egyptian vessels, pinioned to the shore with only forward-facing cannons, proved overwhelming, killing their chained slaves at the oars. The crews abandoned ship and made for land.

Out in mid-channel the viceroy, dressed magnificently in a suit of mail and a superbly worked helmet and breastplate, observed the battle from the *Frol de la Mar*. The *Frol* was the largest and most magnificent ship in the Portuguese fleet, triple-decked and heavily gunned, though now eight years old and feeling its age. It leaked and required continuous pumping. At the start of the battle, eighteen of its cannons opened up a mighty broadside on the Gujarati carracks. The vibrations of the guns shaking the four-hundred-ton vessel were so violent that it began to come apart at the seams. The danger of foundering became a sudden cause of concern—the sinking of the flagship could have turned the tide of battle. Its survival was attributed to divine miracle; the rope in the seams swelled with the water, stanching all leaks so that it remained sealed and required no further pumping.

With the battle raging, Ayaz finally felt compelled to order the commander of the fustas and small dhows, the one-eyed Sidi Ali, "the Crooked," to sweep down on the Portuguese from behind. The *Frol*, however, was specifically positioned to snuff out this threat. The armada, rowing furiously at combat speed, attempted to hurtle past the flagship, but the wind and the current slowed their progress, and as they came abreast of the *Frol* they presented an easy target. Three heavy shots hit them as they rowed past, shattering the front line, splintering the vessels, and hurling men into the water; chaos broke out in the closely packed formation. Those coming up behind were unable to avoid the debris and smashed into the broken ships; three more shots caught the whole group. The attack disintegrated. Those behind backpedaled and half-turned to avoid further catastrophe; a few braver ships, judging that they could row past before the Portuguese fired again, kept going, but the speed at which the gunners reloaded took them by surprise. This essential part of Hussain's plan collapsed.

The Muslims had fought bravely, but their lack of trained fighters, the professional skill of the Portuguese, and the weight of their artillery made the outcome inevitable. One by one, their ships were captured or abandoned. Hussain's flagship eventually surrendered, by which time Hussain himself had slipped away in a small boat and ridden off. Other vessels, in some of which the soldiers could not swim, cut their forward anchor cables and tried to haul themselves back to shore. Again the Portuguese launched their small boats to stab and massacre men in the water, so that "the sea was red with the blood of the dead." Some of the small Calicut dhows managed to get out to sea and away down the Malabar Coast with the doleful news, and the largest of the Gujarati carracks, a twin-decked ship of some six hundred tons, manned by four hundred men, held out all day. It was pulled too close to shore for the Portuguese ships to board, and its hull was extremely stout. It took a sustained general bombardment by the whole fleet to sink it, sending it to settle on the bottom with its superstructure still above the water. Its crew fled to land.

At the day's end, Almeida went from ship to ship, embracing his captains, inquiring about the wounded. In the morning there was a ceremonial gathering on the flagship to the sound of trumpets, then a counting of the costs. Numbers varied between thirty and a hundred dead, and perhaps three hundred wounded—mainly by wooden shrapnel and arrows—but the victory had been complete. The Egyptian fleet had been annihilated. All its ships had been sunk, captured, or burned. Apart from Hussain and twenty-two who fled with him, few of the Rumes survived to tell the tale. According to Portuguese sources, thirteen hundred Gujaratis had died, and an unknown number from Calicut. Three of their carracks, including the flagship, were incorporated into the Portuguese fleet, along with two galleys and six hundred pieces of artillery. The battle had been devastating.

The morning also brought a small fusta flying a white flag. Ayaz played his cards cautiously to the end. He promptly returned the Portuguese captives he had been so carefully nurturing since Chaul, all dressed magnificently in silk and supplied with purses stuffed with gold. He offered the unconditional surrender of Diu and vassalage to the king of Portugal and sent the fleet plenteous gifts of food.

Almeida did not want Diu; he considered it impossible to defend with his existing force. He demanded substantial compensation from the Muslim merchants who had subsidized the fleet in Diu, which he got, and terrible revenge. Since Lourenço's death, the viceroy had lost any reasonableness; his reputation was to be tarnished by pitiless and sadistic paybacks. Ayaz had to surrender all the Rumes he was sheltering in the city to a variety of ghastly fates. The governor smoothly acquiesced. Some had their hands and feet chopped off and were burned alive in a great pyre; others were tied to the mouths of cannons and blasted to pieces or put shackled into captured vessels that were sunk by gunfire. Some were compelled to kill each other. The city gates were decorated with bloody rosaries of dismembered body parts "because through these gates the Muslims who had killed his son had gone in and out." Some he kept alive on the ships. The wrath of the Franks would be remembered for a long time. It was met in the Islamic world with stoical grief: "These cursed interlopers sailed away victorious, such being the decree of God most high, and such his will which is indisputable, and against which nothing can prevail."

Almeida sailed back to Cochin as he had come, traumatizing the coast as he went. The seaports they passed were treated to volleys of heads and hands; at Cannanore, captives were lynched by the sailors and hanged from the masts; more corpses adorned the yardarms as he made his triumphant return into Cochin to the blaring of trumpets. The royal standards of the Mamluk sultan were dispatched to Portugal and hung in the convent of the Order of Christ at Tomar. If the outcome of Diu was perhaps inevitable, its consequences were profound. It destroyed once and for all the credibility of the Mamluk sultans and Muslim hopes that the Portuguese could be swept from the sea. The Franks were in the Indian Ocean to stay.

When Almeida stepped ashore at Cochin to the celebration of his victory, Albuquerque was waiting on the beach. He had come to applaud and to claim his command. Almeida brushed past him. He refused to give up his post, citing that it was too late in the year for him to sail home and that the king had told him to govern until he sailed. Behind this lay fierce factionalism surrounding the Ormuz mutineers and the fiery reputation of Albuquerque. Charges were laid against Albuquerque that he was mentally and morally unfit to govern. "In my opinion," one of his enemies testified, "India is now in greater peril from Afonso de Albuquerque than ever from the Turks!" Men threatened to leave India rather than serve under him; an indictment was got up against him for misgovernance. In September, Almeida ordered him out of Cochin; the fortress elephant demolished his house, and the ship carrying him to Cannanore was so worm-eaten that Albuquerque thought they were trying to kill him. At Cannanore he was effectively confined to prison, though the Portuguese administration there was largely sympathetic to his cause. Albuquerque seems to have borne this situation with considerable patience; quick to anger, he was also quick to forgive. When João de Nova, the man whose beard he had abused and who had defected, died in poverty that year, he paid the funeral expenses.

The situation was resolved only when the year's spice fleet reached Cannanore, in November, commanded by the young but highly self-important Dom Fernando Coutinho, marshal of Portugal, a man who came with full royal authority. He carried Albuquerque with him back to Cochin and demanded the handover of power. Albuquerque finally assumed the governorship of India, to the alarm of many of his subordinates. The next day Almeida departed from India forever, to face the king's displeasure back in Lisbon.

A fortune-teller had predicted that Almeida would not pass the Cape alive; at sea he spent the days composing his will. He left alms to prisoners, a large diamond to the king, money for his servants, and freedom for his slaves. In March 1510, his ship rounded the Cape without incident, then put in to Table Bay to take on wood, water, and supplies, and there he was killed in a pointless and obscure battle with the Khoikhoi that probably arose over the attempt of his men to steal some cattle and possibly to abduct children. The Portuguese must have been caught off guard. It was, by all accounts, a major disaster. Fifty men died that day, including a dozen captains and high-ranking nobles, almost as many as may have lost their lives at the battle of Diu.

Almeida's epitaph was said to have been placed in a church in Portugal:

HERE LIES
DOM FRANCISCO DE ALMEIDA
VICEROY OF INDIA
WHO NEVER LIED OR FLED.

But his mortal remains lay buried in an impromptu grave on the African seashore.

PART III

Conquest

THE LION OF THE SEA

1510–1520

AFOSO DALBOQVERQVE

16

The Doors of the Samudri

January 1510

I F ALBUQUERQUE THOUGHT THAT the departure of Almeida would
at last free him to fulfill his duties as governor of India, he was mistaken. Dom Fernando Coutinho might have been a relative, but he
was also marshal of Portugal, the highest-ranking official yet to visit
the Indies, an important personage at the royal court and much in
favor there. He now laid before Albuquerque trumping orders from
the king, namely to destroy Calicut, still a thorn in the side of the Portuguese and a continuous prick to royal pride. Coutinho had come
with a large fleet and the authorization to act independently of the
governor, who was requested to help.

This was to be Coutinho's show. The marshal was young, head-
strong, dismissive of advice, desperate for glory, and somewhat corpu-
lent. He had promised to return to the king with a souvenir of the
mission with which he had been charged. Overlooking the beach at
Calicut, the samudri had an ornately decorated pavilion called the
Cerame, "made of richly carved wood," to which he came to enjoy the
pleasure of the sea breeze, and which was adorned with fabulously
beautiful doors, embellished with the images of "animals and birds on
plates of silver and gold." This exotic object of desire, much talked up
in the Portuguese court, was to be the trophy of the heroic deed that
Coutinho would undertake. He had effectively come for the purpose

of military tourism. He would show the old India hands how to settle the Calicut problem at a stroke.

There was some justification for believing this to be a propitious moment. Spies from Cochin informed the marshal that the samudri was ill and out of the city; the visiting merchant ships, drawn up on the beach before departure to Arabia, were vulnerable. Their destruction would severely damage the samudri's tax revenues—his sole source of wealth. At the council of war to discuss the plan, Albuquerque remained unconvinced. Privately he was temperamentally averse to joint operations. He felt that while Calicut was at peace with Cochin, as at present, it was vastly to the advantage of the Portuguese pepper trade, and he knew more about the tactical difficulties of the assault than the marshal. Calicut had no harbor of its own, and the beach in front of it was a difficult landing place. Currents ran along its shores, and the sea could be boisterous. Coutinho sharply reminded him that "the council of war couldn't act contrary to the king's orders. It was only to decide how the attack was to be organized. It had no other purpose." And he threw in the rallying call to all the captains present that might serve both for the most magnificent moments of Portuguese courage and for its most disastrous military misjudgments, namely that "the best thing in all the world, after the love of God, was honor." "Honor": a word that rang down through all the decades of Portuguese conquest, resistance, and defeat. Albuquerque was outvoted.

There was seldom any element of surprise possible in military operations along the Malabar Coast. The samudri quickly got wind of the large fleet at Cochin and guessed its intentions. He sent an ambassador to sue for peace on the best terms he could. Whatever sympathy Albuquerque had for the overture—and he had good reason to trust this particular visitor—he had frankly to admit that the man had come too late. The ambassador was too frightened to return to Calicut with bad news. He elected to remain with the Portuguese. On the last day of December 1509, the fleet sailed—some twenty ships and sixteen hundred men, as well as twenty small boats from Cochin, carrying sailors familiar with the sea conditions at Calicut to help with disembarkation.

By the evening of January 2, 1510, the fleet was rocking off the city's beach. The city lay before them, a long ribbon of sand lined with fishermen's straw huts; behind, shops and warehouses, then white-washed merchants' houses glimpsed among palm trees, nobles' houses of wood and stone, minarets and the roofs of Hindu temples. Calicut sprawled over a large area and had no visible defenses; it was a laby-rinth of narrow lanes between high walls, winding back on rising ground to the foothills of the Ghats, where the samudri's palace was situated, some three miles from the sea.

Calicut from the sea, backed by the Western Ghats

The intruders were not unexpected. In his absence the king had appointed a regent, who had assembled all the Nayars at his disposal, as well as archers and whatever artillery he had; the Cerame, the marshal's ardent objective, prominently situated a bowshot back from the water, had been fortified with barricades and a number of bombards, and armed men were positioned among the houses behind, ready to de-fend it.

In the marshal's cabin, the captains met to plan the attack. They would land in two groups—Albuquerque's "India" men to the south of the Cerame, Coutinho's "Portugal" force to the north—and fall upon it in a pincer movement, each contingent to be led by its com-mander, who would have the honor of stepping ashore first with their banners, before the rest of the men. No one was to touch the Cerame's doors, because these were for Manuel. Then they would take the city gates and fall on Calicut.

Throughout the night the troops waited, sharpening their weapons, receiving general absolution from the priests, and commending their souls to God. Alongside these preparatory rituals for battle there was a widespread mood of covetous expectation. The city was held to be fabulously rich, and the prospect of easy plunder whetted appetites. Two hours before dawn, Coutinho lit the signal fire on his ship; the men climbed into longboats and were rowed toward the shore. A bright moon outlined the land before them, the houses among the palm trees, the copper roofs of the temples, and the spikes of the mosques. Albuquerque's force of about six hundred men landed close to the Cerame and drew up in good order. They proceeded to march toward it. The marshal's men, however, were carried along the shore by the current and found themselves at some distance from their objective.

Albuquerque was expected to wait for Coutinho, but his men, spurred on by the lure of plunder, could not be restrained. Discipline broke down. Rather than risk a shambles, Albuquerque ordered the trumpets to sound and raised the battle cry "Santiago!" to signal a full-scale attack. The Nayars rushed out of the houses near the Cerame with loud shouts, and fierce fighting ensued. From the vantage point above the beach, the cannons opened up with a deafening roar, but the inexperienced gunners fired too high. Relentlessly the Portuguese pushed on with their pikes; they stormed the barricades and killed a number of men. The rest turned and ran back among the houses. Meanwhile, men with axes were prying the famous doors out of their frames. They were carried down the beach and loaded onto a ship. To stop the men from proceeding into the town before the marshal and to forestall any sudden counterattacks, Albuquerque put a guard on the entrance to the streets.

The marshal was proceeding slowly up the beach. He could hear the shouts and the boom of guns, see fire rising from burning houses. By the time he arrived, the doors were gone. Coutinho was beside himself with fury. He could only believe that Albuquerque had deprived him of his rightful triumph and snatched the glory himself. He

rounded petulantly on the governor. Albuquerque attempted to soothe
him with pacific words, larded with talk of glory and honor: "You are
the first captain to have landed men and entered the city of Calicut,
and you have gained what you sought—the doors of the Cerame are
now on board." This had no visible effect other than to reduce
Coutinho to an apoplexy of rage. "What is this Afonso de Albuquerque?" he spat back. "Your words are nothing but a puff of air . . ." He
would not be appeased: "This honor is yours . . . I don't want any of it.
I'd be ashamed to go and fight naked little savages who flee like goats."
In a fit of petulance, he ordered the famous doors to be thrown into
the sea, took off his helmet, handed it to his page together with his
shield and lance, and demanded back from him a red cap and a stick.
Calling Gaspar de Almeida, the interpreter, he ordered him to show
the way to the king's palace, from which he would take other doors
with greater honor than those that had been stolen from him on the
beach. And "the king my lord will know that with a stick in my hand
and a cap on my head, I went to the king's houses . . . in this so highly
famed Calicut, which contains nothing but little black men."

In this scene, the chronicler Gaspar Correia pictured Albuquerque
leaning on his lance, his shield dropped at his side, surrounded by
fighting men and trying to reason with the marshal. He was now
alarmed. The troops were tired, and the enraged Coutinho had no idea
what he was proposing. Albuquerque tried pleading with him:

> May the Lord help you. I must tell you that if you take that road,
> these little naked blacks, who flee like goats, you'll find very formi-
> dable merchants whose goods will cost you dear. I beg you for pity's
> sake don't take that road. . . . From here to the houses of the king it's
> a long way, the roads are bad, men can only go in single file, you will
> put yourself in deep trouble getting there. You'll arrive exhausted
> and find many of these little black men there, highly-spirited and
> well-armed. I'm telling you the truth. I beg you with all my heart,
> for pity's sake, don't go.

"For that," sneered the marshal, "I'm going. Return to the ships. You
can embark and be quite happy with your great deed."

He prepared to advance, with a knight leading with a flag and Gaspar de Almeida indicating the way. A *berço,* a light swivel gun, was pulled along on its carriage with supplies of powder and shot. "And the men, avid for what they could plunder from the houses of the king, followed after the marshal." Albuquerque returned to the beach with his own men, saying, "We must be ready. Today we will see what God wills. Many of those you see going won't come back." He left a guard on the longboats on the beach, making sure they were ready to embark the wounded. He took what troops remained—many had followed the marshal—and burned the beached dhows and light sailing boats. He was preparing for the worst.

The marshal and his four hundred men were now heading directly toward the palace—a distance of some three miles. They had to go in single file through narrow lanes sunk down beneath stone walls with houses above set among palm trees. They met with no resistance. "The little black men" fled before them, seeming unwilling to fight. As they went, the marshal's men fired the empty houses. The wind off the Ghats billowed thick smoke back down the path, so that those coming behind were choked by the fumes and the heat of the raging fires. Soon the whole city seemed to be alight. Many turned back. Albuquerque, trying to follow up with his contingent in good order, found it difficult to proceed.

The marshal and his men pressed forward. When they reached a square with grander houses belonging to the nobility, they encountered a large band of Nayars, fully armed and ready to resist. The fighting became fierce. The square was cleared, but at some cost to the *fidalgos:* "Lisuarte Pacheco fell with an arrow in the throat, and António da Costa fell to the ground decapitated"; many suffered arrow wounds to the legs, unprotected by plate armor. Some turned back to the ships, finding the way now increasingly choked with the dead of both sides. Among the Hindu corpses lay that of the regent who had led the resistance.

The marshal battered on, reaching the outer doors of the royal palace, where his force was again confronted by a sizable body of men firing a blizzard of arrows. After a fierce fight, they were put to flight and the Portuguese poured into the royal enclosure. Within "there was a large courtyard, surrounded by many pavilions with highly decorated doors faced with plates of worked copper and gold, and above great balconies of exquisite workmanship."

The samudri's wooden palace

The looting began. Locks were smashed off with axes. Inside was an Aladdin's cave: chests stuffed with rich cloths worked with silk and gold thread, velours and brocades from Arabia, and wooden reliquaries ornamented with gold and silver. The *fidalgos* got their servants to pile up their private stashes, guarding them jealously in a furious competitive grab. The chance to become fabulously wealthy swept away all caution. They left their lances outside, the better to scoop up armfuls of prizes. A hundred men had been detailed to guard the front gate under one Ruy Freire, "crooked in one eye." These men, jealous of their exclusion from the plunder, carried out their own secondary collections. When piles gathered by the looters were left unattended in the palace square, Freire and twenty of his compatriots grabbed what they could and made off back to the ships. For two hours the plundering continued. The morning wore on. The day was becoming hot.

The looters failed to see what was coming. Word of the regent's death, along with three Portuguese heads, had been run to the samudri in retreat up above the city. Furious, he called for revenge. The Nayars regrouped and started to force their way into the courtyard, past the remnants of the guard detail. Treasure fever had by this time rendered the plunderers oblivious to danger. Smashing open one door, they found chests stuffed with gold coins, "which they hauled outside and each one guarded what he could." Inside this room a second inviting door, locked from within, gleamed with panels of beaten gold. This, according to Gaspar the interpreter, was the king's treasure room. Dizzy with the prospect of what might lie within, the soldiers hurled themselves at the door, smashing at it with the butts of their lances. It failed to budge.

Outside four hundred more Nayars had gathered, sent by the king, all determined to avenge the regent's death or die in the attempt. The arrows were starting to fly thick and fast when Albuquerque also arrived with a detachment of his own. He cleared a space around the outer gate and ordered his secretary, Gaspar Pereira, to go inside to rouse Coutinho to the perilousness of his situation. Pereira attempted to get the marshal to comprehend: there were many enemies out there, and the number was increasing by the minute. It was time to go: "he should be content with the deed, which was considerable . . . he lacked men, all had departed with their plunder; they had a long and difficult route; it was already hot and midday."

Coutinho was oblivious, obsessed by the unyielding door. His only message back to Albuquerque was that "he came without him and would return without him." Albuquerque set guards on the outer gate to prevent further men being lured into a death trap. He went in person to try to shift the marshal: "In the name of the king we ask you to leave, we mustn't stay here a moment longer. If we don't, we're all dead. The route by which you came is all on fire and we're going to have great trouble getting away." The marshal was haughty to the last: reluctantly he would go, but like Lourenço at Chaul he would mark his personal courage by being the last to leave, and he would fire the palace as he went. They departed, Albuquerque and his men in front clearing a path, then Coutinho's men, and lastly the marshal himself, trailed by his gun crew firing the *berço,* which, for a time, forced the Nayars back from pursuing them down the street.

They were in the narrow lanes again, half a spear's length wide. The Nayars changed their angle of attack. Climbing up onto the walls and the higher ground above, they pelted the harassed Portuguese with arrows, stones, and javelins, and rolled rocks and branches into the street to bar their way. It soon became impossible to haul the *berço* over these obstacles. It was abandoned. No longer intimidated, the Hindus surged back into the lane and swept down on the stragglers, falling on them with their own spears, which had been left outside the palace doors during the plunder.

Coutinho, overweight and tired, defending himself with a shield, was flanked by a group of *fidalgos*. The lanes were in the shade, but the day was hot, and in the confined space their plate armor put them at a disadvantage. Their adversaries would leap back to avoid a laborious sword thrust, then turn and harass the file of retreating men, now forced to shed their cumbersome armor as they went. When the lane broadened into a wide street, the situation deteriorated further. Another detachment of warriors was lying in wait, this time with room to surround the marshal's entourage. Coutinho himself turned to face this onslaught bravely but was struck from behind. His heel was sliced clean off. He collapsed to the ground. A triumphant shout went up from the Hindus. Those around him tried to get the heavy man back on his feet but, hemmed in, they found it impossible. Pushed back, they fought a gallant rearguard action: Vasco da Silva with his two-handed sword and a host of others went down in a roll call of honor as men "who all performed valiant deeds, and who fought until they could no longer lift their arms and they all died, and their heads were hoisted aloft with the royal flag."

Albuquerque, a musket shot ahead of this rear guard and closer to the beach, was also in growing trouble but had clustered around him a reasonable number of men under intense fire from enemy archers. He wanted to wait for the marshal, but news came that Coutinho had fallen in the fighting. He turned to give help, only there were few volunteers: "no one wanted to go back." Almost immediately he was met by scores of fleeing men; after them came the Hindu warriors shouting triumphantly. Men just dropped their weapons and streamed toward the beach, leaving Albuquerque and forty or fifty others to face the enemy and try to prevent a total rout. Falling back under sustained pressure, Albuquerque was hit in the left arm by an arrow that lodged in the bone; a few minutes later he was hit again, in the neck by a dart that penetrated his throat guard. Then a bullet caught him in the chest. He called out for the protection of Our Lady of Guadalupe as he collapsed to the ground. The shout went up that he was dead; men nearby started to panic. The Nayars closed in for the kill.

But by what Albuquerque came to regard as a miracle, the shot to the chest had not finished him off. While the rank and file fled, four men lifted him onto a shield and ran toward the beach, while a second group closed ranks behind him, preventing total disaster. The commanders on the beach began to ferry the wounded out to the waiting ships; from the longboats they fired their *berços* to deter the pursuers and to give hope to those rushing through the streets that the beach was near. Later the big guns from the ships opened up, too. Keen to the last to prove their fighting qualities, two of the *fidalgos,* António de Noronha and Diogo Fernandes de Beja, led a band of three hundred back into the city. They met a large number of men and women running toward them, thinking that the Portuguese were all dead—and slaughtered them mercilessly. Some of the natives ran down onto the beach to escape, which threw the Portuguese waiting to embark into fresh panic. Assuming these fleeing people to be pursuing them, many hurled themselves into the sea, despite the shouts of their comrades, and drowned trying to reach the ships.

Evening fell. No one was left on the beach but the two captains, to the very end contesting which should be the last to depart. Finally Diogo Fernandes and Dom António embarked simultaneously, to preserve their precious honor. The fleet lingered at Calicut for two days, during which the wounded were attended to, the dead thrown overboard, and Albuquerque himself recovered and made up his dispatches.

The casualties on both sides were heavy. The marshal's glorious escapade had been costly to the Portuguese. Out of eighteen hundred men, three hundred were dead, "of which seventy were noblemen"— the chroniclers were always scrupulous to record their names—and four hundred wounded, "of which many died or were permanently disabled." A snapshot of the losses from those who plundered the palace can be found in the fate of the twenty or so men with Ruy Freire, the crooked-eyed gatekeeper who absconded with some of the plunder: "who all died, except for a single slave, badly wounded, who reached the boats to give news of what had happened to the marshal." Among the uncertainties is the fate of Gaspar de Almeida. The converted Jewish interpreter who first met Vasco da Gama and who provided Manuel with so much information about the Indian Ocean may have died on that day; thereafter he disappears from the records.

The losses to Calicut had been more grievous. The samudri had the head and the banner of the marshal, but these were scant consolation for the death count and the destruction of the city and the royal palace by fire, and the loss of the merchant fleet on which his tax revenues depended. He feared the repercussions. He ensured an honorable burial for the marshal, with an engraved tombstone and his banner hanging above. It was an insurance policy against inevitable Portuguese revenge. As for Albuquerque, he would never fully regain the use of his left arm, but he honored the miracle of his survival. The bullet that had felled him was retrieved by a servant and sent with a sum of money to the shrine of Our Lady of Guadalupe in the Algarve; the bullet was laid before her image and the money paid for a lamp that "might burn forever" there.

There was one bright spot for the governor in all this. He inherited all but three of the marshal's ships, which returned to Portugal. It provided him now with a substantial fleet to deploy as he wished—and he had plans to do so. He spent the next day writing to the king about everything that had happened recently, without a word about the Calicut fiasco. The men returning to Portugal could explain that. His silence was eloquent. Calicut itself remained a problem to be solved. Three years later, he would find a solution to the samudri; it would be far simpler, and almost bloodless, but without honor or glory. Meanwhile, he pondered the lessons of the disastrous collapse of discipline, in which the emphasis on individual bravery outweighed tactical organization, and how the hunger for booty, which was the compensation for continual late pay, could reduce an army to a rabble that might break and run.

17

"What the Portuguese Win They Never Give Up"

January–June 1510

N<small>O ONE KNOWS EXACTLY</small> when or why Albuquerque decided to attack Goa, but within a few weeks of the massacre at Calicut he hatched a plan that would launch the Portuguese on a huge campaign, almost three years of continuous contest that would radically alter the axis of power in the Indian Ocean.

He had returned to Cochin badly wounded. One chronicler claimed that in January 1510 the doctors feared for his life. If so, his recovery was extraordinary. Albuquerque was a driven man, impelled by the shared Manueline dream of destroying Islam, as if he knew, too, that time was short. He saw how quickly India used men up—the sapping climate, the change of diet, the blows of dysentery and malaria all took their toll on energy and life expectancy. "The caulkers and carpenters," he wrote to the king, "what with their dealings with the local women, and the work in this hot climate, within the space of a year are no longer men." He set about his duties as governor in Cochin with ferocious zeal, overhauling the fleet for a new campaign, organizing supplies, shaking up perceived slackness in the fulfillment of duties—and writing. Where Almeida had been sparse in his accounts to the king, Albuquerque was lavish. He had concluded that the chronically insecure Manuel wanted to know everything—and the egocentric Albuquerque wanted to justify everything.

"There is nothing," he wrote to his monarch, "in India or within myself that I do not report to you, save only my own sins." Over the next five years he would supply Manuel with a torrent of detail, explanation, justification, and recommendation on all the doings of India, hundreds of thousands of words dictated to a team of long-suffering secretaries by day and night. They took down his words on horseback, at table, on the deck of a ship, in the small hours of the night. Letters, orders, petitions were signed on his knee and dispatched in multiple copies, composed in tearing haste in an impulsive style, restless and urgent, with sudden changes of subject and shot through with a passionate sense of self.

One of these hapless scribes, Gaspar Correia, not only wore out his fingers writing and copying these letters but somehow found the time to compose his own compendious and brilliantly vivid chronicle of this whirlwind in action. Albuquerque seemed to attend to everything. His ability to frame huge geostrategic initiatives was matched by an inexhaustible attention to detail. While sending envoys to the raja of Vijayanagar, he would be inquiring into the foot of a wounded elephant, considering the use of coconut shells as a packing material, arranging for gifts to loyal potentates, overseeing the loading of ships and the hospital facilities for wounded men. He was aware that while the Portuguese were lords of the ocean, they had only fragile leaseholds on the Indian coast at Cannanore and Cochin. He had personal scores to settle—in Calicut and Ormuz—and imperial edicts to fulfill. The list of objectives that had eluded Almeida was long: the destruction of Calicut, capture of Ormuz, blockade of the Red Sea, and control of Malacca, the southernmost hub of the spice trade, as well as exploring the seas beyond. Behind this, hidden from all but the inner circle of the royal court, Manuel's final contest: the destruction of the Mamluks in Egypt and the retaking of Jerusalem.

Manuel, chronically fearful of entrusting power to any one man, had decided to create three autonomous governments in the Indian Ocean. Nominally Albuquerque had authority to act in only the central segment—the west coast of India from Gujarat to Ceylon. The coasts of Africa, the Red Sea, and the Persian Gulf were the domain of Duarte de Lemos. Beyond Ceylon, Diogo Lopes de Sequeira had responsibility for Malacca and the farthest Orient. This dispersal of forces was strategically flawed, as neither of the other two commanders had sufficient ships for effective action. Albuquerque not only saw the pointlessness of this division, he also believed that no one was as capable as himself. Over a period of time, he found ways of obtaining the ships of the other commanders and integrating them into one unified command, without royal say-so. It made for an effective deployment of military resources; it also made him enemies, both in India and back at court, who would snipe at his methods and malign his intentions to the king.

Equally unpopular was the issue of military organization. The massacre at Calicut had highlighted the shortcomings of the way the Portuguese fought. The military code of the *fidalgos* valued heroic personal deeds over tactics, the taking of booty and prizes over the achievement of strategic objectives. Men-at-arms were tied by personal and economic loyalties to their aristocratic leaders rather than to an overall commander. Victories were gained by acts of individual valor rather than rational planning. The Portuguese fought with a ferocity that stunned the peoples of the Indian Ocean, but their methods were medieval and chaotic and, not infrequently, suicidal. It was in this spirit that Lourenço de Almeida had refused to blast the Egyptian fleet out of the water at Chaul and Coutinho had attempted to march into Calicut with a cane and a cap. The laudatory roll calls of *fidalgos* who went down to the last man pepper the pages of the chronicles. Yet it was clear, too, though cowardice was the ultimate smirch on a *fidalgo's* name and the merest whisper of a refusal to fight had ultimately cost Lourenço his life, that the ill-disciplined rank and file could crack under pressure.

Albuquerque was certainly in thrall to Manuel's messianic ideas of medieval crusade but, like the king himself, he was also keenly aware of the military revolution sweeping Europe. In the Italian wars of the late fifteenth century, bands of professional Swiss mercenaries, drilled to march and fight as organized groups, had revolutionized battlefield tactics. Highly maneuverable columns of trained men, armed with pikes and halberds, had steamrollered their opponents in tight mass formations. Albuquerque, with the energy of a zealot, set about reorganizing and instructing men in the tactics and disciplines of the new warfare. At Cochin, he formed the first trained bands. Immediately after his return from Calicut he wrote to Manuel, asking for a corps of soldiers practiced in the Swiss techniques and for the officers to instruct the India men. As it was, he proceeded anyway. Men were formally enrolled in corps, taught to march in formation and in the use of the pike. Each "Swiss" corps had its own corporals, standard-bearers, pipers, and clerk—as well as monthly payment. To encourage the status of this new regimental structure, Albuquerque himself would sometimes shoulder a pike and march with the men.

Within a month of his return from Calicut, he was again sailing north up the coast of India, this time with a revitalized fleet: twenty-three ships, 1,600 Portuguese soldiers and sailors, plus 220 local troops from the Malabar Coast and 3,000 "fighting slaves," who carried baggage and supplies and in extreme cases might be enrolled in the fight. The initial objective of this expedition appears to have been ill-defined. There were rumors that the Mamluk sultan was preparing a new fleet at Suez to avenge the crushing defeat at Diu. But Albuquerque kept his cards close to his chest. Anchored at Mount Deli on February 13, he explained to his commanders that he had letters from the king to go to Ormuz; he also dropped in news of the Red Sea threat—and casually mentioned the subject of Goa, a city that had never figured in Portuguese plans. Four days later, to the surprise of almost everyone, they were embarked on its capture.

What had happened in the interim was a visit to the fleet by Timoji, the Hindu pirate who had once troubled Vasco da Gama. Timoji, a somewhat ambivalent figure, had thrown in his lot with the Europeans during the time of Almeida, and he came to see Albuquerque with a proposition. Despite the apparent coincidence of this meeting, it is likely that it had been set up: Timoji's emissaries had visited Albuquerque in January. In all probability, the two men had secretly prepared this encounter well in advance. Timoji came with a well-rehearsed tale to tell.

The city of Goa, situated on a fertile island between two rivers, was the most strategically positioned trading post on the west coast of India. It lay on the fault line between two rival empires competing for

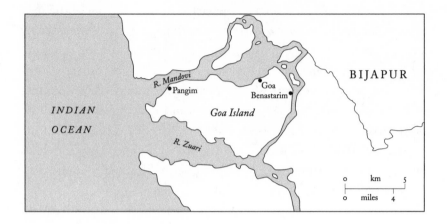

Goa at the time of Albuquerque

the heart of the southern subcontinent: to the north, the Muslim kingdom of Bijapur; to the south its rivals, the Hindu rajas of Vijayanagar. Goa was fiercely contested between these two dynasties. It had changed hands three times in the past thirty years. Its particular value, and its wealth, derived from its role in the horse trade. From Ormuz it imported animals from Persia and Arabia, indispensable to both sides in their frontier wars. In the tropical climate, horses quickly succumbed and did not breed successfully, so stocks required continual replenishment. Goa had other advantages. It had an excellent deep-water port sheltered from the monsoon winds. The area was extremely fertile, and the island on which the city itself was located, Tiswadi or Goa Island, allowed all goods coming in and out to be efficiently taxed at customs points. As an island, it also suggested the possibilities for effective defense.

Timoji had pressing reasons as to why the Portuguese should attack Goa now. Whereas the Malabar cities had Muslim communities but were ruled by Hindus, here the majority Hindus were presently ruled by Muslims, who were not popular. The Hindus were heavily taxed. Unrest was further increased by the presence of a band of Rume fighters, fugitives from the battle of Diu, who oppressed the local population. Of greater concern to Albuquerque was that these men had plans for revenge. They were constructing a good number of carracks along

Portuguese lines, probably with the help of European renegades. They had appealed to the Mamluk sultan for further aid. In effect, Goa was being prepared as a base for a Muslim counterattack in the war with the Franks.

Timoji stressed that it was the moment to strike. The sultan of Bijapur had just died; his young son, Adil Shah, was away from the city putting down an insurrection. The garrison left on the island was not large. Additionally, Bijapur was further distracted by a state of almost permanent hostility with Vijayanagar. There would be support within the city for a Portuguese takeover. Timoji said that he personally could arrange it. He knew the city well, its topography and means of access; he had relationships with the leaders of the Hindu community, who would welcome deliverance from the Muslims. The pirate's exact motives might be hard to fathom, but he had recently proved to be a loyal ally, and his spy network was evidently extensive. Albuquerque was inclined to believe him. Goa fitted his personal vision of an Indian empire. Only ownership of territory would make the India enterprise secure. Goa's strategic position was ideal for controlling the spice trade, while a monopoly of the horse trade would allow the Portuguese to intervene in the complex political and military game of southern India. The city could be defended easily—and there was no religious controversy with the Hindus.

The capture of Goa was just as easy as Timoji had suggested—though holding it would prove otherwise. The Hindu pirate collected his own force of two thousand men to help the operation. On February 15 or 16, Albuquerque sent exploratory ships into the mouth of the Mandovi River to take soundings. The depth was suitable for even his largest carracks. A pincer movement was prepared by land and sea. Timoji's men captured and dismantled an artillery position on the landward side. Albuquerque's nephew attacked the matching battery on the island at the mouth of the river. After a short, sharp fight, the defense collapsed and its captain retreated into the town. Meanwhile, Timoji had infiltrated the city. Two representatives came out to meet the armada and offered peaceful surrender. Albuquerque sent a message to the populace, granting complete religious tolerance for both resident Muslims and Hindus and a lowering of taxes. His only condition was that the Rumes and Adil Shah's mercenary garrison should be expelled. They took chaotic flight out of the city.

On March 1, the governor took possession of Goa with great ceremony. The men of the new trained bands were assembled on the quay, their pikes glittering. Albuquerque stepped ashore in richly worked armor to be met by eight of the principal citizens of Goa on bended knees. They offered him the keys of the city. He rode through the gates on a horse with a silver chased saddle to the shouts of the people and the drums and pipes of the trained bands, a friar holding forth a jeweled cross, and the banner of the Order of Christ, a red cross on a white background, proclaiming the Christian conquest.

From the moment he set foot on the island, Albuquerque considered Goa to be a permanent possession of Portugal. He acted accordingly. Strict discipline was imposed on the men. There was to be no plunder, and he forbade acts of violence, robbery, or sexual assault on people who were now subjects of King Manuel. The governor would maintain this position with unswerving ferocity in the face of extraordinary setbacks and fierce criticism during the years ahead.

They explored the city thoroughly. The shah's palace, with its great square, perfumed gardens, and pavilions of finely worked wood, was as splendid as that at Calicut. They found 150 Arabian horses in the royal stables and a hundred elephants. Timoji's account of the war preparations of the Rumes was also discovered to be correct. Large carracks were under construction in the dockyard; the arsenal contained stockpiles of war materials—cannons, gunpowder, swords—and forges and tools for manufacturing all the equipment for a substantial maritime expedition. The governor ordered the ships to be completed as a welcome addition to the fleet.

Albuquerque set about the creation of Portuguese Goa with zeal. This was the first territorial acquisition in Asia. To mark its permanency, within a fortnight he had ordered the establishment of a mint "to mint new currency, in the service of His Highness, in this his new realm." The circumstances surrounding this reflected his sensitivity to the local situation. The leading figures of the city had quickly approached him about the lack of coinage in Goa, necessary to reinvigorate trade. The new flagship coin was to be the cruzado—or the

Manuel—a glittering gold disk bearing the cross on one side, on the other an armillary sphere, the symbol of the Portuguese king, struck at a weight of 4.56 grams, the local Goan standard, heavier than its Portuguese equivalent. To announce its inception publicly, the new coinage was carried through the streets in silver basins to the sound of drums and pipes, accompanied by clowns and dancers and heralds proclaiming in Portuguese and the local language that "this was the new currency of the king our lord, who ordered that it should run in Goa and its territories."

The attention to detail over the new coinage reveals Albuquerque in all his complexity: a practical and flexible administrator, sensitive to local conditions, able to rethink solutions in new frameworks—and yet touched by a blind and often insufferable sense of self that was to cause many problems. On the lesser coins the sphere was controversially obversed with the letter A, "to show who had minted them." It was the kind of action that would provide ammunition for Albuquerque's enemies and stoke rumors back in Portugal that the governor was intending Goa for his own fiefdom.

The first faltering steps in colonial administration were not error-free. Timoji was initially put in charge of tax collecting, but this promised to stir dissent from both communities and his remit had to be altered. And although Albuquerque had promised religious freedom, he recoiled in horror at the practice of suttee—the immolation of Hindu widows on their husband's funeral pyres—and banned it. The underlying sense of Christian mission and his own obduracy also led him to order summary executions that were to cause unrest.

In the midst of this two ambassadors turned up, one from Shah Ismail, the Shia ruler of Persia, the other from Albuquerque's old adversary Hwaga Ata in Ormuz, asking for help from Adil Shah against the Portuguese. They were nonplussed to find Adil Shah gone and Albuquerque in occupation. However, Albuquerque spotted a strategic opportunity in relations with Ismail, the sworn enemy of the Sunni Mamluks. He proposed a joint operation. The Portuguese would attack from the Mediterranean and the Red Sea, the shah from the east. "Then if God wills that this alliance be concluded, you could descend with all your power upon the town of Cairo and the lands of the sultan, and my lord the king would pass over to Jerusalem and conquer all the country on that side"—giving Albuquerque the chance to fulfill Manuel's crusading dream. He sent an ambassador back to the shah with this message, together with a conciliatory letter to be delivered along the way to the puppet king of Ormuz, overlooking the past. The unfortunate chosen for this role, Ruy Gomes, never made it to Persia. Hwaga Ata poisoned him in Ormuz.

Urgency informed the governor's actions in Goa. He was aware that the city's defenses were insufficient, and it was clear that at some point the young Adil Shah would reappear and demand his valuable trading port back. Repairs were hampered by a lack of lime from which to make mortar; the walls had to be rebuilt with stone packed with mud. Knowing that time was pressing, he detailed teams of men to work round the clock in rotation to shore up the defenses against a possible attack; the governor was on site night and day urging on the work. He was determined to hold Goa at all costs. By April, however, the mood among the Portuguese was restive. Many of the *fidalgos* did not share their governor's vision. The monsoon season was on the way, and distant rumors reached Goa that Adil Shah was preparing a substantial army. Relations with the citizens had soured somewhat over the severity of his justice, and some of his captains began privately to chafe for a return to Cochin. Failure to leave soon would mean being trapped by the rains and forced to sit out a long season, possibly under siege. It was already evident that the favored tactic of Portugal's enemies was to wait until the heavy rain and rough seas isolated their forces from outside help. Albuquerque was not to be shaken. Goa was Portuguese and would remain so.

In fact, by April Adil Shah had put down the rebellion in his kingdom. Unbeknownst to Albuquerque, he had also brokered a truce with the rival kingdom of Vijayanagar. He was ready to spring the monsoon trap. That month he dispatched his general Palud Khan with a large force, speculatively calculated at forty thousand men—trained fighters from Iran and central Asia—to dislodge the intruders. When this force reached the banks of the Mandovi River, it quickly routed Timoji's impromptu fighting band. Across the narrow creeks and crocodile-infested rivers that separated Goa Island from the mainland, the defenders could now see the tents and banners of a large army. It was apparent that the perimeter of the island, some eighteen miles, would stretch Albuquerque's forces to the limit in the attempt to guard the swampy fords, which at low tide might allow an enemy across. Palud Khan kept the Portuguese captains watchful and at full stretch with a series of feints and tentative probes across the lagoons. He slipped letters to the Muslims of Goa. Men from the city started to desert and join the Islamic army. Palud waited for the weather to worsen.

One day, as the defenders stared uneasily across the narrow creek that separated the two sides, they saw a man come down to the water's edge, waving a white flag. A voice called out in their language, "My Portuguese lords, let someone come and speak with me to relay [the information] that I come with a message for the governor." A boat was sent out. The man identified himself as a Portuguese named João Machado, and he begged a safe-conduct to speak to Albuquerque.

Machado had been a convict dropped on the Swahili coast a decade earlier and was in the service of Adil Shah, but he seemed to come with a lingering nostalgia for his own people. He brought helpful advice. His message was a simple one. Palud Khan's forces would soon be further augmented by Adil Shah himself. The monsoon was approaching. Leave the island now, before it was too late. Return the women and children from the sultan's harem who had been left behind when the shah's garrison fled. The shah wished to be on good terms with the governor. In return, he would grant him another place on the coast to build a fort.

The message contained a threat, a sweetener, and an appeal to common sense. Albuquerque ignored them all. There would be no terms. "What the Portuguese win they never give up" was his proud reply. Nor would he return "either the children or the women, whom he was keeping as [Portuguese] brides, and whom he hoped to make Christians." Not for the first time, Albuquerque's intransigent negotiating style shocked people. When his decision was relayed back to Palud Khan, the general "was completely amazed, because he well knew how few men the governor had." He returned to his tent and started to order the construction of large rafts, platforms mounted on canoes lashed together, for transporting an invasion force across the river.

Stubbornly clinging to his imperial vision, Albuquerque did not heed advice. He believed that he could hold out during the monsoon until the next fleet arrived from Lisbon, in August. He was unaware how much Adil Shah's truce with Vijayanagar had freed the young ruler's hand, and he chose to ignore the growing discontent among his own men. Incessant forays across the shallow creeks kept them at full stretch, when they were not being exhorted to work harder at the walls. Over the straits, they could see how large the enemy force was. Sapped by the heat and on tightening rations, there was a sullen and uncomprehending spirit among many of the *fidalgos* as well as their men. Even Timoji had fallen out with the unyielding Albuquerque. As the rain started to lash down and the seas to roughen, the Portuguese could feel the jaws of the trap closing. The governor was becoming increasingly isolated, as he had been at Ormuz. He was reliant on a small band of noblemen personally loyal to him, the most prominent of whom was his nephew, the young António de Noronha, enterprising and brave. Elsewhere, the inhabitants of Goa, Hindus as well as Muslims, were sizing up their chances and concluding that it might be better to side with the army outside the gates.

Palud Khan, informed of the growing dissent among the Portuguese captains, timed his all-out assault well. On the night of May 10 or 11, with the monsoon rain lashing down, the wind whipping the palm trees, and the tide out, so that the fords were more easily traversable, swarms of rafts pushed out across the shallow river. In the confusion of the night, the mixed force of Portuguese and local Malabar troops was taken by surprise. There was a lack of cohesion between the two units. They were overtaken so fast and fled in such panic that they left their cannons behind. In a short while, the Portuguese were forced back into the town. Some of the local troops defected. In the city, the Muslims rose against their new masters. There was street-to-street fighting as Albuquerque struggled to control the situation.

Soon the Portuguese were bottled up within the citadel. For twenty days the governor urged the men to resist, endlessly doing the rounds of the command posts, eating as he rode, but the hastily rebuilt walls bonded with mud were inexorably crumbling. Revolt among the population was spreading. It was clear that he no longer had enough men to hold out indefinitely. Adil Shah himself arrived in person. From the walls they could see the sea of tents and the blue and red flags—"and all their tents fluttered with banners and their terrible cries broke the spirits of our men." A growing number of captains petitioned for withdrawal before it was too late. The chances of making it out of the harbor and to the safety of Cochin were getting slimmer by the day. The governor, supported by his coterie, stubbornly insisted that the city could be held and that Adil Shah would need to return to his fight with Vijayanagar. It was only when news reached him of the truce between the two potentates, João Machado came again to warn him of a plan to burn his boats, and a ship was sunk in the channel to block their escape that he realized that the situation was untenable.

The escape from the beleaguered citadel was planned for the night of May 31. Preparations were taken in the utmost secrecy. A single bell was to be rung at midnight. The ships were readied to sail. Retreat back to the quays was to be covered by an elite group of captains. Suggestions to fire the town were vetoed by Albuquerque. He vowed to return and make Goa his own. Otherwise, he was ruthless. He ordered Timoji to kill all the Muslim men, women, and children they were holding. None was to be left alive. Cannons were to be spiked and horses destroyed to prevent their use in the retreat. The arsenal and military supplies were to be burned.

Timoji set about his grim task. In small groups, the Muslim men were requested to be seen by the governor, then killed in the street. However, Timoji was selective. Many of the women and children he left locked in a house. The most beautiful of the women he stripped of their jewelry, dressed as men, and stowed away on his ships. Despite the stealth of the retreat, it quickly became clear that the Portuguese were leaving. Adil Shah's men poured through the gates. Albuquerque had devised a final stratagem to slow their advance. He had pepper and bars of copper strewn in their way, so that the pursuit was slowed down by men stopping to pilfer the takings. Others were frozen with horror at finding their relatives slaughtered in the street. Despite these attempts, there was fierce fighting all the way down the quays. Only a desperate rearguard action ensured that the ships got away. The armada pushed off into the channel, which the sunken vessel had failed to block. Probably all except the governor were relieved to escape. Their troubles, however, had only just begun.

18

Prisoners of the Rain

June–August 1510

THEY SAILED DOWNSTREAM UNDER a parting bombardment of missiles. Behind them, the sound of Adil Shah's trumpets celebrating the recapture of the city mingled with cries of grief as the Muslims discovered their menfolk slaughtered in the street, their wives and daughters abducted. The fleet anchored close to the mouth of the Mandovi River, where it widened under the lee of the strategic fort of Pangim.

They had left late. It was now the start of June. The monsoon announced itself in earnest. Torrential rain battered the ships; winds whipped through the bending palms. With the river in spate, the ships had to be tethered at both bow and stern to prevent them from twisting in the current. On board there were fierce debates among the senior commanders about whether they could make it out of the river mouth and plow the seas to the island of Anjediva. The mood among the captains was surly. They blamed Albuquerque personally for this plight: they should have sailed sooner. They demanded an escape from the trap. The pilots were equally insistent that it could now not be done. Albuquerque finally agreed to risk one ship under Fernão Peres in an attempt to pass out through the sand spits at the river mouth. The fierce currents swept his vessel onto the shoals. It was lost to the battering of the waves, though the men escaped and the cannons were salvaged from the wreck. Another captain tried an unauthorized escape but was intercepted and stripped of his command. The Portuguese were trapped, facing a river siege that might last until August. It was a situation of unique and grave difficulty.

As they lay tethered midstream, a boat appeared sporting a white flag. Adil Shah had again dispatched João Machado to try to negotiate, ostensibly to offer peace terms. In fact, the shah was buying time. Fearful that the intruders might storm and occupy the fort at Pangim, he wanted to tie them up for long enough to reoccupy it himself. Albuquerque gave a short and sharp reply to the effect that "Goa belonged to his lord, the king of Portugal, and there would never be any peace with the shah unless he changed his mind and handed it back along with all its territories."

The effrontery of Albuquerque's style shocked the shah. This man—hemmed in, defeated, facing starvation—was brusquely dictating terms. The most polite oath that passed his lips was "sons of the devil." He tried again, returning Machado with two important men of the town and a revised offer: he could not give up Goa. Instead, he would present Albuquerque with Dabul and all the Ormuz horse revenues. Albuquerque bluntly told the messengers to go: he would hear nothing more until Goa was returned. It was the start of a new contest that was psychological as much as physical. During this pretense at negotiation, Adil had regarrisoned the fort at Pangim with a large company of men and installed cannons in wooden bastions. A further battery had been positioned on the mainland opposite. From their uneasy position midstream between the two, the Portuguese could gaze up at the banners flying from the twin batteries and hear the shouts of their enemies and the blaring of their drums and trumpets. They were held squarely in the jaws of the trap.

Torment was to be visited on the Portuguese in many forms. First the artillery bombardment: the ships were caught in the cross fire from both banks. Their hulls were too stout to be seriously damaged by the caliber of the shah's guns, but the incessant gunfire, by day and night, induced a dreadful sense of insecurity. Albuquerque's ship, the *Frol de la Mar,* identifiable by its captain's banners, was the most obvious target, sometimes receiving fifty shots a day. It became unwise to appear on the bridge or mount the crow's nest. They had to keep shifting the position of the vessels to limit the threat, which was difficult and dangerous work. No attempts were made to reply. It was better to preserve stores of powder for a later occasion. Cooped up below deck, with the rain drumming furiously overhead, the men started to sicken.

And then, sometime in June, the rain stopped. For fifteen days the skies cleared—and another problem arose: lack of drinking water. Rainwater could no longer be collected, and the Mandovi was too salty to be drunk. Men started to gasp in the sapping heat. Adil guarded all the water sources around the river and waited. He was certain he could crush the intruders just by holding them there long enough. The only consolation for the fleet was the continuous help of Timoji, who knew the terrain, and his intelligence sources. With his aid, a commando raid was launched to tap a spring in the jungle. There was fierce fighting for small rewards: "with great difficulty we managed to fill sixty or seventy caskets with water, but none of our big barrels, because many men were wounded." In the words of another account, "a drop of water cost three of blood."

The unexpected reappearance of fine weather reanimated the faction clamoring for an attempt to escape the hellhole of the river. The captains importuned Albuquerque unceasingly to weigh anchor and try again. Albuquerque and the pilots held firm, citing the fate of Peres's ship. As at Ormuz, their commander's obstinacy was stoking a slow-burning resentment. Among the men, there was a widely held belief that they were being led by an obsessive madman who would push pride to the point of death: "that out of stubbornness he wanted to die and kill them all."

When rain and turbulent seas returned, confirming that an attempt to sail away would probably have ended in disaster, the thirst eased. Water could be collected on the ships in barrels, and the water coming downstream was now fresh enough to be drinkable, as long as the mud was left to settle for a day or two; but hunger was also beginning to sap the morale and physical stamina of the men. Supplies were running low. Albuquerque imposed strict rationing. He kept the storeroom tightly under lock and key, opened only on his signature. Men were issued four ounces of biscuits a day. The small quantities of fish that could be caught from the river were reserved for the sick. Meanwhile, Timoji scouted out whatever he could find, putting his men ashore stealthily in small boats. On board the men hunted rats; those with sea chests stripped off their leather coverings, boiled, and ate them. "The common people did this who couldn't put up with the hunger, with which they were totally desperate," Correia observed, implying that the nobility were above such things, though there is no record as to whether they shared the same diet. Men came to the governor begging for something to eat, and the storekeeper received particular abuse. The captains pointed the finger of blame at Albuquerque for subjecting them to this torment: "If they had not wintered here—and they had advised him not to—they would have avoided this suffering. . . . He was a maniac keeping them there." People's faces darkened with fear. In the rain, with the continuous gunfire, in a tropical hell, soaking and sweating in their rotting clothes, they were increasingly gripped by morbid terror that they were all going to die.

Then the desertions started. Three men dived overboard and swam to the shore. They were received with open arms by Adil, fed well, and pumped for information about the dissent in the ranks and the desperate food shortage. The captains were forced to spend as much time watching their own men as the riverbanks occupied by an implacable foe.

For Albuquerque, everything was at stake. All the principal figures of the Indian administration were besieged in the Mandovi in the rain, with the shots of the enemy crashing in; the men and their captains cursed him for the lack of food, for his obstinacy, his obsessiveness, his vanity. All he had was his belief in a certain strategic vision, encouraging words, and the severities of discipline. It was perhaps his supreme moment of crisis. He had failed to carry men with him at Ormuz; he had experienced a vote of no confidence at Cochin; he was facing disaster in his self-invented project at Goa. In his darkest hour, he "shut himself up in his cabin and looked up to heaven and prayed." Only a small group fully supported the governor; Albuquerque's nephew António de Noronha played a critical role as a softening intermediary between the intemperate commander and his increasingly restive captains.

In his palace in Goa, Adil Shah had been listening attentively to the accounts of the enemy's plight from the renegades. He wanted to test the words of these men, perhaps overly keen to tell their new master what he wanted to hear. He devised a new tactic for breaking his intransigent rival. Sometime in June (the dates are unclear), a vessel laden with food—sacks of rice, chickens, figs, and vegetables—approached the *Frol de la Mar* flying a white flag. A ship's boat was put out to ascertain its mission and was told that the shah wished to win an honorable war, not defeat his enemy through hunger. Keeping the messenger waiting in the river, Albuquerque arranged his own response to such mind games. He ordered a barrel to be cut in two and filled with wine; the dwindling stock of biscuits was also brought up from the storeroom and displayed in buckets. A group of sailors were tipped to disport themselves on the deck in attitudes of jollity, singing and enjoying themselves. When the messenger was finally allowed on board to survey this tableau of plenty and good spirits, Albuquerque was ready with steely words: Take your food away, we have plenty; there will be no peace until Goa is returned. Adil Shah may have concluded that the deserters had lied, or he may have seen through the charade as one more shot in the war of nerves. Albuquerque's men probably muttered unspeakable oaths under their breath as they watched the provisions being rowed away. The cannon fire continued to taunt and unsettle.

Albuquerque knew that Adil Shah did not want to be detained in Goa indefinitely. He had other threats and obligations throughout his kingdom. The Portuguese leader was counting on the shah cracking first. In the meanwhile, to raise morale, he proposed an attack to destroy the shore guns. The mood among the *fidalgos* was sullen. It proved impossible to get their assent. Exasperated, he decided to push ahead anyway: "I am your governor. With God's will, I'm landing on the shore at Pangim with the royal flag. . . . When I embark I will order the sounding of Timoji's trumpets. Come if you want or stay behind." They all signed up.

Timoji's fleet of shallow river craft was essential for an amphibious landing. Before dawn, the Portuguese fell upon the artillery emplacements outside the castle, routed the surprised defenders, and carried off the cannons and a supply of food. The guns on the opposite shore were also silenced. It was evening before Adil dispatched reinforcements to counterattack, by which time his enemies were safely back on board.

Adil had presumed that he could starve the Portuguese into submission, but the attack on Pangim dented his pride. It was now necessary to go on the offensive. In Goa harbor he ordered the secret preparation of a large number of incendiary rafts to destroy the fleet. Yet it proved impossible to hide these activities. The indispensable Timoji was always able to put spies ashore to seek information. Albuquerque decided to launch his own preemptive counterstrike, using light cannons in the boats. The surprise raid was entirely successful, despite resistance. The rafts were simply blown apart by the destructive power of Portuguese gunnery. António de Noronha, carried away by excitement and seeing a light galley temptingly beached, tried to tow it away as a prize. He was hit in the knee by an arrow and had to withdraw. Leg wounds were the blight of Portuguese battles in this sea; they often proved to be mortal blows, either because an arrow had hit a vein or artery or because of infection and the complete lack of medical supplies. Noronha took to his cabin and was dead within three days. Albuquerque seems to have been deeply affected by his nephew's death. Noronha had acted as a mediator between the governor and disaffected captains; he had been the governor's designated successor in the event of death. It was a blow that Albuquerque tried, without success, to keep from Adil Shah.

In their floating prisons on the Mandovi, the weary days drew on: the rain, the lack of food, the weakening men. The only bright spot for Albuquerque was the news that Adil's truce with Vijayanagar was over: the shah was needed elsewhere. For Albuquerque, it was a further incentive to hold out. But the men continued to desert. Eight days after the fight at Goa, a man named João Romão swam ashore with fresh news about the plight on the ships: Dom António dead, people ill and dying of hunger, people wounded in the battles for whom there was no cure. More desertions followed: five, ten, then fifteen, dropping over the side at night and swimming to shore. Morale on the ships was dwindling, but Adil Shah badly needed peace. It was becoming a test of wills.

The shah tried to wrestle the initiative back again: more peace messengers were sent. Albuquerque was tired of the comings and goings of these visitors. He distrusted their motives, undermining morale, wearing down resistance. Additionally, the shah supplied the renegade Romão with a horse. He appeared on the beach in Arab dress, well fed, taunting the men with his better fortune as a Muslim convert. Albuquerque again refused the shah's emissaries, but this time the *fidalgos* demanded that he at least listen to their proposals. He acceded but resolved to fix the desertion problem once and for all.

An exchange of hostages was agreed for the next day. Adil Shah sent his regent, the most distinguished noble in the city, to parley, accompanied by a large cavalcade and an ostentatious show of ceremony. A tent of black satin was set up on the beach, where the regent awaited the negotiator with the necessary interpreters, cavalry, and foot soldiers. Albuquerque sent his auditor, Pêro d'Alpoym, an important figure in the Indian administration, to fetch the ambassador to his ship, and with him, in one of Timoji's boats, a crack marksman named João d'Oeiras, armed with a crossbow. As they approached to the ceremonial beating of drums, they could see the deserters among the throng, well dressed, on horses; among them was Romão, in a silk caftan, armed with lance and shield taunting the Portuguese. Oeiras crouched down in the bow in front of the oarsman as they drew near the beach. Now they could make out Romão's words. He was telling the governor and everyone else to go and eat shit. A word from Alpoym, and the archer stood up, took aim, and fired. The bolt caught Romão full on, passed straight through him, and dropped him dead on the spot. There was a stunned silence, then uproar on the beach at this breach of a truce. It was explained that the renegades were speaking ill of the governor, that he would not tolerate this, and that they should not appear again.

When the regent finally made it on board, he was equally surprised by the brevity of the negotiations. He offered flowery salutations in the style of Oriental diplomacy, a site for a fortress outside Goa with a good port, fifty thousand gold cruzados in cash—with just one concession. He asked for Timoji to be handed over. Albuquerque sighed and gave a short, sharp response. It was Goa or nothing; Timoji would never be surrendered. He hustled the astonished man off the ship in a style distinctly short of diplomatic protocol, with the parting request to send no more messengers unless they were bringing the keys of the city.

Adil Shah gave up trying to negotiate with a man who disdained all the rules. The crossbowman received ten cruzados for his shot, but it failed to deter deserters. Men continued to swim away at night. The situation was at a stalemate. The fleet remained in the river. And almost from nowhere, the dissent of the *fidalgos* suddenly erupted into open rebellion in the strangest circumstances.

It involved the Muslim women and girls, some from the harem, who had been spirited away by Timoji when the city fell. It was suggested that they could now be used as bargaining chips. Albuquerque was startled. He had forgotten their very existence. He quizzed Timoji as to their whereabouts and why he had not been informed. Timoji was evasive: they had been handed over to the captains and divided among the ships "and many of them had turned Christian." The governor was furious at this conspiracy of silence and the implications for discipline of having women aboard the ships, not to mention the obvious opportunities for sin. He demanded that the women be produced. Digging deeper, he was told that some of them had got "married" to men in the fleet, who would not be separated from their paramours. Pragmatically, and fearing trouble in the ranks, he decided simply to legalize these unions without formal ceremony, to the scandal of his chaplain, who declared that this was not in accord with church law. "Then according to the law of Afonso de Albuquerque," the autocrat replied.

There remained another group of harem women and girls who had not converted. These included the more beautiful among them, who would not consort with the common sailors but were the subject of the attention of some of the young nobles. Albuquerque had this group transferred to the *Frol de la Mar* and sequestered in a cabin at the rear of the ship, under lock and key and guarded by a eunuch. This move was the subject of covert bitterness among the young *fidalgos* whose dalliances had been cut short. Soon the eunuch reported suspicious goings-on to the governor; he was sure that men were finding their way into the locked cabin at night, though he had no idea who they were. Albuquerque set a boat to watch. Over the following nights, the observers saw men, sometimes one, sometimes three, swimming over from the nearby *Frol da Rosa*. Stealthily one climbed up onto the rudder, a hatch was opened, and he slipped into the harem. He was positively identified as a young nobleman named Ruy Dias.

Albuquerque called together his two closest advisers. He was furious at the secrecy, the disobedience, the threat to decency—on his very flagship—with the whole fleet under siege. They agreed that "because of the crime of sleeping with the Muslim woman, in such a place at such a time, with such flagrant insolence," there was only one punishment: Dias should be sentenced to death by hanging.

Ruy Dias was at chess with the captain of the *Frol da Rosa*, Jorge Fogaça, when he felt a firm hand on his shoulder: "You are taken in the name of the king!" A boarding party of marines manhandled Dias to the poop deck and tied a noose round his neck; they were preparing to string him up when all hell broke loose. Fogaça stepped forward, cut the rope, and called out that they were hanging Ruy Dias. All the resentment of the noble captains boiled over. Word passed from ship to ship that they were executing the honorable Ruy Dias without due explanation. A hubbub broke out in the fleet. A party of *fidalgos* climbed into a boat, raised a flag, and passed down the line spreading rebellion. The fleet was on the brink of mutiny. From the bank, the watching Muslims cheered and yelled at the growing discord.

Meanwhile, the leader of the marine guard had shouted across to the *Frol de la Mar* that the prisoner had been snatched. Albuquerque, in thunderous mood, climbed into a boat and went to meet the mutineers. The revolt was a challenge to the unbridled authority of their captain: they complained that he was hanging Dias by "arbitrary absolute power, without discussing this with his captains," and, almost worse still, showing his complete contempt for noble etiquette by hanging a *fidalgo* like a common criminal, rather than having him beheaded, as befitted a gentleman of rank. Albuquerque ignored everything they said, clapped the ringleaders in irons, and strung Dias up from the mast of the *Frol da Rosa,* leaving him dangling as a warning.

The revolt had been the fruit of months of tension and difficulty, and the execution of Ruy Dias remained a controversial incident, a blot on Albuquerque's name. In extreme moments he was inflexible, authoritarian, unable to take advice. António da Noronha had acted as a buffer to his style of leadership, but Noronha was dead. The incident was a reprise of the events at Ormuz. His inability to lead men judiciously was making him notorious. But if Albuquerque was quick to anger, he was also quick to repent. He tried to patch up relations with the four imprisoned ringleaders, who were crucial in the struggle to survive. Like the captains at Ormuz, they refused to cooperate; Dias would haunt Albuquerque to the end of his life.

Albuquerque knew that Adil Shah needed to depart. He had other wars to fight. It remained an arm wrestle. But as July dipped into August, the weather started to improve; the rain eased. There was a possibility of escape from their pestilential prison in the Mandovi. Albuquerque wanted Timoji to go for supplies and return, keeping the siege going until Adil Shah's patience was exhausted, but the men could take no more. They begged to leave. Against his will, he relented. "And on 15 August, the Day of Our Lady, on a good wind, with which the governor departed from the river with all the fleet, and made his way to Anjediva." They had been trapped in the Mandovi River for seventy-seven days of rain, hunger, and bombardment. Endurance and survival were almost a victory. For Albuquerque, however, it was unfinished business. As with Ormuz, he vowed to return to Goa and win. The speed with which he did so was astonishing.

19

The Uses of Terror

August–December 1510

A T THE ISLAND OF Anjediva, Albuquerque was surprised to meet
a small squadron of four ships bound for faraway Malacca, on
the Malay Peninsula, under the command of Diogo Mendes de Vasconcelos. Manuel had airily ordered this insignificant force to conquer
the place. Some of the financing had been provided by Florentine investors; their representatives included Giovanni da Empoli, who had
accompanied Albuquerque on an earlier voyage. Empoli found the
governor "very displeased at the defeat sustained in Goa and also about
many other things."

Empoli's surviving account, written probably two years later during
a bout of scurvy while becalmed off the coast of Brazil, is sour and
peevish. He recounts how Albuquerque was obsessed with Goa, determined to return and take it as soon as possible; he needed all the forces
he could muster, including the squadron bound for Malacca, and,
given the wearisome ordeal in the Mandovi River, he needed to be sly
about his tactics in order to get consent from his commanders. Albuquerque had seen the potential of the island, and he feared that the
return of a Rume fleet could render it an impregnable base against
Portuguese interests. He stressed the approaching threat of a new armada. To Empoli, the Egyptian menace had become a phony war: "the
news about the Rume was what had been expected for many years

past, but the truth had never been known ... at present such news could not be considered as certain because of the lack of credibility on the part of the Muslims." Privately, he accused Albuquerque of concocting letters, with the aid of Malik Ayaz in Diu to bolster his case.

Whatever the truth of this, Albuquerque quickly managed to reason, bully, or cajole the fleet, including the Malacca squadron, into a new strike. Given the sensitivity of the Portuguese factions in Cochin and Cannanore, this was a considerable feat. Word from the ever-alert Timoji informed him that Adil Shah had left Goa to fight new wars with Vijayanagar; the moment was right. Two months of frenetic refitting and reprovisioning readied the fleet. At a council in Cochin on October 10 he imposed his will on the captains: let those who would follow him, follow. Those who refused must give their explanations to the king. The matter of Malacca and the Red Sea would be rapidly returned to afterward. Again, by sheer force of personality, and some threats, he carried the day. Diogo Mendes de Vasconcelos, with the reluctant Florentines in tow, agreed to postpone the visit to Malacca. Even the mutineers in the Ruy Dias episode, who had preferred to stay in prison, were released and joined up. On October 16, Albuquerque was writing a letter of justification to the king, explaining yet again why he persisted with Goa: "You will see how good it is, Your Highness, that if you are lord of Goa you throw the whole realm of India into confusion ... there is nowhere on the coasts as good or secure as Goa, because it's an island. If you lost the whole of India you could reconquer it from there." This time it was not just a matter of conquest. Goa was to be utterly purged of a Muslim presence.

On the following day he set sail with nineteen ships and sixteen hundred men. By November 24, the fleet was back in the mouth of the Mandovi. Increasingly the Portuguese did not fight alone. Within the fractious power struggles of coastal India, they were able to pull small principalities into their orbit. The sultan of Honavar sent a reputed fifteen thousand men by land; again Timoji was able to raise four thousand and supply sixty small vessels. Adil Shah, however, had not left Goa undefended. He had placed a garrison of eight thousand men—White Turks, the Portuguese called these men, experienced mercenaries from the Ottoman empire and Iran—and a number of Venetian and Genoese renegades with good technical knowledge of cannon founding.

Deciding not to wait, on November 25, St. Catherine's Day, Albuquerque divided his forces in three and attacked the town from two directions. What followed was not a triumph for the organized military tactics he had been trying to instill. It was the traditional berserker fighting style of the Portuguese that won the day. With cries of "St. Catherine! Santiago!" the men rushed the barricades below the town. One soldier managed to jam his weapon into the city gate to prevent it from being closed by the defenders. Elsewhere a small, agile man named Fradique Fernandes forced his spear into the wall and hoisted himself up onto the parapet, where he stood waving a flag and shouting, "Portugal! Portugal! Victory!"

Distracted by this sudden apparition, the defenders lost the tussle to slam the gate shut. It was ripped open, and the Portuguese poured inside. As the defenders fell back, they were hit by another unit, which had smashed through a second gate. The fighting was extremely bloody. The Portuguese chroniclers reported acts of demented bravery. One of the first through the walls, Manuel de Lacerda, was pierced just below the eye by a barbed arrow, which embedded itself too deeply to be removed. He snapped off the shaft and fought on with the ghastly stump protruding from his bloody face. Another man, Jerónimo de Lima, fought until he collapsed to the ground. His brother João found him and wanted to stay and comfort him as his life ebbed away. The dying man looked up and reproached him for pausing in the fight. "Brother, go on your way" is one of the versions of his reply. "I will go on mine." João returned later to find him dead.

The Muslim resistance collapsed. Men tried to flee from the city across the shallow fords, where many drowned. Others who made it across were met by the Hindu allies. "They came to my aid via the fords and from the mountains," Albuquerque later wrote. "They put to the sword all the Muslims who escaped from Goa without sparing the life of a single creature." It had taken just four hours.

Albuquerque shut the gates to stop his men intemperately chasing their enemies. Then he gave the city up to sack and massacre. The aftermath was bloody. The city was to be rid of all Muslims. Albuquerque later described his actions to the king without apology.

> Our Lord has done great things for us, because he wanted us to accomplish a deed so magnificent that it surpasses even what we have prayed for. . . . I have burned the town and killed everyone. For four days without any pause our men have slaughtered . . . wherever we have been able to get into we haven't spared the life of a single Muslim. We have herded them into the mosques and set them on fire. I have ordered that neither the [Hindu] peasants nor the Brahmans should be killed. We have estimated the number of dead Muslim men and women at six thousand. It was, sire, a very fine deed.

Among those burned alive was one of the Portuguese renegades who had swum ashore during the siege in the Mandovi. "No one escaped," wrote the Florentine merchant Piero Strozzi, "men, women, the pregnant, babes in arms." The bodies of the dead were thrown to the crocodiles; "the destruction was so great," remembered Empoli, "that the river was filled with blood and dead men, so that for a week afterwards the tides deposited the corpses on the banks." Evidently the reptiles were unable to cope with the glut.

"Cleansed" was the word Albuquerque used to describe this process to Manuel. It was intended to be exemplary. "This use of terror will bring great things to your obedience without the need to conquer them," he went on. "I haven't left a single grave stone or Islamic structure standing." In fact, he didn't kill quite everyone; a few of the "white and beautiful" Muslim women were spared to be married off. By all accounts the plunder was magnificent. Strozzi was dazzled by the wealth of the Orient that he saw being dragged away. "There you can find all the riches of the world—both gold and jewels. . . . I think they are superior to us in infinite ways, except when it comes to fighting," he wrote to his father. He ended on a rueful note, while still counting his blessings. "I was unable to loot anything because I had been wounded. Still, I was lucky it wasn't a poisoned arrow."

Toward the end of St. Catherine's Day, Albuquerque personally greeted his triumphant captains and thanked them for their efforts. "Many were knighted," recorded Empoli, "among whom he was pleased to include me," though this did little to soften his attitude to the governor. "It is better to be a knight than a merchant," he added, reflecting on the comparatively low regard in which the Portuguese nobility held commercial activities. Among the first to welcome Albuquerque into the city was Manuel de Lacerda. He was riding a richly caparisoned horse that he had taken from a Muslim he had killed. The arrow stump still protruded from his cheek. He was bathed in blood, "and seeing him thus with an arrow in his face, his armor covered in blood, [Albuquerque] embraced him, kissing his face and said, 'Sir, you are as honorable as a martyred St. Sebastian.'" It was an image burned into Portuguese legend.

Surprise gripped the Indian empires that Goa had fallen to a few Portuguese. Albuquerque's astonishing coup called for strategic reconsideration. Ambassadors came from far and wide to pay their respects, to assess and consider what this might mean.

Albuquerque had innovative ideas for securing this new empire. Aware of how few the Portuguese were, of their high mortality rate and their lack of women, he immediately set about promoting a mixed-marriage policy, encouraging the union of the Portuguese rank and file—soldiers, masons, carpenters—with local women. These were generally low-caste Hindus, who were baptized and granted dowries. The married men, known as *casados,* were also given financial incentives for entering into binding ties. Within two months of the reconquest of Goa, he had arranged two hundred such marriages. This policy was pragmatic in its attempt to create a local Christianized population loyal to Portugal, but Albuquerque also showed some enlightened concern for the general welfare of women in Goa, attempting to outlaw suttee and granting them property rights. His marriage policy, in the face of considerable opposition from scandalized clergy and government officials, set in motion the creation of a durable Indo-Portuguese society.

Meanwhile, the waylaid Diogo Mendes de Vasconcelos, who had orders from the king to capture Malacca, was chafing to be on his way. It was patently obvious that his four ships, unaided, could achieve nothing, and Albuquerque was in receipt of a letter from Ruy de Araujo, one of sixty Portuguese hostages being held there from a previous expedition, which he had received in August. Araujo's message was desperate: "We await your arrival. . . . Please God that you'll be coming here within five months or you won't find us alive." He supplied a great deal of information about the politics and military capacity of the city, to the effect that it was huge but not well defended, and adding that "Your Grace must come here with all force, even if it's not strictly necessary, to inspire terror on land and sea." In April 1511, Albuquerque set sail on a new conquest. He had been in Goa for only four months.

The same year, unknown to Albuquerque, the Portuguese struck another significant blow against the Mamluks, this time from within the Mediterranean basin. In August, a squadron of war galleys led by André do Amaral, a Portuguese knight of the crusading Order of St. John on Rhodes, intercepted and destroyed a fleet of ships carrying timber from Lebanon to Egypt. This was intended for the construction of a new fleet to avenge Diu. The Mamluks were totally dependent on the import of wood from the eastern Mediterranean; without it they were hamstrung. The disaster set their naval capability back years.

20

To the Eye of the Sun

April–November 1511

I N THEIR FIRST DECADE in the Indian Ocean, time, for the Portuguese, moved both fast and slowly. The process of communication
between Lisbon and India was certainly torturous—at least a year and
a half for a royal order to receive a reply—and yet, the learning curve
had been extraordinary: the collation of geographical, cultural, and
linguistic knowledge, the drawing of maps and the nuancing of political understanding had been so rapid that from the perspective of 1510,
the first coming of Vasco da Gama seemed almost like a legend. When
his weather-beaten ships returned in 1499, they brought with them
distant hearsay about Malacca to the effect that "it is forty days' sail
from Calicut with a good wind...all cloves come from there....
There are many big parrots in this country, whose plumage is red like
fire." By 1505, the king was casually ordering Almeida to pry open
new seas: to "discover" Malacca along with Ceylon and China and
"whatever other parts have still not been known" and to plant pillars
as he went. The restless Portuguese were avid for new horizons.

A year later, in 1506, Malacca had moved up to a major strategic
objective: Almeida was ordered to set out at once for these seas, leaving
just a skeleton force on the Malabar Coast. What had jolted the king
was the nagging fear of competition: news of "a certain Castilian
fleet ... that was being got ready this summer to go in search of the

said Malacca." This was tied up with the uncertainties of the Tordesillas treaty. The demarcation line drawn up in 1494 ringed the earth, and the Castilians believed that Malacca lay within their zone of influence in the opposite hemisphere. As Columbus also persisted in the belief that his discoveries were a direct sea route to the Orient, there was grave concern in Lisbon that the Spanish might be capable of sailing west. It seemed like a straight race. Almeida was unable to do more than dispatch two men on a merchant ship that never arrived; as for going himself, the viceroy believed this to be impossible given the threats to his fragile footholds on the Malabar Coast. Impatient of what he perceived to be willful foot-dragging, in 1508 Manuel had sent a small flotilla of ships directly from Lisbon to establish a trading post in Malacca. It was the survivors of this ill-fated expedition who were now being held hostage by the sultan of Malacca, and whose letters were imploring Albuquerque to come.

The Portuguese were also spurred on by a growing appreciation of the value of this city. Strategically situated on the western coast of the Malay Peninsula, dominating the seaway to India, Malacca had grown in less than a century from a poor fishing village to one of the major centers of world trade. "Men cannot estimate the worth of Malacca, on account of its greatness and profit," wrote the Portuguese merchant Tomé Pires. "Malacca is a city that was made for merchandise, fitter than any other in the world; the end of the monsoons and the beginning of others. Malacca is surrounded and lies in the middle, and the trade and commerce between the different nations for a thousand leagues on every hand must come [there]." It connected the trade from the Indian Ocean and all points west with that of the China Sea and the Pacific Ocean. It was the terminus for Chinese trading junks after their withdrawal from the west coast of India. Malacca was called the Eye of the Sun. It was the most cosmopolitan city on earth, where, according to Pires, eighty-four languages could be heard; he listed a whole alphabet of the trading peoples beyond Europe—men from Cairo, Ormuz, Goa, Cambodia, Timor, Ceylon, Java, China, Brunei. Even the parrots were said to be multilingual. It traded the woolen cloth, glass, and ironwork of Venice, the opium and perfumes of Arabia, the pearls of the Persian Gulf, the porcelain of China, the nutmeg of the Bandas, the cloth of Bengal, and the spices of the Moluccas. Larger than Lisbon, it had a population hardly smaller than Venice's, somewhere over 120,000 people. "There is no doubt that Malacca is of such importance and profit that it seems to me it has no equal in the world," wrote Pires. And it was ruled by a Muslim sultan. It was Malacca's wealth as much as the rescue of hostages that Manuel was racing for.

The major players in the arena were the Muslims of Java and of Gujarat. It was too far for the Arabian dhows to make the voyage in one monsoon. Gujarati merchants acted as middlemen for the trade from the western Indian Ocean and were the most potent influence on the sultan of Malacca. Sensing commercial rivalry as in Calicut, they had persuaded the sultan to destroy the Portuguese trading post and take the hostages.

Araujo's letters had given Albuquerque a great deal of information about the city. He had followed the hostages' advice to come with all the force he could muster with the aim of intimidating: he brought eighteen ships, of which twelve were carracks. Manpower was more of a problem. There were only seven hundred Portuguese and three hundred Malabar troops to confront probably an enormous native army, and this was an extremely daring long-range strike. It was fifteen hundred miles across the eastern Indian Ocean, with no easy fallback in case of difficulties. Ships were lost on the way, and Albuquerque's own flagship, the *Frol de la Mar,* was now nine years old and increasingly unseaworthy.

The fleet also followed Araujo's advice to spread fear as they went, capturing Muslim ships and paying threatening visits to Malacca's small vassal principalities on the coast of Sumatra. For many this was a new sea; the dhows of the western Indian Ocean had given way to the sighting of junks from Sumatra and Java, stout, high-sided ships with four masts, "which differ much from the fashion of ours being built of very thick timber." They had ample opportunity to wonder at these vessels. When they encountered a junk that overtopped the mighty *Frol de la Mar,* "no less strong than a castle, because it is of three or four decks one on top of another so that artillery does not harm it," it resisted bombardment from Portuguese cannons for two days. It was only when they succeeded in shooting away the rudder that the vessel was sufficiently disabled to surrender. "And they came down the gangplank on a twenty-degree slope so tall was the junk."

Giovanni da Empoli was again among those who had been dragged along by Albuquerque. He was employed, unwillingly, to land and make overtures to the hostile princes of Sumatra. "He acted like a man who cared little for me," the Florentine complained. Sometime around July 1, the fleet arrived at Malacca, "and having hove to in front of the city, we let down the anchors of the ships without firing artillery or anything, waiting for an embassy from the king to come out from the shore." According to Empoli, the city was "situated near the sea shore, well populated with houses and residences, and it is well over three leagues long, which is a most beautiful thing to see." It sprawled along the shore—palm-thatched houses interspersed with the minarets of mosques in low-lying swampy terrain. At its midpoint a river flowed out into the sea, crossed at the mouth by a stout bridge that divided the city in two.

Malacca lived entirely by trade; behind lay a hinterland of malarial tropical jungle, the lair of tigers and crocodiles. The climate was equatorial, a humid heat capable of sapping the life out of a man in armor. The port was thronged with ships: "between ships and junks, about a hundred sail, besides a great number of rowing boats and sampans of thirty and forty oars," Empoli noted, remarking that "the port is very beautiful, and safe from every wind.... More than two thousand loaded ships can be accommodated ... because the least depth of water over the bar is four fathoms." There were a number of junks from China carrying "white men [who] dress like us in the German fashion with French boots and shoes." Both the Chinese and the Hindu merchants appeared friendly.

What followed was an edgy standoff between sultan and governor. Sultan Mohamed wanted a peace agreement guaranteeing the safe passage of ships, on which his wealth depended, before handing over the hostages. Albuquerque wanted the hostages first. There was a stalemate. The sultan, advised by the Gujarati and Javanese Muslims, was playing the monsoon game, slowing down negotiations until the weather forced the Portuguese out. At the same time, he had the in-

Low-lying Malacca divided by its river. This drawing by Gaspar Correia
was made after its capture and the construction of a fort.

truders carefully watched: he knew how few men they had—and he
prepared his defenses.

Albuquerque lost patience. In mid-July he bombarded the town and
burned some houses on the waterfront, along with the Gujarati junks.
The sultan hurried back to the negotiating table. He dressed the hostages in fine clothes and released them. Albuquerque simply upped his
demands: allow a trading post and a protective fort to be built and pay
a handsome indemnity for losses incurred. He was probably counting
on these stipulations ultimately being rejected and was prepared to
fight. He was helped immensely by the amount of information leaking
out of the city from Araujo and the Chinese. The sultan had a nominal
twenty thousand men, twenty war elephants, cannons, and archers.
Digging down, these numbers were less impressive than they seemed.
The cannons were of poor quality, there was a shortage of powder and
skilled gunners, and in reality there were probably only about four
thousand men armed and ready for combat. The sultan continued to
prevaricate and started to build stout barricades on either side of the
bridge; at the same time, he protected the beach in front with iron
spikes hidden under straw, and sacks of gunpowder.

Araujo pressed the governor to waste no more time; the longer he left it, the more firmly entrenched the defense would become. At the customary war council, Albuquerque urged the captains to support the plan and to understand the full implications: they needed a trading post there because Malacca "is the most populous city of the Indies, positioned at the center and terminus of all the rich commerce and trade that flows through it," but this installation depended on the building of a secure fort. He was insistent on this point. It seemed to be agreed.

The attack was carefully prepared. The key to Malacca was the central bridge over the river: take that and the city would be cut in half. Albuquerque accordingly divided his forces in two—one wing to land on the west bank, where a mosque and the royal palace were situated; the other, led by the governor himself, on the opposite bank, where most of the city was located. The two forces would meet on the bridge. The Chinese offered to assist, but Albuquerque decided to exclude them from the fighting; instead he requested that they provide transport boats to help in landing the men. Two hours before dawn on July 24— the eve of St. James's Day—they launched their attack. Wooden boards were flung down on the beach to protect the men from the booby traps as they advanced to the barricades. The Malaccan cannon fire was largely ineffective and the Portuguese were stoutly armored, but they were met with flights of arrows and by short, thin darts shot from blowpipes, envenomed with poison from a species of fish; once this entered the bloodstream, death was certain within a few days.

Fighting for the bridge became fierce, with Albuquerque's men advancing rapidly. On the other side, as the Portuguese finally stormed the barricade, the sultan decided to enter the contest in person. His twenty war elephants came rampaging down the street, smashing everything in their way, followed by a large body of men. From their castles, archers shot arrows down on the intruders, the mahouts urging on their beasts, which had swords swinging from their tusks. The sultan led the way on the royal elephant. In the face of this terrifying cohort, the Portuguese started to retreat. Just two men stood their ground, confronting the enraged elephant of the king with their lances. One stabbed it in the eye, the other in the stomach. Maddened with pain, the wounded beast, roaring furiously, turned, grabbed its driver, and dashed him to the ground. Pandemonium and wild trumpeting broke out among the elephants following behind. The king managed to slip from his beast and escape, but the charge was halted; the elephants stampeded off, scattering trampled bodies in their wake.

In the smoke and the roaring confusion, amid the whistle of the blow darts and the shouts of "St. James," the Portuguese finally stormed the bridge. It was midday. The sun was at its zenith; after hours of fighting in their plate armor and without food, the men were totally drained by the humidity. Albuquerque ordered the erection of awnings from sails, but the soldiers were simply exhausted—incapable of rousing themselves to reconstruct the barricades needed to secure the hard-won bridge. Albuquerque took the unilateral decision to withdraw, to the fury of his captains, who were anticipating the spoiling of the city. To raise morale in the face of this check, he sent out squads to fire the mosque and some buildings of the king. They came upon a magnificent wooden pavilion mounted on a giant chariot that had thirty wheels, each as high as a room. It had been constructed for the ceremonial marriage procession of the sultan's daughter to a neighboring king, "decked out with silk hangings within and flags without—and it was all burned." This was at least a consolation for a strategic failure. The bridge was abandoned. The Portuguese took with them seventy-two cannons and their wounded. "None of those who had been poisoned by darts survived, except Fernão Gomes de Lemos, whose wound had been scalded with pork fat as soon as he received it. That treatment, after God, was his salvation."

There was an uncertain pause. The sultan declared himself perplexed that his city had been attacked after the release of the hostages, and offered peace. He was temporizing, waiting for the weather to change. The failure of the Portuguese filled him with new confidence. He rebuilt his defenses—the barricades, the booby traps on the beach, whose spikes were now tipped with poison—and he erected internal barriers within the city streets. But Albuquerque had made a solemn vow on his long white beard that vengeance should fall on Malacca, and he would not be denied.

The problem remained the high bridge that commanded the entrance to the city, now more heavily fortified than before. The solution was to overtop it. Probably remembering the remarkable two-day fight with the junk in the Straits of Malacca, which had revealed how tall and how stoutly built these ships were, he commandeered one of the four-masted Javanese junks in the harbor, filled it with cannons, and towed it forward toward the bridge, under the command of António de Abreu. The deep draft of the vessel meant it could advance only on the incoming tide; eventually it was stuck on a sandbar overlooking the bridge. Threatened by the defenders' field of fire, the junk became the focus of intense bombardment. It remained undamaged. Fire rafts packed with wood, pitch, and oil were floated down the river to set it alight. They were prodded away by men in small boats with long iron-tipped harpoons. A musket shot caught Abreu in the face, smashing his teeth and carrying away part of his tongue, but when Albuquerque ordered the injured man to be replaced, Abreu refused point-blank, declaring "as long as he had feet to walk, hands to fight, some tongue left to give commands, that whatever life left that he had he wouldn't give up his post to anyone." Abreu stayed on the junk, ready to pound the bridge.

Albuquerque's preparations for this second attack were more considered. As well as good supplies of crossbows, he ordered the preparation of barrels, pickaxes, spades, and axes so that barricades could be quickly erected once the bridge was stormed; wooden screens were prepared in greater numbers to protect the advancing men from the musket shots and the venomous darts, and more planks to lay down as they splashed onto the beach over the booby-trapped sand. Everything was ready. He gave the Chinese permission to sail away with gifts and blessings. On August 9, he called all the captains and *fidalgos* to another meeting.

It was apparent that many were disgruntled after the failed attack and the governor's unilateral decision to withdraw. The deadly work of the Malaccan blowpipes also genuinely frightened; nor was the idea of building a fortress in the tropical heat appealing. The *fidalgos* always saw this work as demeaning to their status. They would prefer to plunder and go home. In variously reported versions, Albuquerque made an impassioned speech. He sketched out the whole strategic plan for the Indian Ocean. If strangling Muslim trade in the Red Sea was the ultimate goal, Malacca, "the center and terminus of all the rich merchandise and trades," was a critical and connected part. It was "the source of all the spices, drugs and riches of the whole world . . . the route by which more pepper came to Mecca than via Calicut." Its capture would throttle Cairo, Alexandria, and Venice and hinder the spread of Islam: "whoever is lord of Malacca has his hand on the throat of Venice," in the words of Tomé Pires.

Albuquerque understood exactly the nerve centers of Indian Ocean trade and why Malacca mattered. He attempted to reassure the *fidalgos* that, taken and ruled fairly by the Portuguese, it could be held through local alliances, no matter how few men they had. Albuquerque was building an empire, not just sacking a city, but—and here he came to his main point—Malacca could not be held without a fort. Looking his commanders in the eye, he wanted to be certain that they would commit to its construction. He was clear about this. He was not prepared to "disembark the men, nor to fight if the place could not be held with a fort—to risk a single man, no matter how much booty could be taken, would not seem to me in the service of the king my lord." It was a powerful appeal linking empire to crusading zeal, knightly duty—and self-interest. "The golden wall" of Malacca certainly shone brightly in the minds of the listening captains, but Albuquerque would not proceed without the commitment to the fort. It was sheer strength of will that won the day. The *fidalgos,* while probably hoping that Malacca was too short of stone for the construction of forts, declared themselves "ready for everything, and would build a fort"—or, rashly, "even two if necessary." Albuquerque, watching his own back, wisely had their entire testament written down and retained.

On August 10, 1511, on an incoming tide, which they hoped would dislodge the castellated junk from its sandbank and float it even closer to the strategic bridge, the Portuguese prepared to conquer a city of 120,000 people with some thousand men and two hundred Malabars.

It was probably the most disciplined, carefully planned military venture they had yet undertaken. Albuquerque was haunted by the lessons of Calicut and the ghost of Coutinho—the fear that, if they broke the barricades at the sea and took the bridge, the dream of imagined treasure would lure the men feverishly forward into the tangled lanes of an unknown city, where, weighted down with plate armor and exhausted by the stifling heat, they could be picked off and massacred.

The lessons of the first failed attempt had been learned: not to split the men into groups; to take the bridgeheads, dig in, and consolidate; to manage a supply chain to ensure that they could not be repulsed. It worked brilliantly. The junk towered over the bridge, raining shots down on the unprotected Malaccan and Javanese troops. The landing on the west side was efficient and quick; protected by screens and planks, they stormed the barricades and put the sultan's men to flight. The efficient unloading of building materials ensured that stout defenses for the bridge could be constructed at either end. The sultan's men were now divided into two groups. A mosque was taken on the eastern end of the bridge; another spirited attack by the elephants was repulsed. Cannons from the ships fired half shots overhead into the city to intimidate reinforcements. The Portuguese dug in, fortifying two houses near the mosque and planting a battery of cannons on their roofs.

The heat was overwhelming. Albuquerque again constructed awnings to protect his men from the sun; the supply of food and drink was efficient, and the troops were rotated. If the sultan thought that he could lure the Portuguese into an ambush, he was mistaken. Advance into the city was expressly forbidden, on pain of death. Albuquerque resolved to move forward little by little, above all to reduce casualties— the Portuguese were few enough—and to restrain the fervor to loot. Days passed. "We made our stand on the land," according to Empoli, "with our armor on our backs for at least twenty days, guarding the post by day and by night, because from the sea and the land the attacks came every hour, and they gave us a great deal of trouble." The attacks diminished. It was then that the military discipline Albuquerque had started to instill in the men came into its own.

He called out the trained bands to systematically clean out pockets of resistance. They were formed up in squares six by six deep, the iron points of their raised pikes bristling, and marched into the city, with orders not to break ranks and led by local guides who knew the streets. These armored phalanxes, marching to trumpets and the beat of drums and shouts of "Santiago!," were brutally effective. Their orders were not to "spare the lives of the Muslims, their wives, and children wherever they are found." They pushed through the city spearing and trampling. The sultan's soldiers, "who had never seen pikes before," turned and fled. In eight or nine days, the trained bands had swept the city clean. The sultan, together with his family, his retainers, and his elephants, retreated into the jungle. And the *fidalgos,* to whom this style of warfare was distasteful and unheroic, stood by and watched. The city had been secured.

The men, who had endured the heat, the repeated attacks, the mortal dread of the venomous blowpipes, and the governor's iron discipline, were desperate for their reward: a thorough sack of this fabulous Oriental souk. Albuquerque acknowledged that this was their right, but he wanted to preserve a living city, not a smoldering ruin. He imposed a rigorous order on the proceedings. They were allowed one day of looting. The houses of the Hindus, the Javanese, and the Burmese, with whom the Portuguese had formed alliances, were to be excluded from the pillage—their principal residences were marked with flags. No buildings were to be burned. The sultan's palace was not to be touched; its contents were reserved for the crown. Everyone was given a fair turn. The sailors, usually the losers in the free-for-all after a victory, had first pickings. Each cohort was recalled by trumpet signal blast. When they staggered back to the beach with all they could carry, the governor required them to remain with their loot and the next band was dispatched, in a relay that ended at nightfall. The underground cellars of the merchants' houses yielded extraordinarily rich rewards.

Each man decided what to take and what to leave behind in a dash for booty. To the Portuguese, Malacca was an *Arabian Nights* treasure-house of the wealth of the farther Orient. It was a glimpse of what lay to the east of India—and it put the economy of the Malabar Coast into perspective. "Believe me," Empoli wrote to his father, "things here are of great substance, and there are very great things and great walled cities, trade in merchandise and wealth, different customs and ways of living. We are mere nothings; India is the least and poorest thing there is here."

At the end of the day, with the collapse of the sun into the western straits, the streets of Malacca were left strewn with extraordinary merchandise of all sorts: jewels, jars of musk, chests crammed with damask cloth, silks, taffetas, and camphor. "There were rooms full of sandalwood not worth the trouble of carrying away," and rare blue-and-white Chinese porcelain, too fragile and bulky to be worth the bother. Gold bars, jars of gold dust, perfumes, and rare gemstones were the plunder of preference. A large number of iron cannons were carried off, some of which were thought to have been sent by the samudri of Calicut. From the sultan's palace, men under Albuquerque's orders gathered objects of dazzling opulence as gifts for the king, while the governor, who lived with the idea of his own death as much as his life, took for himself six bronze lions to adorn his tomb. The palace was then burned to the ground.

The capture of Malacca, with its huge population, by a few hundred Portuguese in leaky ships had been an extraordinary coup, a risky feat of breathtaking daring and outrageous self-belief, undertaken against vastly superior numbers armed with their own gunpowder weapons. In purely military terms, it stands easy comparison with any of the asymmetrical victories of the Spanish conquistadors in the Americas. However, as Albuquerque had anticipated, the will to hold the city was another matter.

Enriched, the captains, and doubtless the men, were ready to leave. They petitioned the governor to return to India—the fleet could come back another time. Albuquerque had anticipated this reaction. He pointed out that he had their written depositions on the subject of the fort, and declared that if they were to depart without leaving the city "held and secure in the king's name . . . I would deserve to have my head cut off and soul sent to hell . . . don't talk about such a thing. All of us must put ourselves to work with goodwill to make our fort—and do it quickly." Albuquerque was a man in a hurry: the need to consolidate the Portuguese position, the need to leave before the monsoon, the fear of what might be happening in Goa—all these things drove him on.

The doubters were correct to be less than enthusiastic about the task. Constructing a fort by the river in the center of the city turned out to be another kind of hell. Empoli, never one to underplay the difficulty, gave his own account: "The captain-major with some of the men, with great haste by day, and by night with torches, built a fort with wooden planks with many heavy logs around it and much artillery, and in a month made it strong." It was a process of continual consolidation: "as soon as it was strong enough, we set about making one of stone." Doubtless much to the disappointment of the workforce, sufficient stone was pillaged from mosques and houses.

> It was a difficult task carrying the stone on our backs, and every man was laborer, bricklayer, and stonemason.... The fort was built with our arms always besides us in the unbearable heat of the sun, because the position of this country is two degrees north of the equator. The land is low-lying and marshy, inhabited by wild beasts, and this produces in it a great stench and unhealthy air. We had nothing to eat but rice, with the result that all our men became ill.... There was not a man left who was not suffering from a diabolic fever, so that there were dead men in the captain's barracks for two or three days because no one could be found to bury them. I took ill at the beginning of October, and for fifty days I had a continual fever, so severe that I was completely unconscious.

The miasmic conditions, the poor diet, and malaria felled so many Portuguese that they were almost incapable of proceeding. It was left to the local labor to push the work forward. Albuquerque himself shivered with fever but continued to oversee the construction.

The fortress, fear of counterattacks, and sickness had delayed Albuquerque. By the end of 1511, it was time to go or be trapped in Malacca for another year. Albuquerque left a garrison of three hundred men and eight ships, to be crewed by another two hundred. The remaining three ships, the *Frol de la Mar,* the *Emxobregas,* and the *Trini-dade,* were to return to India, carrying with them the bulk of the treasure. He also put fifteen men on a captured junk, to be crewed by Javanese slaves.

The *Frol de la Mar* was one of the trophy ships of the Portuguese fleet. At four hundred tons, it was the largest carrack yet built; equipped with forty cannons, distributed on three decks, its stacked high stern and forecastle made it an intimidating presence among the dhows of the Indian Ocean—a floating fortress that could fire in all directions. At the battle of Diu, it had slammed six hundred cannonballs into the Egyptian fleet in the course of a single day, but its size made it awkward to maneuver in tricky conditions, and it was now old. The average life of a ship on the India run was perhaps four years; the battering of the long voyages and the ravages of the teredo worm turned stout planks to pulp in a short time. By 1512 the *Frol* had been at sea for ten. It was seriously leaky and required continuous patching and pumping. Albuquerque wanted to nurse it back to Cochin and conduct repairs, but the common consensus was that the ship was a death trap. Many of those leaving flatly refused to sail in it. Only the formidable confidence of the governor ensured a crew. Because of its size, it carried the bulk of the treasure as well as many of the sick and wounded and some slaves as presents for the queen.

Empoli, sailing in the *Trinidade,* left his own eyewitness account of what followed. "And so we set out, sailing in very bad weather, because it was already late even if one left Malacca for India on the twentieth day of December." In fact, they were leaving a month later. Six days out, the flotilla was hit by a hurricane.

> At about three o'clock in the night, we heard a thundering noise.... We found ourselves with our ship in barely four fathoms of water. We cast anchor immediately.... The wind was strong and blowing onto the shore, and, when day came, we saw the sea breaking all around us for four or five leagues, because we were in the midst of the shoals. The captain-general's ship was in the shallowest part; a huge wave hit it in the forecastle, and swept away sixteen men, drowned in the sea.

The *Frol* was in trouble, now leaking badly and unable to maneuver with the burden of its cargo and the growing weight of water. It had also anchored to ride out the storm, but water was coming in so fast that the pumps were useless. According to Empoli, "another wave struck it, and the rudder broke off, and it swung sideways and ran aground. It immediately filled with water; the crew gathered on the poop deck, and stood there awaiting God's mercy."

It was time to abandon ship. Albuquerque ordered some of the masts cut down and lashed together to make a crude raft. The sick and wounded were put in the one ship's boat, while the remaining crewmen were transferred to the raft in a rowboat. Albuquerque, with one rope tied around his waist and the other tethered to the *Frol,* steered the skiff back and forward until all the Portuguese had been taken off. Disciplined to the last, he ordered all to leave the ship in just jacket and breeches; anyone who wanted to keep any possessions could stay behind. As for the slaves, they could fend for themselves. Their only recourse was jumping into the sea; those who could not swim drowned. Some were able to cling to the raft but were prevented at the point of a spear from climbing aboard and overloading it. At sea, it was always survival of the most important. Behind them the *Frol* broke in two, so that only her poop deck and mainmast were visible above the water. The ship's boat and the raft drifted through the night, "and so they stayed with their souls in their mouths begging God's mercy, until dawn, when the wind and the sea abated."

In the confusion of the night, the *Emxobregas,* farther ahead, took soundings and decided to save itself, sailing away from the wreckage. The captive crewmen of the junk, seizing the moment, murdered their Portuguese masters and made off with the ship and a vast amount of valuable merchandise. Only the *Trinidade* was close enough to help, but it was also in great trouble, according to Empoli, "and touching bottom, so that we had to throw overboard all the deck fittings and the artillery and part of the spices, commending ourselves to God, because I could see no other solution, as there was no hope of anyone being saved by swimming because of the great extent of the water." With the morning light and the sea calming, they were able to make out the raft, with a makeshift flag hoisted on a spear as a signal.

The survivors were taken aboard the *Trinidade.* "In the ship . . . there were about two hundred of us, and we did not have enough to eat and drink for so many people . . . so many people came on board . . . that it threw us into great confusion." Despite the shortage of food, Albuquerque, anxious about the state of Cochin and Goa in his absence, refused to agree to a landing for supplies, "urging the need in which India stood, and many other reasons." The governor's intransigence made the voyage to Cochin a nightmare, if Empoli is to be believed. "We found ourselves in great trouble and want; we were reduced to six ounces of rotten biscuit and a mouthful of water. . . . The complaints and murmuring [were] so great . . . that the captain shut himself in his cabin so that no one saw him." Some Muslim captives were thrown overboard while they slept to reduce the number of mouths to feed. And so they "made their way to Cochin, where they arrived with a great deal of work at the pumps, half dead," with nothing but the clothes they stood up in. According to one source, Albuquerque had saved a crown, a sword of gold, and a ruby ring sent by the king of Siam as a present for Manuel.

Behind them, only the superstructure of the *Frol de la Mar* remained visible above the Sumatran reef, and somewhere beneath the sea lay all the treasure from the king's palace and a great deal more beside. "I heard [him] say," wrote Correia in a rare personal reminiscence, "that in the king's house they had found a four-legged table with stones worth seventy thousand cruzados." In the *Frol* "was lost a greater wealth of gold and jewels than were ever lost in any part of India, or ever would be." All of this had vanished into the depths, besides the gems and bars of gold intended for the king and queen, along with beautiful slaves drowned in the catastrophe and the bronze lions Albuquerque had reserved for his own memorial. And there was something else, equally precious to the geographically hungry Portuguese as they attempted to take more and more of the world into their comprehension and their grasp. It was a fabulous world map, of which only a portion survived. Albuquerque lamented its loss to the king:

a great map drawn by a Javanese pilot, which showed the Cape of Good Hope, Portugal and the land of Brazil, the Red Sea and the

Persian Gulf, the spice islands, the sailing routes of the Chinese and the people of Formosa [Taiwan], with the rhumbs [lines marking compass bearings] and the courses taken by their ships and the interiors of the various kingdoms which border on each other. It seems to me, sire, that it's the best thing I've ever seen, and Your Highness would have been delighted to see it. The place names are written in the Javanese script. I had a Javanese who knew how to read and write it. I send this fragment . . . in which Your Highness will be able to see where the Chinese and the Formosans really come from, and the routes your ships must take to the spice islands, and where the gold mines are, the islands of Java and Banda, source of nutmeg and mace, and the kingdom of Siam, and also the extent of Chinese navigation, where they return to and the point beyond which they don't voyage. The main map was lost in the *Frol de la Mar.*

But Albuquerque was already using the new bridgehead of Malacca to seek out and explore these seas for himself. He sent embassies to Pegu (Bago in Burma), Siam (Thailand), and Sumatra; an expedition visited and mapped the spice islands of eastern Indonesia in 1512; reaching farther east, ships sent to China in 1513 and 1515 landed at Canton and sought trade relations with the Ming dynasty. He was tying together the farthest ends of the world, fulfilling everything Manuel could demand.

Unfortunately for the Portuguese, these bold extensions had unforeseen consequences. The Malacca strike had been partially undertaken to snuff out Spanish ambitions in the Far East. Instead it provided the personnel, the information, and the maps to advance them. Among those at Malacca was Fernão de Magalhães (Magellan); he returned to Portugal, wealthy from the booty, with a Sumatran slave, baptized as Henrique. When Magalhães quarreled with King Manuel and defected to Spain, he took Henrique with him, as well as Portuguese maps of the spice islands and detailed letters from a friend who had made the voyage. All these he put to use a few years later in the first circumnavigation of the world, under the flag of Spain, during which Henrique was to prove an invaluable interpreter—knowledge that allowed Portugal's rival to claim the spice islands of the East Indies as its own.

21

The Wax Bullet

April 1512–January 1513

Albuquerque arrived in Cochin like a man back from the grave, dressed just in a gray jacket and breeches. His arrival was not a completely pleasant surprise. Since the return of the Ormuz mutineers in 1508, Cochin had become the center of a strong faction opposed to the governor. Every fleet returning to Lisbon carried letters to the king detailing his excesses. "Those who wanted to take revenge on your undertakings," Albuquerque wrote to Manuel, "they proclaimed that I was dead, lost along with the whole fleet."

The apparently indestructible governor stepped ashore to find that corruption, abuse, and incompetence had reigned in his absence. His orders had not been obeyed; his appointees had been slighted; the *casados* married to local women had been excommunicated; men stole and absconded; discipline was lax. Over the next few months, he fired off twenty thousand words of high-voltage rhetoric to the king, in which he laid before his sovereign exactly what should be done to control the ocean, and he claimed the authority of long experience: "I am fifty years old and I have seen two kings before you and what they did in their time." This was not exactly flattering to the present incumbent.

It is a letter that reveals the empire builder in action—exasperated, direct, passionate, and apparently all-seeing. At times he is breathlessly blunt, railing against the *fidalgos* for their indiscipline (they "feel free to do as they please ... and care not a jot for my decisions"); castigating his monarch for lavishing resources on campaigns in Morocco, "yet you abandon India"; irate at the lack of men, materials, and money—not least the rotten ships—and bitter at the dire results: "Does Your Highness know the consequences of neglect and the necessity in which I find myself? I've had to take Malacca twice, Goa twice, make two attacks on Ormuz, and travel on the sea on a raft to remedy your affairs and fulfill my duties."

At times he is downright rude but always fiercely loyal, full of advice but strangely humble, boundlessly self-confident but afflicted by a sense of sin. No detail seems too small to convey to the king. He is sending pulleys to Malacca, along with "two fine robes" for church vestments; he needs church organs and medium-sized missals, "people to dig ditches and make walls," masons to build forts and construct water mills at Malacca, "where there is a great flow of water at high tide"; he puts in requests for carpenters and captains experienced in the Swiss tactics to train his companies. He frets over attempts by clergymen to subvert the mixed-marriage policy and notes that "in Cochin I found a chest of books for teaching children [to read] and it seemed to me that Your Highness had not sent them to rot away in a chest, so I ordered a *casado* here to teach the little boys to read and write"; he comments that "they are very intelligent and learn what they are taught in a short time. They are all Christians." Above all, he asks for men. He is forever counting the numbers available. They are always too few. Over and over: "And again I come back to saying that if you want to avoid war in India and have peace with all the kings here, you must send plenty of troops and good weapons."

In the torrent of words Albuquerque addressed to Manuel he sketched all the dimensions—military, political, economic, social, and religious—of the empire he was single-handedly trying to build with just a few thousand men. This highly intelligent, tortured man reiterated a core of cast-iron principles for dominating the Indian Ocean: "Sire, put your trust in good fortresses"; "Kings and lords cannot easily take fortresses from Portuguese soldiers with helmets on their heads among the battlements.... Places here, controlled by Your Highness with a good fort, once taken will remain so until Judgement Day."

Good forts linked to the control of the choke points of the seas would grant the Portuguese a complete domination. His praise for his key military architect, Tomás Fernandes, was boundless.

"Trust in good fortresses": Tomás Fernandes, Albuquerque's military
architect, built a network of stout forts along the Indian coast
capable of withstanding prolonged sieges.

In the process, Albuquerque was consolidating a revolutionary concept of empire. The Portuguese were always aware of how few they were; many of their early contests were against vastly unequal numbers. They quickly abandoned the notion of occupying large areas of territory. Instead, they evolved as a mantra the concept of flexible sea power tied to the occupation of defendable coastal forts and a network of bases. Supremacy at sea; their technological expertise in fortress building, navigation, cartography, and gunnery; their naval mobility and ability to coordinate operations over vast maritime spaces; the tenacity and continuity of their efforts—an investment over decades in shipbuilding, knowledge acquisition, and human resources—these facilitated a new form of long-range seaborne empire, able to control trade and resources across enormous distances. It gave the Portuguese ambitions with a global dimension.

Yet up close, the India venture often seemed surprisingly ramshackle, dependent on extraordinary individual initiative. "Sire," Albuquerque wrote in complaint to the king, "to make fortresses requires planning and here in India we are not able to do this. We set out in the fleet with a little rice and a few coconuts, and each man with his own weapons, if he has any. . . . The equipment is in your storehouses in Lisbon." It is the frustration of the man on the ground, tugging at the sleeve of a distant superior, desperate to be heard—"Your Highness should not ignore the things that I say"—and aware of malicious counterbriefing. Rumors of his replacement were continually circulated. "I fear that you don't want to favor this endeavour during my time here, because of my sins, old and new," he wrote. "I am kept down and I lack Your Highness's trust." Above all, he was fearful of being swept away before his work could be done. India was the project of Albuquerque's life.

Linked to the fortress policy was a belief he shared with all the commanders who had preceded him in the necessity for exemplary violence:

> I tell you, sire, the one thing that's most essential in India: if you want to be loved and feared here, you must take full revenge . . . it makes no small impression in India seeing the vengeance taken at Malacca and Goa and no small amazement the burning of the samu-dri's palaces and the habitations, mosques and ships of the Muslims. The events that I speak of brought us much credit and favor in the affairs of India.

He knew exactly what the king wanted: "to destroy the trade of Mecca, Jeddah and Cairo," and this involved "taking the main centers of this trade from the Muslims." Now crucial was the long-delayed entry into the Red Sea. What remained unspoken in the correspondence, but understood by both men, was that this was to be the platform for the total destruction of the Mamluks and, in Manuel's millennial plan, the recapture of Jerusalem.

The cornerstone for this final assault on the centers of Muslim power remained Goa. Goa was Albuquerque's mantra and his obsession. Again and again in the face of sniping from his enemies that the fort there should be demolished, he made the case for the island:

"Strongly support Goa and you will thus gain all its territory. . . . [It is] certain to become peaceful and of great service to you." "Sire, it would greatly please me if Your Highness could but see Goa and how it has destroyed the fantasies of the Muslims and pacified India." It took a man with Albuquerque's strategic genius and self-confidence to understand the value of the place.

In fact, at the time of writing, Goa was again under siege. His anxiety while in Malacca had been justified. Instructions for the maintenance of the island had been neglected. Adil Shah had sent a large army back to claim his rightful territory; his soldiers had forced a passage across the fords and erected a substantial fort of their own on the island, at the strategic crossing of Benastarim. From there they had surrounded the city and were holding it under tight siege. Yet again, the expedition to the Red Sea was to be postponed until Goa was secured.

For once, Albuquerque did not hurry. The monsoon was about to render relief impractical. The returning survivors of the Malacca campaign were exhausted; warfare, death, and the need to leave a large number of men and ships in Malacca rendered his forces too small to be effective. He needed to wait until the annual fleet arrived from Lisbon. In the meantime, Albuquerque put his faith in the Goa fort. "With God's help," he had written to the king, "if there is no treachery, there is no need to fear the Muslims attacking your fortresses."

After a desperate start, Portuguese morale in Goa improved over the summer of 1512. It was raised particularly by the defection back to Goa of João Machado, Adil Shah's renegade interpreter, fervent to return to the religion of his birth. The circumstances of this were tinged with a terrible pathos. Machado had a Muslim wife and two children, whom he had secretly baptized as Christians. When the moment came to slip away, he could take only his wife; rather than leave his children in the infidel faith, he drowned them, that they might go directly to heaven. Machado brought with him only a handful of men, but he was privy to the inner plans of the shah's generals, understood their tactics extremely well, and was informed on their resources and the shortcomings of their fort. Spirits were further raised when word reached the fort at Goa that the governor was still alive. Bells pealed from the converted mosque; the garrison wrote that they could hold out but that he needed to come in force.

In mid-August, the Lisbon fleet arrived at Cochin. It did not, as Albuquerque's enemies hoped, bring a replacement governor; instead it provided the governor with as much as he could hope for by way of reinforcements and equipment: twelve ships and fifteen hundred extremely well-equipped men. He was overjoyed: "Sire, now it seems you have decided to treat India worthily." Of particular delight, Manuel had answered his request for trained officers. He sent two captains who were veterans of Swiss tactics in the Italian wars, and company sergeants, as well as three hundred pikes, fifty crossbows, and a supply of muskets. Under their direction, a corps of eight hundred men was formed, divided into thirty-two platoons. Serious training began. The soldiers were bidden to shooting practice on a regular basis, with money prizes for the best shot, and drilled in squad maneuvers, so that they wheeled in synchronized formations as an effective unit rather than in a ragged free-for-all. Best of all, these men were now under Albuquerque's direct command.

With the monsoon over, the governor was ready to move, supremely confident that he could dislodge the Turkish troops, despite the usual disparity in the numbers. The Red Sea beckoned. He wanted to take Goa back quickly and then to use this powerful new force to at least block the throat of the Red Sea within the span between monsoons.

Albuquerque arrived at Goa in late October 1512. By the end of November, it was all over. Throwing caution to the wind, he first isolated Benastarim from the mainland by destroying its defensive stakes in the river. From there he was able to go to the city of Goa to conduct operations against the shah's forces. After a short, sharp field battle and a siege that, for once, saw the Portuguese on the outside pummeling city walls, the shah's general was ready to raise the white flag.

The captains fought with their usual heedless gallantry. The river fighting was particularly fierce. From the walls of Benastarim, accurate artillery fire wiped the surface of the water, raking the Portuguese boats, which had been armored with stout coir padding. The weight of fire left men temporarily deaf. Even Albuquerque had to scold the ship commanders for taking unnecessary risks. "I often upbraided them for exposing recklessly their persons and their lives ... and they would walk upon the castles of the ships and stand about in the most dangerous places. ... Sometimes I was quite pained to see their disregard of all precaution." Yet he never shielded himself from the dangers of battle. A cannonball from the Muslim fort smashed into his small boat, annihilating two of the oarsmen. The Turks thought they had killed him and yelled triumphantly, at which Albuquerque stood up in full view of the fort to show their mistake. His legendary escapes made his enemies, as much as his friends, believe that he must be indestructible. When it came to the final artillery bombardment of Benastarim, he was again in the front line, scrutinizing the disposition of the troops. He was spotted by the enemy gunners, who directed their fire at him. Diogo Mendes de Vasconcelos, one of the *fidalgos* with whom he was at odds, suggested that he take cover. For once, Albuquerque acted on advice. He was ducking behind a rock when a cannonball caught a man beside him, spattering him with blood.

The tactical disagreement between the honor fighting of the *fidalgos* and the strategic deployment of men that Albuquerque wanted remained a running sore. Where the nobles wished to wield their enormous two-handed swords in heroic single combat, winning booty and polishing their reputations, the governor wanted to deploy organized bodies of men in coherent tactics. The trained bands proved effective. The compact body of men, composed of pikemen, archers, and musketeers, wheeling across the battlefield in good order, forced the loose skirmishing Turks back to the walls in open fighting. They comprised "a phalanx well ordered ... locked together, their pikes bristling and eight regimental flags and drums and pipes"; they advanced slowly in close formation firing "many muskets which came this year from Portugal." Albuquerque had seen the future of warfare—and it was not popular. That cannon fire rather than scaling the walls decided the outcome went deeply against a medieval military culture. In the face of bitter opposition from those who wanted to storm and sack the town with a pointless loss of life, he negotiated a surrender. All the Muslims, their wives and children could depart unharmed. Everything else—cannons, horses, weapons—must be left behind. The people would be conducted safely across the river in the clothes they were wearing and nothing more. Just one sticking point remained: there were a number of Portuguese and other renegades in the shah's army, who must be surrendered. The general was deeply reluctant to give them up as converts to Islam. Finally a deal was brokered. Albuquerque would spare their lives.

The Muslims were safely evacuated without being harmed. Albuquerque kept his word with the renegades, too: their lives were spared—just. For three days they sat in the stocks being jeered at, pelted with mud, having their beards plucked out. On the second day they had their noses and ears cut off; on the third, their right hands and their left thumbs. Then their wounds were dressed. Many died; those who survived "bore their sufferings with much patience," saying that "their grievous sin deserved an even greater punishment." Albuquerque's evolving methods of warfare had been clinical, economical on manpower, and quick, but in many quarters they were unpopular. His detractors spread it about that he had let the enemy go to fight another day in return for a hefty bribe. In fact, Albuquerque was confident that he did not need to kill all these men. He realized that Benastarim was the key to the island. He rebuilt its fort, reorganized the defenses at all the other fords, and locked the island tight shut. The trained bands continued their drills. He knew that Goa was permanently secured for the Portuguese crown—all that could undermine it was the sniping from the factions in Cochin and Cannanore.

With this further defeat of Adil Shah, Portugal became an Asiatic power. When Goa had first been taken, in 1510, a Cochin merchant had declared that "the governor has turned the key that gives India to his king"—by this he meant the coastal trade of the Indies. The great continental powers of the subcontinent, Bijapur and Vijayanagar, were hardly under any direct threat from such puny forces, but the Portuguese were now a player in the game. It had been Albuquerque's genius to understand the strategic importance of Goa, on the fault line between the two warring powers and a better commercial hub than Calicut or Cochin could ever be. Crucially he now controlled the Persian horse trade; ships bringing the animals from Ormuz were funneled into Goa by his warships, where the merchants and their valuable cargo were extremely well provided for. A thousand horses a year

passed through the island; the profits for the crown were huge—
between 300 and 500 percent.

Albuquerque himself was the first European since Alexander the
Great to establish an imperial presence in Asia. With his long white
beard and his frightening demeanor, he was regarded across the Indian
Ocean with superstitious awe. Along the Malabar Coast, they named a
local fish afonso-de-albuquerque after him, and used it in magic spells.
His Bengali enemies cursed him as the Great Dog of India. He turned
his fierce intelligence to the interlocking commercial and imperial
contests of the ocean—Hindus and Muslims, Shias and Sunnis, Mamluks and Persians, Vijayanagar and Bijapur, Ormuz and Cambay, Calicut and Cochin, and the survival stratagems of the wily Malik Ayaz in
Diu. He entered this political game with great astuteness, playing one
faction off against another, and without illusions. He put no faith in
pacts and pledges of friendship and wrote accordingly to disabuse
Manuel of the realities of Indian Ocean diplomacy:

> You aim to lay your hands on their trade and to destroy the Mecca
> trade and you're astonished that they do all they can to prevent
> you! ... Your Highness thinks one can keep them with good words,
> offers of peace and protection ... but the only thing they respect is
> force. When I arrive with a fleet the first thing they try to find out
> is how many men and what armaments we have. When they judge
> us invincible they give us a good reception and trade with us in
> good faith. When they find us weak, they procrastinate and prepare
> unpredictable responses. No alliance can be established with any
> king or lord without military support.

Everyone was forced to address the new reality of a permanent Portuguese presence. Ambassadors flocked to Goa at the end of 1512 to
pay their respects. Albuquerque had come to understand the extent of
the Muslim presence in the Indian Ocean and that realistically, it was
ineradicable. He moved to seek a skillful accommodation with rival
Islamic potentates in his pursuit of the destruction of the Mamluks. He
manipulated Vijayanagar and Bijapur, both anxious for the horse trade.
He entered into relations with the Muslim sultan of Gujarat and sent

another ambassador, Miguel Ferreira, to the Shia shah Ismail in Persia; this envoy was more fortunate than his poisoned predecessor. The samudri at last appeared to accept the permanence of the Portuguese and sent offers of peace and the site for a fort. Albuquerque accepted but made other plans. His old sparring partner in Diu, Malik Ayaz, was particularly keen to know his intentions. Albuquerque was petitioning Ayaz's lord, the sultan of Cambay, for permission to build a fort at Diu, and Ayaz was fervently hoping this would not be granted.

Ayaz's emissary was treated to a master class in intimidation. João Machado, the returned renegade, took the unfortunate man on a tour of the shattered defenses of Benastarim, wrecked by Portuguese cannon fire, shunted him around the impressive stabling for the horse trade, the armories and warehouses, and showed him the massive bombards that had done the damage, into which he was invited to thrust his turbaned head to get a true sense of their mighty size. To finish off, he was strapped into a steel breastplate and stood against a wall while a soldier aimed a musket at his chest. With the crack of the shot, the man thought his last hour had come. The bullet bounced harmlessly off. Albuquerque explained to his trembling visitor that Portuguese armor was bulletproof and told him to take the breastplate to his master as evidence. It was all intended to unnerve. Doubtless if Malik Ayaz had risked the same experiment—which might possibly have been at the very back of Albuquerque's mind—he would have been killed. The bullet had been a wax dummy.

As for the samudri, who was now petitioning for peace, Albuquerque had a more cynical solution. He suggested to the samudri's brother, who was pro-Portuguese, that a simple poisoning might clear matters up. The samudri duly died; his successor became a Portuguese puppet. The governor could write to Manuel that he had finally got "this goat by the neck." The Calicut problem was solved, almost bloodlessly. In due time the city would become a regional backwater, its active trade siphoned off to Goa. The same fate befell the two ports that had actively supported the Portuguese, Cannanore and Cochin. There were no long-term rewards for supporting monopoly imperialists.

In the midst of this, an ambassador arrived in Goa from Ethiopia, a dubious character named Matthew who brought a letter and a frag-

ment of the True Cross from Eleni, its dowager queen, on behalf of the
adolescent king, the long-hoped-for Prester John. This direct contact
elicited both fervent excitement and the suspicion that Matthew was
a charlatan. The Ethiopians proposed an alliance with the Portuguese
to break the power of the Muslims to their north; they even suggested
a scheme to divert the course of the upper Nile, which watered the
fertile deltas of Egypt. It was the kind of grandiose idea likely to appeal
to Albuquerque, who believed that Matthew was genuine and sent
him back with the spice fleets that winter to Manuel, by whom he was
well received. It seemed that everything was falling into Albuquerque's
hands.

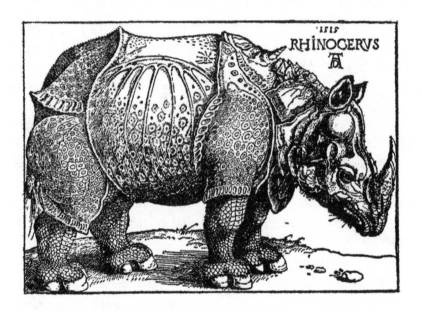

Dürer's impression of King Manuel's rhinoceros

It was probably at the same time that he sent two rare animals to
Manuel, one a white elephant, a gift from the king of Cochin, the
second an equally rare white rhino, from the sultan of Cambay—the
first live rhinoceros seen in Europe since the time of the Romans.
The animals caused a sensation in Lisbon. The elephant was paraded
through the streets and a fight arranged between the two animals in a

specially built enclosure, in the presence of the king. The elephant, however, taking the measure of his opponent, fled in terror. In 1514, Manuel determined on a spectacular public projection of the majesty of his reign and his conquests of India. He delivered the white elephant to the pope under the command of his ambassador, Tristão da Cunha. A cavalcade of 140 people, including some Indians, and an assortment of wild animals—leopards, parrots, and a panther—entered Rome, watched by a gawping crowd. The elephant, led by his mahout, carried a silver castle on his back with rich presents for the pope, who christened him Hanno, after Hannibal's elephants in Italy.

At the papal audience, Hanno bowed three times and amused and alarmed the cardinals of the Holy Church by spraying the contents of a bucket of water over them. He was an immediate animal star—painted by artists, memorialized by poets, the subject of a now lost fresco and a scandalous satirical pamphlet, *The Last Will and Testament of the Elephant Hanno*. He was housed in a specially constructed building, took part in processions, and was greatly loved by the pope. Unfortunately, Hanno's diet was ill-advised, and he died two years after his arrival, aged seven, having been dosed with a laxative laced with gold. The grieving Leo X was at his side and buried him with honor.

Even less fortunate was Manuel's follow-up gift, the rhinoceros, dispatched from Lisbon in a green velvet collar. The ship was wrecked off the coast of Genoa in 1515. The chained animal drowned and was washed up on the seashore. Its hide was recovered, returned to Lisbon, and stuffed. Albrecht Dürer saw a letter describing the creature, and possibly a sketch. He produced his famous print without ever having set eyes on the animal.

The wealth pouring into Lisbon was fabulous. If little of it was plowed back into India, which was Albuquerque's constant complaint, it was in part because Manuel knew how to spend it. The most diverse goods of the world were on sale: objects in ivory and lacquered wood, Chinese porcelain and Oriental carpets, tapestries from Flanders, velvets from Italy. The city was a swirl of color, a febrile gold rush of floating populations of many races and colors. There were gypsies and converted

Jews, and black slaves who arrived in terrible conditions, "piled up in
the holds of ships, twenty-five, thirty or forty at a time, badly fed,
shackled together back to back." New luxurious crazes infected the
city; black household slaves became commonplace; the influx of sugar
produced a revolution in taste. And Lisbon was a theater for permanent spectacle, enlivened by gypsy music and the exotic singing and
dancing of the Africans in religious processions. Here one might watch
the king processing through the streets with five Indian elephants "that
went in front of him, preceded by a rhinoceros—so far ahead that it
couldn't be seen by them—and in front of the king a horse covered
with a rich Persian cloth, at the heels of which came a Persian hunter
leading a jaguar, sent to him by the king of Ormuz."

The echoes of the Orient on the shores of the Tejo were reflected
in the style and grandeur of the building projects Manuel initiated in
the years after 1500. Most ambitious was the construction of the immense monastery at Belém, close to the Restelo beach from where
ships sailed for the Orient. The Jerónimos Monastery, three hundred
yards long, whose monks were bidden to pray for the souls of mariners, was designed both as a fitting pantheon for Manuel's dynasty and
as a celebration of the new worlds discovered in his reign. Funded
from the immense proceeds of the pepper trade, its Gothic medieval
structure was overlaid with a riot of carvings bursting from the stone-
work, as exuberant as the ornamentation on a Hindu temple. This
extraordinary Manueline decoration, developed in a host of churches,
castles, and palaces, sprouting from arches, window frames, and the
roofs of buildings, depicted the symbolism of the maritime voyages
and the discoveries of the Indies. Wreathed around Manuel's proprie-
tary heraldic symbol—the navigational device of the armillary
sphere—were stone anchors and anchor chains, twisted ropes, corals
and seaweed, seashells, pearls, and exotic foliage.

The exuberant organic forms lend these buildings sometimes the
air of a tropical forest or an encrusted submarine cavern sunk on the
floor of the Indian Ocean. The symbols, repeated in stone again and
again, along with the distinctive cross of the crusading Order of Christ,
conjured the rewards and the novelty of the Indies venture. Offshore
at the Restelo beach, Manuel ordered the construction of a defensive

The tower of Belém

The Jerónimos Monastery

fort: the tower of Belém, a fantasy construction as much as a military bastion, standing alone in the sea and emblazoned with these decorative devices. Among the hemispherical watchtowers, like ribbed pineapples girded by ropes, and battlements bearing the shields of the Order of Christ, the stone carvers modeled the head of the white rhinoceros, lifting its horned snout out to sea—an image of marvel and surprise at what the Portuguese had done.

In Goa in the winter of 1513, Manuel's executive officer, Afonso de Albuquerque, was preparing the final encirclement of the Indian Ocean: entry into the Red Sea.

22

"All the Riches of the World in Your Hands"

February–July 1513

THE RED SEA HAD been waiting for years. Its importance had been stressed in Almeida's *regimento* as early as 1505. Another eight were to pass before the Portuguese were ready. By the start of 1513, Goa's fort was redoubtable, the samudri had been poisoned, and Albuquerque had secured the peace of the Indian coast to his satisfaction. The moment had come for the crucial assault.

The ostensible objective was finally to sever the Mamluks' supply line to the East, killing their spice trade—and that of Venice in the process. Behind it lay the messianic dream—to bring Islam to its knees; to regain Jerusalem; for Manuel to be acclaimed the king of kings. The recent arrival of the Abyssinian ambassador had heightened anticipation that they could link up with the army of Prester John and destroy "the Whore of Babylon." These deeper purposes, controversial even within court circles, the governor kept close to his chest as he sailed from Goa in February 1513. The rank and file, pious as they might be, were more interested in the material opportunities for plunder than the triumph of a Christian Kingdom of Heaven on earth.

The Red Sea, a fourteen-hundred-mile gash in the desert separating Arabia from the African continent, was inhospitable terrain. Shallow, lacking in sources of fresh water, made treacherous to navigation by its low-lying islands and hidden shoals, blasted by desert winds and subject to the meteorological rhythms of the Indian Ocean, whose rain failed before its mouth, it could be entered only at certain seasons. It was impossible to sail without local pilots, who would have to be captured or coerced. The Bab el Mandeb strait, the "Gates of Woe," formed the half-open jaws of a potential trap—a suffocating furnace where men might dream of water in vain. Once inside, the Portuguese would be entering the ancient heartlands of the Islamic world. From there it was 650 sea miles to Jeddah, 1,350 to Suez; tracks across the desert from Suez reached Cairo in three days; from Jeddah to Medina, where the body of the Prophet lay, in nine. The men of the Iberian Peninsula felt they were sailing toward the temple of the Antichrist. They were spurred on by centuries of crusading zeal.

Albuquerque's first objective was the fortified port of Aden, 110 miles outside the Gates. Captured, it could provide a secure base camp for a final push. The sheikh of Aden and the sultan in Cairo were not on the best of terms, but with the dislocations to the spice trade caused by the Portuguese, Aden had become an important stopover for Red Sea dhows.

On April 22, 1513, the governor's fleet was rocking off the port. Aden lay before them, cradled in the crater of a dormant volcano, encircled by nine formidable and utterly barren peaks of purple rock, each surmounted by a fort. It was effectively situated in a desert, "surrounded by bare rock, without trees or grass, two or three years pass without any rain falling," Albuquerque later observed. The seaward mouth of the town was sealed by a long and high fortress wall, with one gateway and punctuating towers. Behind, they could see minarets, tall whitewashed houses dazzling in the sun, and the dominating cube of the sheikh's palace—and another line of fortifications enclosing the town from behind. It was unclear at the time to the watching Europeans whether Aden was situated on an island—only subsequent exploration would reveal that it was connected to the mainland by a causeway. To their left, a projecting headland was capped by a fort with a battery of cannons. The harbor, a crescent-shaped bay, was full of ships. "As our carracks were big . . . we stayed a little outside it," Albuquerque wrote of their approach.

It was Good Friday. The weather was already hot. The arrival on the day of Christ's death was both an incentive and a provocation. Crusading fervor was high: "the men were ready, fully armed and keen to set their hands to the task of fighting," Albuquerque later wrote to Manuel during the course of a long explanatory letter. The sheikh was away from the city, but its governor, Amir Mirzan, politely dispatched a messenger to find out what the visitors required. Albuquerque went straight to the point. He was on his way to Jeddah and Suez to destroy the Mamluk fleet. He refused the food the governor sent, as "it was not my practice to accept presents from principalities and rulers with whom we had not agreed peace treaties." He demanded that Amir "should open the city gates and admit our flag and our men." Amir offered to come in person to parley. Pointless, said Albuquerque. The men started sharpening their weapons.

Albuquerque knew he had to work fast, before reinforcements could be fed into the town from the surrounding desert. More important, the severity of Aden's climate made the window of opportunity perilously narrow. They were already encountering the key strategic problem of the Red Sea: "because of our lack of water it seemed to me that, if we captured the city but did not take the gate out to the mountains behind, all our efforts would be wasted and because of our need we would have to withdraw to the ships." There was no debate, no hesitation—just a simple plan, which in retrospect he admitted to be almost none at all. "We had no other plan than to arm ourselves and serve you in spirit and deed. All we did was agree to attack in two places and to split our men into three units." Otherwise, given the auspicious Easter moment, there was a trust that "Our Lord would provide us with everything else." The *fidalgos* and their men-at-arms had to be kept apart from the trained militia, because of the rivalry between the two. Each group was given scaling ladders. "We took battering rams, crowbars, spades and pickaxes, to destroy a stretch of the wall with gunpowder." Two hours before dawn, the trumpet sounded. The men embarked in small boats and pushed off to the shore. "The sight of the city at dawn with the sun coming up was an awe-inspiring prospect," according to Correia, one of the governor's secretaries, who left not only a written account but also a drawing of Aden, "stretched out along the sea shore, shaped like a curved bay, which the boats

Gaspar Correia's drawing of the attack on Aden

could only reach at high tide, fronted by an intimidating wall with many round towers."

It started badly. The boats grounded in the shallows, a crossbow shot from the beach, and they had to wade a considerable distance ashore. The captains were drenched; the musketeers' powder was spoiled in the surf. The *fidalgos* neglected to line their men up properly. Desperate for personal glory, they preferred to climb the ladders themselves for the honor of being first onto the wall—"which grieved me considerably," Albuquerque later wrote, "because they did their duty as knights but neglected their men remaining at the foot of the wall in disarray." The walls were high and the ladders too short to reach to the top, so that the front men had to haul themselves laboriously over the parapet. The first up were two *fidalgos,* Garcia de Sousa and Jorge da Silveira, accompanied by a page with a flag. Lower down, an eager scrum of men attempted to scramble up behind them, but the delay at the top caused a jam on the rungs; very quickly, the attack descended into chaos. Albuquerque described how "the ladder of the trained bands, which could carry a hundred men up to the top of the wall at a time" began to give way. "When I saw the great weight of men on it, I ordered it to be supported by the halberdiers ... who propped it up on both sides with their halberds, but the ladder still collapsed and shattered the halberds into pieces and badly injured the men."

By this time, the Muslim defenders, sensing confusion, had roused themselves and were putting up a determined resistance, hurling rocks and arrows down on the men below the wall. Attempts to batter open the main gate failed. It had been comprehensively blocked. Eventually gunpowder blasted a hole in the wall. It now required one man to take the lead. The commander on the spot, Dom Garcia de Noronha, Albuquerque's nephew, failed to do so. A subsequent judgment suggested that jealousy, if not cowardice, was at stake: "he refused to enter, because of envy of Garcia de Sousa who had entered first, so that if the city were taken, he would get all the glory ... and not wanting to enter, none of the other men wanted to either. If they had, the city would have been taken." The day was to be a series of "ifs."

At the walls there was confusion and incoherent leadership. The governor and Dom Garcia de Noronha were busy with the crucial but menial task of trying to get the ladders repaired. The men on the top, sensing that support was faltering, wanted to withdraw. In the absence of ladders, ropes were being thrown up to enable men to escape. Meanwhile, a small number, including Garcia de Sousa and Jorge da Silveira, had barricaded themselves in a tower and fought on. For once, Albuquerque, for all his self-confidence, admitted to personal indecision. "I didn't know whether to rally the captains, knights and *fidalgos* [who had climbed back down] and Dom Garcia, who was at the foot of the wall urging on the fight, or help those on top, and because of this we sustained some casualties."

On the embattled turret, the men were coming under increasingly heavy fire from arrows and spears. Glimpsing the governor, Jorge da Silveira shouted down: "Sir, help us, otherwise we're all going to die." "I can't help you," Albuquerque called back above the din. "Climb down on the ropes." Some managed to shin down again; others took their chances; others refused. One man balanced himself on the parapet, glanced down, made the sign of the cross, and jumped. He broke his leg in the fall and died some days later. A gunner from one of the ships was luckier; with a crossbow in his hand, he leaped and survived. Garcia de Sousa refused Albuquerque's offer. "I'm not the man to flee death down a rope," he called back. It was pointlessly brave. Shortly afterward, an arrow pierced his brain and he fell dead. A row of heads was soon being brandished on spears from the vanquished tower. There was nothing for it but to withdraw.

Albuquerque was literally left to pick up the pieces; the shattered fragments of the failed ladders were collected as they retreated "so that they shouldn't be left as a testimony to the chaos of our troops." According to the chroniclers, the governor was "so aghast at losing the city in this way, lost so shambolically, that he was unable to speak."

The mood in the camp was frustrated. On Easter Saturday, trusting in divine help, they had failed. The men were desperate to make another attempt, bring up their heavy cannons, and blast a hole in the wall, but Albuquerque knew that the moment had passed. The shortage of water was pressing, and the season of the easterly monsoon was near its end. If they did not go now, they could be trapped in a desperate situation, unable either to enter the Red Sea or to return across the Indian Ocean.

Aden had been a check, although at the time he was unaware how serious it would prove. Albuquerque put the best gloss on events that he could in writing to the king:

> What I can say to Your Highness about the deeds at Aden is that it was the most fiercely fought and rapid engagement that Your Highness could ever imagine.... The desires of the men to serve you doubled their efforts and the ladders only broke because of the weight of the mass of men who wanted to do you outstanding service that day.

He blamed the ladders, he again blamed the knights' lack of discipline, he tacitly blamed Dom Garcia, of whom "I don't dare to say more about my opinion of him that day, as he's my nephew"—and because he was an honest man, he blamed himself: "I think that if I had reconnoitered Aden first, I would not have launched our attack where I did." In the end, he did not disguise the facts—the attack had been badly planned and chaotically executed.

The fleet sailed on, regardless, toward the Bab el Mandeb and the

Red Sea. It was not a popular move. The pilots and captains wanted a return to India before the monsoon started; they had no desire to be trapped in this sea between deserts, whose reputation had preceded it. There was, as at Ormuz, some suppressed muttering that they were in the hands of a madman taking them to a place where there was no food or water, and "they clearly perceived that they were going to die." Albuquerque brushed all objections aside: he was simply following the king's orders. He did not divulge his deeper plan—if the weather permitted, to sail the length of the Red Sea and destroy the sultan's fleet at Suez.

By the end of April, they had entered the narrow strait, "only a cannon shot wide" according to Correia, Albuquerque's secretary. It was taken to be a historic moment, the first time Christians had penetrated the sea at the heart of the Muslim world, but also within reach, on the western shore, of what they took to be the kingdom of Prester John in the Ethiopian highlands. "We arrived at the mouth of the Straits," according to Albuquerque, "and put on the best show we could, with cannon fire, trumpets and flags." For the governor, it was something of

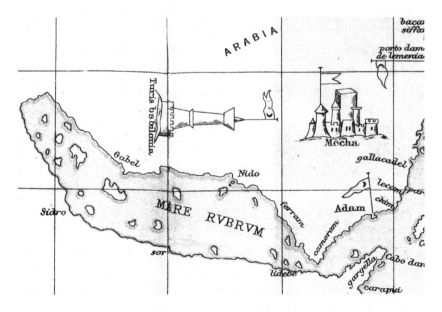

Before Albuquerque's incursion, Portuguese maps of the Red Sea are almost a blank, though Kamaran is marked (Camoram).

an emotional moment, as though they were on the threshold of the final conquest. The problem of acquiring pilots was simply solved by the expedient of capturing a passing Arab dhow, hiding twenty men belowdecks, putting in at the port where pilots were taken on board, and seizing them.

They worked their way up the sea, "always in sight of Prester John's lands and the coasts of Arabia." According to Correia, the prospect on either side was bleak: "no storms, only strong blasts of hot wind . . . on both sides, the land very dry, nothing green, great mountain ranges." The treacherous shallows meant that they sailed only by day, plumb line in hand, anchoring at night. As it was, one ship nearly grounded because of a mistake by a pilot. Albuquerque practiced the intimidatory tactics that had made the Franks so feared along the coast of India. Passing vessels were captured and ransacked for provisions. The unfortunate crews had their hands, noses, and ears cut off and were put ashore to announce the terror and majesty of Portugal. The ships were then burned.

Albuquerque's first objective was the sandy, low-lying island of Kamaran, two hundred miles past the strait, hard against the Arabian Peninsula, the only source of water along the whole stretch of coast. Having taken a supply on board, he was eager to push on to Jeddah, but already the wind had become fickle. It turned to the west, making forward progress impossible; when it spun east again, Albuquerque hustled his ships out of their sheltered anchorage. In due course, it swung back again. For twenty-two days he kept the fleet anchored in the middle of the sea, waiting for the chance to sail north, while his men fretted. When the water ran out, there was no option but to return to Kamaran. "And there they sat," according to Correia, "during May, June and July, with never any rain," effectively trapped with only goats and camels for company, which they ate, along with fish from the sea, among mangrove swamps and sandy scrub under the hot sun. Albuquerque remained boundlessly optimistic, sending out small caravels on scouting expeditions, capturing passing ships and pumping their hapless crews for intelligence. To the terror of his put-upon men, he ordered his masons to experiment with making lime. It could be done, they reported, and "we found plenty of suitable rock and much stone and masonry in the houses, mosques and ancient buildings. . . . For a fort it has the best site and amenities in the world," he wrote back to the king. "A harbor protected from all winds ... plentiful water ... a great abundance of good fish." The men were petrified that he was going to demand the construction of yet another fort.

To the court in Lisbon, Albuquerque presented the island as the healthiest place in the world. The reality of the situation was otherwise. When he set out from Kamaran to Jeddah, there was another great clamor against the decision, the men saying that "he was taking them to die." Contrary to his optimistic accounts to the king, they did perish in large numbers. Food was evidently in short supply on the island, and they were worked hard overhauling the ships. They started to succumb to a mysterious epidemic: "after only two or three fits of fever and great pain in the chest, an unknown illness, blood clogging the chest, many men died, more than five hundred [out of a total of seventeen hundred] and almost all the native troops—of work and poor food." Not a word of this surfaced in his report to the king.

If Albuquerque believed in a God-given mission, it was reinforced by a miraculous sign in the night sky. One moonless night,

> while we were anchored in that place, over the lands of Prester John there appeared to us a sign in the heavens in the shape of a cross, shining brightly, and a cloud hanging over it. When the cloud reached the cross, it split into pieces, without touching it or muffling its brightness. It was visible from many ships and a great number of the men fell to their knees and revered it. Others of those who reverently adored it wept many tears.

Albuquerque tried to persuade the pilots and captains to cross the sea against the wind to the western shore, but they refused to budge.

During these months in the hot sun among the sand dunes, Albuquerque continued to compile a detailed report on the Red Sea, which he filed back to Lisbon. He collected every scrap of information he could on its climate, geography and navigation, ports, politics, and tribal affiliations. He sent out caravels to investigate the pearl fisheries, inquired about the rich gold mines of Prester John, and finally came to the conclusion—to the relief of his men—that Massawa, on the western shore, would be a better place for a fortress than the island he was presently on, because "the coasts behind it are ruled by Prester John," and the belief in the power of the semimythical Christian remained strong. "I now have full information on all aspects of the Red Sea," he told Manuel.

The restless inquisitiveness of Portuguese intelligence gathering took many forms. There were always men prepared for adventure, however reckless. In the spirit of Pêro da Covilhã, the spy King João had sent to India, a man named Fernão Dias volunteered himself for long-range spying duties. Dias was either a Muslim who had been converted to Christianity or a Portuguese who had been captured and held by the Moroccans on Gibraltar for a long time—the sources are unclear. At any rate, he spoke good Arabic and had an excellent knowledge of Islamic rituals, prayers, and Koranic verses. He offered to be landed on the desert shores of Arabia and travel by way of Jeddah, Mecca, and Suez to Cairo, pick up a Venetian ship at Alexandria, then return to Portugal with information for the king. His alibi was to be that of a runaway slave. To this end, a shackle was put on his leg and he was ferried to the mainland in a canoe, with gemstones sewn into his clothing to sell as he went along. He made the journey back unscathed and reported to Manuel. Dias subsequently returned to India and apparently had a long further career spying in the Red Sea. Correia, who knew him, said that "he died very poor."

Albuquerque was particularly keen to seek out information about Suez, at the northern end of the Red Sea, and the composition of the Mamluk fleet. He came to a conclusion, from sources he believed to be reliable, confirming what he had thought for years: that it hardly existed. The defeat at Diu, followed by the interception of wood supplies from Lebanon by the Knights of St. John, had dealt the sultan's naval capacity a fatal blow. Suez, Albuquerque claimed, was a ruin. There were only fifteen pinnaces (small sailing boats) there.

> After Hussain left India, enthusiasm [for naval combat] waned, and they carried out no more shipbuilding of any kind. They had at Suez only thirty men to guard the boats against attacks by occasional Arab

raiders ... [they] water the boats every morning, to stop the sun splitting the planking. There are no carracks left there, no wood, carpenters, masts or sails.

In effect, the annual rumors of a major Islamic fleet were a chimera.

Albuquerque, with his usual way of putting things, went on to claim that the Portuguese probe into the sea had been devastating. "I can assure Your Highness that no boat or canoe sailed the sea, even the birds did not alight there, so terrified was the Red Sea at our entrance and so empty." His analysis concluded that there was a shortage of food in Jeddah and Mecca now, and that the sultan's regime was tottering.

If there was an element of exaggeration in this, overall his assessment was surprisingly accurate. The incursion into the Red Sea stunned the Islamic world. After the attack on Aden, its sheikh had dispatched fast racing camels with the news up the Arabian Peninsula to Jeddah and Mecca. The Mecca garrison marched to Jeddah ready for a last-ditch defense. Another camel hurried the news from Mecca to Cairo in just nine days. By May 23, it was common knowledge there. In the city, panic. The sultan was in consternation; there were special invocations at Friday prayers. A regimental corps was hurriedly gathered for inspection in the hippodrome: "they were presented dressed in mail tunics, helmets on their heads, scimitars in bandoliers. Three hundred men were enrolled on the list for departure ... a contingent of the sultan's Mamluks were given the mission to base themselves at Suez and undertake shipbuilding." In mid-June, the sultan ordered the director of the arsenal and his men to escort cannons to Suez "without payment."

The Cairo chronicler Ibn Iyas recorded the unfolding of this initiative. No men actually left. Reassembled in the hippodrome on June 15, they refused to budge: "'We won't go unless we get a bonus. We don't want to die of hunger and thirst in the desert.' The sultan immediately left the parade ground in a fury." In fact, the regime was tottering. There were fears of a revolt in the city. By September, Iyas could report that the situation was unchanged and the news from the Red Sea had worsened. He documented "the audacity of the Europeans impeding the Red Sea commerce, seizing the cargoes; they have occu-

pied Kamaran, a vital entrepôt on the route to India." Month by
month, stretching through into 1514 and 1515, this litany of paralysis
went on, detailing the effects of the Portuguese on one side and the
naval blockade by the Knights of St. John on the other. "The port of
Alexandria hasn't received any ships in the past year; nothing reaches
Jeddah because of the European corsairs roaming the Indian Ocean; it
has been all of six years since goods have been unloaded at Jeddah." In
July 1515, Hussain, the commander at Diu, who was now in Jeddah,
was still begging the sultan "to send reinforcements as quickly as possible before the Europeans occupy the whole coast of India, and besides he feared an attack on Jeddah . . . everywhere the sultan has real
causes for concern." Not until August 1515, and after a certain number
of men had been weeded out as being "too weak or stricken with
venereal disease," did any sizable body of troops leave for Suez.

Albuquerque had summed the situation up extremely well. He believed that there existed a window of opportunity; that the Red Sea
could be effectively cut in two; that there was no fleet capable of resist-
ing the Portuguese; that the heartlands of the Islamic world lay open;
and that with one concerted effort, the Mamluks could be destroyed:
"The sultan's position is very weak. As well as having few troops he
does not leave Cairo in person or go anywhere to fight, nor does he
leave his fortress. He has Shah Ismail at his gates, pursuing him re-
morselessly."

In the culmination of a long letter sent in December, he presented
King Manuel with a clear but fervent strategic vision and laid before
him the prospect of the ultimate prize:

> It seems to me that if you make yourself powerful in the Red Sea
> you will have all the riches of the world in your hands, because all
> the gold of Prester John will be available to you—such a huge sum
> that I don't dare speak of it—traded for spices and the merchandise
> of India. . . . I take the liberty of writing like this to Your Highness
> because I have seen India on both sides of the Ganges and I observe
> how Our Lord is helping you and placing it in your grasp. Great
> tranquillity and stability have come over India since Your Highness
> gained Goa and Malacca and ordered us to enter the Red Sea, seek

out the sultan's fleet and cut the shipping lanes to Jeddah and
Mecca.... It is no small service that you will perform for Our Lord
in destroying the seat of perdition and all their depravity.

This was lightly encoded for the destruction of Mecca and Medina,
and the body of the prophet Muhammad himself, a project so breathtaking in its daring that it was kept from all but the smallest group of
Manueline ideologues. It was to be undertaken with the help of Prester John.

I have been told that he greatly desires to destroy the city of Mecca
and it seems to him that, if Your Highness provides shipping, he
would send a great number of cavalry, infantry and elephants....

Manuel represented as king of the sea in the 1516 world map of
the German cartographer Martin Waldseemüller

The Muslims themselves believe that Prester John's horses and elephants will feed in the very shrine at Mecca.... It will please Our
Lord to give Your Highness help in such a feat and it will be your
ships, your captains and your men who will perform it because the
crossing only takes two days and a night.

Albuquerque was projecting the idea that tiny Portugal could control the center of the world, that Manuel might be the greatest of
Christian kings, and he indicated how it should be done. He would
construct fortresses at Aden and Massawa, consolidate a position and
station fleets there, but make no attempt to penetrate the hinterland of
Arabia. He would link up with Prester John; then "your fleet can get
to Suez, only three days from Cairo. This will create turmoil in the
capital, because the sultan's power is not as great as you have been led
to believe." He noted, "The business of India we will leave behind.
Goa will keep your affairs calm and peaceful." Albuquerque's strategy
had swiveled the globe: no longer were the Indies the objective. Now
they were the base camp. The summit was to be the destruction of
Islam and the recapture of Jerusalem.

But this would have to wait. By mid-July the wind had shifted, the
monsoon season was over. It was time to sail back to India. On the way,
he again visited Aden, bombarded it, and worked out exactly how to
capture it the following year by cutting off its water supplies.

23

The Last Voyage

July 1513–November 1515

"YOUR HIGHNESS BLAMES ME, blames me, blames me!"
Letters from Portugal reached Goa once a year, with the arrival of the spice fleet in September; replies returned with it the following January or February. These mal-coordinated communications provided ample scope for misunderstandings and misconceptions. Manuel's were becoming increasingly tetchy at the failure to achieve objectives that seemed, viewed down a distant telescope in Lisbon, to be simple. The Red Sea must be locked up, the spices must be sent promptly, the men must be paid. "Men who are well paid will serve with greater satisfaction and be happy to remain abroad," he informed Albuquerque sententiously. "Our pleasure is therefore that they be well paid and content ... but, we enjoin you, let this be done with other people's money [plunder]—not our own." This was a particularly sore point with the governor, who never had enough money or men to fulfill the king's ambitions. Worse still for Albuquerque, he airily doubted the value of Goa. Fortunately for the governor, he was fully backed up by his captains in a vote to hold the island. Manuel was also exasperatingly inconsistent. "Do you know that you change your policy every year," Albuquerque wrote back in frustration. But the voices raised against him were growing louder; he made enemies easily, and

they sent their own accounts home in the yearly mail. The failure at
the walls of Aden went down particularly badly.

It had been his intention to return there in January 1514, but that
did not happen, for the simple reason that he lacked seaworthy ships.
One had sunk on the voyage back to Goa from Aden; there was a
shortage of skilled carpenters and dockyard workers to carry out
repairs—refitting the spice fleet for the return voyage always took pre-
cedence. After the shipwreck of the *Frol de la Mar*, Albuquerque always
sailed with some trepidation, "with one hand upon my beard and the
other on the pump," as he graphically put it to Manuel. It was necessary to await reinforcements in September.

Instead he spent the whole year in Goa, building the colony and
negotiating with the potentates of the Indian subcontinent. A great
deal of time was taken up with preparations for the delayed Aden campaign. He stockpiled quantities of gunpowder and cannonballs, oversaw the manufacture of weapons, particularly pikes, the baking of ship's
biscuit, and the creation of siege equipment. After the humiliating
failure to scale the walls, particular attention was paid to the construction of many very stout ladders, tall enough to top the city's ramparts.
Albuquerque was keen to increase the number of musketeers. A proclamation issued in Goa, Cochin, and Cannanore offered financial rewards for those willing to come forward for training. On Sundays and
the first Saturday of each month, shooting practice took place, with a
prize of a cruzado for those who could hit the target. Twice a month
the trained bands were drilled in the Swiss fighting tactics; their pikes
were stored in the armory in secure conditions—those among the
nobility opposed to the new military fighting style that were threatening to render their role redundant had taken to trying to break their
weapons. On Sunday afternoons Albuquerque went out personally
with the horsemen to practice skirmishing maneuvers and to familiar-
ize them with the Muslim style of saddle. He did not return to the
stables until after nightfall, by the light of torches.

Albuquerque oversaw everything, ruled everything, worked tire-
lessly. His secretary Gaspar Correia left a picture of his daily round:
"The governor used to get up before dawn and go with his guard to
hear Mass, and then ride alone with a cane in his hand and a straw hat

on his head, and with his halberdiers he toured the shore and the walls to inspect the work that was in hand, so that he saw everything with his own eyes and commanded what was to be done." The hapless Correia could not resist a personal note: "His four secretaries trailed after him, servants of the king, with paper and ink, so that he issued orders and dispatches, which he signed there on horseback as he went. And I Gaspar Correia, who am writing this history, I went around in this way as his secretary." "Whenever I receive a petition," Albuquerque could write to Manuel with justifiable pride, "I answer it on the spot."

Albuquerque, the imperial visionary, was intent on building a Portuguese presence in the Indian Ocean that might last forever. The practical man saw to the material defenses of the city—the walls that were bonded with dried mud had to be continually repaired against the battering of the monsoon rain; the stern moralist worked to create a durable and just social order. He was aware of the propensity of his men, alongside their bravery and their talent for spontaneous self-sacrifice, for unruliness, violence, and greed. It required constant oversight. "So long as I am present all goes well, but the minute my back is turned each man acts according to his nature," he observed. He labored unceasingly to stamp out corruption and injustice toward the local population. He understood that the battle for hearts and minds was as important as successful campaigns. He was fully aware that his men needed to be paid, else they would inevitably revert to corruption and looting. The good name of Portugal mattered, and he feared the consequences should "the sugar turn to poison," as the king of Cannanore had once put it. He sought to protect local women against sexual violence and vigorously promoted the mixed-marriage policy. He banned all forms of gambling; only chess and checkers were allowed; he sent men to the galleys for misdemeanors and packed the quarrelsome and unruly back to Lisbon with the spice fleets. He provided monthly handouts for orphans and fatherless children, and paid a tutor to teach them to read and to draw them into the Christian faith. There was a heavy element of social engineering.

Albuquerque might appear a stern autocrat, but there was enjoyment, too. In the ceremonial hall of the raja's palace he had inherited with Goa, he sat down to eat at night with four hundred men to the sound of trumpets. On Sundays the local Goan troops would perform in front of the palace to the music of their native instruments; the twenty-four working fortress elephants, brought from Ceylon, would parade before the governor and, at the command of their mahouts, perform obeisance to him, and dancing girls would sing and dance by torchlight during the meals. Part of Albuquerque deeply loved the spectacle, the sounds, the colors of India: he was going native.

If the Portuguese were tolerated because they were peripheral to the imperial interests of India, they were also closely watched. Albuquerque continued to play the diplomatic game with the potentates of the subcontinent and the wider ocean with great skill. When the ruler of Vijayanagar sent his ambassador, he was treated to a military display. The trained bands marched past him through the city streets. The ambassador stood and watched. For two hours soldiers filed by, pikes at the ready, in a solid stream, to the music of pipes and drums. The astonished man, to whom all Europeans doubtless looked alike, counted ten thousand.

Elsewhere Albuquerque was busy managing the affairs of the Portuguese Malabar Coast. Although not given to holding grudges, his blunt style created antagonisms. He was scornful of the commercial ability and probity of the factors, and cynical, too: "They would not know how to buy ten *reis* of bread at the market . . . it would be more advantageous for Your Highness to let yourself be robbed by Florentines, because they are born to business and they understand it." In return, the cabal of opponents to his style of rule, particularly in Cochin, lost no time in counterbriefing to Manuel. Every packet of mail back to Lisbon contained vociferous complaints: that the governor was mad and dangerous, a slave trader, a corrupt taker of bribes who was amassing a vast fortune at the king's expense. Albuquerque was aware of this: "When they have nothing to say, they make it up," he reported to Manuel. When he intercepted letters containing certain accusations intended for the king, he certainly felt the damage. Their content, he declared, "has made my morale sink to the ground . . . doubled the numbers of my white hairs." Eventually he confronted the ringleaders, António Real, Lourenço Moreno, and Diogo and Gaspar Pereira, and packed some of them back to Lisbon with the spice fleet, a move that would prove counterproductive.

Quelling the riotous and envious *fidalgos,* holding corrupt officials to account, trying to cope with his vacillating monarch's excessive and wavering demands, ordered to do too much with too little— Albuquerque was pushing himself to the limit. During the closing months of 1514, he was shaken by an attempt on his life in Cochin. A brave but reckless man named João Delgado was being held in prison for the rape of a local woman. Somehow he managed to persuade a Muslim slave in the kitchens directly above the dungeon to slip poison into a dish of eggs for the governor's table. Albuquerque survived, but it touched him with a prescience of his own mortality. He said "that he was already just a sack of straw, that he was heading toward his grave every day, and couldn't delay long; but he must wait, and he didn't want to die from poison." When the slave confessed, Delgado was brought before the governor. With nothing to lose, he spoke out with astonishing frankness to the effect that if Albuquerque was aware of how his enemies were eager for his death, he probably did not suspect how much some of those he considered friends wished it, too. Delgado was found guilty and hanged, drawn and quartered, but no one was able to discover who had supplied him with the poison in prison.

At the start of 1515, all was ready for a new expedition. The plan was to take Aden, enter the Red Sea, build a fort at Massawa, on the western shore, and advance on Jeddah. Albuquerque was fully aware of Manuel's commands and ambitions. But in the circumstances, it did not happen. The matter of Ormuz intervened. Although it was a tribute-paying subject of the Portuguese king, the island city-state had remained unfinished business for Albuquerque since he had been forced to withdraw in 1507. Ormuz was one of the nodes of the Indian Ocean, the axis of trade with the Persian Gulf and the export of horses, but its politics were severely dysfunctional. Though it was nominally ruled by juvenile puppet kings, power was in the hands of the chief vizier and his clan, who routinely replaced the incumbent by either poison or blinding. Ormuz housed a number of deposed previous incumbents, all blind. The viziers ruled.

The vizier with whom the governor had treated in 1507, Hwaga Ata, was dead. In his wake a complex palace revolution had taken place. The young king at the time had been killed by the new vizier, Rais Nuruddin, who imposed another puppet ruler, Turan Shah. Then Rais Nuruddin himself had effectively been sidelined by a more ruthless relative, Rais Ahmed. The likelihood was that Ahmed would take the throne himself under the protection of the Persian shah. The prospect made Portugal's position tenuous. Albuquerque therefore decided that Ormuz must trump Aden as a priority.

Albuquerque left Goa with his fleet in February 1515. When he reached Muscat, on the Arabian Peninsula, now an obedient vassal, he got a more detailed account of the situation from its sheikh. Rais Ahmed kept both king and vizier in trembling fear of their lives. He had flooded the town with four hundred Persian archers. Albuquerque hurried on. He reached Ormuz in March, at evening, and gave the town a stern greeting: a blast of trumpets and an impressive volley of stones shot over the rooftops, so fierce, according to Correia, "that it seemed that the ships were on fire." Rais Ahmed was evidently expecting him: the streets down to the shore were stoutly barricaded and mounted with artillery.

At dawn the town's inhabitants could see the fleet shimmering in the morning sun: flags flying, the decks bristling with men armed with pikes and lances. Suits of armor, too hot to wear in the burnished heat of the Persian Gulf, hung glittering from the rigging. A boat approached carrying a man in Portuguese dress. As it drew near he called out, "God save the Lord Governor, the ship and its company!" It was Miguel Ferreira, back from his embassy to the Persian shah. He had reached Ormuz with a return ambassador from the shah, who was awaiting an audience with Albuquerque. Ferreira gave a detailed account of his mission; he had been in Ormuz for two months and he was also well placed to explain the situation in the town. With the arrival of the fleet, overnight Rais Ahmed had released the vizier, Rais Nuruddin, who was an old man, and Ferreira was waiting to see what would happen next. Meanwhile the king, Turan Shah, lived with the continuous prospect of imminent blinding or death; Ahmed kept him secured in the palace, under close scrutiny.

If the arrival of the fleet threatened to upset Ahmed's plans, for the wretched Turan Shah Albuquerque seemed like his only chance: "he had no hope unless he put himself in the hands of the governor." For his part, Ahmed was hoping that he might lure Albuquerque ashore, catch him unguarded, and kill him. The governor entered a poised and delicate situation with decisiveness and cunning—and inside information provided by Ferreira and his Jewish interpreters. When the king suggested, in words dictated by Ahmed, that after an uncomfortable voyage Albuquerque might like to come and relax ashore, he politely declined: he was quite accustomed to life afloat and never found relaxation ashore, but his captains would—and could they have put at their disposal some houses along the shore? Ahmed tried to forbid this, but with a sudden independence born of desperation, the king consented. The Portuguese thus obtained a secure position on shore protected by their own men. Albuquerque refused to acknowledge Ahmed in any way; he would speak only to the king or his vizier. In the security of one of these houses, in the cool of its cellar, away from the growing heat, the governor met the young king alone—and got to work on him. He persuaded him to unblock the streets; he tried first with the vizier, then with the king himself, to get permission to rebuild the fort. Rais Nuruddin prevaricated, despite handsome gifts: it was inconveniently close to the royal palace. To the king, Albuquerque suggested that he needed a fitting place ashore to receive the Persian ambassador, that he came in peace. Turan Shah, in another bid for freedom from the malevolent hand of Rais Ahmed, acquiesced.

Albuquerque needed no further permission. He moved fast. In one frantic night, he quietly unloaded a large detachment of men and prefabricated building materials—wood, baskets to be filled with sand, protective screens—that had been prepared in Goa, and constructed a temporary stockade, guarded by cannons and topped by flags, "that could be defended against all the powers against it." The stockade overlooked the royal palace and blocked access from town to shore. The Portuguese had secured a foothold.

The town's population awoke to this sight next morning with

amazement. Rais Ahmed was furious with his puppet, saying that "he would give the governor his treasure before taking the city captive"—an accurate assessment of the probable consequences. But Turan Shah held firm: the Portuguese came in peace; otherwise the city would be devastated. For Ahmed, killing Albuquerque was now vital.

Beyond its strategic value, the stockade was to be the setting for a theatrical reception for the shah's ambassador. An alliance with the Shia monarch was both a critical part of Albuquerque's power politics and a hedge against any intentions of Rais Ahmed's. He constructed an impressive tableau of Portuguese magnificence. A dais, approached by three steps, backed by rich tapestries and covered with carpets, was prepared for the reception. Here Albuquerque waited for the ambassador on the appointed morning. He sat on a beautifully inlaid chair, a figure of stern majesty, dressed completely in black velvet offset by a gold cross gleaming on his chest and the startling white of his long beard. Behind him were arranged the captains in their finery, swords at their waists, and farther back their pages, caps in hand, holding their masters' lances and shields. Lining the route were the native troops, Goans and Malabars, shouting and beating cymbals, and his own men with banners, pipes, fifes, and drums. The ambassador was preceded by his gifts—a parade of hunting panthers on leashes, horses with elaborately worked saddles, men in file two by two carrying four hundred pieces of rich cloth, turquoises, gold bowls, an exquisite suit of chain mail, inlaid daggers—and a particular present from the shah himself: a sumptuous embroidered gown. Then came the ambassador himself with the shah's letter, written on gold leaf, tucked into the folds of his immense turban. The principal people of the town followed to the cries and the clash of musical instruments. Offshore the fleet, bedecked with flags, fired thunderous salutes.

Albuquerque sat completely motionless as the ambassador approached. Just a movement of his right hand beckoned the man forward. With an exquisite exchange of ritual gestures, the letter, written in Portuguese, phrased in the orotund language of Muslim diplomacy, was read out. It recognized Albuquerque's status and reputation: "For the Great Lord who commands, stay of the governors and great ones of the religion of the Messiah, Mighty warrior, strong and great-hearted Lion of the Sea, you stand high in my esteem, and this is certain as the light of dawn, as unmistakeable as the scent of musk!" It promised all the blessings of friendship and asked for the loan of some master gunners.

Albuquerque accepted the gifts with courtesy but personally profited from none of them. He only draped the magnificent gown over his shoulders, declaring that he could not wear it—it was fit only for a king. He sent the choicest gifts to the queen in Lisbon, the hunting panthers to the king of Ormuz, and the remainder he disbursed to his captains. When he perceived the envy this was provoking among those excluded, and among the wider rank and file, he decided to make a general distribution of money—which he did not intend to pay for. Sensing the desperation of Turan Shah, he sent along with the hunting panthers a suggestion that the king might like to lend him a hundred thousand serafins from his large tax revenues. The king obliged. The money was delivered in person by Rais Ahmed, coming to sense the mood, and ostentatiously paid out to the men at a table at the entrance to the stockade to the sound of trumpets, watched by a gawping population. When it did not suffice, he simply asked for more. A further message from the king: Ahmed was planning to come with presents to the governor and kill him. Albuquerque replied that he had the matter in hand and made his counterplans.

He decided to invite all parties—the king, Ahmed, Nuruddin—to a meeting at a house on the beach. Eight would come from each side; their armed troops were to remain outside. The meeting was to take place on April 18. Secretly Albuquerque prepared a large contingent of soldiers in the stockade nearby. The cannons on the ships were primed and ready.

It was understood that everyone was to attend unarmed. None did. Albuquerque's seven captains came carrying caftans as gifts that concealed their daggers; Albuquerque also carried a hidden weapon. They were equipped for a stabbing. Rais Ahmed was the first to arrive. He walked confidently into the courtyard, openly carrying a sword at his side, a dagger in his belt, some knives, and a small ax. Through his interpreter, Albuquerque remonstrated: "It was agreed no one should carry arms, so why like this?" It was only his usual practice, Ahmed replied. He turned and discarded some of these weapons, though not all. By this time, the king and Nuruddin had arrived and the door was locked behind them.

As Ahmed turned to make a gesture with his hand, it all happened in a flash. Albuquerque seized his arm, drew his own dagger, and shouted to his captains, "Take him!" The two men grappled. Ahmed grabbed the governor's collar with one hand. With the other he tried to clutch the dagger. Missing, he attempted to whip out his own sword. It was too late. The captains fell on him with their weapons and stabbed him so violently that they wounded each other. Ahmed dropped dead on the spot. The king, who had been given some indication of the plan, had assumed that Ahmed would just be captured and taken back to Portugal. Seeing the body on the floor, the young man was terrified, thinking his own time had come. He tried to flee, but the door was still locked. Outside, Ahmed's men cried that their masters were all being killed. They started battering at the door.

Albuquerque had prepared with care. The trained bands advanced into the streets, pikes bristling, and forced the people back. As the trembling king waited for his doom, Albuquerque took him by the hand, reassured him, dressed him in silks, and took him up onto a terrace to show him to his people. For a time, Ahmed's supporters barricaded themselves in the palace; eventually they were pried out under a promise of safe conduct, and they left the city. The day ended in feasting throughout Ormuz. Turan Shah was conducted back to his palace with great solemnity and a rousing speech from the governor:

> Lord Sultan Turan, you are lord and king of this kingdom of Ormuz, and . . . you will always be for as long as God grants you life, and no one can take it from you. And I will assist you with all the power of the king of Portugal, who commands me, because he is your great friend, which is why I will be the friend of your friends, enemy of your enemies. To protect your person, if you wish, we will sleep here, armed as we are.

It was a perfect coup. In effect, Turan had become a puppet of the Portuguese, if one whose life was secure. Albuquerque quietly picked away at the last obstacles to complete control. Whenever he asked for money, he got it. He planted in the king's mind the seeds of new insecurities: there were no guarantees that all Ahmed's supporters had gone; he could so easily be killed by an arrow shot from a balcony or window as he walked to the mosque; it would be better if everyone in the city was disarmed; from now on the Portuguese would provide complete protection. It was done. Moving up the scale, he hinted at rumors of a new Rume fleet. If the king were to hand over his artillery, his men could better protect Ormuz from attack. The cannons had been deliberately buried to prevent the Portuguese from acquiring them. The king and Nuruddin were dumbstruck at this; their only retort was that it was impossible to disinter them. No trouble, Albuquerque replied; the sailors could do it. Overriding further resistance, they recovered 140 artillery pieces. Portuguese justice, nominally in the hands of the king, was severe. Albuquerque constructed a pillory in the market for punishment and execution, and presented it to the king. When four Portuguese sailors were induced to desert and convert to Islam with promises of great wealth, he tracked them down, bound them hand and foot, and had them burned alive in their boat in front of the town. It was intended to be exemplary to all concerned: "the Muslims remained extremely frightened, seeing the very great lengths the governor went to capture these men to inflict justice upon them."

It was the king, too, who was asked to pay for the construction of a stone fort on the site of the stockade—the last piece in place for complete Portuguese control. Albuquerque suggested that the cost was only the settling of an outstanding debt going back to Hwaga Ata.

The work was meticulously organized under Albuquerque's master architect, Tomás Fernandes. Stone was ferried across in boats from another island; mortar came from kilns on the mainland. Everyone was impressed for the task: the Portuguese and their native Indian troops as well as local Muslims. Three hundred men were to be put to the work, arranged in twelve teams, of which two worked each day, laboring two days out of five. On May 3, Albuquerque and the captains formally inaugurated the groundwork, opening the trench with hoes to the chanting of prayers. Three days later, Albuquerque, with a cloth over his shoulder, carried the first stone for the foundations and, after dropping five gold coins underneath, placed it in position.

In the stunning summer heat, the project advanced. The site presented difficulties. The fort was situated on the fringe of the sea, so close that some of the foundations had to be laid underwater with waterproof cement. By preference, the Portuguese worked at night by torchlight and the moon, but exhaustion, fever, and dehydration were taking their toll. An epidemic of dysentery broke out, and the men started to die. Albuquerque grew exasperated by the doctors' failure to help and their high fees. "You get doctor's pay and yet have no idea about the illness that afflicts the men who serve the king our lord," he thundered. "Very well, I will teach you what they're dying of." He compelled them to a strenuous day's work carrying stone under the hot sun by way of explanation. When they were finally released, he turned on them again. "Now that I've taught you, henceforward you'll be able to cure them and give them some of the money that you get so pleasantly. I'm advising you as friends," he added, "because I wouldn't like to see you sitting on the benches of those galleys."

The governor was always at hand to encourage. He slept little, ate little, seldom left the fort. When he did, he was followed by crowds of people who wanted to catch a glimpse of him. They came to the entrance of the fort to kiss his hand. He had become a legend across the Indian Ocean: the Lion of the Sea, who "dispenses justice and commands on sea and land." Neighboring kings from the Persian Gulf and beyond wrote seeking friendship. Persian rulers addressed him as "First of the First, Captain of many Captains, Fortunate Lion, Captain General and Governor of India." Others sent painters "to draw him from life." For Albuquerque, it was the crowning moment of his life. "With this achievement," he wrote to the king, "we shall have settled everything in India except the Red Sea and Aden, to which Ormuz brings us very near and greatly increases our prestige in India." He envisaged a rapid advance into the Red Sea, a fort at Massawa, control of the pearl fisheries, Portuguese hands on the throat of Islam and the Mamluk sultanate. Total control of the Indian Ocean seemed within reach. But in August, dysentery seized him.

Albuquerque had been in the Indian Ocean for nine years. He had worked continually and at a furious pace to build Manuel's empire, during which time he had endured the incessant voyaging, the wars, the intriguing, the rigors of the climate. He had been wounded at Calicut, shipwrecked on Sumatra, imprisoned in Cannanore, poisoned in Goa; for three months he had been besieged in the Mandovi River in the rain. He had negotiated, intimidated, persuaded, and killed. To outsiders he appeared indestructible. The bullets and the spear wounds had not felled him; the cannonballs had whistled past his head; he had stood up in his boat to taunt the Turkish gunners of Benastarim. But he was nearly sixty years old, and to those who saw him up close, such as his secretary Gaspar Correia, "he was old and very wasted in body." Now, in the atomizing heat of Ormuz, between the brilliant blue of the sea and the blinding sunlight on the barren rocks, he was dying.

At his side was a man named Nicolau de Ferreira, returned from Lisbon as an ambassador from Ormuz. When Albuquerque asked how he stood at court, Ferreira, perhaps putting the best gloss on things, replied that the king valued him so highly that he wanted him at his side to advise on India. The old man replied sadly, "There is no honor in Portugal that can equal being governor of India. In Portugal one can have a rest from work. But how long can my body enjoy rest? And what could be better for me than to end my days, of which I now have very few, in these labors, which make me feel alive?" India had been the adventure of his life, and he wished to die in his command.

There were days when he did not leave his room. He saw no one but his immediate retinue. People put it about that he had died and the body had been hidden. The work slackened. Albuquerque showed himself at his window overlooking the fort, from where he could speak to his captains and be seen. In September, he confessed himself and called the captains to him. He took each man by the hand in turn and made him swear to obey whomever he appointed as successor.

Their oaths were recorded on the twenty-sixth of the month. The captain designate of the fort, Pêro de Albuquerque, a cousin, took over control of its building.

But Albuquerque was still alive in November. He would neither leave nor die without seeing Ormuz secured. Though incomplete, the stone fort was now a defendable structure, armed with the king's artillery. The doctors believed that the sea would do the governor some good. On November 8, he embarked on the *Frol da Rosa,* a ship with memories for him; it was from its yardarm that he had hanged Ruy Dias five years earlier. He ordered the captain to slip anchor during the siesta, while Ormuz lay stunned in the noon heat, to avoid goodbyes. Anchored offshore, he sent a final farewell and apologies back to Turan Shah. The king returned messages of sorrow; he had wished to see Albuquerque before he left: "I cannot restrain my tears at this departure, which I think will be forever." The *Frol da Rosa,* with three other ships, raised its anchors. "And as night fell they set sail for India."

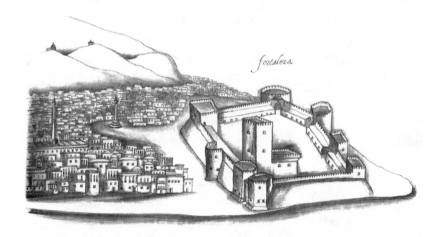

Albuquerque's fort at Ormuz drawn by Gaspar Correia

Close friends on board tried to console him, but Albuquerque was gloomy that he might die stripped of his governorship. Crossing the Gulf of Cambay, they captured a small dhow and questioned its captain. The word was that a new governor had come with many ships

and captains; he had been at Goa a month and now had gone to Cochin; the names he did not know. For the dying man, it was a heavy
blow.

Worse followed. Off Dabul, they came across a Portuguese ship; on
board was a man whose path had repeatedly crisscrossed Albuquerque's voyages through all his years in India: the Florentine merchant
Giovanni da Empoli, who harbored grudges. It is not clear exactly
what passed between the two but, according to one account, Empoli
"very confidentially told him things that were poison to his health,
and most damaging to his peace of mind ... [and] that hastened his
death." Perhaps he maliciously emphasized the extent of Albuquerque's downfall in the king's eyes. At any rate, the dying man learned
the name of his successor, Lopo Soares de Albergaria, and other appointees in his fleet to key positions in the Indian administration. They
were largely his enemies, and they included Diogo Pereira, whom he
had packed off back to Portugal. He turned to his friend Diogo Fernandes and said, "What do you think of that? Good news for me that
the men I ordered home and of whom I wrote critically are honored
and rewarded. Certainly my sins before the king are great. I am condemned before him for love of men, and by men for love of him."
With this news, he lost the will to live. He ordered the royal standard
to be lowered on the ship: he no longer had authority.

December 6, 1515. His last letter to the king:

> Sire, I do not write to Your Highness in my own hand, because at
> the making of this letter I am dying.
> I, sire, leave behind a son to perpetuate my memory. To whom I
> bequeath all my property, which is little enough, but I also leave him
> what is owed me for all my services and that is much—the affairs of
> India will speak for him and for me. I leave India with all the princi-
> pal points taken and in your power, the only difficulty that remains
> being to close, very securely, the straits. This is what Your Highness
> committed to me.... I place my confidence in the hands of Your
> Highness and the Lady Queen. I commend myself to you both to

promote my affairs, since I die in your service and I have deserved it of you.... I kiss your hands....

Written at sea, the 6th day of December of 1515

Then in his own shaky handwriting:

The servant of Your Highness

A de Albuquerque

Signature of Afonso de Albuquerque

He wished to live until he was in sight of Goa again, and asked to be dressed in the surcoat of the military order of the Knights of Santiago, of which he was a member, and to be buried in the same. He had made his will. Among his bequests: money to say ninety Masses for the soul of Ruy Dias, hanged in a hotheaded moment; a cannonball that had miraculously missed him at Goa to be covered in silver and sent with other gifts to the church of Our Lady of Guadalupe in the Algarve. He was still just clinging to life as they sighted Goa in the predawn of December 15. The senior clergyman of the city came out to give him absolution, and a doctor helped him drink some Portuguese red wine. As they entered the Mandovi, with the faint light flushing over the Ghats, he struggled to get up and was helped to the cabin window for a last look at the place he had envisioned as the seat of empire. After that, he said nothing more. The body was taken ashore on a bier by torchlight. All the people of Goa turned out to watch the Lion of the Sea being carried to the church, the native Goans lamenting as much as the Portuguese. Monkeys chattered in the trees. Smoke rose from the morning fires.

March 20, 1516. Before the spice fleet brings the annual news from India, King Manuel writes a letter:

Afonso de Albuquerque, Friend!

News has reached us via Venice that the sultan's fleet has gone to India, in which case, though we have commanded your return, we deem it imperative that you should stay! From the experience we have had of you and your service, and the victory which Our Lord has always given you, we feel it would be the greatest comfort to know we have you there. . . . We rely wholly upon you, and if you execute these our commands, we shall feel as much at rest as though we could attend to them in person!

If it was too late for Albuquerque, it was also too late for Manuel's great crusading dream. With Albuquerque's death, it would never recover.

Epilogue

"They Never Stop in One Place"

Enough for us to know that the hidden half of the globe is brought to light, and the Portuguese go farther and farther beyond the equator. Thus shores unknown will soon become accessible, for one in emulation of another sets forth in labors and mighty perils.

—PETER MARTYR D'ANGHIERA (1493)

O N THE NIGHT OF October 19, 1520, a small Portuguese expedition to the Ethiopian highlands was ushered into a richly carpeted tent; on bended knees, to the low tolling of a stone bell, they waited and watched. A curtain was slowly drawn aside to reveal a man seated above them on a rich throne, his face concealed by a blue cloth suspended from invisible cords. And as the bell sounded, the final covering was briefly lowered to allow a tantalizing glimpse of the mythic figure that had provided much of the motivation for the Portuguese maritime adventure: the Christian king of Ethiopia, Dawit II, the man they called Prester John—who they believed would help fulfill Manuel's crusading dreams. It was a meeting the Portuguese had anticipated for almost a century, the whole of western Christendom for much longer:

And there we saw Prester John sitting on a platform of six steps very richly adorned. He had on his head a high crown of gold and silver . . . and a silver cross in his hand. . . . The Prester was dressed in a rich robe of brocade, and silk shirt of wide sleeves. . . . From his knees downward he had a rich cloth well spread out like a bishop's apron, and he was sitting as they painted God the Father on the wall. . . . In age, complexion and stature, he is a young man, not very dark . . . an elegant man of middling stature, they said that he was twenty-three years of age, and he looks like that, his face is round, the eyes large, the nose high in the middle, and his beard is beginning to grow. In his presence and state he fully looks like the great lord he is. We were about a space of two lances distant from him.

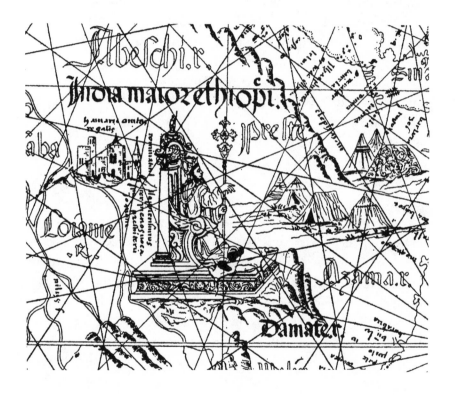

The kingdom of Prester John in a sixteenth-century Portuguese map

When the news of Prester John reached Manuel, the following spring, he fired off a letter of rejoicing to the pope. In June 1521, the king publicly declared that the destruction of Mecca and the recapture of Jerusalem were in sight. Yet the truth was otherwise. Manuel was as yet unaware that, impressive as Dawit II was in person, he was not the all-conquering king whose golden image had embossed medieval maps. Up close, it was obvious that the Ethiopians were in no position militarily or economically to launch any attack on the Islamic world; on the contrary, they were hemmed in by Muslim enemies. When Dawit was killed fighting in 1540, it was a heroic expedition of four hundred Portuguese volunteers that saved Christian Ethiopia. Like the gradual revelation of the face of the real Prester, the first century of Portuguese discoveries saw a successive stripping away of layers of medieval mythology about the world and the received wisdom of ancient authority—the tales of dog-headed men and birds that could swallow elephants—by the empirical observation of geography, climate, natural history, and cultures that ushered in the early modern age.

Manuel died in December 1521. Though no one knew it at the time, his crusading plans had first faltered years back with Albuquerque's failure at the walls of Aden, the ladders cracking like fatal pistol shots, then with the governor's dismissal and death. He was replaced, in turn, by three fumbling and timid men, none blessed with his strategic nous. Lopo Soares de Albergaria, equipped with a huge fleet, actually refused the sheikh's offer to build a fort at Aden because it was not in his orders, then flunked an attack on Jeddah—"the most sad and miserable tragedy ever" was the verdict of João de Barros. "Neither before or after was anything seen like it, a vast fleet just vanishing without a fight." Albergaria did worse: he turned back the clock, abolishing the professional trained bands in favor of the *fidalgos,* relaxing the prohibition on private trading—which had been at the heart of Albuquerque's quarrel with his opponents in India—and favoring the factioning self-interest of piratical captains. Corruption and abuses of power crept in.

Other blows had fallen on Manuel's great project. In 1515 his army in Morocco, the second arm of an intended pincer movement against the Islamic world, suffered a significant defeat. His queen, Maria, the most fervent supporter of his millennial dreams, died in 1517. The same year, the Mamluk dynasty collapsed. The Ottoman sultan, Selim "the Grim," shattered its army and hanged the last ruler from Cairo's gates. Henceforward the Portuguese would face a far more formidable Muslim opponent in the Indian Ocean.

In Almeida and Albuquerque, Manuel had had the luck of two incorruptible and loyal commanders, the latter one of the great conquerors and visionary empire builders of world history. With never more than a few thousand men, makeshift resources, worm-eaten ships, and breathtaking ambition, Albuquerque gifted him an empire in the Indian Ocean, underpinned by a matrix of fortified bases. In the process, the Portuguese surprised the world. No one in the European arena had predicted that this tiny marginalized country would make a vaulting leap into the East, join up the hemispheres, and construct the first empire with a global reach. "Why does not the king of Castile, the king of France or the Signoria of Venice send men here?" seemed a reasonable question to ask when Gama first landed at Calicut. Only Portugal could: the answer lay in the long decades of acquired knowledge and tenacious effort on the prow of Europe, during which discovery became an organ of state policy.

With Manuel's death, India ceased to be the launchpad for the destruction of the Islamic world; it had reverted to being an end in itself. During the sixteenth century, the Portuguese endured decades of bloody warfare, defending these acquisitions from continual Ottoman-led attacks that tested Albuquerque's fortress policy to the limit. Small pockets of men, often hopelessly outnumbered, fought with a spirit that defied the odds. Even a massive pan-Indian assault on Goa and Chaul in the years 1570–71 died at the walls. The Franks could not be dislodged. Goa, "the Rome of the East," justified Albuquerque's strategic vision. It would remain a Portuguese colony for four hundred years, home to a remarkable mixed-race culture.

In time, the counterpressure of the Ottoman Empire rendered the economic blockade of the Red Sea impossible to maintain. Henceforth the spice trade would be shared between Cairo and Lisbon. The Portuguese effectively enlarged the market: European spice consumption doubled during the course of the sixteenth century. For Portugal's overseas possessions, commerce within the Indian Ocean and the seas beyond became as important as that with the home country itself, and Portuguese expansion, now increasingly in the hands of private traders, reached out to the seas beyond Malacca—to the spice islands, China, and Japan.

As with all imperial adventures, the judgments of history have been mixed. Albuquerque, despite his ferocity, adhered to a robust ideal of justice. He was clear-eyed about the risks and consequences of the Portuguese adventure. Surveying the walls of Ormuz, he declared:

> So long as they are upheld by justice and without oppression, they are more than sufficient. But if good faith and humanity cease to be observed in these lands, then pride will overthrow the strongest walls we have. Portugal is very poor and when the poor are covetous they become oppressors. The fumes of India are powerful—I fear the time will come when instead of our present fame as warriors we may only be known as grasping tyrants.

The samudri then and many Indian historians since have labeled the Portuguese incursions as acts of piracy; the Malaysian government has constructed a replica of the *Frol de la Mar* as an object lesson. At its entrance a notice reads, "The ship's cargo consisted of precious treasures of the country plundered by the colonialists after they had conquered Malacca in 1511. But thanks to God the vessel was shipwrecked on 26 January 1512 in the straits of Malacca on its voyage to Europe."

Yet for all the nostalgia for a dream time before the coming of the Franks, this vast and largely pacific trade zone was an enclosed sea. The Portuguese, with their bronze cannons and capable fleets, both ruptured a self-sufficient system and joined up the world. They came as harbingers of globalization and the scientific age of discovery. Their explorers, missionaries, merchants, and soldiers fanned far across the world. They were in Nagasaki and Macao, in the uplands of Ethiopia and the mountains of Bhutan. They trudged across the Tibetan Plateau and battled upstream the length of the Amazon. As they went, they mapped, they learned languages, and they described, with a "pen in one hand, a sword in the other." Luís Vaz de Camões, whose epic poem *The Lusíads* created a founding mythology for the heroism of exploration, exemplified in person the sometimes desperate qualities of their adventure. He was the most widely traveled poet of the Renaissance, a man who lost an eye in

Morocco, who was exiled to the East for a sword fight, who was destitute in Goa and shipwrecked in the Mekong Delta—he swam ashore clutching his manuscript above his head while his Chinese lover drowned. "Had there been more of the world," Camões wrote of the Portuguese explorers, they "would have discovered it."

Though its supremacy lasted little more than a century, Portugal's achievement was to create the prototype for new and flexible forms of empire, based on mobile sea power, and the paradigm for European expansion. Where it led, the Dutch and the English followed.

In the process, the Portuguese set rolling endless global interactions, both benign and malign. They brought firearms and bread to Japan and astrolabes and green beans to China, African slaves to the Americas, tea to England, pepper to the New World, Chinese silk and Indian medicines to the whole of Europe, and an elephant to the pope. For the first time, peoples from opposite ends of the planet could view one another—subjects for description and wonder. Japanese painters imaged their strange visitors in enormous ballooning trousers and colorful hats. The Sinhalese were perplexed by their endemic restlessness and their eating habits, declaring the Portuguese to be "a very white and beautiful people, who wear hats and boots of iron and never stop in one place. They eat a sort of white stone and drink blood." Such images, impressions, and trades left a huge and long-lasting influence on the culture, food, flora, art, history, languages, and genes of the planet. They also marked the start of five hundred years of domination by the West that is reversing only now; in its wake, multistory container ships plow the oceans, returning with the manufactured goods of the Orient. China projects new forms of soft power across the Indian Ocean and into the heart of Africa.

In Belém today, close to Vasco da Gama's tomb, the statue of gruff Albuquerque, and the shore from which the Portuguese sailed away, there is a venerable pâtisserie and café, the Antiga Confeitaria de Belém. It is perhaps a shrine to the more benign influences of Portugal's global adventure. People flock here to eat its specialty, the *pastéis de Belém,* sweet custard tarts, baked golden brown and sprinkled with cinnamon, accompanied by hits of coffee, black as tar. Cinnamon, sugar, coffee: the tastes of the world first landed here in sailing ships.

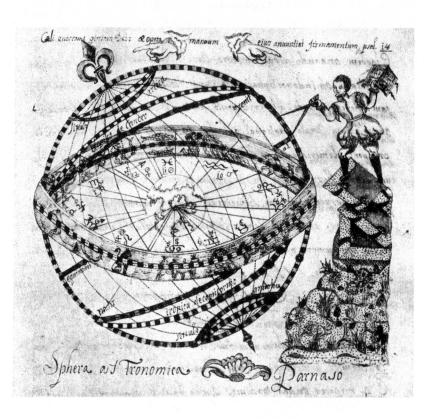

Sphera astronomica   Parnaso

ACKNOWLEDGMENTS

Writing about the Portuguese discovery of the world has been a fascinating personal adventure, and I am deeply grateful to the many individuals and organizations who helped along the way.

First, to Pascal Monteiro de Barros, who sent me an email and launched a hundred thousand words, for suggesting this project and then supporting it throughout, and to Patrick Monteiro de Barros. They opened doors for me in Lisbon, and I have received much kindness and good advice—not all of which I have been wise enough to follow—both in the city where all the voyages begin and end and in England. My thanks to Mary-Anne Stillwell d'Avillez and Isabel Stillwell and their families, to Isabel Cruz Almeida for a personal tour of the Jerónimos Monastery, João Lúcio da Costa Lopes for a chance to step aboard the caravel the *Vera Cruz,* Admiral José Vilas Boas Tavares and Admiral Bossa Dionísio for access to the library at the Museu de Marinha, Pedro de Avillez for invaluable books, Ricardo Noronha for translation help, and Carlos Damas at the Center for the History of Banco Espírito Santo. I also had much hospitality and fascinating conversations with Francisco de Bragança van Uden and his guests, with Eduardo Costa Duarte and his guests (who introduced me to the lines of Pessoa at the front of this book), Francisco Andrade, Francisco and

José Duarte Lobo de Vasconcellos, Joaquim and Alison Luiz Gomes, Manuel de Melo Pinto Ribeiro, and Francisco Magalhães Carneiro.

Thank you, too, to Stan and Tom Ginn and Ron Morton for reading and commenting on the manuscript, to Julian Loose, Kate Ward, and Eleanor Rees for their care in refining and producing this book, to Andrew Lownie, and, as always, to Jan. Many others, not mentioned above, contributed insights and ideas. I can only apologize for not thanking all of you personally.

Finally, I would like to express my gratitude to the Authors' Foundation at the Society of Authors for its grant that supported the writing of this book.

NOTES

The following abbreviations are used in the notes below:

CAD: Albuquerque, Afonso de [1500–80]. *The Commentaries of the Great Alfonso de Albuquerque.* Translated by Walter de Gray Birch. 4 vols. London, 1875–84.

CPR: Albuquerque, Afonso de. *Cartas para El-Rei D. Manuel I.* Edited by António Baião. Lisbon, 1942.

JVG: Ravenstein, E. G., ed. and trans. *A Journal of the First Voyage of Vasco da Gama, 1497–99.* London, 1898.

VPC: The *Voyage of Pedro Álvares Cabral to Brazil and India,* trans. W. B. Greenlee, London 1938.

VVG: Teyssier, Paul, and Paul Valentin, ed. and trans. *Voyages de Vasco de Gama: Relations des Expéditions de 1497–1499 et 1502–1503.* Paris, 1995.

Epigraph **"The sea with limits"**: from "Padrão," Pessoa, p. 59.

PROLOGUE: THE PROW OF EUROPE

xxiii **"with the body of a deer"**: Sheriff, p. 309.

xxiii **"its hoofs do not tread"**: Hall, p. 84.

xxiv **"Our sails . . . loftily unfurled"**: ibid., p. 81.

xxiv **"to go to the [barbarians'] countries"**: Ferguson, p. 32.

xxiv **"The countries beyond the horizon and at the end of the earth"**: Sheriff, p. 297.

xxv "the flower of all other cities": Diffie and Winius, p. 53.

xxvi "Ethiopia, Alexandria, Syria": ibid.

xxvi "Our poor houses looked like pigsties": Rogerson, p. 287.

xxvi "beyond the axis": Diffie and Winius, p. 53.

xxviii "Of late we have dispatched missions": http://www.ceylontoday.lk/64
     -75733-news-detail-galles-fascinating-museums.html.

1 THE INDIA PLAN

3 "In the era of 6681": http://www.socgeografialisboa.pt/en/coleccoes/
    areas-geograficas/portugal/2009/08/05/padrao-de-santo-agostinho.

6 "to invade, search out, capture, vanquish": The Bull *Romanus Pontifex*
    (Nicholas V), January 8, 1455, in http://www.nativeweb.org/pages/legal/
    indig-romanus-pontifex.html.

8 "more powerful than any other man": Russell, p. 122.

9 "an air of such gravity": Fonseca (2005), p. 179.

9 "a man who commanded others": ibid., p. 181.

9 "the deep desire to do great things": ibid.

10 "a sea route from here to India": letter from Toscanelli to Fernam Mar-
    tins, canon of Lisbon, June 25, 1474, in http://cartographic-images.net/
    Cartographic_Images/252_Toscanellis_World_Map.html.

11 "The king, because he saw this Cristóvão": Garcia, p. 67.

11 "the well-founded hope of exploring": ibid., p. 69.

12 "He shall have dominion": Psalm 72:8.

13 "Here arrived the ships": Winius, p. 97.

2 THE RACE

15 "information of all new discoveries . . . by ocular inspection": Kimble,
    p. 658.

18 "to carry extra provisions": Fonseca (2005), p. 105.

18 "a man who by his experience": ibid.

19 "the king ordered that they were to be dropped . . . called Prester
    John": ibid., p. 106.

21 "with woolly hair, like those of Guinea": Barros, Década I, part 1, p. 187.

21 "when Dias was taking in water": *JVG,* p. 10.

21 "with one voice began to murmur": Barros, Década I, part 1, p. 187.

22 "when [he] departed": ibid.

22 "He saw the land of India": Peres, p. 300.

22 "because it promised the discovery of India": Barros, Década I, part 1,
    p. 190.

23 "from the joy of seeing his companions": ibid., p. 191.

23 "Note, that in December of this year": Ravenstein (2010), p. 20.

24 "every day we are trying": "La Configuration Cartographique du Continent Africain Avant et Après le Voyage de Bartolomeu Dias," in Randles, p. 115.

25 "he had seen and found out": Ficalho, p. 107.

25 "caravels that frequent Guinea": ibid., p. 108.

25 "the desire he had for his friendship": Diffie and Winius, p. 165.

26 "puffed up in manner": Fonseca, pp. 120–21.

27 "from the Arctic to the Antarctic pole": Gardner, p. 90.

29 "Show me the clause in Adam's will": Fuentes, p. 159.

3 VASCO DA GAMA

30 "Among all the western princes of Europe": Oliviera e Costa, p. 176.

31 "the first shall be last": Matthew 19:30.

32 "And giving as an overriding reason": Barros, Década I, part 1, pp. 269–70.

32 "an unmarried man and of the age": Gois (1926), p. 49.

33 "bold in action, severe in his orders": Bouchon (1997), p. 101.

34 "bigger than Nuremberg and much more populous": Vasconcelos, p. 27.

34 "an enormous and extraordinarily well-made golden map": ibid., p. 22.

34 "of which they gave us a lot": ibid., p. 27.

35 "an enormous workshop": ibid.

38 "They were built by excellent masters": Duarte Pacheco Pereira, p. 166.

40 "the oriental riches so celebrated": Barros, Década I, part 1, p. 273.

40 "a place of tears for those going": ibid., p. 278.

41 "for so many centuries hidden": ibid., p. 276.

41 "in this discovery and conquest": ibid., p. 278.

41 "In this ceremony everyone wept": ibid.

41 "And with one party looking back at the land": ibid., p. 279.

43 "In the name of God. Amen!": JVG, p. 1.

43 "And having got speech with him": ibid., p. 3.

43 "On Thursday 3 August": ibid.

44 "as if making for the land": ibid., p. 4.

44 "On Friday 27 October": ibid.

44 "and we lay to under foresail": ibid., p. 3.

44 "the watch is changed": Disney and Booth, p. 89.

46 "we had soundings in 110 fathoms": JVG, p. 5.

46 "tawny colored . . . bark like them": ibid., pp. 5–6.

46 "they speak as if they have hiccups": Bouchon (1997), p. 111.

46 "one of the sheaths which they wore": *JVG*, p. 7.

47 "All this happened because we looked upon these people": ibid., p. 8.

47 "that we had the means of doing them an injury": ibid., p. 12.

47 "They brought with them about a dozen oxen": ibid., p. 11.

48 "Henceforward it pleased God . . . thus always!": ibid., p. 16.

48 "Black and well-made . . . nothing which we gave them": ibid., p. 20.

49 "They invited us to proceed further": ibid., p. 22.

4 "THE DEVIL TAKE YOU!"

52 "God . . . had given the sea in common": Sheriff, p. 314.

52 "They came immediately on board": Castanheda, vol. 1, p. 19.

53 "gold, silver, cloves . . . collected in baskets": *JVG*, p. 23.

53 "Prester John resided not far from this place": ibid., p. 24.

53 "we cried with joy and prayed God": ibid., p. 24.

53 "with all of which he was much pleased": Castanheda, vol. 1, p. 21.

55 "We anchored here with much pleasure": *JVG*, p. 35.

55 "who showed them a paper": ibid., p. 36.

55 "And when this torture was being applied": ibid., p. 37.

55 "seeing themselves discovered": ibid.

56 "because the climate of this place is very good": ibid., p. 39.

56 "and at once gave chase": ibid.

56 "gold, silver, and an abundance of maize": ibid.

56 "would rejoice to make peace with him": ibid., p. 41.

56 "he was not permitted by his master to go on land": ibid., p. 42.

57 "much pleased, made the circuit of our ships": ibid.

57 "they prostrated themselves": ibid., p. 45.

57 "Christ! Christ!": ibid.

57 "These Indians are tawny men": ibid.

57 "We remained in front of this town during nine days": ibid., p. 46.

58 "for a city called Calicut": ibid.

59 "he told us that they were above Calicut": ibid., p. 48.

59 "thanks to God": Castanheda, vol. 1, p. 35.

60 "The Devil take you!": *Roteiro da Viagem*, pp. 50–51.

60 "We came . . . Signoria of Venice send men here?": ibid., p. 51.

60 "Good fortune! . . . where there are such riches!": Subrahmanyam (1997), p. 129.

60 "We were so amazed": ibid.

61 "gladly receive the general as ambassador": Castanheda, vol. 1, p. 42.

61 "In Calicut . . . no matter where a ship is from": Subrahmanyam (1997), p. 104.

61 "Formerly . . . there was a king": Sheriff, p. 188.
62 "It is not my intention": Castanheda, vol. 1, p. 44.
62 "We put on our best attire": *JVG*, p. 51.
63 "They had all come to see us . . . entered his palanquin": ibid., p. 52.
63 "of a tawny complexion": ibid., p. 49.
63 "as a rule, short and ugly": ibid.
63 "well-disposed and apparently of mild temper": ibid., p. 50.
63 "a large church": ibid., p. 52.
64 "within this sanctuary stood a small image": ibid., p. 53.
64 "gave us some white earth": ibid., p. 54.
64 "painted variously, with teeth protruding": ibid., p. 55.
64 "We passed through four doors": ibid., p. 56.
64 "a great hall, surrounded with seats": Castanheda, vol. 1, p. 48.

5 THE SAMUDRI

65 "The king was of a brown complexion": Castanheda, vol. 1, p. 48.
65 "On the right side of the king": *JVG*, p. 56.
66 "some poured the water into their throats": Castanheda, vol. 1, p. 49.
66 "the possessor of great wealth of every description": *JVG*, p. 58.
67 "the poorest merchant from Mecca": ibid., p. 60.
67 "he was no merchant but an ambassador": ibid., pp. 60–61.
67 "As to us others": ibid., p. 61.
67 "this separation portended no good": ibid., p. 62.
68 "What had he come to discover": ibid.
68 "Not golden . . . own country": ibid.
68 "we ate, notwithstanding our fatigue": ibid., p. 64.
69 "The captain said that if he ordered his vessels": ibid., p. 65.
69 "who was a Christian like himself": ibid.
69 "none of us being allowed to go outside . . . bear it": ibid.
69 "with orders to go back to the ships": ibid., p. 66.
69 "once inside they could easily be captured": ibid.
69 "We passed all that day most anxiously": ibid., pp. 66–67.
69 "better faces": ibid., p. 67.
70 "it was the custom of the country": ibid.
70 "At this we rejoiced greatly": ibid.
70 "They spat on the ground": ibid., p. 68.
70 "This was done": ibid.
71 "bracelets, clothes, new shirts and other articles": ibid., p. 69.
71 "to eat or to sleep": ibid.
71 "sometimes it was night . . . and not evil": ibid.

71 "island called Ceylon . . . Malacca": ibid., p. 77.

72 "wore their hair long . . . like those of Spain": ibid., p. 131.

73 "if he [the samudri] desired it": ibid., p. 70.

73 "that then he might go": ibid., p. 71.

73 "that we were thieves": ibid., pp. 71–72.

74 "all were made welcome by us": ibid., p. 72.

74 "six persons of quality": ibid.

74 "until the ships of Mecca": ibid., p. 73.

74 "as is the custom of the country": ibid., pp. 74–75.

74 "Vasco Gama, a gentleman of your household": ibid., p. 75.

74 "promised to surrender if on the morrow": ibid.

75 "be careful, as he hoped shortly to be back": ibid., p. 76.

75 "We therefore set sail and left": ibid.

75 "About seventy boats approached us . . . we pursued our route": ibid., p. 77.

76 "although at heart still a Christian": *JVG*, p. 84.

76 "we might have anything in his country . . . who had come to attack us": ibid., p. 85.

76 "said that it was not for sale": ibid.

77 "frequent calms and foul winds": ibid., p. 87.

77 "all our people again suffered from their gums . . . that all the bonds of discipline had gone": ibid.

78 "much desired by our sick": ibid., p. 89.

78 "desired to go with us to Portugal": ibid., p. 90.

78 "the rain fell so heavily": ibid., p. 92.

78 "at times nearly dead from the cold": ibid., p. 93.

79 "did reach and discover . . . with much pleasure and satisfaction": ibid., p. 114.

79 "His Holiness and Your Reverence": ibid.

80 "God ordered and wished": Subrahmanyam (1997), p. 162.

80 "three caravels belonging to the king of Portugal": Priuli, p. 153.

81 "And it all goes to pay . . . to destroy this venture": *VVG*, p. 182.

6 CABRAL

86 "the Indians . . . might more completely have instruction": *VPC*, p. 170.

87 "and the king went with them to the beach": Correia (1860), vol. 1, p. 155.

87 "when they have the wind behind them": *VPC*, p. 167.

87 "first of a large mountain": ibid., p. 7.

87 "these people are dark . . . with long hair": ibid., p. 59.

88 "beds set up like looms": ibid.

88 "like sparrows at a feeding place": ibid., p. 22.

88 "large as a barrel": ibid., p. 60.

88 "some as large as hens": ibid., p. 59.

88 "it seems impossible to me": ibid., p. 39.

88 "They began to weep": ibid., p. 60.

88 "with a very long tail in the direction of Arabia": ibid., p. 61.

89 "so sudden that we knew . . . give them aid in any way": ibid.

90 "the mouth sickness": ibid., p. 65.

90 "If you encounter ships": ibid., p. 180.

90 "you shall put them all in one of the ships": ibid., p. 184.

90 "food and drink and all other good treatment": ibid., p. 169.

91 "with your ships close together": ibid., p. 261.

91 "because it comes to us by direct succession": ibid., p. 180.

91 "because in this he would comply . . . and much more": ibid., p. 181.

91 "as befits the service of God": ibid., p. 170.

93 "were innumerable, with lances and swords . . . they razed it completely": ibid., p. 84.

93 "and with him fifty and more men . . . all nine of the unloaded ships": ibid., p. 85.

95 "and then they ate with great grief and sorrow": ibid., p. 87.

96 "nothing was saved from it": ibid., p. 89.

96 "and thus the ship came [back] with only six men": ibid., p. 91.

98 "has already told the Venetian ambassador": Subrahmanyam (1997), p. 184.

98 "They took on a heavy cargo": VPC, p. 123.

98 "If this voyage should continue . . . due form with him": ibid., p. 132.

98 "These new facts are of such importance": Priuli, p. 157.

98 "that I should write to Your Serenity": VPC, p. 122.

98 "It is impossible to procure the map of that voyage": ibid., p. 123.

99 "he would forbid the [Mamluk] sultan going for spices": ibid., p. 122.

99 "the worshippers of crucifixes": Zayn al-Dīn 'Abd al-'Azīz, p. 7.

99 "trespass on the property": ibid., p. 79.

7 THE FATE OF THE MIRI

100 "guard the mouth of the Strait": Subrahmanyam (1997), p. 190.

101 "a region with a very agreeable climate . . . ate and drank a lot": VVG, pp. 203–4.

102 "Only two found themselves still together": ibid., p. 205.

102 "We put our clothes out to dry in the sun": ibid.

103 "He did not wish to see me": Subrahmanyam (1997), p. 202.

103 "I am the slave of the king . . . captive of the king of Portugal": Correia (1879), pp. 295–96.

103 "with great noise and manifestations of joy . . . Portugal!": *VVG*, p. 217.

104 "this is the fleet of the king of Portugal": Correia (1860), vol. 1, p. 290.

105 "We took no part . . . to disclose": *VVG*, p. 330.

106 "When I commanded this ship . . . and other commodities": ibid., p. 225.

106 "and we understood that they asked for pity . . . our lord the king": ibid., p. 226.

107 "We could see everything": ibid., p. 227.

107 "so suddenly and with such fury . . . fighting unarmed people": ibid.

107 "As soon as one of us": ibid., p. 228.

107 "they hurled themselves against us": ibid.

107 "We were all wounded": ibid., p. 229.

108 "Tomé Lopes, clerk of this ship": ibid.

108 "They uttered loud shouts . . . nearly all, wounded": ibid.

108 "They killed one of us": ibid., pp. 229–30.

108 "During the battle we sometimes saw a man": ibid., p. 231.

109 "And so it was, after so many fights": ibid.

109 "It is unheard of": Sheriff, p. 314.

8 FURY AND VENGEANCE

110 "as he knew very well": *VVG*, p. 234.

111 "his kaffirs would pay for it": ibid., p. 235.

112 "There remained only one sure solution . . . no intention of acting otherwise": ibid., p. 239.

112 "We could only see a small part of it": ibid., p. 241.

112 "whether merchants or permanent residents": ibid., p. 242.

113 "The Christians took more delight in theft": ibid., p. 243.

113 "At dawn . . . we saw many more people . . . thirty-four were hanged": ibid., p. 245.

113 "a continuous storm and rain of iron balls": Barros, Década I, part 2, pp. 56–57.

113 "like serpents": *VVG*, p. 245.

113 "they fired badly . . . in places hit by shot": ibid., p. 246.

114 "I have come to this port": ibid.

115 "their faces changed, betraying the seriousness of the matter": ibid., p. 247.

116 "Sometimes they asked more for the spices . . . suddenly they stopped": ibid., p. 261.

116 "a rich and very large island": ibid., p. 256.

118 "some without arms or legs": ibid., p. 267.

118 "O miserable man": ibid., p. 268.

9 TOEHOLDS

120 "to find rapid and secret remedies": Weinstein, p. 77.

120 "The audacity of the Franks knows no limit . . . of this piracy": Ibn Iyas, p. 106.

121 "goods could be paid for with money": Correia (1860), vol. 1, p. 308.

122 "a place to the Christians": Subrahmanyam (1997), p. 349.

123 "It seems clear that the loss of the two brothers": Castanheda, vol. 1, p. 116.

124 "I am a man . . . tell good from bad": Sanceau (1936), p. 4.

125 "with a pen in one hand, a sword in the other": Camões, p. 154.

125 "Every ship . . . well garrisoned and fortified": Noonan, p. 142.

126 "God rest the souls of Duarte Pacheco and his men": Sanceau (1936), p. 15.

127 "with little water": Noonan, pp. 144–45.

127 "The wind was against us": ibid.

128 "we will die serving you if necessary": Castanheda, vol. 1, p. 138.

129 "And with this defeat": ibid., p. 203.

133 "horrible prison": Weinstein, p. 81.

10 THE KINGDOM OF INDIA

135 "Dom Manuel, by the grace of God . . . for three years": Silva, p. 260.

138 "all India should be stripped of the illusion": ibid., p. 96.

138 "wage war and total destruction on him": ibid.

139 "whatever other parts have still not been known": Rodrigues and Devezas (2008), p. 212.

140 "out of love for the viceroy": ibid., p. 175.

141 "a noble gentleman": Silva, p. 113.

141 "of white damask emblazoned . . . carrying gilded halberds": Correia (1860), vol. 1, pp. 533–34.

142 "very fertile . . . an intimidating sight": Albuquerque and Domingues, p. 84.

144 "Portugal! Portugal!": ibid., p. 82.

144 "saddled in the Portuguese fashion . . . the king of Portugal": Castanheda, vol. 1, p. 215.

144 "Sire, Kilwa . . . than that in the West": Silva, p. 311.

146 "the fire that ran through the city": Castanheda, vol. 1, p. 221.

146 "that our men did not have time to fire our muskets": ibid., p. 223.

147 "a great number of very rich cloths": Hall, p. 207.

147 "of whom many were light-skinned women": Castanheda, vol. 1, p. 226.

148 "as long as the sun and the moon endured": Silva, p. 126.

148 "God keep you, Said Ali": Hall, p. 207.

11 THE GREAT WHORE OF BABYLON

150 "the sanctity of the House of the Portuguese Crown": Aubin (1990), p. 70.

150 "Christians may therefore hope . . . each time greater": Silva, p. 133.

152 "I have seen the sailing charts": Ca'Masser, p. 31.

152 "pearls to the value of 4000 ducats": ibid., p. 20.

152 "all burned with the spices": ibid., p. 21.

152 "I see that this enterprise can't be destroyed": ibid., p. 32.

153 "Speak to the sultan . . . a large quantity of spices": Aubin, vol. 3, p. 455.

153 "hindering them on their journeys": Zayn al-Dīn 'Abd al-'Azīz, pp. 105–7.

153 "Her arrival occasioned . . . in an original way": Ibn Iyas, p. 77.

154 "according to custom . . . as he always did": ibid., p. 78.

154 "to oppose the incursions of the Franks": ibid., p. 79.

155 "the most certain and swift way . . . cheaper in Venice than Lisbon": Aubin, vol. 3, p. 458.

155 "very high with great peaks": Albuquerque and Domingues, p. 89.

156 "more indignation than pain": Barros, Década I, part 2, p. 273.

157 "ordered hangings to be set up": Albuquerque and Domingues, p. 90.

158 "accepted these things from the hand": Barros, Década I, part 2, p. 357.

158 "that would be the headquarters and seat": ibid., pp. 356–57.

158 "the principal intention of his king": ibid., pp. 353–54.

159 "the viceroy continuously took great care . . . two hours after sunset": Silva, p. 140.

160 "Believe me Your Highness": ibid., p. 144.

160 "my reward is to serve you": ibid., p. 175.

160 "as seen in the books": Ca'Masser, p. 23.

160 "everything is unloaded in the India House": ibid., p. 29.

160 "certainly a very great sum": Silva, p. 33.

161 "It seems to me that Your Highness should strive": ibid., p. 317.

161 "I have decided, My Lord": ibid., p. 313.

12 "THE TERRIBLE"

163 "I, Afonso de Albuquerque": Sanceau (1936), p. 19.

165 "I presumed I could take my ship to India": ibid., p. 21.

166 "Latterly the audacity of the Franks knows no bounds": Ibn Iyas, p. 106.

168 "that in decisions about whether to fight": Barros, Década II, part 1, p. 61.

169 "the sugar of the Portuguese friendship would turn to poison": Bouchon (1988), p. 81.

170 "guard the mouth of the Red Sea": Silva, p. 192.

172 "a very elegant town with very fine houses": CAD, vol. 1, p. 83.

172 "a very large and beautiful edifice . . . nothing remained of it": ibid., p. 82.

172 "he ordered the place to be set on fire": ibid., p. 83.

172 "he ordered the ears and noses": ibid.

173 "a fine large city . . . Ormuz would be the jewel in it": Sheriff, p. 184.

173 "establish treaties": Silva, p. 192.

174 "the great miracle Our Lord performed": Earle and Villiers, p. 56.

175 "Sir, we do this in writing": CAD, vol. 1, p. 169.

175 "I was out of control . . . and had the Devil in him": Silva, p. 194.

175 "The captains were driven to despair . . . grabbed his beard and pulled it out": ibid., p. 195.

176 "when they saw that their complaints": ibid.

13 THREE DAYS AT CHAUL

180 "I want to arm myself . . . you'll still be laughing at nightfall": Correia (1860), vol. 1, pp. 754–55.

180 "and entering the river": Castanheda, vol. 1, p. 390.

181 "that seemed like rain": ibid.

183 "Don't put yourself and your men . . . glory at the point of the sword": Correia (1860), vol. 1, pp. 757–59.

187 "that because their sins demanded that they flee": Castanheda, vol. 1, p. 395.

189 "went back down into the hold": ibid., p. 396.

189 "whether he survived or not was for the honor of Portugal": ibid., p. 397.

190 "the survival of Dom Lourenço lay in his hands": ibid., p. 398.

190 "wanted to row as little as possible": ibid.

190 "fought like men who wanted revenge before they died": ibid.

191 "And so ended Dom Lourenço": ibid., p. 399.

192 "the Europeans who infest . . . remaining European forces": Ibn Iyas, p. 138.

14 "THE WRATH OF THE FRANKS"

193 "If these men had not deserted me": Sanceau (1936), p. 70.

194 "Sir, I remind you": Silva, p. 193.

195 "he who eats the chicken": Rodrigues and Devezas (2008), p. 242.

196 "To the very high and mighty king, My Lord": Correia (1860), vol. 1, pp. 897–98.

196 "there are more Muslims from Malacca to Ormuz": ibid., p. 898.

198 "instill terror in the enemy": Castanheda, vol. 1, p. 428.

199 "finally no living thing was left alive": ibid., p. 430.

199 "May the wrath of the Franks fall upon you": ibid.

200 "I, the viceroy": Correia (1860), vol. 1, p. 927.

15 DIU

202 "be certain that in conquering this fleet": Castanheda, vol. 1, p. 435.

204 "Sirs, the Rumes will not come out": Monteiro, pp. 264–65.

204 "Dom Francisco d'Almeida . . . punished and wiped out": Correia (1860), vol. 1, pp. 937–38.

205 "over everything a rain of shots": Castanheda, vol. 1, pp. 437–38.

205 "the smoke and fire so thick": Correia (1860), vol. 1, pp. 940–41.

205 "so frightening that it seemed to be the work": Castanheda, vol. 1, p. 437.

206 "an infinity of arrows": ibid., p. 437.

206 "so loud that it seemed to be the day of judgment": Correia (1860), vol. 1, p. 941.

208 "highly skilled and extremely accurate": ibid., p. 943.

209 "the sea was red with the blood of the dead": ibid., p. 943.

210 "because through these gates": ibid., p. 952.

211 "These cursed interlopers sailed away victorious": Zayn al-Dīn 'Abd al-'Azīz, p. 44.

211 "In my opinion . . . India is now in greater peril": Sanceau (1936), p. 79.
212 "Here lies Dom Francisco de Almeida": Silva, p. 208.

16 THE DOORS OF THE SAMUDRI

215 "made of richly carved wood . . . plates of silver and gold": Correia (1860), vol. 2, pp. 6–7.
216 "the council of war couldn't act": ibid., p. 9.
216 "the best thing in all the world": ibid.
219 "You are the first captain to have landed men": ibid., p. 16.
219 "What is this, Afonso de Albuquerque": Castanheda, vol. 1, p. 501.
219 "This honor is yours": Correia (1860), vol. 2, p. 16.
219 "the king my lord will know": ibid., p. 17.
219 "May the Lord help you . . . with your great deed": ibid.
220 "And the men, avid for what they could plunder . . . won't come back": ibid., p. 18.
220 "Lisuarte Pacheco fell with an arrow": ibid., p. 19.
220 "there was a large courtyard": ibid.
221 "crooked in one eye": ibid.
222 "which they hauled outside": ibid.
222 "he should be content": ibid., p. 21.
222 "he came without him . . . trouble getting away": ibid.
223 "who all performed valiant deeds": ibid., p. 22.
223 "no one wanted to go back": ibid., p. 23.
224 "of which seventy were noblemen": ibid., p. 25.
225 "who all died, except for a single slave": ibid.
225 "might burn forever": Castanheda, vol. 1, p. 505.

17 "WHAT THE PORTUGUESE WIN THEY NEVER GIVE UP"

226 "The caulkers and carpenters": *CPR*, p. 1.
227 "There is nothing . . . in India or within myself": Sanceau (1936), p. 103.
232 "to mint new currency": Correia (1860), vol. 2, p. 76.
233 "this was the new currency of the king": ibid., p. 77.
233 "to show who had minted them": Sanceau (1936), p. 118.
233 "Then if God wills that this alliance be concluded": Sanceau (1936), p. 119.
235 "My Portuguese lords": Correia (1860), vol. 2, p. 85.
235 "What the Portuguese win they never give up": ibid., p. 87.
235 "either the children or the women": Castanheda, vol. 1, p. 528.

235 "was completely amazed": ibid.

237 "and all their tents fluttered with banners": ibid., p. 540.

18 PRISONERS OF THE RAIN

240 "Goa belonged to his lord": Correia (1860), vol. 2, p. 98.

240 "sons of the devil": ibid.

241 "with great difficulty we managed to fill": ibid., p. 100.

241 "a drop of water cost three of blood": Rodrigues and Oliviera e Costa (2008), p. 43.

241 "that out of stubbornness he wanted to die": Correia (1860), vol. 2, p. 100.

242 "The common people did this": ibid.

242 "If they had not wintered here": Castanheda, vol. 1, p. 555.

242 "shut himself up in his cabin": ibid., p. 556.

243 "I am your governor": Correia (1860), vol. 2, p. 103.

246 "and many of them had turned Christian": ibid., p. 114.

246 "Then according to the law of Afonso de Albuquerque": ibid., p. 115.

247 "because of the crime of sleeping with the Muslim woman": ibid., p. 116.

247 "You are taken in the name of the king": ibid.

247 "arbitrary absolute power": Castanheda, vol. 1, p. 563.

248 "And on 15 August, the Day of Our Lady": Correia (1860), vol. 2, p. 120.

19 THE USES OF TERROR

249 "very displeased at the defeat sustained in Goa": Noonan, p. 183.

249 "the news about the Rume": ibid., p. 185.

250 "You will see how good it is": CPR, p. 2.

251 "Brother, go on your way": Correia (1860), vol. 2, p. 150.

251 "They came to my aid": CPR, p. 7.

252 "Our Lord has done great things": ibid., pp. 7–8.

252 "No one escaped": Bouchon (1992), p. 189.

252 "the destruction was so great": Noonan, p. 189.

252 "This use of terror will bring great things": Bouchon (1992), p. 188.

252 "white and beautiful": ibid., p. 190.

252 "There you can find all the riches . . . a poisoned arrow": ibid., p. 189.

253 "Many were knighted . . . than a merchant": Noonan, p. 189.

253 "and seeing him thus with an arrow": Correia (1860), vol. 2, pp. 153–54.

254 "We await your arrival . . . terror on land and sea": Bouchon (1992), p. 193.

20 TO THE EYE OF THE SUN

255 "it is forty days' sail from Calicut": *JVG*, p. 100.

255 "whatever other parts have still not been known": Rodrigues and Oliviera e Costa (2011), p. 17.

255 "a certain Castilian fleet": ibid., p. 18.

256 "Men cannot estimate the worth . . . must come [there]": Pires, vol. 2, p. 286.

257 "There is no doubt that Malacca is of such importance": ibid., p. 285.

257 "which differ . . . so that artillery does not harm it": Noonan, p. 195.

258 "And they came down the gangplank": Correia (1860), vol. 2, p. 218.

258 "He acted like a man . . . French boots and shoes": ibid., p. 195.

260 "is the most populous city of the Indies": ibid., p. 234.

261 "decked out with silk hangings": Castanheda, vol. 1, p. 634.

261 "None of those who had been poisoned by darts survived": *CAD*, vol. 3, p. 73.

262 "as long as he had feet to walk": Castanheda, vol. 1, p. 638.

263 "the center and terminus": Correia (1860), vol. 2, p. 234.

263 "the source of all the spices": Castanheda, vol. 1, p. 639.

263 "whoever is lord of Malacca": Crowley, p. 374.

263 "disembark the men, nor to fight": Castanheda, vol. 1, p. 640.

263 "The golden wall": ibid.

263 "ready for everything, and would build a fort": Correia (1860), vol. 2, p. 234.

264 "We made our stand on the land": Noonan, p. 197.

265 "spare the lives of the Muslims . . . who had never seen pikes before": Correia (1860), vol. 2, p. 244.

265 "Believe me . . . things here are of great substance": Noonan, p. 196.

266 "There were rooms full of sandalwood": Correia (1860), vol. 2, p. 246.

266 "held and secure in the king's name": ibid., p. 249.

267 "The captain-major with some of the men . . . completely unconscious": Noonan, pp. 199–200.

268 "And so we set out . . . awaiting God's mercy": ibid., p. 200.

269 "and so they stayed with their souls in their mouths": Correia (1860), vol. 2, p. 269.

269 "and touching bottom . . . and many other reasons": Noonan, p. 201.

270 "We found ourselves in great trouble": ibid., p. 202.

270 "made their way to Cochin": Correia (1860), vol. 2, p. 270.

270 "I heard [him] say": ibid., p. 247.

270 "was lost a greater wealth of gold and jewels": ibid., p. 269.

270 "a great map drawn by a Javanese pilot": *CPR*, pp. 148–49.

21 THE WAX BULLET

272 "Those who wanted to take revenge": *CPR,* p. 98.
272 "I am fifty years old": ibid., p. 21.
272 "feel free to do as they please . . . yet you abandon India": ibid., pp. 24–25.
273 "Does Your Highness know the consequences": ibid., p. 27.
273 "two fine robes . . . and make walls": ibid., p. 57.
273 "where there is a great flow of water . . . They are all Christians": ibid., p. 41.
273 "And again I come back to saying": ibid., p. 35.
273 "Sire, put your trust in good fortresses": ibid., p. 31.
273 "Kings and lords": ibid., p. 59.
273 "Places here, controlled by Your Highness": ibid., p. 53.
274 "Sire . . . to make fortresses requires planning": ibid., p. 21.
275 "Your Highness should not ignore the things that I say": ibid., p. 44.
275 "I fear that you don't want to favor": ibid., p. 23.
275 "I am kept down . . . in the affairs of India": ibid., pp. 49–50.
275 "to destroy the trade of Mecca": ibid.
275 "taking the main centers of this trade from the Muslims": ibid., p. 22.
276 "Strongly support Goa . . . [It is] certain to become peaceful": ibid., pp. 59–60.
276 "Sire, it would greatly please me": ibid., p. 62.
276 "With God's help . . . if there is no treachery": ibid., p. 59.
277 "Sire, now it seems you have decided": Sanceau (1936), p. 199.
277 "I often upbraided them": ibid., p. 202.
278 "a phalanx well ordered . . . this year from Portugal": Correia (1860), vol. 2, p. 304.
279 "bore their sufferings with much patience": Sanceau (1936), p. 207.
279 "the governor has turned the key": Bouchon (1992), p. 191.
280 "You aim to lay your hands on their trade": ibid., pp. 220–21.
281 "this goat by the neck": Rodrigues and Devezas (2008), p. 269.
284 "piled up in the holds of ships": *Lisboa Quinhentista,* p. 17.
284 "that went in front of him": ibid., p. 22.

22 "ALL THE RICHES OF THE WORLD IN YOUR HANDS"

288 "surrounded by bare rock": *CPR,* p. 217.
288 "As our carracks were big . . . the task of fighting": ibid., p. 168.
289 "it was not my practice . . . to destroy a stretch of the wall with gunpowder": ibid., pp. 169–71.

289 "The site of the city at dawn ... many round towers": Correia (1860), vol. 2, p. 337.

290 "which grieved me considerably ... and badly injured the men": *CPR,* pp. 173–74.

291 "he refused to enter": Castanheda, vol. 1, p. 752.

291 "I didn't know whether to rally the captains": *CPR,* p. 177.

291 "Sir, help us, otherwise we're all going to die": Correia (1860), vol. 2, p. 342.

291 "I'm not the man to flee death down a rope": ibid., p. 343.

292 "so that they shouldn't be left": Castanheda, vol. 1, p. 755.

292 "so aghast at losing the city in this way": ibid.

292 "What I can say to Your Highness": *CPR,* p. 179.

292 "I don't dare to say more": ibid., p. 174.

292 "I think that if I had reconnoitered Aden first": ibid., p. 217.

293 "they clearly perceived that they were going to die": Castanheda, vol. 1, p. 758.

293 "only a cannon shot wide": Correia (1860), vol. 1, p. 758.

293 "We arrived at the mouth of the Straits": *CPR,* p. 182.

294 "always in sight of Prester John's lands": ibid., p. 183.

294 "no storms, only strong blasts of hot wind": Correia (1860), vol. 2, pp. 345–46.

294 "And there they sat": ibid., p. 347.

294 "we found plenty of suitable rock ... a great abundance of good fish": *CPR,* pp. 194–95.

295 "he was taking them to die": Castanheda, vol. 1, p. 761.

295 "after only two or three fits of fever": Correia (1860), vol. 2, p. 348.

295 "while we were anchored in that place": *CPR,* p. 190.

296 "the coasts behind it are ruled by Prester John": ibid., pp. 222–23.

296 "I now have full information": ibid., p. 201.

296 "he died very poor": Correia (1860), vol. 2, p. 348.

296 "After Hussain left India": *CPR,* pp. 197–98.

297 "I can assure Your Highness": ibid., p. 192.

297 "they were presented dressed in mail tunics": Ibn Iyas, p. 289.

297 "'We won't go unless we get a bonus'": ibid., p. 291.

297 "the audacity of the Europeans ... goods have been unloaded at Jeddah": ibid., p. 335.

298 "to send reinforcements as quickly as possible": ibid., p. 356.

298 "too weak or stricken with venereal disease": ibid., p. 424.

298 "The sultan's position is very weak": *CPR,* p. 225.

298 "It seems to me that if you make yourself powerful": *CPR,* pp. 221–22.

299 "I have been told that he greatly desires": ibid., p. 201.

300 "your fleet can get to Suez": ibid., p. 224.

300 "The business of India we will leave behind": ibid., p. 223.

23 THE LAST VOYAGE

301 "Your Highness blames me": Sanceau (1936), p. 242.

301 "Men who are well paid": ibid., p. 246.

301 "Do you know that you change your policy": ibid., p. 245.

302 "with one hand upon my beard": ibid., p. 232.

302 "The governor used to get up ... as his secretary": Correia (1860), vol. 2, pp. 364–65.

303 "Whenever I receive a petition": Sanceau (1936), p. 247.

303 "So long as I am present all goes well": ibid., p. 232.

303 "the sugar turn to poison": Bouchon (1988), p. 81.

304 "They would not know how to buy": Sanceau (1936), p. 243.

304 "When they have nothing to say ... my white hairs": Bouchon (1992), p. 243.

305 "that he was already just a sack of straw": Correia (1860), vol. 2, p. 398.

306 "that it seemed that the ships were on fire": ibid., p. 408.

306 "God save the Lord Governor": ibid., p. 409.

307 "he had no hope unless": ibid., p. 420.

307 "that could be defended against all the powers against it": ibid., p. 422.

308 "he would give the governor his treasure": ibid., p. 423.

308 "For the Great Lord who commands": Sanceau (1936), p. 271.

310 "It was agreed no one should carry arms": Correia (1860), vol. 2, p. 431.

310 "Lord Sultan Turan, you are lord and king": ibid., p. 436.

311 "the Muslims remained extremely frightened": ibid., p. 438.

312 "You get doctor's pay ... benches of those galleys": ibid., pp. 440–41.

312 "dispenses justice and commands on sea and land": Castanheda, vol. 1, p. 857.

312 "First of the First, Captain of many Captains": Sanceau (1936), p. 281.

312 "to draw him from life": Castanheda, vol. 1, p. 858.

312 "With this achievement ... we shall have settled everything": Sanceau (1936), p. 280.

313 "he was old and very wasted ... which make me feel alive?": Correia (1860), vol. 2, p. 452.

314 "I cannot restrain my tears ... set sail for India": ibid., p. 456.

315 "very confidentially told him things": Barros, Década II, part 2, p. 491.

315 "What do you think of that?": Correia (1860), vol. 2, p. 458.

315 "Sire, I do not write to Your Highness": Sanceau (1936), p. 296.
317 "Afonso de Albuquerque, Friend!": ibid., p. 299.

EPILOGUE: "THEY NEVER STOP IN ONE PLACE"

318 "Enough for us to know": Boorstin, p. 145.
318 "And there we saw Prester John": Alvares (1881), pp. 202–3.
320 "the most sad and miserable tragedy ever": Rodrigues and Devezas (2008), p. 284.
321 "Why does not the king of Castile": *Roteiro da Viagem,* p. 51.
322 "So long as they are upheld by justice": Sanceau (1936), p. 286.
322 "The ship's cargo consisted of precious treasures": Rodrigues and Devezas (2008), p. 329.
322 "pen in one hand, a sword in the other": Camões, p. 154.
323 "Had there been more of the world": Pyne, pp. 18–19.
323 "a very white and beautiful people": Suckling, p. 280.

BIBLIOGRAPHY

PRIMARY SOURCES

Albuquerque, Afonso de. *Cartas para El-Rei D. Manuel I.* Edited by António Baião. Lisbon, 1942.

Albuquerque, Afonso de [1500–80]. *The Commentaries of the Great Alfonso de Albuquerque.* Translated by Walter de Gray Birch. 4 vols. London, 1875–84.

Albuquerque, Luís de, and Francisco Contente Domingues, eds. *Grandes Viagens Marítimas.* Lisbon, 1989.

Alvares, Francisco. *Narrative of the Portuguese Embassy to Abyssinia During the Years 1520–1527.* Edited and translated by Lord Stanley of Alderley. London, 1881.

———. *The Prester John of the Indies.* Edited and translated by C. F. Buckingham and G. W. B. Huntingford. Vol. 2. Cambridge, 1961.

Azurara, Gomes Eannes de. *The Chronicle of the Discovery and Conquest of Guinea.* Edited and translated by Charles Raymond Beazley and Edgar Prestage. 2 vols. London, 1896 and 1899.

Barbosa, Duarte. *The Book of Duarte Barbosa.* Translated by Mansel Longworth Danes. London, 1918.

Barros, João de. *Da Ásia.* Décadas I–II. Lisbon, 1778.

Cadamosto, Alvise. *The Voyages of Cadamosto.* Translated and edited by G. R. Crone. London, 1937.

Ca'Masser, Leonardo da. "Relazione di Leonardo da Ca'Masser, alla Serenissima Republica di Venezia Sopra il Commercio dei Portoghesi nell'India." *Archivio Storico Italiano,* appendice, vol. 2, 1845.

Camões, Luís Vaz de. *The Lusíads.* Translated by Landeg White. Oxford, 1997.

Castanheda, Fernão Lopes de. *História do Descobrimento e Conquista da Índia Pelos Portugueses.* Edited by M. Lopes de Almeida. 2 vols. Porto, 1979.

Correia (or Corrêa), Gaspar. *The Three Voyages of Vasco da Gama.* Edited and translated by Henry Stanley. London, 1879.

———. *Lendas da India.* 2 vols. Lisbon, 1860.

Davenport, Frances Gardiner, ed. *European Treaties Bearing on the History of the United States and Its Dependencies to 1648.* Washington, D.C., 1917.

Earle, T. F., and John Villiers, ed. and trans. *Albuquerque, Caesar of the East: Selected Texts by Afonso de Albuquerque and His Son.* Warminster, 1990.

Góis, Damião de. *Crónica do Felicissimo Rei D. Manuel.* Vol. 1. Coimbra, 1926.

———. *Lisbon in the Renaissance.* Translated by Jeffrey S. Ruth. New York, 1996.

Greenlee, W. B., trans. *The Voyage of Pedro Álvares Cabral to Brazil and India.* London, 1938.

Ibn Iyas. *Journal d'un Bourgeois du Caire.* Translated and edited by Gaston Wiet. Paris, 1955.

Major, R. H., ed. and trans. *India in the Fifteenth Century.* London, 1857.

Pereira, Duarte Pacheco. *Esmeraldo de Situ Orbis.* Edited and translated by George H. T. Kimble. London, 1937.

Pires, Tomé. *The Suma Oriental of Tomé Pires.* 2 vols. Edited and translated by Armando Cortesáo. London, 1944.

Priuli, G. *Diarii.* Edited by A. Segre. In *Rerum Italicarum Scriptores,* vol. 24, part 3. Città di Castello, 1921–34.

Ravenstein, E. G., ed. and trans. *A Journal of the First Voyage of Vasco da Gama, 1497–99.* London, 1898.

Roteiro da Viagem Que em Descobrimento da India pelo Cabo da Boa Esperança Fez Dom Vasco da Gama em 1497. Porto, 1838.

Teyssier, Paul, and Paul Valentin, ed. and trans. *Voyages de Vasco de Gama: Relations des Expéditions de 1497–1499 et 1502–1503.* Paris, 1995.

Vasconcelos, Basílio de, ed. *Itinerário do Dr. Jerónimo Münzer.* Coimbra, 1931.

Zayn al-Dīn 'Abd al-'Azīz. *Tohfut-ul-Mujahideen.* Translated by M. J. Rowlandson. London, 1883.

MODERN WORKS

Albuquerque, Luís de, and Francisco Contente Domingues, eds. *Dictionário de História dos Descobrimentos Portugueses.* 2 vols. Lisbon, 1994.

Aubin, Jean, ed. *La Découverte, le Portugal et l'Europe.* Paris, 1990.

———. *Le Latin et l'astrolabe: Recherches sur le Portugal de la Renaissance, Son Expansion en Asie et les Relations Internationales.* 3 vols. Lisbon, 1996–2006.

Axelson, Eric. *The Portuguese in South-East Africa, 1488–1600*. Johannesburg, 1973.

Baião, António, Hernani Cidade, and Manuel Múriàs, eds. *História da Expansaó Portuguesa no Mundo*. Lisbon, 1937.

Baldridge, Cates. *Prisoners of Prester John: The Portuguese Mission to Ethiopia in Search of the Mythical King, 1520–1526*. Jefferson, 2012.

Bedini, Silvano A. *The Pope's Elephant*. Manchester, 1997.

Blake, John W. *European Beginnings in West Africa, 1454–1578*. London, 1937.

Boorstin, Daniel J. *The Discoverers*. New York, 1986.

Bouchon, Geneviève. *Albuquerque: Le Lion des Mers d'Asie*. Paris, 1992.

———. *Inde Découverte, Inde Retrouvée, 1498–1630*. Lisbon, 1999.

———. *Regent of the Sea*. Translated by Louise Shackley. Delhi, 1988.

———. *Vasco de Gama*. Paris, 1997.

Boxer, C. R. *The Portuguese Seaborne Empire, 1415–1825*. New York, 1969.

Campos, José Moreira. *Da Fantasia à Realidade: Afonso d'Albuquerque*. Lisbon, 1953.

Casale, Giancarlo. *The Ottoman Age of Exploration*. Oxford, 2010.

Catz, Rebecca. *Christopher Columbus and the Portuguese, 1476–98*. Westport, 1993.

Chandeigne, Michel, ed. *Lisbonne Hors les Murs, 1415–1580: L'Invention du Monde par les Navigateurs Portugais*. Paris, 1990.

Cliff, Nigel. *Holy War*. New York, 2011.

Costa, A. F. de. *Ás Portas da Índia em 1484*. Lisbon, 1935.

Coutinho, Gago. *A Náutica dos Descobrimentos*. Lisbon, 1969.

Couto, Djanirah, and Rui Manuel Loureiro. *Ormuz 1507 e 1622: Conquista e Perda*. Lisbon, 2007.

Crowley, Roger. *City of Fortune*. London, 2011.

Danvers, Frederick Charles. *The Portuguese in India*. Vol. 1. London, 1966.

Delumeau, Jean. "L'Escatologie de Manuel le Fortuné." *Journal des Savants*, no. 1 (1995): pp. 179–86.

Diffie, Bailey W., and George D. Winius. *Foundations of the Portuguese Empire, 1415–1580*. Minneapolis, 1977.

Disney, Anthony, and Emily Booth, eds. *Vasco da Gama and the Linking of Europe and Asia*. Delhi, 2000.

Domingues, Francisco Contente. *Navios e Viagens*. Lisbon, 2008.

Donkin, R. A. *Between East and West: The Moluccas and the Trade in Spices up to the Arrival of the Europeans*. Philadelphia, 2003.

Ferguson, Niall. *Civilization: The West and the Rest*. London, 2011.

Fernández-Armesto, Felipe. *Columbus*. Oxford, 1991.

———. *Pathfinders: A Global History of Exploration*. Oxford, 2006.

Ficalho, Conde de. *Viagens de Pero da Covilha*. Lisbon, 1988.

Fonseca, Luìs Adão da. *The Discoveries and the Formation of the Atlantic Ocean*. Lisbon, 1999.

———. *D. João II*. Rio de Mouro, 2005.

Frater, Alexander. *Chasing the Monsoon*. London, 1990.

Fuentes, Carlos. *The Buried Mirror: Reflecting on Spain and the New World*. New York, 1999.

Garcia, José Manuel. *D. João II vs. Colombo*. Vila do Conde, 2012.

Gracias, Fátima da Silva. *Kaleidoscope of Women in Goa, 1510–1961*. Delhi, 1996.

Granzotto, Gianni. *Christopher Columbus: The Dream and the Obsession*. London, 1986.

Hall, Richard. *Empires of the Monsoon*. London, 1996.

Jack, Malcolm. *Lisbon: City of the Sea*. London, 2007.

Kimble, George. "Portuguese Policy and Its Influence on Fifteenth-Century Cartography." *Geographical Review*, 23, no. 4 (October 1933).

Krondl, Michael. *The Taste of Conquest*. New York, 2007.

Lisboa Quinhentista, a Imagem e a Vida da Cidade. Lisbon, 1983.

Magalhães, Joaquim Romero. *The Portuguese in the Sixteenth Century*. Lisbon, 1998.

Marques, A. H. de Oliviera. *History of Portugal*. Vol. 1. New York, 1972.

Monteiro, Saturnino. *Portuguese Sea Battles*. Vol. 1, *The First World Sea Power, 1139–1521*. Lisbon, 2013.

Newitt, M. *A History of Portuguese Overseas Expansion, 1400–1668*. London, 2005.

Noonan, Laurence A. *John of Empoli and His Relations with Afonso de Albuquerque*. Lisbon, 1989.

Oliviera e Costa, João Paulo. *D. Manuel 1*. Rio de Mouro, 2005.

Page, Martin. *The First Global Village: How Portugal Changed the World*. Lisbon, 2002.

Panikkar, K. M. *Asia and Western Dominance*. London, 1953.

———. *Malabar and the Portuguese*. Bombay, 1929.

Parry, J. H. *The Age of Reconnaissance*. London, 1966.

Pearson, M. N. *Coastal Western India: Studies from the Portuguese Records*. Delhi, 1981.

———. *The New Cambridge History of India*. Part 1, vol. 1, *The Portuguese in India*. Cambridge, 1987.

Pereira, José António Rodrigues. *Marinha Portuguesa: Nove Séculos de História*. Lisbon, 2010.

Pereira, Paulo. *Torre de Belém*. London, 2005.

Peres, Damião. *História dos Descobrimentos Portuguêses*. Coimbra, 1960.

Pessoa, Fernando. *Mensangem*. Lisbon, 1945.

Pissara, José Virgílio Amarao. *Chaul e Diu: O Domínio do Índico*. Lisbon, 2002.

Pyne, Stephen J. "Seeking Newer Worlds: An Historical Context for Space Exploration." www. history.nasa.gov/SP-2006-4702/chapters/chapter1.pdf.

Ramos, Rui, et al. *História de Portugal*. Lisbon, 2009.

Randles, W. G. L. *Geography, Cartography and Nautical Science in the Renaissance: The Impact of the Great Discoveries*. Farnham, 2000.

Ravenstein, E. G. *The Voyages of Diogo Cão and Bartholomeu Dias, 1482–88*. England, 2010.

Rodrigues, J. N., and T. Devezas. *1509*. Famalicão, 2008.

———. *Pioneers of Globalization—Why Portugal Surprised the World*. Famalicão, 2007.

Rodrigues, Vítor Luís. "As Companhias de Ordenança no Estado Português da Índia, 1510–1580." In *Oceanos—Indo Portuguesmente*, no. 19/20, 212–18. Lisbon: CNCDP, 1994.

Rodrigues, Vítor Luís Gaspar, and João Paulo Oliviera e Costa. *Conquista de Goa, 1510–1512*. Lisbon, 2008.

———. *Conquista de Malaca, 1511*. Lisbon, 2011.

Rogerson, Barnaby. *The Last Crusaders: East, West and the Battle for the Centre of the World*. London, 2010.

Russell, Peter. *Prince Henry the "Navigator": A Life*. New Haven, 2000.

Sanceau, Elaine. *Indies Adventure*. London, 1936.

———. *The Perfect Prince*. Porto, 1959.

Santos, José Loureiro dos. *Ceuta 1415: A Conquista*. Lisbon, 2004.

Sheriff, Abdul. *Dhow Cultures of the Indian Ocean*. London, 2010.

Silva, Joaquim Candeias. *O Fundador do Estado Português da Índia—D. Francisco de Almeida*. Lisbon, 1996.

Subrahmanyam, Sanjay. *The Career and Legend of Vasco da Gama*. Cambridge, 1997.

———. *The Portuguese Empire in Asia, 1500–1700: A Political and Economic History*. London, 1993.

Suckling, Horatio John. *Ceylon: A General Description of the Island*. London, 1876.

Teixeira, André. *Fortalezas: Estado Português da India*. Lisbon, 2008.

Thomaz, Luís Felipe. *De Ceuta a Timor*. Lisbon, 1994.

Thompson, William R., ed. *Great Power Rivalries*. Columbia, 1999.

Villiers, Alan. *Sons of Sindbad*. London, 1940.

Weinstein, Donald. *Ambassador from Venice: Pietro Pasqualigo in Lisbon, 1501*. Minneapolis, 1960.

Whiteway, R. S. *The Rise of Portuguese Power in India, 1497–1550*. London, 1899.

Winius, George D., ed. *Portugal, the Pathfinder: Journeys from the Medieval Toward the Modern World, 1300–c. 1600*. Madison, 1995.

INDEX

Page numbers in *italics* refer to illustrations.

ABOUT THE AUTHOR

ROGER CROWLEY is a UK-based writer and historian and a graduate of Cambridge University. As a child of a naval family, his fascination with maritime and world history started early, on the island of Malta. He has lived in Istanbul, walked across much of Western Turkey, and traveled widely across the region. His particular interests are the Byzantines, Venetian and Ottoman empires, and seafaring and eyewitness history. He is also the author of three books on the empires of the Mediterranean and its surroundings: *1453: The Holy War for Constantinople and the Clash of Islam and the West, Empires of the Sea: The Siege of Malta, the Battle of Lepanto, and the Contest for the Center of the World*, and *City of Fortune: How Venice Ruled the Seas*.

rogercrowley.co.uk

@crowley_roger

ABOUT THE TYPE

This book was set in Bembo, a typeface based on an old-style Roman face that was used for Cardinal Pietro Bembo's tract *De Aetna* in 1495. Bembo was cut by Francesco Griffo (1450–1518) in the early sixteenth century for Italian Renaissance printer and publisher Aldus Manutius (1449–1515). The Lanston Monotype Company of Philadelphia brought the well-proportioned letterforms of Bembo to the United States in the 1930s.

909.0971 Crowley, Roger,
CRO   1951-

        Conquerors.

$30.00